# JESUS
# POTTER
# HARRY
# CHRIST

The fascinating parallels between two of
the world's most popular literary characters.

# Derek Murphy

*holyblasphemy press*
Portland, Oregon

Biblical passages are taken from the New Jerusalem Bible unless otherwise noted.

JESUS POTTER HARRY CHRIST:
The fascinating parallels between two of the world's most popular literary characters
ISBN-13: 9780615430935
ISBN-10: 0615430937

First paperback edition, February 2011
Copyright 2011 by Derek Murphy

Publisher: Holy Blasphemy
www.holyblasphemy.net


Cover Design by Derek Murphy
Author Photo by Steven Vigar


10 9 8 7 6 5 4 3 2 1

# Contents

# Preface

At the beginning of J.K. Rowling's internationally popular phenomenon, Harry Potter was first viewed with suspicion, and then damned outright by religious conservatives claiming that Rowling's stories encouraged children to embrace witchcraft. The fallout from this controversy has included law suits, worker strikes, book burnings, and several campaigns to educate Christian families against the evils of Harry Potter. The "boy who lived" became Jesus' arch-nemesis: the icon or rallying point behind which infuriated Christians could gain support (and a much needed platform) against a society embracing vampires as boyfriends, witches as heroes, and monsters as merely misunderstood. None of this slowed the success of Harry Potter, whose books, and then the movie franchise produced by Warner Bros, have been not only an unchallengeable model for marketing strategy and economic success, but also an integral part of the lives of millions of fans who have watched Harry grow up – and grown up with him.

As we reached the end of this journey, the final coming of Harry Potter was being treated as Messianic; blogs were calling the release of the first installment of Harry Potter 7 (*Harry Potter and the Deathly Hallows* Part I) "a historic event." However, the tension between Jesus and Harry has not been forgotten. A few extremist groups continue to burn books or protest movie openings or mount the pulpit in frothy defense of Christianity against the madness of modern culture's obsession with wizardry. At the same time, the general Christian stance towards Harry Potter has taken a profound shift after the publication of the final book, in which Harry is tortured using the Cruciatus curse, dies a sacrificial death, and has an afterlife experience of sorts at "King's Cross" station. Potter then comes back to life and triumphs over his evil adversary, Voldemort. These motifs have guided many Christians to ask whether Rowling consciously crafted the Harry Potter story after the Passion of Jesus Christ. *Is Harry Potter a Christ-Figure?* In fact this question had been asked by sharp-minded readers since the early days of Potterdom. Many bloggers correctly guessed that the details of Harry Potter's final conclusion would mirror the sacrificial death of Jesus. In 2002 Beliefnet.com hosted an online debate between several scholars who had published books on the subject, called "Harry Potter, Christ Figure?" Now that the 7th book has been released, these early musings have been justified; especially in light of comments by Rowling herself to the effect that she knowingly crafted parts of her story around the biblical story of Jesus Christ. Suddenly preachers are making headlines, not for burning Harry Potter, but for championing him. Harry Potter is claimed to be a Christian story, which parallels the story of Jesus Christ and thus can help open a dialogue between Christians and the broader public.

And yet the most fascinating question has so far been ignored: *Why do these similarities exist at all?* Although it is easy to accept that Rowling crafted the literary character of Harry Potter after the figure of Jesus, shouldn't it pique our interest that Jesus – a monumental figure in modern world religion generally believed to have been historical – has so much in common with the obviously fictional fantasy world and character of Harry Potter? This book will trace the genesis of the story of Jesus Christ and examine the controversy concerning the historical founder of Christianity, to see if Jesus can be distinguished from Harry based on the claim that Jesus was a real historic figure, while Harry Potter is obviously a fable.

# Introduction

The primary aim of this investigation is to increase awareness of the fact that a debate over the reliability of the historical Jesus exists, that the evidence for Jesus is insufficient to prove a historical founder, and that a strong case can be made in favor of a mythological, literary character that was mistakenly assumed to be historical by later Christian converts. To that end, Jesus Potter Harry Christ begins by comparing the similarities between Jesus and J.K. Rowling's Harry Potter and claims that the only difference between the two is that Jesus has traditionally been regarded as historical – that is, a real person in history.

Rather than launching into dated arguments from Christ-Myth theory, Jesus Potter Harry Christ moves very slowly – establishing the historical basis and controversy surrounding the historical Jesus, analyzing the modern assumptions and pre-established beliefs, and re-examining critical evidence in the debate. Only after exploring and appreciating the history of the controversy, does it move into concrete parallels between Jesus Christ and earlier mythology and literature that may have been assimilated into the Jesus tradition. Next, the book traces the universal source of many religious myths and symbols to astrology: the fact that Greeks and Romans identified all of the planets as gods, and believed that mythological figures and events were 'placed in the heavens' as constellations, gives this premise firm ground. Finally, Jesus Potter Harry Christ concludes that the figure of Jesus Christ may have been a deliberate attempt to bridge Judaism and pagan thought, and that stories about this figure were embedded with historical details until a few believers actually began to think he was a real person.

These claims will be substantiated by a thorough examination of pagan and Jewish sources, early Christian and Gnostic writings, biblical and apocryphal literature as well as corresponding religious art and sculpture. Moreover, I will demonstrate not only that the time was ripe for a deliberate creation of a Jewish national figure based on pagan mystery gods, but also explore the astrological roots linking these pagan faiths and modern religious traditions. I will show how central symbolism from ancient spiritual mythologies continues to manifest themselves in popular fiction and literature, and finally explore the exact process of how a pagan mystery cult assumed Jewish trappings and how its founder was eventually mistaken for a historical figure; a process that can be outlined entirely based on biblical texts.

Once we recognize that the stories, parables, deeds, words and stories told about Jesus in the gospel reflect older traditions, we are faced with the very challenging task of trying to situate a historical founder of Christianity within or behind the tales associated with him. The most common approach, shared by both Christian and secular scholars, is to insist that Jesus was a historical person upon which pagan tales and stories were naturally assimilated. I hope to demonstrate convincingly that this is a very weak position.

At the same time, I recognize that the idea of a historical Jesus Christ is so deeply ingrained in modern times that it is difficult to raise an alternative theory – one in which the savior figure of the gospels may not have been historical. To a large extent, this is due to the consequences of postmodernism and the dissolution of Objective Truth in favor of local narratives. The 'failure' of historical criticism, with the realization that each researcher projects their own meaning into the evidence, provides the illusion that any interpretation of history is possible, regardless of the corroborating evidence.

Unfortunately, this loose perception of history as immaterial and essentially meaningless has been applied to Christianity in order to safeguard its very insubstantial history from the voracious criticisms of rationalism. The current disengagement with historical evidence cannot be maintained, however, precisely because Christianity's faith is fixed firmly upon its own historical foundation: that Jesus, the son of God, really and truly died on the cross for our sins and was resurrected.

This book is not meant as an attack on religion, on faith, on belief, or on anybody's conception of God. It is simply an attempt to tell, perhaps for the first time ever, the actual history of the Christian Church – a history that is clearly discernible even after a millennium of misdirection and wishful thinking; a history that *really* happened, in one particular, concrete way, and can be reconstructed based on reliable evidence and testimony. Although some of the ideas in this book have been raised before, much of the evidence and arguments presented are new. Moreover, Jesus Potter Harry Christ provides answers that no other book on the subject has been able to provide: exactly how this transformation from myth to history occurred, why anyone would want to combine Judaism and pagan mythology, how followers of Jesus could believe so fervently in his existence to become martyrs, and how a movement as powerful and long-lasting as Christianity could have begun around a myth.

It should be pointed out that this book is not (unlike contemporary biblical scholars) concerned with trying to find some historical figure who was not named Jesus Christ but something else, and who did not do the things described in the gospels, but may have been somehow tenuously tied into the tradition that later became Christianity. Instead we are looking for the character of Jesus we know – the character fully proclaimed by the Bible, who has so much in common with Harry Potter – and asking whether the deeds and events ascribed to this Jesus really happened, and are thus distinct from other mythical or fictional characters like Harry Potter. Conversely, if it can be shown that the points of similarity are due to Christianity's inclusion of literary symbolism from older spiritual traditions, then Jesus' originality (and hence his separation from Harry Potter) dissolves. Our question then is not whether Jesus Christ *existed,* but whether the literary character recorded in the New Testament was primarily inspired by a historical figure or previous literary traditions and characters.

# PART ONE

## The Historical Controversy

CHAPTER ONE

# Sacrificial Half Breed Warlocks: Harry Potter as Christ Figure

*Warlocks are the enemies of God! And I don't care what kind of hero they are, they're an enemy of God and had it been in the Old Testament, Harry Potter would have been put to death! –Becky Fischer, Pentecostal children's pastor, 2006*

LET'S SKIP THE INTRODUCTIONS. YOU DON'T need me to tell you that Jesus Christ and Harry Potter are two of the most famous celebrities in the world, whose stories have been translated into dozens of languages and found international support in diverse cultures. What you may not be aware of, however, is the mysterious, complicated and intriguing relationship between them. For example, did you know that the topics "I read Harry Potter and Jesus still loves me," "Even Jesus reads Harry Potter" and "Harry Potter will return sooner than Jesus" each have their own Facebook group, or that Wikipedia has a page dedicated to "Religious debates over the Harry Potter Series"? Much more remarkable than their respective popularity is the significant tension – and unexpected affinity – between them.

At first glance it may seem that J.K. Rowling's boy wizard and the crucified Jesus prophet who became the Christian savior have absolutely nothing to do with each other – and yet the unease and sometimes outright animosity between the followers of these two figures suggest otherwise. Harry has been banned, burned, and abused by religious fundamentalists for over a decade. Just what is it about Harry Potter that Christians find so threatening?

On the surface, the conflict appears simple. The Bible prohibits witchcraft absolutely, on pain of death. Consequently, some Christians argue that the popularity of Harry Potter can lead children to accept that magic is OK – if used for the right reasons – and thus lure them into evil practices that lead to damnation. At the release of Rowling's final book, however, many readers were surprised to discover parallels between Jesus and Harry that, in such apparently diverse world-views, had no right to be there. As a result, recent years have witnessed a revolution in Christian responses to Harry, with many groups, writers and religious leaders praising Rowling's young sorcerer as ultimately Christian and a clear metaphor for Jesus Christ. A few of the similarities that have been raised include the following:

- ★ Magic father, human mother
- ★ Miraculous birth, foretold by prophecy
- ★ Threatened by an evil ruler, had to go into hiding as a baby
- ★ Power over animals, time, and matter
- ★ Symbolized by a lion/ enemy symbolized by a snake
- ★ Descended into the underworld
- ★ Broke seven magical seals
- ★ Went willingly to his death
- ★ Suffered and died (or appeared to die) willingly, was mourned
- ★ Came back to life
- ★ Defeated his enemy in a glorious final battle

Can this list really be applied to both Jesus Christ and Harry Potter equally? If so, where do the apparent similarities come from? More importantly, why do some Christian groups deem Harry Potter satanic, while Jesus Christ is revered as the Son of God? What key differences allow Christians to make the distinction between them? In order to answer these questions, this chapter will trace the raging controversy over the Harry Potter series, examine the

Christian responses to J.K. Rowling's protagonist, and then explore the potential similarities themselves. I will conclude by arguing that the key variance between the two is that Harry Potter is obviously a fictional character, while Jesus Christ is almost universally accepted as a historical figure.

## Background

The character of Harry Potter popped into Joanne Rowling's head in 1990, when she was returning by train to London after flat-hunting in Manchester. She didn't have a pen, so for the next four hours she simply sat and thought; dreaming up the story of the scrawny, black-haired, bespectacled boy who didn't know he was a wizard.[1] She started writing *Philosopher's Stone* as soon as she got back to her Clapham Junction flat.

Rowling's "rags to riches" has been an inspiration for millions of would-be authors. After years of personal challenges, including a failed marriage and problems with depression, Rowling crafted her novel in nearby cafés while her daughter was sleeping, surviving on state welfare support. After some initial rejection, Rowling found her agent, Christopher Little. The book was submitted to twelve publishing houses; all of which rejected the manuscript. Then in August, 1996, Christopher called to tell her that Bloomsbury, a small publishing house in London, had made an offer.

*Harry Potter and the Philosopher's Stone* became an overnight sensation when it hit bookstores. It was the first children's book to make it onto the *New York Times* best-seller list since E.B. White's *Charlotte's Web* in 1952, and was followed shortly by Rowling's next two books, *Harry Potter and the Chamber of Secrets* and *Harry Potter and the Prisoner of Azkaban*. These three books held the top three positions on the New *York Times* best-seller list in 1999. On December 18th, 2001, *USA Today* announced that J.K. Rowling had become the best-selling author in the world, displacing mystery writer John Grisham, and in 2004, they named Rowling the most successful author of the decade, landing five of the top six spots on the list of the 100 best-selling books of the past 10 years. In 2007, *Harry Potter and the Deathly Hallow*s, the seventh and final volume of J.K. Rowling's fantasy series, sold 11 million copies in just 24 hours, and 8.3 million copies in another week; making it the fastest selling book in history.

Bookstores and publishers have been surprised, not only by the sales, but by the passion of supporting fans, who find the books irresistible. Part of this can be chalked up to a brilliant marketing campaign, but even so, it is clear that Rowling has presented an intriguing story, with central characters that fans identify with and a rich magical world.

It would be a mistake to identify the series exclusively as children's literature; the books have received an enthusiastic reception from adults as well, and in the seriousness of the later books it is clear that Rowling had a mature audience in mind. Horror writer Stephen King notes that the great secret of the Harry Potter series is that Rowling's kids *grew up*. The books, which certainly began as children's literature, developed into something much more sober as Rowling's depiction of the conflict between good and evil, her characters, and her writing skills reached maturity:

> These books ceased to be specifically for children halfway through the series; by Goblet of Fire, Rowling was writing for everyone, and knew it. The clearest sign of how adult the books had become by the conclusion arrives — and splendidly — in Deathly Hallows, when Mrs. Weasley sees the odious Bellatrix Lestrange trying to finish off Ginny with a Killing Curse. "Not my daughter, you bitch!" she cries. It's the most shocking bitch in recent fiction; since there's virtually no cursing (of the linguistic kind, anyway) in the Potter books, this one hits home with almost fatal force. It is totally correct in its context — perfect, really — but it is also a quintessentially adult response to a child's peril.[2]

The popularity of Harry Potter has also drawn the attention of academic research and popular non-fiction titles about the series. As such a universal element of contemporary culture, Harry Potter has been used to shed light on more complex social and political issues. In "Harry Potter and the Goblet of Colonialism," Tracy Douglas seeks to place Harry Potter "within the wider context of the British literature canon's tendency to define the foreigner against a characterization of English identity."[3] Gwen A. Tarbox, in

"Harry Potter and the War on Terror," reflects "If the earlier books in the series were designed to engage children's sense of wonder, it would appear that the later texts are designed to encourage children's skepticism of the current geopolitical situation."[4] Nancee Lee-Allen, meanwhile, in "Understanding Prejudice Utilizing the Harry Potter Series," claims:

> Harry Potter's world is full of prejudicial ideas, though not the ones found in our world. In Harry's world, people are not discriminated against for the color of their skin, religious affiliation, or sexual identity; it is all about blood – pure, half or muggle. Teens easily identify with characters and are able to relate to the idea of prejudice in the magic world. These books allow us to explore inner feelings about people who are different without identifying anyone as a real-world racist, which can lead to a better understanding of ourselves and begin to build respect for those who are different.[5]

Academics have also tried to isolate what gives Harry Potter its distinctive appeal. Tricia Sindel-Arrington writes, "J.K. Rowling's Harry Potter books are modern Gothic novels which incorporate symbols to create vivid imagery while connecting to the adolescent's self-discovery journey."[6] Janet Neilson finds that "J.K. Rowling draws from global sources for inspiration for everything from spells to magical creatures. These sources are woven throughout the text to create depth and a sense of cultures beyond the one in which Harry lives."[7] John Granger, one of the first writers to comment on the Christian symbolism in Harry Potter, notes that Rowling "wields the tools of narrative misdirection, literary alchemy, the hero's journey, postmodern themes and traditional symbolism to engage and entrance us well beyond suspended disbelief."[8]

The academic interest in the Harry Potter phenomenon has inspired over a dozen literary conferences focused on the Harry Potter series. In 2008 alone, the list of Potter conferences included *Terminus* in Chicago, *Convention Alley* in Ottawa, *Portus* in Dallas, and *Accio* in England, and even more have been held in the years since. For serious researchers, a 275-page hardcover called *Scholarly Studies in Harry Potter: Applying Academic Methods to a Popular Text* was released in 2005 and sold on Amazon.com for $109.95.[9] According to Debbie Mynott, Area Children's Librarian at Solihull Metropolitan Borough Council (UK), the articles in the book "demonstrate the richness Harry Potter and his world provide for literary critics and scholars."[10]

Harry's quickly expanding fandom has even inspired comparisons to be made between the Potter series and the Bible, which popular culture has dubbed the "best-selling book of all time." Although the Bible is still winning, Rowling's novels are catching up:

> According to Rowling's agent, Christopher Little, the seven Harry Potter books have so far been translated into 67 languages, amassing the 400m figure since the publication of the first book in the series, Harry Potter and the Philosopher's Stone, in 1997. Despite the furious pace of sales, Harry Potter will still have his work cut out to catch The Bible, which, according to the Guinness Book of Records, has sold 2.5b copies since 1815, and has been translated into 2,233 languages or dialects.[11]

Along with its success, however, came controversy. The overwhelming popularity of the Harry Potter series might have been what first raised the suspicions of conservative Christians, who – citing the examples of magic and witchcraft in Harry Potter's world – have declared Rowling's fiction satanic propaganda designed to lead children into the occult. The continuing debate among Christian communities over whether children should be allowed to read the Harry Potter series has frequently been reported by the media; for example in news reports of lawsuits attempting to ban Harry Potter books from school and public libraries, or the even more startling accounts of public book burnings. Aside from evolution, Harry Potter is one of the most controversial subjects in the heated debate over what we should be teaching our children. (While these issues are predominantly constrained to U.S. politics and culture, the spread of evangelical forms of Christianity abroad have resulted in similar issues). On August 2, 2000, *Education Week* reported that:

> The American Library Association reports that at least 13 states witnessed attacks on the Harry Potter novels last year, making them the most challenged books of 1999. Given the enormous publicity

and forecasted sales of Harry Potter and the Goblet of Fire, we can expect the attacks to escalate when schools reopen in September.[12]

These initial responses were enflamed by a spoof article called "Harry Potter Books Spark Rise in Satanism Among Children," posted by the satire news site the Onion on July 26, 2000. Using made-up interview statements and provocative language, it painted a frightening picture of Harry's Satanic influence on kids:

> "I used to believe in what they taught us at Sunday School," said Ashley, conjuring up an ancient spell to summon Cerebus, the three-headed hound of hell. "But the Harry Potter books showed me that magic is real, something I can learn and use right now, and that the Bible is nothing but boring lies."

> "I think it's absolute rubbish to protest children's books on the grounds that they are luring children to Satan," Rowling told a London Times reporter in a July 17 interview. "People should be praising them for that! These books guide children to an understanding that the weak, idiotic Son of God is a living hoax who will be humiliated when the rain of fire comes, and will suck the greasy cock of the Dark Lord while we, his faithful servants, laugh and cavort in victory."[13]

Although the article was meant to ridicule the fears of Christian parents protesting the Harry Potter books and poke fun of the controversy, it was unexpectedly used by Christians (either deliberately or without realizing that the Onion is a satire site) as definitive proof against the series. Soon after the article appeared, a chain letter was created and forwarded in a massive email campaign which heavily cited the passages of the Onion's fabricated news story. By mixing truth with fiction, it proved a powerful motivator in the fight against Rowling's young wizard:

Date: Fri, 4 Aug 2000 01:59:13 EDT

Subject: Fwd: Harry Potter Books?

This is the most evil thing I have laid my eyes on in 10 years... and no one seems to understand its threat. The Harry Potter books are THE

NUMBER ONE selling children's books in the nation today. Just look at any Barnes & Noble or Waldenbook storefront. Go to Amazon. com and read the reviews. Hear the touting by educators and even Christian teachers about how "It's great to see the youth so eagerly embracing the reading experience!"

Harry Potter is the creation of a former UK English teacher who promotes witchcraft and Satanism. Harry is a 13 year old 'wizard.' Her creation openly blasphemes Jesus and God and promotes sorcery, seeking revenge upon anyone who upsets them by giving you examples (even the sources with authors and titles!) of spells, rituals, and demonic powers. It is the doorway for children to enter the Dark Side of evil.

. . . My hope is that you will see fit to become involved in getting the word out about this garbage. Please FWD to every pastor, teacher, and parent you know. This author has now published FOUR BOOKS in less than 2 years of this "encyclopedia of Satanism" and is surely going to write more. I also ask all Christians to please pray for this lost woman's soul. Pray also for the Holy Spirit to work in the young minds of those who are reading this garbage that they may be delivered from its harm. Lastly, pray for all parents to grow closer to their children, and that a bond of sharing thoughts and spiritual intimacy will grow between them.

Letters such as this one ignited outrage and inspired a deliberate movement against J.K. Rowling's novels. In 2001, several book burnings were held with Harry Potter as the main stimulus. In early January 2002, the Christ Community Church of Alamogordo, New Mexico, became the topic of international media attention for its book burning after the pastor, Jack D. Brock, preached a sermon on the topic "The Baby Jesus Or Harry Potter?" Brock stated he considered the Harry Potter books to be "an example of our society's growing preoccupation with the occult. The Potter books present witchcraft as a generally positive practice, while the Bible expressly condemns all occult practices." The event became the topic of news features in both the United States and England.[14] Pastor Brock admitted to never having read any of the Potter novels. In

August 2003, the Jesus Non-denominational Church in Greenville, Michigan, also burned Harry Potter books. According to the report, "The pastor says stories like Harry Potter that glorify wizardry and sorcery will lead people to accept and believe in Satan."

Evangelical Protestants were not the only ones worried that positive depictions of wizardry would mislead children. In a letter from March, 2003 Cardinal Ratzinger (now Pope Benedict XVI) thanked the author of *Harry Potter – Good or Evil,* who argued that Rowling's novels corrupt young people and harm a child's developing relationship with God, for her "instructive" book:

> It is good, that you enlighten people about Harry Potter, because those are subtle seductions, which act unnoticed and by this deeply distort Christianity in the soul, before it can grow properly.[15]

Harry Potter has also been a dividing factor in many communities. For several years, J.K. Rowling's series topped the American Library Association's lists of most-challenged books, for reasons including "anti-family, occult/Satanism, religious viewpoint and violence" (reasons cited in 2001). Attempting to educate Christians about the dangers of Harry Potter, Robert McGee of Merritt Island, Florida, released a documentary in 2001 (*Harry Potter: Witchcraft Repackaged; Making Evil Look Innocent*) claiming that Rowling's books introduce kids to human sacrifice, witchcraft and even Nazism.[16] School boards in Cedarville, Arkansas, and the Eastern York School district in Pennsylvania were challenged on decisions regarding whether Harry should be allowed in school libraries. In 2002, the police department of Penryn, Pennsylvania refused to direct traffic for the YMCA triathlon because Harry Potter was read to kids attending the YMCA after-school program. In a letter sent to the YMCA, the town's police captain questioned whether it was "serving the will of God by reading Harry to children," adding "As long as we don't stand up, it won't stop. It's unfortunate that this is the way it has to be."

Although the controversy softened with the continued success of Harry Potter and its endorsement by many mainstream religious organizations, pockets of resistance remain. In 2006 the conflict resurfaced with the documentary *Jesus Camp*, which shadowed a Christian camp aimed at using children to proselytize. Leader Becky Fischer's bold comments on Harry Potter were quoted at the beginning of this chapter. Traces of the early email campaign based from the Onion article continue to condition Christian responses to Harry Potter. In July 2009 Reverend Douglas Taylor and his "Jesus Party" received media attention for protesting the opening of "Harry Potter and the Half-Blood Prince"; these protests were mocked by satire site *Land Rover Baptist* as part of their continuing (fictitious) campaign against Harry Potter:

> Each night in July during the release of the Satanic film, "The Half Blood Prince," JESUS YOUTHS will be armed with fire-extinguishers filled with compressed lamb's blood. "Our brave Baptist youths will innocently approach theater lines and spray unsaved moviegoers with the warm blood of the Lamb. They'll shout the name of Jesus and throw Chick Tracts into the dazed crowd," says Pastor. "They need to run like their dickens are on fire after witnessing time is over because they are outreaching for Jesus outside of church property! And there might be some unsaved police officers about! Church vans will be waiting a quarter mile away from each theater to escort JESUS YOUTHS back to the Main Sanctuary for a de-brief with the Board of Deacons. Then it's off to Friendly's for 20-minutes of ice-cream fellowship.[17]

As recently as October 24, 2010 the following article was posted on the blog *Everyday For Life Canada*:

> As the Harry Potter phenomenon continues to contaminate the hearts and minds of Canadian youth, I felt it necessary to address my concerns and that of so many other like-minded Christians, who clearly understand the Harry Potter controversy, that it glorifies and propagates the occult. Make no mistake, the Harry Potter story line is about witches and wizards, the practice of divination, necromancy and sorcery. It is all presented in a glorifying way through the exciting adventures of a young boy's life.[18]

## What's the big deal? Christian Responses

It is tempting to simply dismiss or discredit these reactions as fundamentally misinformed or baseless. However, there is a very real anti-Harry sentiment among conservative Christian churches – and it has a biblical foundation. Thus it is important to look more deeply into the issue and to understand what the religious debate against Harry is all about. As esteemed author Judy Blume points out, it would be a mistake to overlook the real impetus behind the protests:

> The real danger is not in the books, but in laughing off those who would ban them. The protests against Harry Potter follow a tradition that has been growing since the early 1980's and often leaves school principals trembling with fear that is then passed down to teachers and librarians. What began with the religious right has spread to the politically correct. . . . And now the gate is open so wide that some parents believe they have the right to demand immediate removal of any book for any reason from school or classroom libraries. The list of gifted teachers and librarians who find their jobs in jeopardy for defending their students' right to read, to imagine, to question, grows every year. ... I knew this was coming. The only surprise is that it took so long – as long as it took for the zealots who claim they're protecting children from evil (and evil can be found lurking everywhere these days) to discover that children actually like these books. If children are excited about a book, it must be suspect.[19]

At the same time, from a Christian perspective the issue is very clear: the Bible explicitly forbids witchcraft. The command "Thou shalt not suffer a witch to live" of Exodus 22:18, which was used to justify the persecution of women during the Inquisition and later during the Salem witch trials, is also cited against Harry Potter. The other biblical passage quoted often in arguments against the Harry Potter series is from the book of Deuteronomy:

> There must never be anyone among you who makes his son or daughter pass through the fire of sacrifice, who practices divination, who is soothsayer, augur or sorcerer, weaver of spells, consulter of ghosts of mediums, or necromancer. (Deut. 18:10-12)

While this passage clearly forbids believers to practice sorcery, ambiguity remains. Is reading about witchcraft the same as practicing it, and therefore also banned? As Connie Neal clarifies in *What's a Christian to Do with Harry Potter*:

Reading Harry Potter is a disputable matter because we are not debating whether it is okay for Christians to practice witchcraft of spells. The Christian position on that is clear. We agree that we should never participate in or practice anything listed in Deuteronomy 18:9-14. But reading Harry Potter is not the same as practicing witchcraft or even – as some assert – promoting it. However, some can *take it to mean just that*. Therein lies the disputable part of these issues that Christians debate in earnest.[20]

To a skeptical reader who doesn't believe in magic, this controversy might seem exasperating; but the root of the issue is that Christians *do* believe in a super-natural world (and hence, the possibility of magic), and also that the Bible outlines appropriate responses to that world. A literal reading of the Bible makes it clear that magic, spell-casting, divination and communion with spirits are not only real, but also very dangerous. The fear is that children reading the Harry Potter books and playing around with make-believe spells and magic may end up being drawn towards more occult practices later, or even accidentally contacting real evil spirits.

Although these biblical prohibitions may be the root of the criticisms made against Harry Potter, as J.K. Rowling's novels grew in popularity, Christians opposed to Harry Potter searched for further ways to demonstrate the potential dangers of the books for children. The following is a summary of some of the early Christian responses to the Harry Potter series. It should be noted that critics who are against the reading of the Harry Potter series have rarely read the books themselves. This means that their information about the novels comes only from 2nd or 3rd place testimonies, book jackets, literature reviews and conjecture. Moreover, many of the following responses were formulated after only the second or third Harry Potter novel, and are inadequate to deal with the Potter series as a whole.

## Promotes the Idea that Magic is Just Fantasy

The belief that witches and wizards are harmless because they don't really exist is a dangerous fallacy for Christians who believe that magic and witchcraft are real and condemned by God. This point is demonstrated admirably by the preface of Michael D. O'Brien's *Harry Potter and the Paganization of Culture.* O'Brien describes how he was inspired to write the book after hearing from three independent and unconnected Christian sources whose attempts to read Harry Potter caused them to experience physical nausea. He then claims that when he started publishing, he was cursed by three witches, whose spells were only broken by his faith in Jesus. The fantastic elements in his account are worth quoting in full:

> The witches' spells against me were utterly terrifying, nearly paralyzing, and only when I cried out the name of Jesus were the spells broken and pushed back. I had to keep repeating His name to preserve the defense, and woke up in a state of terror that did not dissipate in the manner of bad dreams. My wife woke up too and prayed with me, and finally we were able to go back to sleep in peace. In a similar dream the following night, the three witches returned, now accompanied by a sorcerer, and once more they cast a hideous spell against me. Again it was repelled by the holy name of Jesus and also by the prayers of the saints, especially St. Joseph. A third dream that occurred not long after was the most frightening of all. In it, I had been captured and taken to an isolated house deep in a forest. The building was filled with men and women involved in witchcraft and sorcery. They were waiting for a man who was their chief sorcerer to arrive, and I was to be the human sacrifice in the night's ritual. When he entered the room I felt that all hope had been lost, a black dismay filled me, along with terror of a kind I had never before felt. Even then, I was able to whisper the name of Jesus. Instantly the walls fell backward onto the ground outside the house, the cords that had bound me fell from my wrists and ankles, and I ran for my life. Leaping out of the house, I was astonished to find the entire building surrounded by mighty angels, who by their holy authority had immobilized all of the sorcerers within. I leaped and danced with joy, and realized that I had been transformed into a child. Jesus appeared in the sky above and began to descend. I continued to dance in jubilation and relief, crying out greetings to him as he arrived. At which point I woke up, filled with utter joy. And that was the last of the bad dreams.[21]

Like O'Brien, many Christians accept the fact that an invisible spiritual warfare is constantly going on between Jesus and the forces of evil, and live in a world just as incredible as that of Harry Potter.

## Makes a Distinction Between Good Magic and Bad Magic

Fans of Harry Potter would probably agree that Harry and his companions are moral characters who use magic for good purposes, as opposed to their unethical enemies, who use magic for evil and selfish purposes. But this distinction could lead children to the conclusion that magic can be good or "safe," depending on the moral choices made – a dangerous path for Christians who see all magic, for any purpose, as unacceptable. Alison Lentini explores this theme in her article "Harry Potter: Occult Cosmology and the Corrupted Imagination":

> For those who seek conformity with the teachings of the Hebrew Scriptures and the New Testament, "safe magic" is wishful thinking, intellectual dishonesty, and an invitation to the spiritual deviations that the Hebrew prophets bluntly referred to as "harlotry," and the New Testament apostles forbade. As such, the "safe magic" of Harry Potter offers a message that is as morally confusing to a generation of children as the current ideology of "safe sex."[22]

## Introduces Children to the Occult

Wicca = Witchcraft = Satanism. Or at least that's the connection made on many fundamentalist blogs and websites, who view the accepted modern day religion named Wicca as positive proof that New Age ideologies and the contemporary tolerance of pluralism are Satan's ploy to capture the souls of those who wander too far into occult territory. Although Harry Potter, as a fictional character who employs magic to defeat his adversaries, is not unique in children's literature, he is the most popular manifestation of contemporary society's demand for magic and fantasy, and has therefore become a primary target of criticism. The threat is voiced clearly by Alan Jacobs in "Harry Potter's Magic," which claims "such novels could at best encourage children to take a smilingly tolerant New Age view of witchcraft, at worst encourage the practice of witchcraft itself."[23]

The overly zealous author of the website *Exposing Satanism*, who has placed Taoism and Buddhism under the title of "False Beliefs," gives a stronger response:

> The whole purpose of these books is to desensitize readers and introduce them to the occult. What a better way to introduce tolerance and acceptance of what God calls an abomination, than in children's books? If you can get them when they are young, then you have them for life. It's the oldest marketing scheme there is.[24]

## Has No Moral Compass or Ethical Authority

Another criticism raised against the Harry Potter series has been that there is no absolute moral authority. Although there are good characters and bad characters in the books, there is also a lot of moral ambiguity and no supreme authority for establishing and policing universal ethical laws. Moreover, "good" characters often behave very poorly – for example being angry or jealous. Harry himself often lies and breaks the rules, is rude towards authority figures and prone to violent encounters with his enemies. This argument usually goes hand-in-hand with a defense of other, more Christian works like the C.S. Lewis's *Chronicles of Narnia* or Tolkien's *Lord of the Rings* trilogy, both of which (mostly on account that the authors were practicing Christians) are championed as appropriate books for Christian children. As writer Richard Abanes proclaims, "the books clearly present far too much moral subjectivity and patently unbiblical actions to be of any ethical value."[25] Lindy Beam agrees, in an article about the appropriate Christian response to Harry Potter:

> The spiritual fault of Harry Potter is not so much that it plays to dark supernatural powers, but that it doesn't acknowledge any supernatural powers or moral authority at all. Rowling does not write from the basis of Judeo-Christian ethics. So her characters may do "the-wrong-thing-for-the-right-reason," often lying, cheating, or breaking rules in order to save the day.[26]

However, this argument becomes very weak if we agree that the criticism should be applied to every novel equally and not only to the Harry Potter series; there are very few works of literature in which the protagonist is sin-free and ethically meticulous. In response to this argument, Connie Neal points out that the Bible itself is hardly bereft from moral ambiguity itself, and cites a handful of biblical indiscretions worsened by the fact that the characters acted purely out of self interest: Abraham and Isaac lied about their wives, calling them sisters in order to escape persecution; Jacob and his mother deceived Isaac with an elaborate disguise and lied to cover the deception; Rachel stole her father's idols, hid them, and lied about it; ten of the Patriarchs sold their brother into slavery. She concludes, "If we decide that we will only read stories to kids where those on the good side never do wrong, we would not be able to read the Bible."[27]

### Uses Satanic Symbols

Still others have found Satanic symbols in the Harry Potter stories. Arguments following this kind of logic mention that the Bible often depicts Satan as being a snake (Genesis 3:1-4; 2 Corinthians 11:3; Revelation 12:9; 20:2), and that in book two of the Potter series, we discover that Harry has a gift of speaking with snakes (*Chamber of Secrets* 145-147). This language is called Parseltongue, and is already openly associated with the dark arts in the series. Harry, however, got this power from the truly evil character, Voldemort, and always uses it for the greater good.

Another connection is made from the lightning bolt figure on Harry's forehead. Associating lightning with Satan based on the passage, "I saw Satan fall from heaven like lightning" (Luke 10:18), and noting that the forehead is meant to be a place reserved for the name that God will put on those who love Him and serve Him ("And they will see His face; and His name will be on their foreheads" (Rev 22:4)), some fundamentalists have argued that to put any other mark there, especially a Satanic mark, is a mockery to God.

As we've seen, arguments like these, when used in conjunction with anti-Potter propaganda and riveting "proofs" of Harry's Satanic influences, stirred up the fury of religious extremists enough to cause public demonstrations, lawsuits or book burning events. Although in today's liberal culture of tolerance, book burning is generally frowned upon (in nearly every case more liberal members of the community protested the burnings – ashamed that their towns had become harbors for such violent and discriminatory practices), the burning of books on witchcraft is a biblically sanctioned practice. The following story is found in the Acts of the Apostles:

> And many that believed came, and confessed, and shewed their deeds. Many of them also which used curious arts brought their books together and burned them before all men: and they counted the price of them, and found it fifty thousand pieces of silver. So mightily grew the Word of God and prevailed. (Acts 19: 18-20)

It should be pointed out, however, that this episode is a bit of ecclesiastical advertising and rather than denounce witchcraft, it actually acknowledges its power. Early Christian communities believed that Jesus Christ eclipsed all magical spells; not because they weren't real, but because Jesus had a higher magical efficacy than the best alternative methods. This is why new converts could converge and cast their expensive books into the fire. This is not the same as burning books about magic simply because they are *evil*.

## Positive Christian Responses

The fact that there have been a few isolated cases of Harry Potter book burning by fundamentalist religious groups should not lead us to the assumption that all Christians are anti-Potter. On the contrary, many of the most authoritative sources have given the series their support. On January 10th, 2000, for example, *Christianity Today* published the editorial "Why We Like Harry Potter," which claims:

> Rowling has created a world with real good and evil, and Harry is definitely on the side of light fighting the "dark powers." Third, and this is why we recommend the books, Rowling's series is a Book of Virtues with a preadolescent funny bone. Amid the laugh-out-loud scenes are wonderful examples of compassion, loyalty, courage, friendship, and even self-sacrifice. No wonder young readers want to

be like these believable characters. That is a Christmas present we can
be grateful for.[28]

Christians who have read the series even find that they can be
useful instruments for spreading the gospel message. John Killinger,
for example, says glowingly "The Potter stories, far from being
'wicked' or 'Satanic'... are in fact narratives of robust faith and
morality, entirely worthy of children's reading again and again, and
even becoming world classics that will be reprinted as long as there
is a civilization."[29]

Christians who approve of Harry Potter have trouble accepting
the argument that Narnia or the Lord of the Rings – which also
feature magic, spells, warfare, mythological symbols, talking
animals and half-breeds like elves and centaurs – are better material
for Christian children. Indeed there is no argument that can hold
against Harry Potter and not also be used against hundreds of
other classic and contemporary children's stories. Neal contends
that the content of the stories, rather than the intention of the
authors, must be honestly appraised; and if we ban one book
based on specific criteria, all others should be judged similarly:
"Must we say that Lewis's stories promote Wicca and conclude
that they are unsuitable for children and Christians? If we take this
position about the Harry Potter stories, then the answer is yes."[30]
This argument can be extended to include most other popular fairy
tales: the Good Witch in The Wizard of Oz; the magic in Disney
stories like Cinderella, Beauty and the Beast or the Little Mermaid
– many of which are allowed by Christian parents. As Marcia
Hoehne observes in a letter to the editor of Christianity Today:

> Rowling's story, which she has described as an epic novel in seven
> parts rather than a book with six sequels, is an epic novel of good
> versus evil, where the heroes require help beyond natural strength,
> and where good wins out. Are Hogwarts's witches more sinister than
> Oz's? Than Mary Poppins? It would be refreshing if Christians would
> look up from the pulp fiction and animated videos long enough to
> educate themselves in the field of literature, so they might think
> through and discuss its complexities and themes as ably as the world
> does.[31]

Supporters of Harry Potter point out that the plot revolves around a battle between good and evil, and also that Jesus Christ has at least a little in common with Harry Potter. In addition, the two stories share moral themes like love, sacrifice, honor, bravery, honesty and friendship; as well as challenging moral lessons that must be learned as the characters struggle through the plot. Harry Potter therefore, it can be argued, stems from a Judeo-Christian ethos. The willingness of non-Christians to discuss an interesting and "neutral" topic such as Harry Potter can even be used as a platform towards more in-depth conversations about spiritual themes. Chuck Colson instructs that interest in Harry Potter can be used to turn readers towards "more Christian" books:

> If your kids do develop a taste for Harry Potter and his wizard friends, this interest might just open them up to an appreciation for other fantasy books with a distinctly Christian worldview. When your kids finish reading Harry Potter, give them C.S. Lewis's Narnia books and J.R.R. Tolkien's Lord of the Rings trilogy. These books also feature wizards and witches and magical potions – but in addition, they inspire the imagination within a Christian framework – and prepare the hearts of readers for the real life story of Christ.[32]

It is also noted that the Harry Potter series and Christianity share a certain number of esoteric symbols, such as the lion for bravery and righteousness, the snake for evil, the phoenix for rebirth, and the unicorn for purity – although the reason for these similarities is debated. Neal stresses that while Christians can interpret the symbols in Harry Potter within a biblical paradigm, these associations were not deliberately intended by Rowling:

> We Christians can associate the symbol of the Lion for Gryffindor House with the Biblical symbol of Jesus (supremely good) being the "Lion of the tribe of Judah." We can associate the snake of Slytherin House with the biblical symbol of the evil one represented as a serpent. . . . However, we must remain absolutely clear on this point: The author of Harry Potter never makes any association between Harry Potter's fantasy world and Satan the devil, or any other aspect of occult spiritual forces revealed in The Bible as real in our spiritual

world. If we choose to create such an association, it is our own choice.[33]

Others, however, have noted the similarities and claimed that Rowling's inspiration must have come directly from the Bible. After quoting a lengthy passage from the Book of Revelation, Killinger comments, "The sweep and imagery are not that different from those employed by Rowling. In fact, there can be little doubt where Rowling got the idea of the King of Serpents for her story, whether she did so consciously or unconsciously."[34]

The strength of the Christian arguments in support of Harry Potter, however, depend upon the ability to see Harry Potter as a Christian story built around a Christian framework. Killinger remarks, for example, that the Potter mythos "is not only dependent on the Christian understanding of life and the universe but actually grows out of that understanding and would have been unthinkable without it."[35]

However, in this passage we can detect an extremist worldview that, while prevalent among a few fundamental Christian groups, is academically impermissible. This is that all love and goodness came into the world only after Jesus Christ, and no true ethics can be found before him. Therefore anything good in Harry Potter, deliberate or not, must have been influenced by Christianity.

> There has been only one great plot engine for all fiction since the coming of Christ, and that is the struggle of good to overcome evil. Before Christ, in the eras of great Hellenistic and Roman literature, this was not true. There was struggle in The Iliad, The Odyssey, and The Aeneid, but it was not about the conflict between good and evil; this essential ingredient in all great Western literature (and even many of the lesser writings) is derived from Hebrew and Christian theology, and especially from the Gospels, with their portrayal of the battle between Christ and the forces of darkness.[36]

Killinger's conclusion – that any good and evil struggle where good wins is a *Christian Story* – is hard to accept. Incidentally, this argument reveals a troubling inconsistency in Christian dogma: strictly speaking, in Christian theology there should be no struggle at all between good and evil: Judeo-Christian monotheistic belief makes it very clear that there is only one God, and he is omnipotent. There never was, nor can there be, any real conflict between good and evil in such a scenario. It is not possible for evil to win the battle against God. Although it can be argued that the battle is waged for the soul of each person, based around the issue of "free-will," it is more likely that instances of light against dark imagery and the epic battles between the forces of good and evil are vestiges of Zoroastrianism, a Persian religion from which Christianity has always tried, with little success, to distance itself. It would seem that in this case Harry Potter and Christianity (against its better judgment), are both borrowing themes from older traditions. However, the theme of light and dark, good versus evil, is so universal that it would be reckless to suggest that a story based on such conflict is guilty of plagiarism.

Embracing the Harry Potter fad as a way to reach children, in 2003 Trudy Ardizzone of St. Peter's Episcopal Church of Del Mar California created the Vacation Bible School program "Wizards and Wonders"; a kind of Harry Potter role-play with biblical substitutions. According to the online description, God "delights in any path that leads to us him," so there's no reason not to use Harry Potter as a fun and engaging activity:

Through drama, crafts and games, participants connect the hero's story to Bible stories. In an engaging set of experiences, mirroring some of Harry's, you will explore issues of identity, alliances, team work, spiritual gifts, life's direction, temptations, moral choices, courage and faith. Two thousand years ago, Jesus taught the public through parable, metaphor, and simile. How could he make simple people grasp such vast and impossible ideas such as God, heaven, and grace? He did so by relating them to objects and experiences the people understood. The glory and majesty of our Lord and his divine plan were in no way tarnished or diminished by comparing them to humble shepherds and sheep, mustard seeds, yeast and lost coins. The task of each generation is to read the Bible through the fresh filter of its own experience. If we believe we are a people led and inspired by the Holy Spirit, we should have no problem finding new metaphors for grace, love, forgiveness, and even the divine in our contemporary world. I believe God infuses his creation with the holy and makes many diverse opportunities available for our connection and revelation. My religious imagination thinks that God delights in any path that leads us to him, even if it is in tales of lonely but courageous orphan boys, silly spells, school friendships and loyalties, magic, and evil wizards.[37]

In 2010, a congregation in the Episcopal Diocese of Iowa used Trudy's program to run a successful Vacation Bible School with 30+ children, which was picked up by the local Iowa City newspaper and then spread through online news services. The event was newsworthy because of the inherently volatile tensions that continue to be perceived between Harry Potter and Christianity.

# Changes Since 2007

The landscape for Christian-Potter relations significantly changed, however, after the publication of Rowling's final book, *Harry Potter and the Deathly Hallows*, on July 21st, 2007. Not only did the book sell 11 million copies in the first 24 hours of release (in only three markets) – breaking all previous sales records and becoming the fastest selling book in history it also shattered the religious opposition to Harry Potter with its inclusion of specifically Christian motifs, themes and plot events. According to Paul V.M. Flesher, director of the religious studies program at the University of Wyoming and the author of an article about Harry Potter for the *Journal of Religion and Film*:

> At the end of the last book, we have a dying and rising Potter – he has to be killed to deliver the world from the evil personified by Voldemort. There's a Christian pattern to this story. It's not just good versus evil. Rowling is not being evangelistic – this is not C.S. Lewis – but she knows these stories, and it's clear she's fitting pieces together in a way that makes sense and she knows her readers will follow.[38]

These revelations, and the increasing support from religious leaders, have spurred the proliferation of articles like the one published in *Boston Globe* of August 16, 2009, titled "The Book of Harry: How the Boy Wizard Won Over Religious Critics."[39] The sudden praise of J.K. Rowling's boy wizard also allowed some religious leaders to gain an instant platform simply for approving of the boy wizard and encouraging other Christians to do the same. Mary Hess, for example, of Luther Seminary in St. Paul, Minnesota, writes in the journal *Word & World*:

> Rather than decrying as wicked certain elements of the series – as far too many Christians have done – we ought to be inviting our communities into deeper appreciation of both the similarities and the contrasts between the stories and our Christian faith[40]

This task has been taken up with remarkable passion by numerous writers, both online and in print. Although books on the spiritual or religious symbolism in Harry Potter are not new, there has been a marked increase in interest and media coverage. A few of the available titles include:

- ★ Harry Potter Power
- ★ The Seeker's Guide to Harry Potter
- ★ Looking for God in Harry Potter
- ★ The Hidden Key to Harry Potter
- ★ Harry Potter and Torah
- ★ What's a Christian to Do with Harry Potter?
- ★ A Charmed Life: The Spirituality of Potterworld
- ★ Harry Potter and the Meaning of Life
- ★ Harry Potter and the Bible: The Menace Behind the Magic
- ★ Harry Potter's Bookshelf
- ★ Does Harry Potter Tickle Sleeping Dragons
- ★ How Harry Cast His Spell
- ★ The Wisdom of Harry Potter
- ★ The Mystery of Harry Potter
- ★ The Gospel According To Harry Potter

One of the most recent books exploring the Christian symbolism in Rowling's work is *One Fine Potion: The Literary Magic of Harry Potter* by Baylor University professor of English, Greg Garrett.[41] Answering the question "How would C.S. Lewis respond to the Harry Potter series?" in an online interview, Garret responds,

> I have no doubt that the Christian apologist part of Lewis would have celebrated the fact that there is no more powerful contemporary

retelling of the gospel narrative than Rowling's 4100 pages. (...) Now that the series is complete, we know that the shape of the finished Potter narrative is the shape of the Christian story: A prophesied savior willingly lays down his life in order to defeat the power of death, fear, and hopelessness, and usher in a beautiful new world. The qualities of love, community, sacrifice, compassion, and courage that Rowling celebrates in the novels seem to me to be the qualities Christians most need to live an authentic and faithful life, so even though no one in the books preaches, the books preach.[42]

## What Does Rowling Have to Say?

*J.K. Rowling* has always been careful responding to questions about her spiritual views, maintaining that she couldn't comment on the books' religious content until the conclusion of Book Seven.[43] In a 2000 interview, she stated:

> If I talk too freely about whether I believe in God I think the intelligent reader, whether 10 or 60, will be able to guess what's coming in the books.[44]

Not surprisingly, along with the final book of the series, which culminates in Harry's sacrificial death, some readers have made the claim that Rowling's early refusals to discuss religion, hinting that it would give away the ending of the story, proves that the entire series has been a conscious and deliberate recreation of the gospels. According to the editorial "Is Harry Potter the Son of God?" (2007) posted on mugglenet.com by Abigail BeauSeigneur:

> The secret to Harry Potter is tied to Rowling's Christianity. The master of the red herring has done it. She has tricked the entire world. What appears to be a book about witchcraft is a story about Jesus Christ... The story of Harry Potter is, and always was, a Christian allegory – a fictionalized modern day adaptation of the life of Christ, intended to introduce his character to a new generation.[45]

And there is some truth to this view. Rowling could not have failed to be aware of the similarities between Harry and Jesus as she was writing. In fact, after the publication of the 7th book she's admitted in several interviews that Harry Potter was, in some sense, modeled on the Christian narrative. In a 2007 interview, when asked by a young reader about Harry's being referred to in the books as the "chosen one," Rowling replied:

> Well, there clearly is a religious undertone. And it's always been difficult to talk about that because until we reached Book Seven, views of what happens after death and so on, it would give away a lot of what was coming. So yes, my belief and my struggling with religious belief and so on I think is quite apparent in this book.[46]

At the same time Rowling, although reported to be a regular churchgoer whose daughter Jessica was baptized into the Church of Scotland, has been careful to say that she didn't set out to convert anyone to Christianity.

> I wasn't trying to do what CS Lewis (author of the Chronicles of Narnia) did. It is perfectly possible to live a very moral life without a belief in God and I think it's perfectly possible to live a life peppered with ill-doing and believe in God.[47]

She reaffirmed this position during her appearance on *The Oprah Winfrey Show* (Oct. 1, 2010), insisting that her books have no religious agenda:

> I'm not pushing any belief system here; although there is a lot of Christian imagery in the books. That's undeniable. But that's an allusion to a belief system in which I was raised.

## Comparisons between Jesus and Harry Potter

Now that we've established that similarities between Jesus and Harry do exist and have been recognized by academics, religious leaders and even Rowling herself, we should take a closer look at the actual parallels before continuing. I've listed a few of the main items below; of course there is no end to this kind of exegesis, and acute readers will be able to find many more connections.

### Miraculous Birth

Both Jesus and Harry have a miraculous birth story, which

includes the survival of an attempt on their lives by an evil power, who tried to kill them because of a prophecy that the child would someday challenge their rule. Jesus goes into hiding in Egypt with his parents when king Herod orders the massacre of all the young male born children in Bethlehem because of prophecy he'd heard from the Magi (Matthew 2:16-18). Harry Potter's parents, meanwhile, weren't lucky enough to be warned by an angel, and Lord Voldemort kills them both. However, when he tries to kill Harry, the powerful magical protection put on Harry by his mother's love makes the killing curse backfire and hit Voldemort. Harry is taken away in secrecy by professors McGonagall and Dumbledore, and left in the house of his only living relative.

### Childhood Miracles

Of both Jesus and Harry, very little is known until after they are older. Rowling reveals a few episodes where, before Harry learned how to use magic properly, it accidentally caused accidents when he was angry. Likewise, although not recorded in the canonical gospels, there are apocryphal writings of Jesus as a child using his miraculous powers for less than noble reasons. In *The Infancy Gospel of Thomas*, for example, Jesus killed a boy for throwing a stone at him, and another for spoiling the pools of water he'd made. The parents of the town came to Joseph and said, "It is impossible for thee to live with us in this city: but if thou wishest to do so, teach thy child to bless, and not to curse: for he is killing our children, and everything that he says is certainly accomplished" (*Infancy Gospel of Thomas*, 4). While the biblical story of Jesus then jumps to his adult years (or year – his ministry as recorded in the Bible appears to be just one year long), Harry's main battles are all completed as a teenager.

### Magical Powers

It may be controversial to suggest that Jesus, like Harry, is a magician; however it is no secret that the figure of Jesus was endowed with miraculous powers, and many of his feats in the Bible may seem to critics little different than party tricks. This claim was raised, for example, by the pagan philosopher Celsus (178AD) who claimed that Jesus had learned magic in Egypt:

> Jesus, on account of his poverty, was hired out to go to Egypt. While there he acquired certain [magical] powers. . . He returned home highly elated at possessing these powers, and on the strength of them gave himself out to be a god. . . It was by means of sorcery that He was able to accomplish the wonders which He performed. . . Let us believe that these cures, or the resurrection, or the feeding of a multitude with a few loaves. . . These are nothing more than the tricks of jugglers. . . It is by the names of certain demons, and by the use of incantations, that the Christians appear to be possessed of [miraculous] power.[48]

Even in his own time, the miracles of Jesus were not particularly impressive; similar – and greater – feats of supernatural prowess were regularly associated with other mythological figures. Early converts confessed they had difficulty separating the miracles done by Jesus and the apostles from those done by the heretics and apostates. In the Pseudo-Clementine Literature, for example, Simon Magus (who was said to be, like Jesus, a disciple of John the Baptist) walks through fire, flies through the air, makes statues walk and turns stones into bread. He becomes a serpent, changes himself into gold, opens locked doors, and makes dishes bear themselves and wait on him.[49] The author admits "if we did not know that he does these things by magic, we ourselves should also have been deceived."[50]

What feats did Jesus perform as evidence of his divinity? He changed water into wine (Harry could have learned to do that in "transfiguration" class), walked on water (Harry would have used the spell, *"wingardium leviosa"*), and multiplied fish and loaves of bread (a similar spell was put on the contents of Bellatrix's bank vault, which Harry broke into in Book 7). The truth is that there is no miracle performed in the gospels that is in any way more astounding than the many magical feats in Harry Potter's world. A large part of what has always made the gospel stories exciting to readers, just like the Harry Potter novels, are the elements of magic, fantasy and power.

*Battles with Evil*

Jesus often battles with demons that have taken possession of a person. He "calls them out" or sends them away. Harry Potter's enemies are also sometimes disguised as or have taken over the appearance of someone else. Jesus' power comes from the One who sent him, and his enemies are all manifestations or pawns of Satan, the deceiver. Harry Potter's challenges are overcome through his faith in Dumbledore, who continuously teaches that Love is the greatest magic, and Potter's enemies are mostly agents of Voldemort. Also, Jesus, while good, is given power to command demons and evil forces, who must obey him. Likewise, Harry is given the gift of Parseltongue, the rare ability to talk with snakes; thus he alone has control over "evil" or dangerous elements in the books; a power he often uses to the benefit of others.

## The Power of Faith and Love

A central theme in Christianity is faith: God has a plan, and people should listen to and heed God's call, and believe in him even when things don't seem clear. A similar theme is found in Harry Potter, between Harry and Dumbledore. Throughout the seven novels, it becomes clear that Dumbledore has more information about the truth of things than he is willing to share, and has a definite plan in store for Harry, even though he won't tell him what it is. Although in the beginning, Harry has enough faith and loyalty in Dumbledore to summon Fawkes, the sorting cap and Gryffindor's sword, as things get more difficult Harry has to continuously struggle to keep his faith in Dumbledore. After the death of Dobby in Book 7, however, Harry's faith is finally given unconditionally:

> He had made his choice while he dug Dobby's grave; he had decided to continue along the winding, dangerous path indicated for him by Albus Dumbledore, to accept that he had not been told everything that he wanted to know, but simply to trust. He had no desire to doubt him again, he did not want to hear anything that would deflect him from his purpose. (*Deathly Hallows*, 454)

Another important Christian theme is Love. The golden rule, "Love your neighbor as yourself," is sometimes recognized as Jesus' single greatest ethical teaching, and the simple claim that "God is Love" is not infrequently given as a definitive statement of Christian belief. Likewise, in the Harry Potter series, we learn that love is the greatest magic; it is more powerful than Voldemort's dark skills. It is the magic that protects Harry from his enemies and guarantees his eventual victory. Dumbledore, the surrogate God-the-Father figure in the novels, promotes the idea that love is more powerful than all other magic, something that Voldemort never accepts:

> "The old argument," he said softly. "But nothing I have seen in the world has supported your famous pronouncements that love is more powerful than my kind of magic, Dumbledore." (*Halfblood Prince*, 444)

Incidentally, a passage from the book of John concerning love can be used in defense of Harry Potter. "Beloved, let us love one another, because love is from God; everyone who loves is born of God and knows God. Whoever does not love does not know God, for God is love" (I John 4:7-12). In the series, Harry Potter knows love and it is this power that enables him to defeat Voldemort. Therefore, it could be argued that Harry Potter is "born of God and knows God."

## Sacrificial Death and Subsequent Resurrection

There is nothing so crucial to Christian theology, nor so sensitive to criticism, as Jesus' sacrificial death (which is believed to break the chains of sin and save all humanity) and his subsequent resurrection (the evidence that Jesus is God's son, savior, and that believers can likewise expect life after death). Jesus' physical resurrection is the *epicenter* of Christian faith. It is revealing that before the last book of Harry Potter was even published, several critics were already forecasting that Harry would face some sort of sacrificial death. Based on the similarities between Harry Potter and Jesus Christ, many bloggers guessed that the seventh novel would have Harry die to defeat his enemies:

> But perhaps Harry will perform the ultimate sacrifice by defeating Voldemort and dying himself so everyone else will have the chance to

live on. We really won't know until the releases of *Half-Blood Prince* and Book 7, but it's still fun to make predictions based on the possible foreshadowing and Biblical symbolism.[51]

His death will be a noble one, it is prophesied in the blogs, a death both sacrificial and necessary to save the world from the satanic Lord Voldemort. I agree with this line. I also expect Harry's death to show that his character's path is modeled on the Gospel accounts of Jesus, and, more significantly, that the link between him and wizardry-school headmaster Albus Dumbledore is patterned on the most essential relationship in the Christian Bible - that between Jesus the Son and God the Father.[52]

As it turns out, the way in which Harry faces his death in Book Seven is more similar to the Passion of Christ than anyone could have guessed. Harry Potter fully realizes that Dumbledore *intended* him to die at Voldemort's hand. Such is his love and faith in Dumbledore that Harry goes willingly to his death; hoping by his sacrifice to stop Voldemort and effectively save the world:

> Finally, the truth. Lying with his face pressed into the dusty carpet of the office where he had once thought he was learning the secrets of victory, Harry understood at last that he was not supposed to survive. His job was to walk calmly into Death's welcoming arms. Along the way, he was to dispose of Voldemort's remaining links to life, so that when at last he flung himself across Voldemort's path, and did not raise a wand to defend himself, the end would be clean, and the job that ought to have been done in Godric's Hollow would be finished: neither would live, neither could survive. (*Deathly Hallows*, 554)

The exact nature of Christ's resurrection is likewise a hotly contested topic – and has been throughout the history of the Church. A central tenet of Christian faith is that the term "resurrection" means the physical, bodily re-animation of a fully deceased human body. As such, the Christian tradition is unique in claiming that Jesus Christ was *actually* raised, in bodily form, from the dead. Any other accounts of figures dying and re-appearing differ substantially, it is argued, because they were only mythological or symbolic. The same criticism will of course be used against claims that Harry Potter resurrected. And perhaps he did not, strictly speaking. However, Rowling's final book includes all of the right literary requirements to designate Harry Potter as a dying and resurrecting savior of the type that has been celebrated in various traditions for thousands of years. How we interpret the differences between Jesus' death and Harry's cannot mask the underlying similarities.

Harry went willingly to his death, gave no resistance, and was hit by a killing curse. It was the intent of his self-sacrifice that sealed his victory over evil. He found himself in a heaven of sorts (significantly it was "King's Cross" station) where he was able to talk to his deceased friend and guide, Dumbledore:

> "But I should have died – I didn't defend myself! I meant to let him kill me!"
>
> "And that," said Dumbledore, "Will, I think, have made all the difference." (*Deathly Hallows,* 567)

Dumbledore told him, that if he so chose, Harry would 'go on' to other things, leaving his body behind.

> "I've got to go back, haven't I?"
> "That is up to you. "
> "I've got a choice? "
> "Oh yes." Dumbledore smiled at him. "We are in King's Cross, you say? I think that if you decided not to go back, you would be able to... let's say... board a train."
> "And where would that take me?"
> "On," said Dumbledore simply. (*Deathly Hallows,* 567)

We must assume that if Harry had "boarded a train," then his physical body would never reanimate and he would be truly dead. He chose, instead, to go back and try and defeat Voldemort once and for all.

Harry was subjected to humiliation by his enemies, as Voldemort (believing Harry to be dead) celebrated his triumph by performing the "Cruciatus Curse" on Harry's body (582). He was believed dead by all of his followers and friends, who wept for him. His body was carried in a procession by Hagrid, and displayed as a symbol of Voldemort's triumph. Briefly, it seemed that evil had won the battle, but then Harry rose up, fought the final battle and defeated Voldemort forever. More important than the scientific nuances of the word "resurrection" are the literary themes found here: the hero appeared dead and was mourned. His followers are then later surprised that he is not actually dead, and celebrate his return. Such a literary motif would apply equally to both Harry and Jesus.

For those familiar with mythology and able to look in the gospels for universal symbols, themes and motifs rather than strictly literal accounts of history, the connections between Harry Potter and Jesus Christ can go even deeper.

## Half-breeds

One common motif in mythology is that of the "half-divine hero." Stories and folklore from nearly all cultures explain their heroes' supernatural strength and powers by giving them a unique parentage; usually a mortal mother and an immortal father. The mother is sometimes referred to as a virgin – but this can mean simply that, rather than becoming pregnant through intercourse with a mortal male, the infant is sired through supernatural means. Often these heroes are raised by a human father, who may not even know that his wife secretly bore the child of a god. These figures are sometimes referred to as half gods or Demi-gods. Dionysus, Hercules, Gilgamesh, Perseus and many more heroes are on this list, as well as historical figures like Alexander the Great. Any sufficiently grand personage could be given a higher status through this mythological motif. The divine parentage manifests in special abilities; or, in other versions, figures are given miraculous gifts and special items later by their divine parent.

To take a familiar example, the sorcerer Merlin was son of a mortal woman and a spirit of the air, giving him his magical ability. Jesus, meanwhile, was born of a mortal woman and the Holy Spirit (a face of the triune God) and announced by an angel. He was raised by his father Joseph, but knew that he also had a divine father. Incidentally, some critics have argued that Rowling's boy wizard is indebted mostly to the Merlin myths. Like Jesus and Harry, Merlin was also terrorized by a powerful ruler (named

Voltigern) as a baby, due to a prophecy by his astrologers. Although Voltigern and Voldemort sound a little alike, there is no indication that Rowling got her inspiration from the Merlin story – although she may well have.

Rowling's treatment of the Demi-god motif is innovative. Rather than having a mortal woman for a mother and a divinity or deity for a father, Harry's mother (Lily) was a "mud-blood," who came from a mundane, non-magical family, while his father (James) was a warlock, who came from the magical world. Harry, like his enemy Voldemort, is a half-blood: half ordinary and half magical.

### Lions and Serpents

Harry Potter is associated with the lion through his placement in Gryffindor, whose symbol is a lion. His enemies are collectively and repeated identified with snakes and serpents: "Draco" Malfoy, placed in "Slytherin," whose symbol is a snake, and Voldemort with his pet companions Nagini, a giant, venomous, hooded snake that Voldemort makes into a Horcrux, and Salazar Slytherin's basilisk, which Harry defeats in Book Two.

Jesus is called "The Lion of Judea" and frequently identified as a lion, and Satan's symbol has always been a serpent – probably because of the snake's role in the temptation episode of Genesis. If these symbolic representations of good and evil were unique to Harry Potter and the Bible, we would probably conclude that Rowling had done the borrowing; the symbols are just too specific for them to be accidental attributes. However, the lion has been a symbol of divinity, righteousness, courage, and the triumph of good over evil for a very long time – at least a thousand years before the Christian era. Likewise, the snake has long been identified with evil, sin, or philosophically, with time and the cycle of death and rebirth.

### A Girl, a Sword, a Snake, and a Flying Hero

A very common motif in mythology, easily recognizable in the second Harry Potter novel and also identifiable, although with more difficulty, in the Bible is the story of a hero with a powerful sword and a magical means of flight that saves a princess or maiden from the captivity of a dragon or sea-monster. Manifestations of this story include, most famously, Perseus on Pegasus the flying horse saving the chained Andromeda from being sacrificed to the sea beast, or the Christian legend of St. George the dragon slayer. It is essentially a battle scene between good and evil, although it has a much deeper esoteric significance.

In *Harry Potter and the Chamber of Secrets*, Ron's sister Ginny is possessed by Tom Riddle (Voldemort's teenage self) and taken deep into the belly of the caverns under Hogwarts. Harry descends into the underworld to save her, and his faith and bravery is rewarded by a magical sword, which he uses to slay a basilisk and "save the girl." He then relies on Fawkes, Dumbledore's phoenix capable of bearing many times its own weight, to fly himself and Ginny to safety. The same motif can also be found in the Book of Revelation, where the battle takes place in the heavens between a snake, a mother fleeing from the snake's venom, and a mighty, armed, winged protector (usually identified as the archangel Michael).

However there is a more symbolic reading as well. Jesus Christ, by his death and resurrection, defeated his enemy, Satan (always represented as a serpent, as he was in the Garden of Eden). Jesus came to save his followers, represented collectively as a feminine entity: "The Holy Mother Church." Although he may not have wings, he can both walk on water and ascend bodily into heaven. Jesus also had a sword – but it is well hidden in the symbol of the cross. The cross and the sword are actually identical figures, symbolically: (†). It is only the Christian interpretation of that symbol and the emphasis on the death and resurrection, rather than the struggle over the adversary, which makes the distinction. Jesus is often thought of as a pacifist, but he makes it clear that he came "not to bring peace, but the sword" (Matthew 10:34). It is perhaps Christianity's unique inversion of classical symbolism from the sword of conflict to the cross of non-violence that is responsible for its peaceful reputation. Ironically, the symbol that has come to represent peace in modern times is an inverted cross with broken arms – although this symbol was actually designed for the Nuclear Disbarment campaign and has no overt religious meaning.

## 7 Seals, 7 Horcruxes

In the Book of Revelation, the plot revolves around the destruction of the seven seals that bind a sacred scroll. The seven seals must be broken to open this manuscript, which will undo the work of God's creation and end the world. Only the Lamb is worthy to open the scroll, because he made the sacrifice that saved many people (Rev. 5-6). Similarly, Harry's quest in Books Six and Seven is the destruction of seven magical objects that contain pieces of Voldemort's soul, called "Horcruxes." All of the Horcruxes must be found and destroyed before Voldemort can be killed.

The symbolism of the number seven, however, predates Christianity and comes from classical cosmology and ancient philosophical traditions. The system of Pythagoras, for example, was very detailed: there were seven known visible planets, and each planet had a certain vibration or sound – which gave rise to the seven notes in an octave (the eighth note being a repetition of the first on a higher scale). Many Greco-Roman religions and spiritual communities believed that to get from this place (earth) to heaven (the source), you had to travel back through the seven planets or heavens.

The similarities in this case are most likely due to Rowling's interest in alchemy (which has preserved classical symbolism, cosmology and thought more accurately than the Bible) rather than any Christian-based inspiration. In a 1998 interview, Rowling remarked:

> I've never wanted to be a witch, but an alchemist, now that's a different matter. To invent this wizard world, I've learned a ridiculous amount about alchemy. Perhaps much of it I'll never use in the books, but I have to know in detail what magic can and cannot do in order to set the parameters and establish the stories' logic.[53]

According to the website *Harry Potter for Seekers*, which aims to "discover the many layers of spiritual symbolism hidden beneath the excitement, mystery and fascination of Harry Potter,"[54] Rowling even consciously crafted the titles and order of the seven books along alchemical guidelines.[55]

| 1 | Earth | STONE |
|---|---|---|
| 2 | Air | CHAMBER |
| 3 | Water | AZKABAN *(island)* |
| 4 | Fire | FIRE |
| 5 | Quintessence | PHOENIX |
| 6 | Soul | BLOOD |
| 7 | Spirit | HALLOW *(Holy)* |

We might wonder whether C.S. Lewis had a similar inspiration for the organization of the seven books of his Narnia series, which ended in *The Last Battle*.

### James, Peter and John

One final surprising Christian parallel we find in Harry Potter are the names of Christ's three most prominent disciples: James, Peter and John. Sirius' three best friends were *James* Potter, *Peter* Pettigrew and Remus *John* Lupin. In both cases it was Peter who betrayed his friend.

## Is Harry Potter a Christ Figure?

Although Rowling is obviously aware of the parallels between Jesus and Harry, it is difficult to claim that Harry is *only* a modern retelling of the story of Jesus Christ. Rowling not only borrows from a wide range of mythological and literary motifs, she also creates innovative characters, plot events and magical items. Hence the claim that Harry Potter is a Christ figure – although it can be made – is problematic.

A "Christ figure" is simply a literary referent used to identify a fictional character that seems to symbolize Jesus Christ in a significant way, such as through the endurance of suffering, a sacrificial death, or a (perceived) rebirth or resurrection. Many literary figures have been called Christ figures by various researchers, including Ahab of *Moby Dick*, Gandalf or Frodo Baggins of *The Lord of the Rings*, Galahad in the *Grail Quest*, and McMurphy in *One Flew Over the Cuckoo's Nest*. Sophocles' *Oedipus Rex* has even been labelled a Christ figure, although his story was written centuries before Christianity. Killinger gives the following brief overview in an online discussion about Harry Potter's relationship with Jesus Christ:

> A Christ figure is a literary device, a particular way of shaping an important character in a novel. He (or she) may not conform in every instance to the biblical image of Jesus, but bears enough of the traits or characteristics to suggest the relationship and send us looking for important messages in the text.[56]

Credible criteria for potential Christ figures include:

- ★ Comes from an extraordinary origin
- ★ Possesses a "secret identity" and dual nature
- ★ Displays a distinctive appearance
- ★ Exhibits extraordinary powers
- ★ Generates awe and wonder
- ★ Gathers and leads disciples
- ★ Saves others
- ★ Suffers a sacrificial death
- ★ Descends into "hell"
- ★ Rises from the dead

Harry Potter certainly meets most, if not all, of these factors. His "descent into hell" occurs during Book One. To get into the Chamber of Secrets, Harry first had to pass the three-headed dog that guards the door. In classical mythology, Cerberus, the three headed dog, guards the gates of Hell. Defeating this monster was one of the twelve feats of Heracles. As we mentioned earlier, "rising from the dead" is open to interpretation.

Given the similarities between Jesus Christ and Harry Potter, it is no surprise that Harry Potter was identified as a Christ figure by some writers even before the final book was released:

> Harry Potter… is a witting or unwitting Christ figure who actually battles the forces of darkness for the souls of the faithful and wins a place in readers' hearts because he so admirably conforms to our expectations of such a redemptive figure.[57]

Other readers have been strongly opposed to this identification. In November of 2002, *Beliefnet.com* hosted an online debate on the topic, "Harry Potter, Christ Figure? Professional Harry watchers on whether J.K. Rowling's hero is meant to resemble Christ." Although the debate ran when only four books of the series were available, the opinions given are worth revisiting. Professor Thomas L. Martin, from Florida Atlantic University writes:

> Leaving aside Harry's "Christlikeness" for the moment, Harry Potter does conform to what (mythologist Joseph) Campbell would call the pattern of the mythic hero. Potter is marked at birth for something special, prophecies foretell the high destiny he faces, the various mentors and rivals he encounters along the way, and then, of course, the ultimate showdown with evil. These characteristics not only link him to Christ – in Campbell's system – but also Cinderella, Odysseus, Buddha, and other heroes of other times and places.[58]

Professor Andrew Blake of King Alfred's College, Winchester (UK) agrees: "My first responses to Harry Potter were that he is being written (and remember, he hasn't yet been fully written) as a redeemer. So far, so Christ-like."[59]

Richard Abanes on the other hand, author of *Fantasy and Your Family*, argues "at best, Rowling's novels are terribly derivative of age-old myths, legends, and stories. In fact, she habitually borrows from older (and better told, I might add) tales to flesh out her stories. Rowling's work is really nothing but a long string of mini-derivations dressed up in 21st century garb."[60] Patrick Rothfuss, author of *The Name of the Wind*, contributes to the conversation by expanding this idea:

> Of all the irritating literary games people play, Find-the-Jesus is one of the most wearying to me. Not every book has Christ symbolism. Let it go. People use stairs. People suffer. People have fathers. People make noble sacrifices. And, in fantastic stories, people come back from the dead. Odin did it. Osiris did it. Sherlock Holmes did it. Buffy did it. Spock did it. Hell... Voldemort died and came back. It takes more than that to make a Christ figure. You want good Jesus symbolism in a fantasy story? Go to Aslan in the Lion the Witch and the Wardrobe. There's a Christ figure for you. Harry is, at best, just following a standard sacrificial hero archetype. It's a storyline that was old before Jesus was born.[61]

Remarkably, both sides of the above argument rely on the *same evidence* to support their claims. On the one hand, those who don't see Harry as a Christ figure argue that any apparent similarities are in fact common in mythology and literature, and J.K. Rowling was simply throwing together ancient mythological symbols that have nothing to do with Jesus – because the story was "old before Jesus was born." Those who do see Harry as a Christ figure, on the other hand, also see Harry as a mythological composite, but in their view, this *connects* him to Jesus Christ, who is also in some way related to mythological tradition.

In other words, everybody agrees that Harry Potter and Jesus Christ have a lot in common but disagree about how important these similarities are or where they came from. In fact the determining factor has very little to do with Harry Potter, and everything to do with the reader's understanding of Jesus Christ. Is Jesus absolutely unique in history, divorced from common universal mythological traditions, making all apparent similarities therefore unbinding or irrelevant? Or is he related to those mythologies, either as founder, or product?

Of course today, in light of Rowling's own admissions on the subject and the parallels in the seventh book that have led even Christians to accept Harry as one of their own, the voices denying the similarities between Jesus and Harry have lessened. And yet the most striking question has so far been ignored: *Why do these similarities exist at all?* Why does Jesus – a monumental figure in modern world religion generally believed to have been historical – have so much in common with the obviously fictional character of Harry Potter?

Now that we've seen the similarities between them, can we spot the differences? The main distinction, it will be argued, is that Jesus Christ is *real*: Jesus has traditionally been viewed as a historical figure, while Harry is instantly recognized as fiction. But does this distinction apply to the many seemingly mythical elements in the gospels? Can Jesus' miracles be separated from Harry's magic tricks because they *really happened* – or will we allow that certain features of the gospels were exaggerated or intended to be literary. And if so, where do we stop? What protects Jesus from the claim that he is, like Harry, a fictional character?

Perhaps the real question we need to ask is not whether Harry Potter is a "Christ Figure" (similar to a historical religious savior), but rather whether Jesus Christ is a "Potter Figure" (a composition of redemptive mythological symbols and philosophies). The remainder of this book will aim at exploring this issue.

## Conclusions and Summary

Similarities between Jesus Christ, Harry Potter, and countless other figures *do exist*; but Jesus Christ is the only figure whose followers have faith that his life and acts (including the nature-defying miracles) have a historical basis.

As long as the biblical account of Jesus is assumed to be historically valid, any apparent connection with mythology (including the modern re-writing of mythology that is Harry Potter) can be automatically discounted. However, if we can present evidence that destabilizes the claim that the Bible records historical events, the boundaries between Harry Potter and Jesus become very thin.

Critics argue that Harry Potter is only borrowing from universal mythological symbols, but if this is true, can Jesus be accused of the same? Could the similarities between Harry Potter and Jesus Christ have resulted from Christianity's inclusion of mythological motifs, rather than Harry Potter's inclusion of biblical ones?

In recent decades, every attempt to demonstrate that Jesus Christ is a literary figure, or that most of his deeds in the Bible are adaptations of pre-existing traditions, has been so strongly repudiated by conservative scholars that any claim to that effect is automatically discredited. As we will see in the next chapter, however, the charge that the life of Jesus has too much in common with pagan gods and mythological traditions has been leveled against Christianity repeatedly and consistently, all the way back to the very earliest periods of the church.

Just how much of the gospel accounts of Jesus are based on pre-existing mythology? Can we find the historical founder of Christianity by removing the mythology from around him? Is there reliable evidence that Jesus Christ was a historical person? These are some of the questions that will be addressed in the next chapter.

CHAPTER TWO

# Doubting Jesus:
# Ancient and Modern
# Controversy

*"To the question, then, on what grounds do you deny that such a person as Jesus Christ existed as a man? The proper answer is, because his existence as a man has, from the earliest day on which it can be shown to have been asserted, been as earnestly and strenuously denied, and that, not by enemies of the Christian name, or unbelievers of the Christian faith, but by the most intelligent, most learned, most sincere of the Christian name, whoever left the world proofs of their intelligence and learning in their writings, and of their sincerity in their sufferings."*
*—Reverend R. Taylor, 1834*

IN THE LAST CHAPTER WE EXPLORED the similarities between Jesus and Harry Potter and ended with the question, is Jesus, like Harry, a purely literary figure? To begin with, we need to understand that this is not a new question. As Reverend Taylor pointed out in 1834, the idea that Jesus Christ existed as a historical man has been denied not only by modern critics, but also by Christian communities (now branded as heretics) since the earliest periods of the Christian movement.[1]

St. Ignatius, for example, who was martyred before 117AD, fought against the Docetist heresy, which denied that Jesus had come in the flesh. Docetists, most likely with the Platonic split between spirit and matter in mind, believed that Jesus had come in the appearance or "semblance" of a human only, but did not have a physical body. Ignatius had to vigorously dispute the claim that Jesus was born, crucified and raised only in appearance. T.R. Glover captures the spirit of his writing:

> Men around him spoke of a phantom crucified by the deluded soldiers amid the deluded Jews. – No! cries Ignatius, over and over, he *truly* suffered, he *truly* rose, ate and drank, and was no daemon without a body – none of it is *seeming*, it is all truly, truly, truly. He has been called hysterical – death before him, his Lord's reality denied, and only time for one word –*Truly.*[2]

Overlooking Ignatius' zeal and emphasis on the Jesus who *truly* existed, how can we reconcile the traditional account of Christian history with the fact that early "heretics" denied that Jesus had come in the flesh? The Docetist understanding of Jesus is not some late schism; the New Testament Epistle of John shows that similar beliefs were active and threateningly popular very early in the Christian communities:

> Beloved, believe not every spirit, but try the spirits whether they are of God: because many false prophets are gone out into the world. Hereby know ye the Spirit of God: Every spirit that confesseth that Jesus Christ is come in the flesh is of God: And every spirit that confesseth not that Jesus Christ is come in the flesh is not of God: and this is that spirit of antichrist, whereof ye have heard that it should come; and even now already is it in the world. (1 John 4: 1-3)

Rather than the traditional account of one, catholic (universal) message of Jesus Christ, in the first few centuries of Christianity there were dozens of factions, each of which believed very different things about Jesus, and many of whom believed that the major events in Jesus' life occurred only in appearance.

At the same time, classically educated scholars familiar with ancient philosophy, poetry or religion have been struck by the similarities between Jesus Christ and other mythological figures. Jesus raised the dead and healed the sick, and so did Asclepius; Jesus provided wine at a wedding feast, and suffered so that humanity might be saved, as did Dionysus; Jesus descended into Hell, and had powers to make the lion and lamb lay down together, just like Orpheus. These parallels were much more obvious in the first few centuries of the Christian movement, when these other figures played an active role in religion, spiritual practices, literature and culture, than they are today. Hence Celsus, a pagan philosopher who wrote a condemnation of the Christian movement in the 2nd century AD, could ask:

> Are these distinctive happenings unique to the Christians - and if so, how are they unique? Or are ours to be accounted myths and theirs believed? What reasons do the Christians give for the distinctiveness of their beliefs? In truth there is nothing at all unusual about what the Christians believe, except that they believe it to the exclusion of more comprehensive truths about God.[3]

This alone should come as a surprise to those familiar with traditional accounts of Christian history. Jesus was supposed to be something entirely new. His miracles, death and resurrection were expected to shock and awe; even his humility and ethics are assumed to be in stark contrast to the wild revelries of the pagans. Actually – as Celsus pointed out – there was nothing in the *doctrine* of Christianity that was at all surprising to their contemporaries.

Writing several decades earlier than Celsus and trying to justify his beliefs to critical outsiders, the apologist Justin Martyr, who converted to Christianity around 130 and was martyred around 165, acknowledges the parallels between Jesus and pagan figures without ever making the modern claim that these similarities are simply coincidental:

> When we say that the Word, who is first born of God, was produced without sexual union, and that he, Jesus Christ, our teacher, was crucified and died, and rose again, and ascended into heaven; we propound nothing different from what you believe regarding those whom you esteem sons of Jupiter (Zeus). For you know how

many sons your esteemed writers ascribed to Jupiter: Mercury, the interpreting word and teacher of all; Æsculapius, who, though he was a great physician, was struck by a thunderbolt, and so ascended to heaven; and Bacchus too, after he had been torn limb from limb; and Hercules, when he had committed himself to the flames to escape his toils; and the sons of Leda, and Dioscuri; and Perseus, son of Danae; and Bellerophon, who, though sprung from mortals, rose to heaven on the horse Pegasus (*First Apology* XXI).[4]

Justin's formal argument is that although other pagan gods are also said to have been "born without sexual union, crucified, died, rose and ascended into heaven," Jesus Christ physically and actually performed these feats, and is therefore unique:

But in no instance, not even in any of those called sons of Jupiter, did they imitate the being crucified; for it was not understood by them, all the things said of it having been put symbolically. (*First Apology* LV)

This argument is no different from the assertion that Harry Potter and Jesus Christ are fundamentally different, because Jesus was real. However, this distinction is only possible with faith that Jesus genuinely performed the supernatural deeds that other figures accomplished only "symbolically"; thus, the critical question is whether Jesus was a historical figure who performed his miraculous feats of power *in the flesh*, rather than just in appearance. The importance of this criterion was not lost on the early church fathers. Faced on all sides with the criticism that the gospel stories were spiritual allegories and not intended as historical truth, the early church fathers argued passionately for the fact of Jesus' physical body. That they needed to argue at all, and so vehemently, that Jesus was a *real person* despite his similarities to other traditions, is an indication that this claim was not widely accepted.

The purpose of this chapter is to show, first, that the claim of Jesus Christ being either in part or in totality comparable to the mythologies of other cultures is not a modern invention of conspiracy fanatics, but has been argued and supported by some of the greatest thinkers in history; and second, that the current academic consensus that there was a historical founder behind Christianity is the product of a specific trend in academic thought, rather than a conclusion based on reliable evidence.

At the same time, the arguments and quotations presented here are not to be construed as an argument for or against the existence of Jesus Christ; many of the works presented have already been criticized, called into question or disputed as academic research into the subject has progressed. My goal is only to demonstrate that a modern controversy over the historical Jesus exists, that it has a long and substantial history, and that, in effect, the jury is still out.

I also want to show that certain claims regarding Jesus are not modern delusions of "fringe" scholars – in fact there are few claims made about Jesus today that were not made centuries earlier. The reason a handful of writers continue to re-raise these arguments is because most people are completely unaware that they can be made at all. After demonstrating that the hypothesis of Jesus Christ as Christianity's historical founder is not the only logical possibility, and that the evidence used to support him is not unanimously accepted, can we move into more speculative theories.

## The Modern Debate

In the year 1600, scientist and astronomer Giordano Bruno reiterated Celsus' argument that the gospel stories of Jesus Christ were akin to pagan mythologies. Unfortunately, at the time, the Church did not permit such blasphemous accusations – after a seven-year trial he was burned on the stake. As R.E. Witt relates:

> Excommunicated by an obscurantist ecclesiasticism he went to the stake for his beliefs. He was convinced that the wisdom and magic-born religion of ancient Egypt excelled the fanatical theory that burnt dissident thinkers as heretics. For the Biblical record was on par with the Greek myths. Refusing to retract his teachings, he met his doom dauntlessly, for he had less cause than his judges to fear the verdict of history and could snap his fingers at them in warning. Giordano Bruno, the unfrocked monk, perished on 16 February 1600, for his intransigent denial that Christianity was unique.[5]

Bruno's death represents perhaps the birth pains of the Enlightenment; an age when mankind flexed its mental prowess and attempted to find logical answers through reason rather than by faith, superstition or revelation. Although most scholars attribute the movement to the 18th or 19th centuries, it can be traced back to Descartes' *cogito ergo sum* (1637), or even the Scientific Revolution that began about a century earlier (Copernicus published *On the Revolutions of the Heavenly Spheres* in 1543). An interest in classicism and the translation of mythologies from newly discovered parts of the world, critical biblical scholarship, along with the weakening power of Church censorship, led to the publication of many dozen treatises investigating the historical nature of Jesus Christ.

One of the earliest of these essays was published by G.E. Lessing (based on notes by Reimarus) under the general title *Wolfenbüttel Fragments,* between 1774 and 1778. It concludes that Jesus was wholly terrestrial and never meant to start a new religion. French Enlightenment writer and philosopher Voltaire (1694-1778), although maintaining the idea of a historical, crucified founder, cautions that very little of the gospels could be taken at face value. Voltaire argued that the Gospels were "written by persons acquainted with nothing, full of contradictions and imposture" and that "the whole history Jesus – only a fanatic or a stupid knave would deny it – should be examined in the light of reason."[6] Constantin-François Volney and Charles François Dupuis, two great thinkers of the French Enlightenment, published works in the 1790's claiming that the stories of Jesus Christ found in the gospels, as well as many other myths, were based on movements of the sun through the zodiac. According to Dupuis:

> Jesus is still less man than God. He is, like all the deities that men have adored, the sun; Christianity is a solar myth. When we shall have shown, that the pretended history of a God, who is born of a virgin in the winter solstice, who is resuscitated at Easter or at the Vernal equinox, after having descended into hell, who brings with Him a retinue of twelve apostles whose chief possesses all the attributes of Janus—a God, conqueror of the prince of darkness, who translates mankind into the empire of light, and who heals the woes of the world, is only a solar fable, ... it will be almost as unnecessary to inquire whether there was a man called Christ as it is to inquire whether some prince is called Hercules.[7]

The writings of Constantin Volney (1757-1820) were also influential in challenging the claim that Jesus was historical. In 1808, Napoleon I was under the influence of Volney when, in a conversation he had with Wieland at Weimar, he said it was a great question to decide whether Jesus had existed.[8] Another theory was raised in Germany around the same time by Bahrdt and Venturini, who introduced a skeptical movement into Jesus' life that "so far forsook the gospel representation as to leave his real historical form largely a matter of conjecture."[9] Jesus, they said, was a protégé of the Essenes, who had drawn upon secret wisdom from Babylonia, Egypt, India and Greece. Thus, he was a revealer of ancient and secret wisdom, but not the savior portrayed in the gospels.

Thomas Jefferson, in a book now frequently called the *Jefferson Bible* wrote under the premise that the gospel authors had incorporated both events and teachings that could not be historically accurate to Jesus himself.[10] In 1829 Reverend Robert Taylor published *The Diegesis,* which professes Christianity did not originate with a historical founder and in fact has far more ancient roots. Prior to this work, Taylor founded the Christian Evidence Society, among whose central claims were that the persons in the gospels never existed and the events in the gospels never happened. Taylor was thrown in jail for blasphemy and conspiracy to overthrow the Christian religion. A more influential (and controversial) work was David Friedrich Strauss's *The Life of Jesus*, first published in 1835 and translated into English in 1846. *The Life of Jesus* is an attempt to remove all of the mythical elements from the gospel accounts in order to search for the genuine figure behind them; as such Strauss is considered a pioneer in the historical investigation of Jesus:

> The first Gospel accounts, in Strauss's opinion, have not been drawn up from an historical point of view. They do not relate the events as these took place, but express certain ideas by means of images and symbols, or, to employ the exact term that Strauss makes use of, by myths. What is important in the notion of the myth is not the idea of unreality, but that of a symbolical expression of a higher truth. The mythical explanation seems to Strauss the synthesis which resolves the

antibook between the naturalist and the supernatural explanations of the life of Jesus.[11]

Strauss's research was continued by Bruno Bauer, who accepted Strauss's premise but focused on the mythical rather than historical Jesus. Starting in 1840, he argued that Jesus was merely a fusion of Greek, Roman and Jewish theologies. In *Christ and the Caesars* (1877),[12] Bauer argued that the language of the New Testament was more in line with Stoicism and Roman culture than Judaism. Hermann Detering notes, "The 'demon' to whom Bauer submitted had whispered to him that all the Pauline letters were inauthentic and that an historical person named Jesus very probably never existed."[13] Wilhelm Wrede would later (1901) repeat many of Bauer's ideas in his book, *The Messianic Secret*. Going back in the other direction, *Vie de Jésus* (life of Jesus) by Ernest Renan in 1863 – mostly a compilation of German criticism – was directed at the public and consequently attracted more attention. Renan's novel paints a literary picture of a (very human) gentle dreamer, and makes the claim that the idea of a risen God comes from the passion of a deluded woman. In 1875 Kersey Graves published *The World's Sixteen Crucified Saviors* (or *Christianity Before Christ*). In his preface, Graves states that Jesus taught no new doctrine or moral precept; that he inculcated the same religion and morality as other moral teachers; and that he differs so little in his character, preaching, and practical life from some of the oriental Gods, that "no person whose mind is not deplorably warped and biased by early training can call one divine while he considers the other human."[14]

Around the same time, the "Rosetta Stone," found by Napoleon's army in 1799 and translated by Egyptologist Jean-Francois Champollion in 1822, inspired a frenzied academic study of Egyptian mythologies. This movement motivated specifically Egyptian comparisons between Christianity and mythology. In 1877 W.R. Cooper published *The Horus Myth in its Relation to Christianity*, in which he writes:

> The works of art, the ideas, the expressions, and the heresies of the first four centuries of the Christian era cannot be well studied without a right comprehension of the nature and influence of the Horus myth.

We cannot ignore these facts. We have as Christians no reason to be afraid of them.[15]

Egyptologist Gerald Massey, (1828-1907) author of *Gnostic and Historic Christianity* and other works, also compared Jesus' biography with Egyptian mythology. Once having made this identification, however, he goes on to conclude that the figure of Jesus is completely mythological, and could never have been historical. In a private edition of his lectures published at the turn of the 20th century (c.1900), he says:

> Nothing is more certain, according to honest evidence, than that the Christian scheme of redemption is founded on a fable misinterpreted; that the prophecy of fulfillment was solely astronomical, and the Coming One as the Christ who came in the end of an age, or of the world, was but a metaphorical figure, a type of time, from the first, which never could take form in historic personality, any more than Time in Person could come out of a clock-case when the hour strikes; that no Jesus could become a Nazarene by being born at, or taken to, Nazareth; and that the history in our Gospels is from beginning to end the identifiable story of the Sun-God, and the Gnostic Christ who never could be made flesh.[16]

John Mackinnon Robertson (1856-1933) wrote several books in his lifetime about the mythical Jesus, who he identified as the solar deity of a Jewish cult. Based on the evidence that everything found in the gospels can be paralleled to pagan mythology, and that the Jesus Paul speaks of is a "speechless sacrifice" rather than a person of action and teaching, Robertson concluded that Jesus was a composite of pagan myths.[17] He is perhaps most famous for *Pagan Christs: Studies in Comparative Theology*, which was published in 1903. Also published in 1903 was G.R.S. Mead's *Did Jesus Live 100 BC*, which finds a Talmudic basis for the Jesus of the gospels. In 1906 Albert Schweitzer published *The Quest of the Historical Jesus*, a classic work of biblical historical criticism. Thomas Whittaker, meanwhile, in *The Origins of Christianity* (London, 1904; 1909), argued "Jesus may not be an entirely fictitious person, yet the gospel stories are almost wholly mythical."[18] These texts influenced Arthur Drews' *The Christ Myth* (1909), which synthesized and strengthened many of the earlier arguments, and W.B. Smith's *Ecce Deus,* that earned a full review in *The New York Times* on August 13, 1911. A little later we find Edward Carpenter's *Pagan and Christian Creeds* (1920) and *Jesus of Nazareth: Myth or History* by Maurice Goguel (1926). According to Goguel:

> Jesus must, then, have been at the beginning the God of a mystery. At the time of Paul neither the God nor the mystery had become historical. They were to become so in the period to follow the creative age, when it would be no longer possible to understand the high spirituality which had inspired the primitive faith, and when the celestial drama upon which Christianity of the first generation had lived had been transported to earth.[19]

After a century of debate over the historical Jesus, by the beginning of the 20th century it was generally conceded that Jesus, even if he existed, was virtually unknowable. The great German scholar Rudolf Karl Bultmann and his new literary critical school of *Formgeschichte* (form criticism), effectively shut down inquiry into the historical Jesus with his memorable 1926 statement, "I do indeed think that we can know nothing concerning the life and personality of Jesus, since the early Christian sources show no interest in either, are moreover fragmentary and often legendary; and other sources about Jesus do not exist."[20] This position – that the historical Jesus is beyond the scope of rational inquiry – was taken for granted in 1927 by philosopher Bertrand Russell in his treatise, *Why I am not a Christian*:

> Historically, it is quite doubtful whether Christ ever existed at all, and if He did we do not know anything about Him, so that I am not concerned with the historical question, which is a very difficult one.[21]

In response to this apparent dead end, research into the historical Jesus led in two distinct directions. The first was a continued emphasis on comparative mythology, wherein the historical Jesus was ignored in favor of the interpretation of the mythos and its importance for understanding the human condition. This was the direction which gained prominence through the writings of Sigmund Freud, Carl Jung, Joseph Campbell, Mircea Eliade, and Sir James George Frazer. The second was a renewed interest in discovering the historical Jesus, *by identifying and removing* all traces of mythology, which focused on identifying dissimilar elements in the Christ movement that might have originated with a historical founder.

## Mythology, Archetypes and the Subconscious

James George Frazer's *The Golden Bough: A Study in Magic and Religion* (first published in 1890) scandalized Europe by equating the story of Jesus Christ with mythologies from more primitive and ancient peoples, and arguing that all mythical heroes that die and come back are really vegetation gods representing the changing seasons.[22] *The Golden Bough* had a major influence on anthropology and many of the poets and authors of the 20th century, and invited the interpretation of mythology and religion as allegories.

Frazer was an early piece of a movement towards the appreciation and universalism of humanity. With the ongoing synthesis and comparison between different religious and mythological traditions, it became clear to many that human beings, rather than gods, were responsible for the creation of their own myths – and moreover that the similarities between these stories reflected some as yet unknown common link between all humans. The study of mythology became seen as a way to access the raw, original *subconscious* desires and motivations of mankind.

In the late 1890's, Sigmund Freud interpreted mythology as the result of repressed sexual desires. For example, Sophocles' classic myth of Oedipus Rex (the King) was considered by Freud to be incestuous in nature, and to support his claim that all men have a subconscious desire to sleep with their mothers and kill their fathers. Freud's studies have become so widely appreciated that few people have not heard of the Oedipal Complex, which Freud explains in his work "The Interpretation of Dreams."

> His destiny moves us only because it might have been ours – because the oracle laid the same curse upon us before our birth as upon him. It is the fate of all of us, perhaps, to direct our first sexual impulse

towards our mother and our first hatred and our first murderous wish against our father. Our dreams convince us that this is so.[23]

It must be pointed out, however, that Freud's thought is rooted in the assumption that dreams and mythology are productions of the subconscious mind, and that subconscious motivations are universal. There may be truth in Freud's theories, but there are also some sensational claims that are not adequately supported. Critics of Freud have christened Freudian analysis the "find the penis" game. Trying to read Harry Potter, for example, along Freudian lines, is both possible and ultimately unsatisfying. In *Harry Potter's Oedipal Issues* (2001), Kelly Noel-Smith explains:

> Given that it is every child's phantasy to remove, by death, his or her father to enjoy exclusive possession of his or her mother (and, inversely, to eliminate one's mother to take her place with one's father), the reader of Harry Potter is able to indulge in wish fulfillment of the most basic phantasies without the grief which would ordinarily attach to them: we know, at a conscious level, that the story is not true; unconsciously, the deaths of Harry's parents represent a wonderful fulfillment of Oedipal phantasies.[24]

Less commonly known about Freud is his interest in comparative mythology. His book *Moses and Monotheism* (1938) explores the link between the Judaic monotheism of Moses and the sun-centered religion of the Egyptian pharaoh Akhenaten, claiming that Jewish monotheism was inspired by this violently intolerant Egyptian religious movement. As Jan Assman writes in *Moses the Egyptian*, "Freud stresses (quite correctly) the fact that he is dealing with the absolutely first monotheistic, counter-religious, and exclusivistically intolerant movement of this sort in history."[25]

Carl Gustav Jung later argued that the human psyche is by nature religious, and that mythology, religions, dreams, art and philosophy can be used to explore the unconscious:

> Myths are original revelations of the preconscious psyche, involuntary statements about unconscious psychic happenings, and anything but allegories of physical processes.[26]

Like many of his peers, interest into comparative mythology

greatly influenced his work. As a student of Freud, his early position was that myth originates and functions to satisfy the psychological need for contact with the unconscious. He was "staunchly committed to independent invention" of myth and asserted there is "no evidence and indeed no possibility of contact among all of the societies with similar myths."[27] Based on the similarities between various world traditions and the presumed impossibility of contact, Jung came up with the concepts of "the collective unconscious" and "psychological archetypes." In other words, since many cultures use the symbol of a dying and resurrecting savior figure, and since these cultures did not share the symbol with each other, it must have come out of universal subconscious forces.

Jung argued that Christianity, although once vital, stopped interpreting its myths and so stopped being relevant to modern people. "Belief is no adequate substitute for inner experience, and where this is absent even strong faith which came miraculously as a gift of grace may depart equally miraculously."[28] Noting the conflicts between the claim of a historical Jesus and comparative mythology, Jung reasons:

> If the statement that Christ rose from the dead is to be understood not literally but symbolically, then it is capable of various interpretations that do not conflict with knowledge and do not impair the meaning of the statement.[29]

According to prominent Jungian Mircea Eliade, all myths are religious myths (except for modern myths, which may be secular). Eliade also continues the Jungian idea that you cannot go from sacred to profane; in other words, it is possible for humans to create religious myths (sacred stories) based on mundane experience (profane), but not the other way around. Mythologist Joseph Campbell continued this emphasis, even subjugating the historical to the mythic. In *The Hero with a Thousand Faces* (1949) his primary purpose was to explore the similarities between Eastern and Western religions. Later, in his four-volume series of books *The Masks of God* (1959-1968), Campbell tried to summarize the main spiritual threads common throughout the world while examining their local manifestations. He made it clear that it is the stories themselves that are important – not whether or not the stories have historical basis:

> We may doubt whether such a scene ever actually took place. But that would not help us any; for we are concerned, at present, with problems of symbolism, not of historicity. We do not particularly care whether Rip van Winkle, Kamar al-Zaman, or Jesus Christ ever actually lived. Their *stories* are what concern us: and these stories are so widely distributed over the world – attached to various heroes in various lands – that the question of whether this or that local carrier of the universal theme may or may not have been a historical living man can be of only secondary moment. The stressing of this historical element will only lead to confusion; it will simply obfuscate the picture message.[30]

Campbell represented mythology studies at its most matured; however, by continuing in the tradition of Freud and Jung, he sought only the universal aspects of humanity which gave rise to specific mythological symbols and was not interested in finding any shared external source for these symbols.

Christian apologist C.S. Lewis reflects many of the humanistic tendencies and shifts Christianity went through in the middle of the 20th century. During the rise of the "modernist heresy" much of Christian thought and writing involved Neo-scholasticism and biblical literacy, along with the adamant refusal of the studies mentioned above. In the 1950's, however, under humanist theologians like Kahr Rahner and John Courtney Murray, Christian theology began to turn towards tolerance, inclusion and interfaith dialogue. The Second Vatican Council (1962) is a record of these changes, although the Catholic Church has since moved back to a more conservative position. An inspired theologian, C.S. Lewis accepts the universal mythology of Jung or Campbell and models a very modern (liberal) Christianity – one which could accept the mythical nature of the gospels without being threatened by it. His conclusion is that all the other figures who are similar to Jesus Christ were legends, stemming from the imagination, and that Jesus Christ was the same story, but as a historical reality:

> The heart of Christianity is a myth which is also a fact. The old myth of the Dying God, without ceasing to be myth, comes down

from the heaven of legend and imagination to the earth of history. It happens—at a particular date, in a particular place, followed by definable historical consequences. We pass from a Balder or an Osiris, dying nobody knows when or where, to a historical Person crucified (it is all in order) under Pontius Pilate. By becoming fact it does not cease to be myth: that is the miracle... God is more than god, not less: Christ is more than Balder, not less. We must not be ashamed of the mythical radiance resting on our theology. We must not be nervous about "parallels" and "Pagan Christs": they ought to be there—it would be a stumbling block if they weren't. We must not, in false spirituality, withhold our imaginative welcome.[31]

Lewis' hypothesis however, is based on the assumption that there is a great deal of evidence for the historical Jesus: "it is all in order." If Jesus existed, then similarities to mythology are simply irrelevant. Thus, the similarities between Jesus and other mythological figures are not threatening to Christians, but *only as long as* the evidence for the historical Jesus is strong enough to silence our incredulity that a historical person should have so much in common with mythology.

One limitation of the focus on psychological undercurrents of universal mythology is that, although popularizing the similarities between various mythological traditions, it also chained the subject into the fixed, limited historical period of the movement. Consequently the rich field of comparative mythology research is unfortunately seen as "dated" or only relevant for psychology majors.

## Criteria of Double Dissimilarity

While mythologists were busy exploring the similarities between Jesus Christ and world mythology and claiming that they were produced out of some universal human need or shared unconscious, biblical scholars continued the quest for the historical Jesus with a shifted focus. Using a methodological tool first advocated by Bultmann, the Criteria of Double Dissimilarity (or "CDD"), scholars tried to identify the genuine historical founder behind the Christian movement by combing through the Bible for ideas that could not be traced either to Judaism or the early church. As Bultmann says in *The History of the Synoptic Tradition* (1921):

> We can only count on possessing a genuine similitude of Jesus where, on the one hand, expression is given to the contrast between Jewish morality and piety and the distinctive eschatological temper which characterised the preaching of Jesus; and where on the other hand we find no specifically Christian features.[32]

Bultmann's CDD was reiterated and expanded by Ernst Käsemann and Norman Perrin, gaining the seal of approval among academics, and has since remained influential in academic research into the life of Jesus:

> We can only sketch in a few bold strokes the embarrassment of critical research. It lies in this; while the historical credibility of the Synoptic tradition has become doubtful all along the line, yet at the same time we are still short of one essential requisite for the identification of the authentic Jesus material, namely, a conspectus of the very earliest stage of primitive Christian history; and also there is an almost complete lack of satisfactory and water tight criteria for this material. In only one case do we have more or less ground under our feet, when there are no grounds either for deriving a tradition from Judaism or for ascribing it to primitive Christianity. (Käsemann )[33]

> Thus we reach the fundamental criterion for authenticity upon which all reconstructions of the teaching of Jesus must be built, which we propose to call the 'criterion of dissimilarity.' Recognising that it follows an attempt to write a history of the tradition concerned, we may formulate it as follows: the earliest form of a saying we can reach may be regarded as authentic if it can be shown to be dissimilar to characteristic emphases both of ancient Judaism and of the early Church, and this will particularly be the case where Christian tradition orientated towards Judaism can be shown to have modified the saying away from its original emphasis. (Perrin)[34]

Although the CDD is a reasonable academic process, it has a few disadvantages. First of all, it is made possible by first completely ignoring the mythological and pagan elements in the gospels. Biblical scholars (of the Bultmann variety) unanimously conclude that these are "later additions" and can tell us nothing about the historical Jesus. In other words – if Jesus *was* pagan, if all of those mythical elements were the core of him and he consisted of nothing else, he would not be historical; thus leading to a dead end in research and the impossibility of knowing any more about him. Therefore, scholars focus on what Jesus, as a hypothesized historical figure, *must* have been. Since many of the elements in the Bible came either from pre-Christian Jewish movements or post-Jesus Christian apologetics, Jesus (according to the CDD) is to be found somewhere between these two.

This has been the motivating reasoning behind research into the historical Jesus for the last few decades. It must be noted, however, that with this type of research, the *historical Jesus* remains only an unproven theory: Jesus the historical figure is the binding element given to any untraceable idea, phrase, philosophy or theology from a specific time period. Based on the fact that the gospel accounts of Jesus Christ are almost completely filled with earlier Jewish ideology, pagan philosophy, or later Christian theology which developed over time (and hence can say little about a historical founder), the only way to talk about the historical Jesus intelligibly is to talk about the type of person he could have been: he was either Jesus the Jew (who became immediately transformed into something very different by his followers) or nothing at all.

This trend is clearly shown by a few of the more popular titles published about Jesus in the last few decades: *Jesus the Jew* (1973); *Jesus and Judaism* (1985); *The Historical Jesus: The Life of a Mediterranean Jewish Peasant* (1991); *A Marginal Jew: Rethinking the Historical Jesus* (1991-2001); and *Jesus of Nazareth, King of the Jews: A Jewish Life and the Emergence of Christianity* (1999). In 2002, Theisen and Winter published *The Quest for the Plausible Jesus*, which uses a softer form of the CDD to envision the Jesus who might have been.[35]

The danger with this line of reasoning is that, when we do a close examination of the Jewish sources, we find very little in the gospels that cannot be traced to earlier movements within Judaism. We could theorize that Jesus was the person who put these pieces together and fueled them with passion, but it is also possible to remove the hypothesis of a historical Jesus without weakening an understanding of the historical developments. Consequently, when searching for the historical Jesus with academic rigor, it is possible to go *too far* and actually weaken the position that there was one at all. This problem was recognized in a 1963 article printed by *TIME* magazine:

> "We Can Know Nothing." During the 1920s, Bultmann sealed the doom of the old quest, as far as Europe was concerned.* He argued that the Gospels were interested not in presenting a dispassionate portrait of Jesus but in expressing the kerygma—the proclamation of the early church's faith in a Risen Christ. This meant that although the New Testament might be a primary source for a study of the early church, it was only a secondary one for a life of Jesus. Since the faith of later generations was really based upon the shining faith of the first Christians and not upon Jesus himself, theologians should forget about seeking the earthly Jesus and analyze the formation of the kerygma. "We can now know almost nothing concerning the life and personality of Jesus," Bultmann wrote in one of the shaping dicta of modern theology. Bultmann himself later moved a step farther to the theological left and argued that to become credible for modern man, the kerygma must be "de-mythologized" – stripped of such unbelievable elements as its heaven-above, hell-below framework. But demythologizing, Robinson points out, threatened to end up with "the conclusion that the Jesus of the kerygma could well be only a myth." Deprived of its link with the historical Jesus, Christianity might end up as some kind of existentialist philosophy, of which Christ was little more than a mythological symbol.[36]

The modern situation has not improved. In an article published by *Christianity Today* in April of 2010, professor of religion at North Park University in Chicago Scot McKnight, who has been intimately involved in "Historical Jesus Research" for the past several decades, describes how after years of passionate research the quest for the historical Jesus has again reached an impasse.

Illustrating this point in his classroom, he asks students to take a test about what kind of person they think Jesus was. Was he outgoing, shy, friendly, pensive, exciting, etc. Then they take the same test, only about themselves. The results show that people picture Jesus to be just like they are; and the same is true, McKnight concludes, of religious historians. McKnight quotes Dale Allison, one of America's top New Testament scholars, who confesses:

> Professional historians are not bloodless templates passively registering the facts: we actively and imaginatively project. Our rationality cannot be extricated from our sentiments and feelings, our hopes and fears, our hunches and ambitions. Maybe we have unthinkingly reduced biography [of Jesus] to autobiography... The fragmentary and imperfect nature of the evidence as well as the limitations of our historical abilities should move us to confess, if we are conscientious, how hard it is to recover the past. We wield our criteria to get what we want.[37]

In other words, with virtually no evidence regarding the historical Jesus, the best historians can do is project their interpretations of him. McKnight also admits that the majority of New Testament scholars are not orthodox Christians: they may be believers, but theirs is a mature faith, which doesn't accept the New Testament at face value. While they maintain that Jesus was at least in part historical, they also accept that much of the New Testament is not historically accurate. At the same time, as believers, they project into their research their own pre-existing theological affirmations. McKnight adds:

> One has to wonder if the driving force behind historical Jesus scholarship is more an *a priori* disbelief in orthodoxy than a historian's genuine (and disinterested) interest in what really happened. The theological conclusions of those who pursue the historical Jesus simply correlate too strongly with their own theological predilections to suggest otherwise.[38]

Incidentally, we might be justified in asking whether historical New Testament scholars are really the experts on the historical Jesus at all; wouldn't someone studying mythology, comparative religion, history or sociology be better qualified to explain the motivations behind the Christian movement than someone who is seeking and *inserting* the savior they need to find in order to justify their beliefs?

Despite the article's subtitle, "Why scholarly attempts to

discover the 'real' Jesus have failed. And why that's a good thing," McKnight concludes without giving any indication of the benefits of the failure to discover the real Jesus. We can only guess that McKnight feels this creates a space for people to believe whatever they want to believe, without any proof or need of justification; "If there is no proof it happened, there is also no proof that it did not happen," believers might argue. McKnight finishes his article with an unintentional demonstration of the way faith can cloud academic judgment:

> As a historian I think I can prove that Jesus died and that he thought his death was atoning. I think I can establish that the tomb was empty and that resurrection is the best explanation for the empty tomb. But one thing the historical method cannot prove is that Jesus died for our sins and was raised for our justification. At some point, historical methods run out of steam and energy. Historical Jesus studies cannot get us to the point where the Holy Spirit and the church can take us.[39]

Would an unbiased researcher conclude that the corpse of Jesus getting up, walking out of his grave and ascending into heaven is more rational than any other explanation, however improbable?

The main problem with the human, Jewish Jesus at the center of modern research into biblical history is that nobody really *believes* in him. He is a necessary hypothesis in order to preserve the possibility of Christian faith, but he is nobody's hero or savior; only a historical premise. Moreover, in stripping away the mythical elements in the gospel, academics are also removing central concepts of Christian belief (the virgin birth, the miracles, the death and resurrection of Jesus). In *proving* the historical Christ, they are also, albeit indirectly, *disproving* the Jesus of faith.

There have been a few contemporary researchers who disagree with the trendy insistence on the historical Jesus. These scholars are aware that the Jewish Jesus, while necessary to preserve the possibility of a historical Jesus of any kind, is very tenuously based on the Bible and the assumption that Jesus was real; and that although he remains the focus of academic investigation, a very different hypothesis, which does not presume the historical Jesus, is also possible. This hypothesis is often referred to as the "Christ-Myth Theory."

Although the following definition does not apply equally to all writers, in brief the Christ-Myth Theory maintains that there is no need for a historical founder to explain the rise of the Christian movement; that all episodes and events in the gospels can be traced to earlier traditions; and that certain early sects of Christianity began to believe (mistakenly) that the stories of Jesus Christ were about a real, historical figure. This theory may sound unbelievable at first, but bear in mind that it is already not so different from the orthodox position. Modern scholars already accept that the early Christian communities, who worshipped Jesus as the dying and resurrecting son of God, glossed over the real historical Jesus in favor of the "Jesus of Faith" – a Jesus that incorporated elements from mythology, philosophy and the theology produced by early Christian writers. The Jesus that they believed in and even died for *was not* the historical Jesus still being investigated by modern scholarship.

The Christ-Myth Theory is in general not supported by the academia because they have already decided to look for the historical Jesus, and believe that comparative mythology cannot shed light onto the object of their investigations. Those few historians and academics that are interested in researching the mythical Christ hope to present an argument strong enough to withstand the foregone presumption of critics that the theory is outdated or has already been adequately disproved. Acharya S., author of several books on the mythical Christ whose research was a key resource for the viral documentary *Zeitgeist*, is forced to argue with those who doubt that the controversy over Jesus is worth exploring; when in fact, as we have seen, it has a long history:

> The most enduring and profound controversy in this subject is whether or not a person named Jesus Christ ever really existed.... when one examines this issue closely, one will find a tremendous volume of literature that demonstrates, logically and intelligently, time and again that Jesus Christ is a mythological character along the same lines as the Greek, Roman, Egyptian, Sumerian, Phoenician, Indian or other godmen, who are all presently accepted as myths rather than historical figures.[40]

Meanwhile biblical historians focus exclusively on Jesus the

Jew, theologians focus exclusively on Christology and theory, and the very real difficulty in putting the two together is ignored.

For the general public however, whether or not Jesus Christ as presented in the gospels was a historical figure is a source of much interest, and books on the subject have been both well-received and heavily criticized. Titles taking the Christ-Myth approach include G.A. Wells' *Did Jesus Exist?* (1975), as well as his later books *The Jesus Legend* (1996) and *The Jesus Myth* (1998). In 1999, three books on Christ Myth theory were published: *The Christ Conspiracy: The Greatest Story Ever Sold* by Acharya S; *The Jesus Mysteries: Was Jesus a Pagan God* by Timothy Freke and Peter Gandy; and *The Jesus Puzzle* by Earl Doherty (an expanded version was published in 2009 under the title *Jesus: Neither God nor Man-The Case for a Mythical Jesus*). There was also Robert M. Price's *Deconstructing Jesus* (2000) and *The Incredible Shrinking Son of Man* (2003), and more recently Tom Harpur's *The Pagan Christ* (2005) and sequel *Water Into Wine* (2007).

Critics respond that modern scholars affirm the historical Jesus and that Christ-Myth Theory is centuries old and based on bad scholarship; which is arguably true (mostly because of advances in research standards). Going further, they reject outright any similarities – which for them either do not exist at all (usually because, as Justin Martyr affirmed, Jesus *actually* existed as opposed to the others who did not) or are a case of reverse borrowing (i.e., Jesus did it first). Unfortunately, they also ignore all of the critical research that has gone into the historical Jesus, cite historical evidences that were discarded as proof by experts centuries ago, and use regurgitated arguments that have no logical foundation to prove that Jesus existed as a historical person. (In fairness, the same can be said for most online supporters of Christ-Myth theory).

## Conclusions and Summary

Part of the confusion surrounding the historical Jesus is the lack of consensus on the subject matter. What *is* Jesus? Is Jesus the Son of God, Savior, miracle worker, who was born of a virgin, died, came back to life and ascended into heaven? Or was Jesus one of dozens of Jewish rebel leaders during the Roman occupation of Jerusalem? Among scholars, the former is generally refuted (or ignored) and the later is affirmed. As a result, conservatives often point out that no "serious" scholar doubts the historical Jesus. However, not only is the historical Jesus of modern academics completely different from the Jesus Christ of the gospels, there is also a very specific reason – one which is not based on evidence – for the current academic support of the historical Jesus.

The common, popular understanding of the historical Jesus goes something like this: scholars and academics still believe that there was a historical founder of Christianity, but disbelieve in the miracles because they aren't scientific (or are too similar to pagan mythology). Christians believe in the historical Jesus as well – which is not irrational because they are supported by the academic community – and also *have faith* in the miraculous events. However, there is a paradox in this situation which is not often pointed out: the method and technique that scholars have been using for centuries to try and find the "historical Jesus" is to first get rid of all the blatant mythological or pagan elements in the Bible usually because they are believed to be additions from alternative (non-Jesus) sources. They are, in effect, the very things *least likely* to have been said or done by Jesus, not because they are unrealistic, but because they are not unique to an authentic, Jesus-inspired tradition. The result is a historical founder of Christianity which, rather than providing a doorway or foundation for Christian faith, is actually diametrically opposed; for if the historical founder of the scholars did exist, it is only possible due to his *dissimilarity* from the Jesus Christ of the gospels.

At the same time, the idea that Jesus Christ was the historical founder of Christianity is so heavily defended by Christians and biblical scholars that to even raise the possibility of an alternative theory – one in which the savior figure of the gospels may not have been historical – is automatically derided. This has unfortunately led to the development of rhetoric, presumption and a great deal of obstinacy on both sides of the controversy. Before we could even begin to look at the actual similarities between Jesus Christ and other mythological traditions, we needed to first explore the history of the debate in modern times and trace the historical developments that have led to the contemporary academic and popular positions on the historical Jesus.

Once we understand that various interpretations of Jesus Christ have been made, ranging from Jesus as only a physical man, to Jesus as only a supernatural deity, and that a definitive conclusion is perhaps more a matter of belief than evidence, we may be able to view the entire matter more objectively and review the evidence based on its own merits. At the same time, the difficulty of approaching this subject without pre-formed opinions and ideological baggage must be acknowledged. The idea that Jesus really existed and that the Bible is at least in part historically valid is a paradigm supported by modern culture even among the non-faithful. Due to the number of magazine articles and TV documentaries exploring the investigation into the historical Jesus, showing new archeological discoveries purporting to prove biblical testimony, reviewing the findings of biblical scholars or debating controversies such as the Turin Shroud, there is a passive acceptance that, whatever Jesus might have been, he almost certainly was historical.

Meanwhile, the dispersion of Christ-Myth ideas such as those found in the documentaries *Zeitgeist* (2007) and *The God Who Wasn't There* (2005), which introduced the Christ-Myth hypothesis to record numbers of people, sparked a new level of Internet fervor over the subject. The controversy now rages stronger than ever – but both sides recycle arguments and evidence that the other side then blithely discredits or ignores. The current state of frenzied disagreement is all too often based on bias, semantics and sophistry rather than a close investigation of the evidence, and also fails to give – on either camp – a clear explanation of Christian history that is fully supported by the available evidence.

An objective analysis of the evidence simply cannot be done without first identifying the general ideologies and assumptions surrounding the historical Jesus; this will be the aim of the next chapter. After examining some of the modern ideas concerning the historical Jesus Christ, which pre-condition how adherents approach the debate, I will identify the evidence and documents used to support the idea of a historical Jesus and question whether they can be accepted as impartial proof.

CHAPTER THREE

# Where's the Proof? An Overview of the Evidence and Arguments for the Existence of Jesus Christ

*Yamauchi's response seemed uncharacteristically strong. 'From time to time some people have tried to deny the existence of Jesus, but this is really a lost cause,' he said with a tone of exasperation. 'There is overwhelming evidence that Jesus did exist, and these hypothetical questions are really very vacuous and fallacious.'*
*—Strobel, The Case for Christ, 81*

WHEN CONFRONTED WITH ARGUMENTS that Jesus may not have been historical, the majority of Christians will refer to the hard evidence that Jesus really existed; but not without first displaying a certain sense of desperation. On the one hand, they are right – any reliable historical records that prove that Jesus was historical would automatically weaken theories to the contrary. But is there really, as Yamauchi claims, such "overwhelming evidence"?

In fact, even academics that believe Jesus was historical openly acknowledge that there are far too few reliable historical records referring to Jesus Christ. The handful that do exist – they maintain – are enough. But before we look at the evidence, it will be worthwhile to review some common preconceptions concerning Jesus Christ that are widespread in popular culture and that influence individuals' beliefs on the subject.

As we've seen, the claim that Jesus was mythological, rather than historical, has a long history. It has "been refuted" time and again by Christian apologists, who are often exasperated to learn that there are still some people who won't let it go. The majority of scholars, as well as the general public – whether religious or secular – believe that Jesus Christ *was* historical (that there was a historical teacher who began the movement); however, the arguments used to support this theory are often a mixture of inferences, deductions and references to common knowledge and unfounded associations. Because many readers will have these same concepts nagging in the back of their minds, it will be worthwhile to review them before moving on.

Isn't there a great deal of evidence for the historical Jesus? Wasn't it necessary for there to have been a founder of the Christian movement? Would the martyrs have died for a myth? Can archaeology or other sources prove the veracity of some parts of biblical narrative? Is there any historical evidence, either from within the Christian communities or without, that can support the idea of a historical Jesus? In order to be thorough, these questions need to be addressed. In this chapter, therefore, we will review the evidence and arguments commonly used to support the idea of a historical Jesus.

## *Archaeological Evidence Confirms Many Biblical Accounts*

Every few years there is an archaeological discovery that "proves" Christianity to be true and makes media headlines. This makes it appear that the Bible records sound historical testimonies of things that really did happen. Although there haven't actually been any archaeological discoveries that prove Jesus was real, there have been, some claim, discoveries which enhance the reliability of the testimonies by confirming real names and places involved. If these places, mentioned by name by the writers of the gospels, really existed, and the authors had included these seemingly innocuous details into their story, it appears to raise the trustworthiness of the source. After interviewing John McRay, professor and author of *Archaeology and the New Testament,* Lee Strobel (whose one-sided *The Case for Christ* continues to be a popular defense of the historical Jesus) concludes:

> Here's the bottom line: 'If Luke was so painstakingly accurate in his historical reporting,' said one book on the topic, 'on what logical basis may we assume he was credulous or inaccurate in his reporting of matters that were far more important, not only to him but to others as well'.[1]

A comparable argument, however, might be that Dan Brown's *DaVinci Code* is a true story because it includes so many true facts and research; or more relevantly – that Harry Potter is true (despite amazing events) because it mentions many real places (like London) and describes accurately minute details and customs from Harry's relatives' muggle household. First of all, reliable testimony about mundane historical events is simply not equal to testimony about miraculous events. If a modern witness gave us a lot of firm details about a suspect, but then said something outlandish like "the suspect flew away on a pink giraffe," we should be less inclined to believe even the commonplace aspects of his account. Why is this not also true when dealing with the Bible? Secondly, this argument avoids the main reason the historicity of Jesus is challenged at all – the similarities to older traditions. And thirdly, there are a few specific historical details recorded in the gospels that go against trustworthy historical sources. As evolutionary biologist Richard Dawkins points out in *The God Delusion*:

> Moreover, Luke screws up his dating by tactlessly mentioning events that historians are capable of independently checking. There was indeed a census under Governor Quirinius – a local census, not one decreed by Caesar Augustus for the Empire as a whole – but it happened too late: in 6 AD, long after Herod's death. Lane Fox concludes that 'Luke's story is historically impossible and internally incoherent,' but he sympathizes with Luke's plight and his desire to fulfil the prophecy of Micah.[2]

### The Martyrs Would not Have Been Willing to Die for a Lie

This emotionally-charged argument goes something like this:

"If there was no Jesus Christ, what did all those martyrs die for?" The online source *All About Religion* uses it the following way:

> In light of the cruel and torturous deaths of the first and second generation Christians, all theories that Christianity is a fabricated myth, created for the personal gain of its followers, must be rejected. Even today, many will die for a belief, but none will die for a lie.[3]

The argument assumes that if Christianity were a myth, its followers would have known about it and therefore been adverse to martyrdom. However, I believe the Christian martyrs were very convinced in their own minds that Jesus Christ was a historical person. Interestingly, not all Christians were willing to be martyrs. Christians who believed in Jesus as a spirit or non-physical entity, or who didn't think Jesus felt real pain or suffered like humans, felt no need to die as martyrs and conscientiously avoided persecution.

St. Ignatius and St. Polycarp, two of the earliest Christian martyrs, were already fighting against these "heretics" who weren't willing to die for their cause. Ignatius, outraged, gives in essence the first instance of the martyrdom argument:

> For if it is merely in semblance that these things were done by our Lord, I am also a prisoner in semblance. And why have I given myself up to death, to fire, to the sword, to wild beasts?[4]

Why indeed? If he did not have an answer then, so close to the time of Christ, nor any proof to offer heretics who denied the physicality of Jesus, how could the mere fact of his *willingness* to die for his beliefs be used as evidence nearly 2,000 years later?

## Christianity Could not Have Started Without a Founder

Some claim that Jesus existed because there is a Church, and it must have had a founder. This argument is given by, for example, W.K.C. Guthrie in *Orpheus and Greek Religion:*

> If there were no other evidence for the real existence of the founder of Christianity, a strong case might still be made based on the difficulty a man might feel in accounting for the rise of Christianity without the impulse of a historic Jesus behind it.[5]

An offshoot of this argument is sometimes that, unlike Christianity, all the various pagan religions died out, and Christianity survived despite very challenging periods of persecution. Either it was "God's Will," or Christianity had something no one else did: a historical founder. German scholar of Greek mythology Walter Burkert raises this argument against the ancient mysteries:

> The basic difference between ancient mysteries, on the one hand, and religious communities, sects, and churches of the Judeo-Christian type, on the other, is borne out by the verdict of history. With the imperial decrees of 391/92AD prohibiting all pagan cults and with the forceful destruction of the sanctuaries, the mysteries simply and suddenly disappeared.[6]

Notice, however, the contradiction implicit in this quote: the mysteries were first outlawed, and then their sanctuaries were forcibly destroyed – after which Burkert makes it sound like the disappearance of the mysteries was mysterious and unexplainable. Not irrelevant to the survival of Christianity is the fact that the early Christian church had both a fixed authority and an organizational structure, not to mention a great deal of wealth; and that all traces of paganism were either destroyed or assimilated. This, more than a physical founder, can account for its preservation.

### The Life of Jesus Was Prophesied in the Old Testament

This is the argument used within the Bible itself to justify Jesus Christ, and it continues to be used today. As written, the New Testament makes Jesus fulfill hundreds of Old Testament prophecies. Most of these prophecies are written in past tense about specific events and give no indication that they are to be used for the future; however, in order for orthodox Jews to accept Jesus as Messiah, he needed to appear as Jewish as possible. Therefore Jesus was made to do a lot of strange and inconvenient things (many of which were done in private or secretly), so that the gospel writers could say, "And Jesus did *this*, to fulfill the prophecy."

For instance, although the "massacre of the infants" or the persecution of the child-hero is a common literary motif, the writer of Matthew links it to a passage from Jeremiah, which reads "A voice is heard in Ramah, mourning and great weeping, Rachel weeping for her children and refusing to be comforted, because her children are no more" (Jeremiah 31:15).

> When Herod realized that the Magi had outwitted him, he was furious, and he gave orders to kill all the boys in Bethlehem and its vicinity who were two years old and under, in accordance with the time he had learned from the Magi. Then what was said through the prophet Jeremiah was fulfilled: "A voice is heard in Ramah, weeping and great mourning, Rachel weeping for her children and refusing to be comforted, because they are no more." (Matthew 2:16-18)

Incidentally, very few biblical scholars consider any of the birth narratives of Christ to be historically genuine, so similar are they to pagan mythology. If this episode *didn't happen*, it makes it all the more easy to see how the writer could take a common theme, apply it to the character of Jesus Christ as a biographical episode, and link it to the Jewish tradition via prophecy. The prophecy argument is also used by Jesus himself in the gospels; however, being Jewish, it would have been natural for him to use phrases and quotes from the Old Testament in reference to his own life.

> "Awake, O sword, against my shepherd, against the man who is close to me!" declares the LORD Almighty. "Strike the shepherd, and the sheep will be scattered, and I will turn my hand against the little ones." (Zechariah 13:7)

> Then Jesus told them, "This very night you will all fall away on account of me, for it is written: "I will strike the shepherd, and the sheep of the flock will be scattered." (Matthew 26.31)

Many of the major biographical details of Jesus in the gospels also arise out of prophecy. He had to be born in Bethlehem, for example, but he also had to be from Nazareth and then move to Egypt. And so that is how the story is written. Moreover (as we saw previously), the fact that these are real, historical cities lends credence to the idea that these events really happened. Since the identical correlation between Jesus' life and the Old Testament prophecies is unlikely to be coincidental, the fact that Jesus actually did these things is taken as proof that he was the coming savior.

However, it takes faith in the historical reliability of the Bible (and the miraculous intervention of an all-seeing God into history) before this proof can be convincing. Thus it is self-referential, equivalent to "I know the Bible is true because the Bible says so." Skeptics will argue that the gospel writers just wrote the story of Jesus to include as many of these prophecies as possible, something that is also acknowledged by biblical scholars. It is also important to recognize that if Jesus had been a historical Jew, he would have been familiar with all of the prophecies in the Old Testament which were later interpreted to refer to him. If he had "fulfilled" them, he would have been doing so deliberately and conscientiously rather than incidentally – leaving him open to the criticism that he was a charlatan.

### Jesus was the Founder of Ethics

This horribly uninformed idea, especially common in American Country music, is that all goodness, love and truth came into the world with Christ, and before him people had limited ethical ability. Alan Jackson, for example, sings:

> I'm just a singer of simple songs
>
> I'm not a real political man
>
> I watch CNN but I'm not sure I can tell you
>
> The difference in Iraq and Iran
>
> But I know Jesus and I talk to God
>
> And I remember this from when I was young
>
> Faith hope and love are some good things he gave us
>
> And the greatest is love
>
> –*Where were you when the world stopped turning*

Anyone familiar with world literature knows that ethical considerations and practical morality have always been a concern for human civilizations. There are many pearls of ethical wisdom that can be found several thousand years before the Christian era; and in the pagan milieu that gave birth to the Christian movement, the philosophical quest for concepts such as "Truth", "Love", "Goodness" and "Virtue" was seen as a pressing issue of ultimate importance. Many contemporary philosophical schools urged restraint, humility, abstinence, or charity. Jesus' teachings on ethics were nothing new. His famous moral precepts "love your neighbor as yourself" or "do unto others as you would have them do unto you" are not unique to him but can be found in much earlier religious literature; a point Bertrand Russell raises in his article, *Why I'm not a Christian*:

> You will remember that He said, "Resist not evil: but whosoever shall smite thee on thy right cheek, turn to him the other also." That is not a new precept or a new principle. It was used by Lao-tse and Buddha some 500 or 600 years before Christ, but it is not a principle which as a matter of fact Christians accept.[7]

Now that we've dispelled some common preconceptions, we can turn to the actual evidence. Although I have neither the expertise nor the aspiration to judge the reliability of the testimonies and documents which have been used as proof in the historical Jesus, they are important to consider – if only because they continue to be heavily cited, scrutinized and bickered over. In the following overview, I will merely point out why they have been questioned by some scholars, why they are not considered universally reliable, and why therefore, they cannot be trusted to bear light on our present study.

# Historical Evidence

In 1944, Alvin Boyd Kuhn wrote the book *Who is This King of Glory? A Critical Study of the Christos-Messiah*. In it he disparages not only the documents used as historical for Jesus Christ, but more keenly the discrepancies that exist in the understanding of these texts and the fact that they are recommended to the faithful without acknowledging that they have been questioned by academic research:

The average Christian minister who has not read outside the pale of accredited Church authorities will impart to any parishioner making the inquiry the information that no event in history is better attested by witnesses than the occurrences in the Gospel narrative of Christ's life. He will go over the usual citation of the historians who mention Jesus and the letters claiming to have been written about him. When the credulous questioner, putting trust in the intelligence and good faith of his pastor, gets this answer, he goes away assured on the point of the veracity of the Gospel story. The pastor does not qualify his data with the information that the practice of forgery, fictionizing and fable was rampant in the early Church. In the simple interest of truth, then, it is important to examine the body of alleged testimony from secular history and see what credibility and authority it possesses. First, as to the historians whose works record the existence of Jesus, the list comprises but four. They are Pliny, Tacitus, Suetonius and Josephus. There are short paragraphs in the works of each of these, two in Josephus. The total quantity of this material is given by Harry Elmer Barnes in "The Twilight of Christianity" as some twenty-four lines. It may total a little more, perhaps twice that amount. This meager testimony constitutes the body or mass of the evidence of 'one of the best attested events in history.'[8]

The information gap between Christians and biblical or historical researchers has not improved in the 50+ years since the publication of Kuhn's book. Although his claims may have been overstated and contemporary scholars generally dismiss him, he correctly mentions the four main historical references to Jesus Christ that continue to be used today. Search online for any one of them and you'll find that they are constantly and readily given as the *definitive historical* evidence for the existence of Jesus, on many thousands of faith-based and apologetic websites. However, among biblical scholars and church historians (even Christian academics) they are not universally accepted. Although all four of them were considered complete forgeries throughout much of the last two centuries, today an uneasy truce has been established that in general recognizes that at least some of the quotes may be partially authentic. The following is a brief overview of the passages.

The first and most widely quoted non-Christian reference to Jesus comes from Romano-Jewish historian Flavius Josephus in his book, *The Antiquities of the Jews*. It is referred to as the "Testimoniam Flavianum" and was written in the late first century AD:

> Now there was about this time Jesus, a wise man, if it be lawful to call him a man. For he was a doer of wonderful works, a teacher of such men as received the truth with pleasure. He drew over to him both many of the Jews and many of the Gentiles. He was the Christ; and when Pilate, at the suggestion of the principal men among us, had condemned him to the cross, those that loved him at the first ceased not, for he appeared to them thereafter again the third day, as the divine prophets foretold these and ten thousand other wonderful things concerning him. And even now the tribe of Christians so named from him is not extinct. (18.63-64)

Some scholars argue that at least some of this passage is genuine, while others see it entirely as an inserted Christian passage (it fits poorly into the surrounding text, and the style stands out as being dissimilar). If a forgery, it may have been written by Emperor Constantine's church historian, Eusebius, who was also the first to quote from it. While Christians today continue to use it as a proof for their faith, it was questioned as early as 1770 by Bishop Warburton of Gloucester, who called it a "rank forgery, and a stupid one, too."[9] Over a hundred years ago it was discounted in more depth, by a book called *Christian Mythology Unveiled*, written by Mitchell Logan in 1842:

> The famous passage which we find in Josephus, about Jesus Christ, was never mentioned nor alluded to in any way whatever by any of the fathers of the first, second, or third centuries; nor until the time of Eusebius, 'when it was first quoted by himself.' The truth is, none of these fathers could quote or allude to a passage which did not exist in their times; but was to all points short of absolute certainty, forged and interpolated by Eusebius.[10]

Below is a more exhaustive treatment of this passage outlined by a Dr. Larner, first published in 1760 and reprinted in T.W. Doane's 1882 book, *Bible Myths and Their Parallels in Other Religions*:

1. It was never quoted by any of our Christian ancestors before *Eusebius.*
2. Josephus has nowhere else mentioned the name or word *Christ,* in any of his works, except the testimony above mentioned, and the passage concerning James, the Lord's brother.
3. It interrupts the narrative.
4. The language is quite Christian.
5. It is *not* quoted by Chrysostom, though he often refers to Josephus, and could not have omitted quoting it, had it been *then,* in the text.
6. It is *not* quoted by Photius, though he has three articles concerning Josephus.
7. Under the article *Justus of Tiberius,* this author (Photius) expressly states that this historian (Josephus), being a Jew, *has not taken the least notice of Christ.*
8. Neither Justin, in his dialogue with Typho the Jew, nor Clemens Alexandrinus, who made so many extracts from ancient authors, nor Origen against Celsus, *have even mentioned this testimony.*
9. But, on the contrary, Origen openly affirms (ch. xxiv., bk. i, against Celsus), that Josephus, who had mentioned John the Baptist, *did not acknowledge Christ.*[11]

As Dr. Larner points out, another passage in Josephus mentions James, the brother of Jesus (20:9); this passage is less passionately contested. Despite arguments like these, the Josephus passage is mostly accepted today as partially genuine. According to Paula Fredrikson, "Most scholars currently incline to see the passage as basically authentic, with a few later insertions by Christian scribes."[12] Earl Doherty, however, in *The Jesus Puzzle,* points to the difficulty these two passages have in supporting the burden placed on them:

> In the absence of any other supporting evidence from the first century that in fact the Jesus of Nazareth portrayed in the Gospels clearly existed, Josephus becomes the slender thread by which such an assumption hangs. And the sound and fury and desperate manoeuverings which surround the dissection of those two little passages becomes a din of astonishing proportions. The obsessive focus on this one uncertain record is necessitated by the fact that the rest of the evidence is so dismal, so contrary to the orthodox picture.

If almost everything outside Josephus points in a different direction, to the essential fiction of the Gospel picture and its central figure, how can Josephus be made to bear on his shoulders, through two passages whose reliability has thus far remained unsettled, the counterweight to all this other negative evidence?[13]

The next passage is from *The Annals* of Roman historian and Senator Tacitus (c. 68). Tacitus is generally considered a reliable historian, which has been used to give this passage added weight:

> Nero fastened the guilt of starting the blaze and inflicted the most exquisite tortures on a class hated for their abominations, called Christians [Chrestians] by the populace. Christus, from whom the name had its origin, suffered the extreme penalty during the reign of Tiberius 14-37 at the hands of one of our procurators, Pontius Pilatus, and a most mischievous superstition, thus checked for the moment, again broke out not only in Judaea, the first source of the evil, but even in Rome, where all things hideous and shameful from every part of the world find their centre and become popular. (Tacitus 15:44)

First of all, Tacitus was not infallible. In referring to earlier references, Tacitus confirms that Moses led a colony of lepers (the Jews) out of Israel, thus giving the rumor that the Jewish people were originally a leper colony a pseudo-historical foundation. Assmann reflects, Tacitus' "authority as a historian imparted the dignity of authentic historical research to this product of imagination, projection, and distorted memory."[14]

Even so, a strong case can also be made against the authenticity of this passage. Larner and Doane point out that it was discovered only in the 15th century (this is confirmed by the *Catholic Encyclopedia*) and that there was "no vestige nor trace of its existence anywhere in the world" before then:

> The original MSS. containing the "Annals of Tacitus" were "discovered" in the fifteenth century. Their existence cannot be traced back further than that time. And as it was an age of imposture, some persons are disposed to believe that not only portions of the *Annals*, but the whole work, was forged at that time. Mr. J. W. Ross, in an elaborate work published in London some years ago, contended that the *Annals* were forged by Poggio Bracciolini, their professed

discoverer. At the time of Bracciolini the temptation was great to palm off literary forgeries, especially of the chief writers of antiquity, on account of the Popes, in their efforts to revive learning, giving money rewards and indulgences to those who should procure MS. copies of any of the ancient Greek or Roman authors. Manuscripts turned up as if by magic, in every direction; from libraries of monasteries, obscure as well as famous; the most out-of-the-way places,—the bottom of exhausted wells, besmeared by snails, as the History of Velleius Paterculus, or from garrets, where they had been contending with cobwebs and dust, as the poems of Catullus.[15]

Nevertheless, the passage is generally accepted as authentic by modern researchers. At the same time, it has been noted that it can offer no information regarding the historical Jesus, since "Christ" is not a name and could have referred to any number of individuals. Another claim is that Tacitus is only repeating Christians' own perception of their history. Moreover it is unclear whether the original "Chrestians" referred to Jesus followers at all.

Pliny the Younger wrote to Emperor Trajan in 112 about certain Christians who refused to worship the emperor. This letter has also been used to justify the historical Jesus – although it refers only to the existence of Christians:

Those who denied that they were or had been Christians, when they invoked the gods in words dictated by me, offered prayer with incense and wine to your image, which I had ordered to be brought for this purpose together with statues of the gods, and moreover cursed Christ – none of which those who are really Christians, it is said, can be forced to do – these I thought should be discharged. Others named by the informer declared that they were Christians, but then denied it, asserting that they had been but had ceased to be, some three years before, others many years, some as much as twenty-five years. They all worshiped your image and the statues of the gods, and cursed Christ. (Pliny the Younger 10:96-97)

Finally, Gaius Suetonius Tranquillus (c. 69-140), a secretary and historian to Emperor Hadrian wrote the following in his *Life of Claudius*: "As the Jews were making constant disturbances at the instigation of Chrestus, he (Claudius) expelled them from Rome" (25:4). That this passage is referring to Jesus Christ assumes the following:

1.  The "Chrestus" causing disturbance in Rome refers to a "Christ" who actually resided some years earlier in Palestine.
2.  The information is not secondhand via Christian sources.
3.  The presence of Christians in Rome by 49 implies the existence of an actual "Christ" rather than a developing legend.
4.  "Chrestus" means "Christ," rather than its translation "Useful One."

Suetonius later mentions that, because of the great fire in Rome of 64AD, "punishment by Nero was inflicted on the Christians, a class of men given to a new and harmful superstition" (*Lives of the Caesars*, 26:2).

Putting aside the question of whether these passages are authentic or forgeries, in fact they are not strong witnesses for the historical Jesus anyway. They were all written after the life and times of Jesus, by non-followers who had only second hand, anecdotal evidence about him. They don't mention any of the miraculous deeds or teachings of the Bible. If anything they only support the idea that there were at the time some Christians *who believed* in a historical Jesus – a point which I have no intention of challenging. As Kuhn pointed out in the quote above, these meager historical sources are incongruous to the claim that the life of Jesus Christ was one of the best-attested events in history.

Some scholars have noticed, with surprise, that there are no contemporary accounts of Jesus of any kind. When used against the idea of a historical Jesus, this is sometimes referred to as the "argument from silence." Kersey Graves, for example, writing in 1875, commented strongly on the lack of historical testimony:

> The fact that no history sacred or profane,—that not one of the three hundred histories of that age,—makes the slightest allusion to Christ, or any of the miraculous incidents ingrafted into his life certainly proves, with a cogency that no logic can overthrow, no sophistry can contradict, and no honest skepticism can resist, that there never was such a miraculously endowed being as his many orthodox disciples claim him to have been. The fact that Christ finds no place in the history of the era in which he lived,—that not one event of his life is recorded by anybody but his own interested and prejudiced biographers,—settles the conclusion, beyond cavil or criticism, that the godlike achievements ascribed to him are naught but fable or

fiction. It not only proves he was not miraculously endowed, but proves he was not even naturally endowed to such an extraordinary degree as to make him an object of general attention.[16]

Defenders of Christianity respond to this argument by claiming that Jesus was a small time preacher living in the backwaters of the Roman Empire, and as such shouldn't be expected to have received much attention anyway. However, in the gospels his death and resurrection were witnessed and believed in by both Roman and Jewish officials; the word would have been sure to spread very quickly. As Mead emphasized in 1903,

> It has always been unfailing source of astonishment to the historical investigator of Christian beginnings, that there is not a single word from the pen of any pagan writer of the first century of our era, which can in any fashion be referred to the marvelous story recounted by the Gospel writer. The very existence of Jesus seems unknown.[17]

Of course the "argument from silence" can't prove that Jesus didn't exist; nor can questioning the authenticity of the passages cited above. For the purposes of the present study, however, the above documents are refuted as proofs for the historical Jesus: the reason for this conclusion has nothing to do with the documents themselves, but is simply based on the perception that controversy and argumentation surrounding these documents continues, and appears irresolvable. For obvious reasons, a document used as evidence to give testimony about an individual should be a reliable and trusted source of information. If experts cannot agree on the validity of the document, and if they argue for centuries about whether or not it is genuine, a forgery, or a well-intentioned interpolation, and if in general there is no consensus, then the document should not be used as valid evidence in a research investigation.

However, that's not to say that these passages couldn't be used as strong supporting or secondary evidence – but only in the absence of other evidence pointing at a different solution, or after an irrefutable (or at least much more secure) primary source of testimony was first established. This is an assertion that most Christians can agree with, maintaining that the most reliable testimony of the life of Jesus Christ can be found in the Bible. On his website, Mark D. Roberts, author of *Jesus Revealed*, quickly dismisses the main Jewish and Roman sources used to support the historical Jesus and even makes the early Christian writings dispensable. In the end, however, he finds in the Bible plenty of evidence for the historical Jesus.

> If all we had were the second-century Christian writings, we'd have a hard time sorting out what Jesus really did and said. The gulf between orthodox and heterodox treatments of Jesus was wide and growing wider in this century as Gnostics claimed Jesus as their heavenly redeemer while orthodox Christians insisted that his ministry included far more than revelation. At its core, they argued, it had to do with his death and resurrection, something the Gnostics rejected, preferring a revealer who didn't really suffer. But, I'm glad to say, we don't have only the second-century writings. In fact we have access to texts from the earliest days of Christian faith, writings which are collected in the New Testament.[18]

But is the Bible really historically accurate? Who wrote the New Testament and for what purpose? What can we learn about Jesus from the gospel stories? These questions will be explored in the next section.

## The Old Testament

The modern Bible is a collection of writings that attempt to link Jesus, as a historical figure, to the much older (and more exhaustive) Old Testament, or Jewish scriptures. It was generally maintained by Christians that Jesus had come as the Jewish Messiah, and as such, the Old Testament writings were interpreted as references to Jesus and his coming kingdom. It is important to note that the New Testament was most likely written by Jews or at least scribes who were very familiar with traditional Jewish writings. Therefore, before we examine whether the New Testament is a reliable historical source, it will be advantageous to examine the Old Testament to develop an understanding of just what kind of writing it is. Specifically, is the Old Testament historically reliable and accurate?

We should also understand that the concept of an "Old

Testament" is completely Christian. Although the bulk of the Old Testament is the Jewish Pentateuch or *Tanach*, as well as collections of Jewish writings, the organization of them into one linear text starting with the beginning of history (creation) and ending in the fulfillment of Jesus Christ (New Testament) is a reflection of Christian ideology. To Jews who continue to maintain the supremacy of their scriptures, the prefix "Old" is insulting; it reflects the Christian paradigm that Christ fulfills and supersedes the Law. It is mostly the Christian understanding of the New Testament as literal history, miracles included, which has likewise spread the view that the Old Testament is also to be read literally – a practice which conflicts with historical records.

In fact, when we study the Old Testament within the social and geographic context in which it was developed, we will see that *the main stories* of the Old Testament – David and Goliath, Moses and the Ten Commandments, Joseph, the Ark, the Garden of Eden – are all refurbished pagan stories; assimilated and transformed to give Jews their own national heroes. This demonstrates that Jewish scribes, rather than writing in a vacuum, were already relying on a rich and very ancient literary tradition. The best example of this is from the *Epic of Gilgamesh*. Gilgamesh, the greatest literary accomplishment of Mesopotamia, was widely translated throughout the ancient Middle East. There are many parallels between the Epic of Gilgamesh, pagan mythology, and the Old Testament. We will focus on just one (the story of the flood) to demonstrate how closely the parallels run and how it can be effectively proven that the Old Testament borrowed from earlier sources. The similarities between the story of Noah should be apparent to anyone familiar with the biblical account of the flood.

The Babylonian Noah was named Utnupishtim, who with his wife became immortal after surviving the great flood. Gilgamesh, in his quest for immortality, seeks him out and gets to hear the story first hand. The gods had decided to destroy mankind, but one god, Ea, was friendly and determined to save Utnupishtim. He told him to disregard his possessions, construct an ark according to exact specifications, and take the seed of all living plants and creatures (as well as his wife, adequate supplies and crew). Cyrus Gordon, an American scholar of Near Eastern cultures, notes that the Babylonian account is "more detailed and realistic than the biblical version because the Mesopotamians were more advanced than the Hebrews in material civilization in general and specifically in the arts of naval construction and operation."[19] Rains came and the ark was carried on the waters. Finally it came to rest on a mountain. The survivors sent out a dove, and then a swallow, and then a raven to determine whether the earth was dry. Utnupishtim got out and sacrificed to the gods, who hovered over the sweet-smelling sacrifice like flies.

Exploring the similarities between these two literary traditions, Gordon makes a clear argument regarding their relationship:

> Here we need to say a special word about the relationship between the flood accounts as preserved in the Bible and in the Gilgamesh Epic. It is obvious that the two versions are strikingly similar and must be related in some way. The consensus of scholars is that the Babylonian version influenced the Israelite version. The reasons for this are manifold. First, all things being equal, a greater society is more likely to influence a lesser society than vice versa. Babylonia was the dominant culture of the Asiatic near East and Israel represented a backwater of sorts. Secondly, the manner of destruction, i.e., by flood, is typical of Mesopotamia, where the great Tigris and Euphrates Rivers regularly flooded their banks and cause havoc and destruction. Israel, by contrast, is very arid; it is unlikely that anyone in that part of the Near East would conceive of a divine destruction of the people through flooding. Third, the geography of the biblical accounts points to a Mesopotamian origin. Noah's ark lands on the mountains of Aratat, at the headwaters of the Tigris and the Euphrates; if the story had originated in Canaan we would expect Mount Hermon (c 7,500 feet high), for example, as the locale of the ark's resting place. Fourth, as we have seen, the Gilgamesh Epic was the literary masterpiece of antiquity, and one fragment even has been found in the land of Israel (at Megiddo). Fifth, the earliest Hebrews come from Mesopotamia, and it is unlikely that Abraham and his entourage would have been unfamiliar with the story.[20]

Interestingly, the fact that flood stories appear also in other cultural myths have been used to support the reliability of the Bible; however in this instance, the parallels are so precisely mirrored – the releasing of the birds, the sweet-smelling sacrifice that pacified the god (Genesis 8:20-12) – that this cannot be an instance of a universal tradition, but rather a direct influence. Although the Bible seems to give a clear picture of the history of mankind from the beginning of creation until the establishment of the Kingdom of Christ, the truth is that there were already extremely advanced and developed civilizations before the Old Testament was written, and the Old Testament authors were undoubtedly influenced by these civilizations.

For example, before Yahweh gave the Jews their 10 commandments, the first king Urnammu of the Third dynasty of Ur (2028-1920BC), developed the first code of laws known anywhere in the world. There are also countless business documents of this period, dated by month and even to the day. Soon thereafter, the king of the Babylonian First Dynasty Hammurapi (1704-1662BC) made an even more advanced code of law. There were three classes of society: rich, middle and slaves. Prices were fixed. Laws were precise and included traffic violation, marriage, care of children, and a Veteran's Bill of Rights. Moreover, it was specifically devoid of legalistic jargon – so that anybody could understand the regulations.

The Jews were heavily influenced by their 70-year Babylonian exile, something that can be seen, for example, in their calendar. "Babylonian unity is reflected by the spread throughout the land of a single calendar, whose month names persisted to the end of Babylonian history and which live on in the religious calendar of the Jews, who adopted it during the Babylonian Exile."[21] This is not to say they assimilated; in fact the extreme disapproval of adapting outsider customs and pagan religions, as well as the ritualistic laws and strict punishments for idolatry, may have been formulated as a way to protect an autonomous Jewish identity.

At the same time, many of the stories in the Old Testament disagree with archaeological evidence. In the story of Exodus, for example, Moses led his people out of Egypt and across the river into Canaan, where they destroyed the Canaanite cities and decimated the local population. As Karen Armstrong, author of *The Bible: A Biography*, points out:

> Israeli archaeologists, who have been excavating the region since 1967, have found no evidence to corroborate this story; there is no sign of foreign invasion or mass destruction, and nothing to indicate

a large-scale change of population. The scholarly consensus is that the story of Exodus is not historical.[22]

The Old Testament is a collection and compilation of Jewish writings, which reflect the Jewish belief in a national divinity and his covenant with them as a people. However, rather than an account of historical events, the Old Testament is an Israel-centered pastiche, which reflects the cultural and ethnographic heritage of the Jews, and for which the various writers freely used and adapted existing literatures from different traditions. It was then organized, translated and copied by Christian scholars, who interpreted it as a foreshadowing of the coming of Christ. Although many of the accounts in the Old Testament may be historical – i.e. the names of specific places or rulers – the writers in general adopted myth, fable and folklore and tied it into current Jewish happenings, as a commentary on contemporary events. In identifying this process in the Old Testament, we already have a working model of how the New Testament gospels may have been written.

## The New Testament

It is awkward to talk about the New Testament as providing proof for the historical Jesus, if only because of the stark contrast in respective beliefs concerning the Bible. Many people believe firmly, without a doubt that the New Testament is not historical; and others believe just as firmly that it is. Although it has long been concluded by literary experts, biblical exegetes, and historical scholars that the four gospels of the New Testament reflect specific theological trends within the early church rather than dispassionate historical reports, they are still considered eye-witness testimonials and historical evidence by perhaps the majority of Christians (and thus a large portion of the world population).

As I mentioned previously, we should not be concerned here with proving the matter one way or another; all that is needed is to fully understand the various reasons why each side claims what it does. To begin with, it can be reiterated that the academic community hasn't considered the gospels as eye-witness accounts since the early days of biblical criticism (although they might say the gospels reflect the genuine or authentic spirit of the early church). In 1986 for example, Robert Funk created the Westar Institute with the aim of exploring the reliability of the New Testament as testimony. He organized the Jesus Seminar, an inter-disciplinary panel of scholars, to investigate the historical accuracy of the New Testament sayings of Jesus. In 1993, the seminar published the findings of their vote-based investigation, in a work called, *The Five Gospels*.[123] Their conclusion was that only 16% of the words attributed to Jesus in the gospels may have actually been spoken by him.

Some of the reasons for this are not difficult to find if reading the Bible objectively. For example, the gospels never say "I saw Jesus do this and was afraid." Instead, they use the third person – as would someone telling a story or legend – and say, "The disciples saw Jesus do this and were afraid." They frequently talk about things that happened behind closed doors or among their rivals, using omniscient narration.

They are also incredibly impersonal; they share no private conversations or anecdotes, no complaints, and no worries or thoughts of the author (which might be expected if the author had traveled in an intimate band of companions for a year). Moreover, scholars generally agree that Mark came first, and the other two Synoptic gospels, Matthew and Luke, copied from him and added their own material to support the agenda of their community. In Mark, the earliest gospel, there was no birth story and no account of the resurrection (the current ending of Mark, which includes Jesus appearing to his disciples, is considered a late addition.) Mark may have been based on an earlier tradition or literature that scholars refer to as "Q." Daniel Wallace of the Dallas Theological Seminary and Executive Director for the *Center for the Study of New Testament Manuscripts,* has written an excellent paper, "The Synoptic Problem," exploring some of these issues.[24]

In fact there is nothing in the text themselves that would give the impression that they are eye-witness accounts; it is only tradition, which later gave the gospels names of specific apostles, which has led to the modern belief that they were written by original followers of Christ. The fact that they were not is universally accepted among scholars; although some claim that they still record genuine testimony, passed down from original witnesses. "Pseudonymity was the rule until 135 at least... then writings were placed under names of apostles to demonstrate that they represented the 'true workings of the spirit' and guaranteed orthodoxy."[25]

What *are* the gospels, if not eye-witness accounts? To understand why and how the gospels were written, we need to remember that the first few centuries of Christianity were filled with controversies. Dozens of schisms, sects, and communities worshipped Jesus independently and called each other heretics. Some groups, in order to claim authority, tried to create a direct link of transmission between themselves and the disciples who actually knew Jesus. The concept of "apostolic succession" was an attempt to strengthen the particular ideology of certain Christian communities. Moreover, communities selected, altered or crafted stories about Jesus to support their own particular theology and to raise the status of the apostle their group claimed to have received direct transmission from.

Many Christian communities were the result of the hard work of the apostle Paul, whose letters (both authentic and those forged in his name) make up nearly half of the New Testament. Interestingly, it seems Paul himself was completely against the idea of apostolic tradition. He argued that believers could experience Jesus personally – without any human intermediary – and that this metaphysical experience of Jesus made them equal to any others: "I did not receive it [the gospel] from man, nor was I taught it, but it came through a revelation of Jesus Christ" (Gal. 1:12); "Am I not an apostle, have I not seen Jesus our Lord?" (1:Cor. 15:7).

Against the teachings of Paul, and unlike the earliest Christian texts (such as the Didache[26] (c. 50-120AD) in which roles are merit based and there is no hierarchy, or the book of Matthew, which rejected fixed forms of ritual) by around 100AD a body of teaching was becoming established to which appeal could be made. Its authenticity could be guaranteed by reference to the apostles and to Christ himself, and it was represented by an ordered hierarchy that could claim descent from apostolic times.[27]

Faced with controversy on all sides, the early church fathers developed a canon (or plumb-line) of "orthodox" writings; the criteria for which was that they could be traced back to a disciple of Christ. Thus, they could claim absolute authority via direct apostolic transmission. However, in order to validate the appropriate texts, pseudepigraphy (forgery) was used to assign the texts to various apostles. As radical critic Hermann Detering comments:

> The history of the investigation of the New Testament writings has led to the generally recognized conclusion that of the all-together twenty-seven writings in the New Testament, apart from those that supposedly derive from Paul – not a single one can be traced back to an apostle, or a student of an apostle – and this is the case even though all the writings of the New Testament claim direct or indirect apostolic authorship, which then constitutes the presupposition for their inclusion in the canon![28]

The communities that insisted on a fixed canon and apostolic tradition were the same communities preaching a Jesus "in the flesh," as opposed to one that came only in appearance; thus they naturally had a stronger claim to the historical transmission of dogma or truth. Other communities with a more integrative, spiritual focus also began to use apostolic tradition to justify their teachings; but without a clear, physical human founder, their claim of authenticity was weakened. This is probably why in the Bible, which is a result of a "normative Christianity," Peter (considered one of the actual disciples) is made the rock on which Jesus founded his church, rather than Paul (who never met Jesus).

In the apocryphal gospel of Thomas, however, Jesus chose James to be ruler. In the gospel of Mary Magdalene, we find it is Mary who was closest to Jesus and had been given ultimate knowledge. In fact it was quite easy for a sect or community to attribute their theology to Jesus – they could just claim another revelation from the spiritual Christ, or a private conversation between him and a disciple not yet recorded. This opportunity was fortified by the fact that Jesus had resurrected, and could appear in the flesh (or in dreams) to anybody, at any time. It was probably this atmosphere of intense competition that made it necessary for the orthodox to deny the spiritual Jesus as much as possible and emphasize his one-time-only historicity. As such, they could codify a set of gospels to which nothing more could be added. (Even so, they constantly had to fight against communities who claimed Jesus had revealed secret knowledge to other disciples).

At the same time, it is worth noting the style of the earliest

Christian documents (which oddly were not deemed worthy of biblical inclusion) with regard to Jesus. Rather than the eye-witness testimonials which we would expect, they refer very generally (if at all) to Jesus, and rarely in a human context. The impression of Jesus Christ was interpreted less in terms of the Gospels than in those of the messianic prophecies of the Old Testament.[29] 1 Clement and the Didache present Christ as "the servant," and quote Isaiah to demonstrate qualities of Christ, rather than any historical events. For example, they would say that Christ was humble; not because of his humility under Pilate, but because Isaiah said he would be.

Likewise, Clement 1 proves the possibility of immortality through a reference to the phoenix, instead of the empty tomb. Ethical teachings of the early communities were based on the "Two Ways" of Job, the Proverbs and the book of Ecclesiastics rather than the Sermon on the Mount. Judith and Esther are used as examples of self-sacrificing, modest women instead of Mary Magdalene or Jesus' mother.

The Jesus of the early Christian communities, rather than a recently deceased historical person, was primarily a literary construct – a synthesis based on an academic exegesis that interpreted Jewish scripture as prophecy about the coming Messiah. Karen Armstrong explains how a "blurring" of several Old Testament motifs was used to form the character of Jesus Christ:

> They were also attracted to the mysterious figure of the servant in Second Isaiah, whose suffering had redeemed the world. The servant had not been a messianic figure, but by constantly comparing the servant with Jesus Christos, using the same 'blurring' technique, they established for the first time the idea of a suffering messiah. Thus three separate figures – servant, messiah and Jesus – became inseparable in the Christian imagination.[30]

As Armstrong continues, this Christian exegesis was so thorough that "there is scarcely a verse in the New Testament that did not refer to older scriptures," and that, therefore, "some scholars have gone so far as to suggest that it would be possible to construct an entire gospel from the Jewish scriptures, without quoting a single word by Jesus himself."[31]

The gospel story about Jesus Christ *begins* with his theological role and relationship with the Old Testament; however at the same time, there are anomalous elements that could not have come from Judaism. The Holy Communion for example, is in direct violation of the command in Leviticus 17:12 not to eat raw blood.

Early writings like the Didache[32] mention Jesus only as the "servant to God" who initiated the Eucharist. The Didache doesn't mention Christ's resurrection; and while it speaks of a "Son of God" and "Lord," this figure is never explicitly identified with Jesus Christ. He was *expected* to arrive, rather than being present. The Didache also lists ethical commands, without linking them to Jesus. *Do not do to others what you would not done to you. Love your neighbor as yourself. Pray for your enemies. If someone takes your cloak, give him your coat. The meek shall inherit the earth.* These maxims were part of the "Way of Life" (as opposed to the "Way of Death") and would later be attributed to the figure of Jesus.[33]

The specific details of the gospel, and the story of the human, physical life of Jesus, were told only when needed by Christian communities to confront the claims that Jesus had not lived a human life. In the second century there was no canon of prescribed texts because there was "as yet, no standard form of Christianity."[34] Jesus Christ was then placed in a historical context, and pre-existing statements (like those from the Didache[35]) were prefixed with "Jesus said –." As W.H.C. Frend confirms in *The Rise of Christianity*:

> Communities needed an account of the life of the Savior for their edification and in order to refute those who denied that he was the Messiah or claimed that his ministry was not real.[36]

Part of the confusion over the gospels is that *they appear* to be historical; they are written in a way, and with the inclusion of historical data, which makes them seem like historical documents. This stylistic feature is often pointed out as evidence. Craig Blomberg for example, Professor of the New Testament at the Denver Seminary in Colorado, argues:

> But if you're going to be convinced enough to believe, the theology has to flow from accurate history. Besides, there's an important piece of implicit evidence that can't be overlooked. Consider the way the gospels are written – a sober and responsible fashion, with accurate incidental details, with obvious care and exactitude. You don't find

the outlandish flourishes and blatant mythologizing that you see in a lot of other ancient writings.[37]

Overlooking the claim that a story about a man who walks on water, pulls coins out of fish and rises from the dead is "sober and responsible" and not "outlandish flourishes and blatant mythologizing," we could easily respond that the gospels were written in this particular style precisely because the authors wanted them to be considered as historical testimonies – which in no way proves that they actually were. The gospels that were canonized were the ones that presented Jesus the man; and they were chosen *because* they focused on the physical Jesus and could support a claim of apostolic tradition and the authority of a particular Christian community (with the exception of John, which presents Jesus in transcendental terms that for many were irreconcilable with a physical human being). Other scholars have claimed that the consistent style of these gospels implies a historical mover behind them. Welsh New Testament scholar and influential Protestant theologian C.H. Dodd takes this approach:

> The Synoptic writers give us a body of his sayings so coherent, and withal so distinctive in style, manner and content, that no reasonable critic could doubt that whatever reservations he might have about individual Sayings, we find reflected here the thought of a single, unique teacher.[38]

Early Christian writings, however, testify that like the Old Testament, the stories in the New Testament were allegories deliberately written as "historical narratives" that held deeper meaning meant to be interpreted. Christian apologist Origen, in *Contra Celsum*, explains:

> It is sufficient however, to represent in the style of a historical narrative what is intended to convey a secret meaning in the garb of history, that those who have the capacity may work out for themselves all that relates to the subject. (Book 5, Chapter 29)

In fact, for much of its existence, it was understood that the Bible was meant to be treated as allegory. Origen's three levels of meaning in exegetical practice formed the basis of biblical study well into the Middle Ages. But along with the Reformation, and the Protestant cry of *sola scriptura,* came an emphasis on a literal reading of the Bible. The complications inherent in mixing spiritual allegory with historical fact are many. Richard Dawkins points out one such example in *The God Delusion.* In Christian theology, Jesus is the "New Adam" necessary to redeem the sin of Adam; but Adam, or "first man," is without question a literary construct – his alleged transgression merely a theological explanation for why there is sin in the world. Even if a real Jesus did come in the flesh, why would his actions remove the "stain of sin" from a mythical figure?:

> To cap it all, Adam, the supposed perpetrator of the original sin, never existed in the first place: an – awkward fact – excusably unknown to Paul but presumably known to an Omniscient God (and Jesus, if you believe he was God?) – which fundamentally undermines the premise of the whole nasty theory. Oh, but of course, the story of Adam and Eve was only ever *symbolic,* wasn't it? *Symbolic?* So, in order to impress himself, Jesus had himself tortured and executed, in vicarious punishment for a *symbolic* sin committed by a *non-existent* individual?[39]

## Jesus and the Stoic Philosophers

What about the teachings of Jesus found in the New Testament? Can they be traced to innovative ideas that may have come from a historical founder? Actually, many "Christian" ideas were already present in Jewish spiritual communities and pagan philosophy. The Pharisees, for example, systematized works of mercy and charity towards the poor, as well as care of the dead (burial of corpses and care of graves), which were to become characteristic of Christian practice. They also already believed in an afterlife and a last judgment:

> Nonetheless, the Pharisaic belief in the afterlife, in its rewards and punishments, in angels and demons, and also in the ability of each individual to repent of sins and earn forgiveness, and of the duty to die for the Torah rather than compromise its prescriptions, were accepted by the people. Lazarus's sister Martha took it as a matter of course that her brother would rise again in the resurrection at the last day.[40]

The Jesus movement appears unique in preaching that, rather than at the end of time, the Kingdom and the resurrection was to be found *right now* – in this lifetime. This passionate and motivating belief, however, can be traced to the community at Qumran:

> Like Jesus himself and the early Christians, the Covenanters expected the rapid end of the age, they were concerned with membership of the future kingdom, and they shared with Jesus' followers a deep interest in discovering signs that might warn them of the approach of the end.[41]

A similar theme is found in the Stoic writings. The Stoic doctrine of the "world conflagration" described the destruction of the present scheme of things so that it may begin anew. Hence, Epictetus teaches non-attachment, and "not to stray too far from the ship":

> On a voyage, when the ship calls at the port and you go ashore for water, it amuses you to pick up a shell or a plant by the way; but your thoughts ought to be directed to the ship and you must watch lest the captain call, and then you must throw away all those things, that you may not be flung aboard, tied like the sheep. So in life suppose that instead of some little shell or plant, you are given something in the way of wife or child nothing need hinder. But, if the captain call, run to the ship letting them all go and never looking round.[42]

Early Christianity developed a similar doctrine of the End of Times, when God would destroy the world with fire and natural disasters, and Jesus would return to judge the living and the dead.

> Immediately after the distress of those days, 'the sun will be darkened, and the moon will not give its light; the stars will fall from the sky, and the heavenly bodies will be shaken.' At that time the sign of the Son of Man will appear in the sky, and all the nations of the earth will mourn. (Matthew 24:29-31, NIV)

> On the earth, nations will be in anguish and perplexity at the roaring and tossing of the sea. Men will faint from terror, apprehensive of what is coming on the world, for the heavenly bodies will be shaken. At that time they will see the Son of Man coming in a cloud with power and great glory. When these things begin to take place, stand

up and lift up your heads, because your redemption is drawing near. (Luke 21:25-28, NIV)

Rather than Epictetus' metaphor of the ship, the gospel writers preferred to imagine Jesus arriving "like a thief in the night":

But the day of the Lord will come like a thief. The heavens will disappear with a roar; the elements will be destroyed by fire, and the earth and everything in it will be laid bare. (2 Peter 3:10, NIV)

Behold, I come like a thief! Blessed is he who stays awake and keeps his clothes with him, so that he may not go naked and be shamefully exposed. (Revelation 16:15, NIV)

The Qumran community used a dualistic system marked by light and dark symmetry – the two ways or two paths – which is in common with early Christian texts. The *Manual of Discipline,* for example, reads "Now this God created man to rule the world and appointed for him two spirits he was to walk with until the final Inquisition."[43] This division between a higher, divine self, and a lower, animal self was also common in most pagan philosophical and spiritual traditions. It was believed that developing the higher self would lead to life while giving in to the passions of the body would lead to death.

Stoicism also taught, like the Gospel of John, that the Word of God (*Spermaticos Logos*) was the creative force through which the universe was created, that existed with the Father in the beginning, and descended even into men. According to Seneca:

This fabric which you see, wherein are divine and human, is one. We are members of a great body. Nature has made us of one blood, has implanted in us mutual love, has made us for society.

The gods are not scornful, they are not envious. They welcome us, and, as we ascend, they reach us their hands. Are you surprised that a man should go to the gods? God comes to men, nay! Nearer still! He comes into men. No mind (mens) is good without God. Divine seeds are sown in human bodies, and will grow into likeness to their origin if rightly cultivated.[44]

As Bultmann pointed out, if the ideas recorded in the New Testament as teachings of Jesus were already present in his environment, they cannot have originated with him. Specifically, although there may have been a Jewish teacher or rebel leader who drew from those beliefs and formulated a synthesis, those teachings – not being original – cannot be used to identify or locate him.

The reverse, however, is also true. Just because the New Testament may not refer to a specific, unique historical person, and instead may be a compilation of Christian theology, beliefs and mythology, doesn't prove that there was not a historical founder behind them. The conclusion can only be that the gospels of the New Testament are not focused on the historical Jesus, and as such should not be expected to give strong evidence of him. Without conflicting evidence, there is no reason not to take them at face value as relating to a specific historical individual:

> In their final form the Gospels are works reflecting the faith and attitudes of Christian communities some two generations after the crucifixion. Their writers were concerned with "the gospel of Jesus Christ, the Son of God (Mark 1:1) and not with historical biography. The story they tell, however, can hardly relate to a situation other than Palestine in the first half of the first century A.D. and to an individual who lived in those times.[45]

The story of the gospels is *about* an individual that lived in a specific period of history and, as recent scholarship has proved, we can generate a lot of details about that individual by researching relevant historical data. But it should not be forgotten that this method begins with the hypothesis of a historical Jesus.

To elaborate this point, consider the novel *Gone with the Wind*. It is about a woman named Scarlett O'Hara, who lived during a specific episode of American history the civil war. *Gone with the Wind* is full of passion, relationship, adventure and dialog, and made realistic by the inclusion of history-specific details, such as descriptions of soldiers' uniforms or references to real battles that took place or real political leaders. However, we recognize that *Gone with the Wind* is a story written in a certain genre: historical fiction or historical narrative. It can move us, inspire us, motivate and entertain us; and a person like Scarlett may really have existed and had similar experiences; but by examining the literary components, we can separate fact from fiction.

Many scholars still believe that the gospels preserve genuine Jesus-inspired traditions, recollections and evidences of Christianity's historical founder, and in the absence of other indicators, biblical studies would do well to continue searching for him. However, there *is* other evidence, which is discarded for being irrelevant simply because it doesn't lead to the conclusion that Jesus Christ was historical. This circular argument is that any evidence which describes Jesus in non-historical terms has no relevance to historical Jesus research. At the same time, some of this evidence comes from *Christ-worshipping* communities and traditions, and therefore can be useful in understanding the development of Christian history and ideology.

## The Gnostic Gospels

In 1979 Professor of Religion at Princeton University Elaine Pagels first published her book *The Gnostic Gospels,* a popular introduction to the ancient manuscripts discovered near the upper Egyptian town of Nag Hammadi in 1943. The word "Gnostic" refers to possessing intellectual or spiritual knowledge. These documents, which were buried to avoid persecution in the 3rd or 4th century, depict a Jesus concerned with illusion and enlightenment rather than sin and repentance. According to Pagels, "Instead of coming to save us from sin, he comes as a guide who opens access to spiritual understanding." Pagels' book revealed that the early Christian communities were diverse, held vastly differing beliefs about their savior Jesus Christ, and treasured several gospels that were not included in the Bible:

> Contemporary Christianity, diverse and complex as we find it, actually may show more unanimity than the Christian churches of the first and second centuries. For nearly all Christians since that time, Catholics, Protestants, or Orthodox, have shared three basic premises. First, they accept the canon of the New Testament; second, they confess the apostolic creed; and third, they affirm specific forms of church institutions. But every one of these – the canon of Scripture, the creed, and the institutional structure – emerged in its present

form only toward the end of the second century. Before that time, as Irenaeus and others attest, numerous gospels circulated among various Christian groups, ranging from those of the New Testament, Matthew, Mark, Luke, and John, to such writings as the *Gospel of Thomas*, the *Gospel of Philip*, and the *Gospel of Truth*, as well as many other secret teachings, myths, and poems attributed to Jesus or his disciples. Some of these, apparently, were discovered at Nag Hammadi; many others are lost to us. Those who identified themselves as Christians entertained many – and radically differing – religious beliefs and practices.[46]

But can the Gnostic Gospels really tell us anything about Jesus? Traditional biblical scholars insist that Gnosticism was a schism or heresy from the original Jesus movement, and that it was mostly pagan and had nothing to do with the authentic teachings of Jesus. This argument was used early by the church, who claimed ultimate possession over the Christian legacy. As Frend relates:

> An assumption, which started early and continues to hold weight today, is that these Gnostic communities came late and as such have no bearing on the historical Jesus. Tertullian, for example, argues that Gnostics had no right to use scripture in any way. They were usurpers, latecomers whose sects had come into being long after the church had established itself and therefore held a possessory right over Scripture.[47]

Today "Gnostic" is commonly used as a broad term to refer to certain groups and ideas of the 2nd century. Anything Gnostic then, by definition, can be satisfactorily restrained to the safety of the second century as an offshoot of mainstream Christianity. Another method used to marginalize Gnostic writings is to say they are not concerned with the historical Jesus, or don't believe in him, and therefore have nothing useful to say about him. It can be demonstrated, however, that the beliefs and ideologies of Gnosticism come directly from traditions that are older than mainstream Christianity. Therefore, rather than offshoots of orthodox Christianity, they actually represent co-existing, contemporary communities which developed around the same time as normative Christianity. Although I will not argue that the Gnostic gospels have more authority or are earlier than the canonical ones, I think it reasonable to accept that they may have at least something to tell us about the diverse early practices of worshipping Jesus, as well as the reliability of the tradition of a historical founder.

Gnosticism is basically a philosophical form of Christianity that focuses on esoteric wisdom and metaphysics. Many Gnostics believed in dualism: the earth is the lowest of seven universes or planets, and our souls (remnants from the perfect light of the first world) are stuck here in corrupted, physical bodies. We can find these beliefs in Saturnius (c.100-120), the disciple of Menander (c.60-100), who was the disciple of Simon Magus. The world was viewed as evil matter, and Christ came to save us from the "seven angels" (planets or powers) – one of whom was the Yahweh of the Old Testament.[48] As was already pointed out, "orthodox" Christianity also had strong dualistic tendencies; but with the emphasis on the historical Jesus and the resurrection of the flesh, it became problematic to vilify the physical body.

Influenced by logical inquiry and pagan philosophy, Gnostics read the Old Testament description of Yahweh (which shows him to be possessive, jealous and angry) and concluded that he could not be the *real* God, who must be perfect. Instead, they called him *Demiurge* – a malevolent force that produced the world by blunder.

Gnostic writings demonstrate a synthesis of Jewish and pagan thought, and also employ New Testament figures like Jesus, Peter, John, Mark, Paul and Mary. A few of the most influential Gnostic teachers were Basilides (c.130-150), Valentinus (c.140-160) and Heracleon (c.170-180). Basilides taught the Demiurge, and claimed the crucifixion was not real (for Christ could not suffer). In Basilides' account of the Passion, Simon of Cyrene takes on the appearance of Jesus, and Jesus stands by and laughs in scorn as the Jews try to kill him. Interestingly, Simon of Cyrene also appears in the gospel of Mark, as the bystander who carries the cross for Jesus (Mark, 15:21).

In the account of Valentinus (c. 140-65), Sophia, a great Goddess, gave birth to the creator of the universe (the Demiurge) but then fell into matter and became trapped (or in some accounts, sacrificed herself.) A savior, Jesus, is sent to Sophia. He separates her from her passions, saving her. Like all Gnostic myths, the symbols are meant to be interpreted. Sophia means "wisdom," and it is she who is also found in the book of Wisdom. The qualities of Wisdom are very similar to those later given to the "Logos," which were then placed onto the person of Jesus Christ:

> Wisdom is quicker to move than any motion; she is so pure, she pervades and permeates all things. She is a breath of the power of God, pure emanation of the glory of the Almighty; so nothing impure can find its way into her. For she is a reflection of the eternal light, untarnished mirror of God's active power, and image of his goodness. Although she is alone, she can do everything; herself unchanging, she renews the world, and, generation after generation, passing into holy souls, she makes them into God's friends and prophets; for God loves those who dwell in wisdom. (Wisdom 7:24-28)

When we reflect that "Sophia" or wisdom is what the Gnostics prized above all else, the book of Wisdom actually seems more attune to Gnosticism than what became orthodox Christianity. Although the above qualities given to Wisdom could also be attached to the Holy Spirit, they certainly reflect a pre-Christian trend which was more common to Gnostics and pagans than to early Christianity. According to the myth, when Sophia fell to the earth she became trapped in "dirt" (humanity); giving human beings the spark of the divine, or reason. Jesus, for Valentinus, was the savior who came to liberate our souls or higher selves from the prison of the flesh.

Clement of Alexandria (c.150-215), considered a saint by the church until the 17th century, believed that Jesus had a true human nature but felt no emotions, pleasure or pain. Clement also quoted from Valentinus, who said that "Jesus ate and drank in a manner peculiar to himself and that the food did not pass through his body" (Miscellanies VI.9.71 1-2). A fragment (in a Latin translation) of a commentary of Clement's on the first Epistle of John contains the following curious statement, which directly contradicts the biblical story of "doubting Thomas":

> It is said in the tradition that John touched the surface of the body of Jesus, and drove his hand deep into it, and the firmness of the flesh was no obstacle but gave way to the hand of the disciple.[49]

Clement was familiar with Indian religions and customs, and it has been pointed out that his spiritual beliefs may have been more Buddhist than Christian. This just shows the ease and ability with which Jesus' Gnostic followers integrated with other traditions.

Basilides also interpreted scripture allegorically and related it freely to other myths. Based on the writings of Paul (Romans 7:9), Basilides taught the "transmigration of souls" (reincarnation), a common theme shared between Orphism, Plato and mystery cults.

According to Heracleon (and most Gnostics), spiritual beings comprehended the passion of the savior as spiritual allegory for their own restoration to the Father. Heracleon, like Paul, criticized the orthodox for still acting like Jews; celebrating Passover in the Eucharist and making the mistake of interpreting literary events historically.[50] Heracleon also taught that the baptism of John was only for the body, and thus imperfect, while the baptism of the Gnostics is spiritual. Significantly, according to New Testament writings, early Christianity originally had *two baptisms* – one of the flesh and one of the spirit. John's baptism is of water, while Jesus' baptism is of fire and the holy spirit. In Acts of the Apostles, St. Paul finds whole communities that did not receive the 2nd baptism. The fact that most forms of modern Christianity celebrate only one baptism is an indication of what has been lost.

Marcion (c.85-165) distinguished between the Demiurge, who symbolized righteousness (reward and punishment) and the real god, which was pure goodness. Citing from Isaiah, Marcion pointed out that Yahweh was the creator of evil: "I make weal and create woe, I am the Lord, who do all these things" (Isaiah 45:7). This vengeful creator god was not the same as the meek, passive Jesus. Jesus is the inner man, and though revealed as a man was not a man; he had a body only in appearance, and was subject to no nativity or passion, except in appearance.

Therefore, Marcion was against tying Jesus to the Old Testament or keeping Jewish Law. After nine years living and teaching in the Christian community in Rome, Marcion was finally expelled. As was customary, he had donated money and property to the church when he joined, and this was returned to him. When he was barred from orthodoxy, he used his fortune to start his own churches, in which membership was restricted to the truly dedicated. In Marcion's churches you had to abandon all family ties and obligations. Baptism was granted only to those ready to abandon the world and its joys.

Frend notes, "This was, however, the way leading to the status of a respected sect, such as the Parsees in India, but not to that of world religion."[51] Marcion's god was not interested in flaming fire and eternal punishment. This passive and meek god was derided by the orthodox, who did not see how a gentile god could make people behave:

> Listen, you sinners, and any of you not yet so, that you may be able to become so. A better god has been discovered, one who is neither offended nor angry nor inflicts punishment, who has no fire warming in hell, no gnashing of teeth in the outer darkness. (Tertullian 144)

The orthodox position, which stressed fear of punishment and hope for reward, blind faith and a fearsome god, proved conducive to establishing a grounded historical movement. The Gnostics, on the other hand, melted too easily into their surrounding environment; however, it should be pointed out that the triumph of Christianity was due more to the specific beliefs of orthodoxy rather than the teachings of a potentially historical founder:

> To worship an unknown God sending Christ as a "healthful Spirit swooshing down from heaven" on an alien world to guide humankind, was to make Christianity into another mystery religion with no roots in the past... The good-natured spirit preached by Marcion was not one to inspire most would-be Christians to break from the world and accept the test of martyrdom.[52]

The main difference between orthodoxy and Gnosticism is that, while orthodoxy was developing a canon, a hierarchy, rules and regulations, and an organizational structure, the Gnostics were searching for truth. Gnostics were "intellectually superior and better attuned to the ideas of their age than were their orthodox rivals, and they were less bound to what was hardening into formal and legalistic tradition."[53] They drew easily from contemporary philosophies and literature; Homer, Plato and Paul were placed on the same level of authority.

When they encountered a contradiction or logical problem within their gospels or beliefs, they fixed them; which led to the rapid expansion of Gnostic sects and literature. Their ideas were based on reason and intelligence rather than revelation. These values made it easy for them to blend into the intellectually progressive environment of the Roman Empire.

> The Gnostic teachers therefore stood in the mainstream of second-century religious speculation. They molded current ideas into their own systems, and associated them with Christ, the heavenly Messenger, who had appeared on earth in historical times.[54]

For the same reason, critics claim that Gnosticism can say nothing about the historical Jesus because it is *too* pagan. However, the synthesis between Judaism and paganism had begun before the arrival of Jesus, and most of the elements used by the Gnostics predate Christianity:

> It is impossible to think of the emergence of Gnosticism in the second century without the background of wisdom literature, of Philo, and the speculative preoccupation throughout Jewry with angelology, with the planets and the zodiac, and with mysteries connected with the sacred name of Yahweh. In these respects, it was one more successful manifestation of that extraordinarily vigorous Jewish culture that flourished at the time of Jesus, and of which Christianity was largely the heir.[55]

As was pointed out earlier, the main reason the Gnostic gospels are discarded in the quest for the historical Jesus is because they do not present the narrative picture of Jesus that we've come to expect. They are talking about some other Jesus entirely; and if Jesus *did* exist as presented in the gospels, the Gnostic gospels must be mistaken.

And yet it is difficult to see how the appearance of the historical figure of Jesus Christ could produce one community which remembered him as a human being and several other communities which worshiped him as an eternal, spiritual entity. On the other hand, a model of how certain Jesus-based communities developed the need of a historical Jesus to justify their unique beliefs about a physical resurrection, which is supported by all available evidence, can be presented very clearly.

It is also possible to show that the tradition of a historical Jesus may have appeared *later* than the Gnostic tradition: Justin Martyr and Irenaeus record that Gnosticism started from Simon Magus, a popular magician-preacher recorded in the Acts of the Apostles. Simon's teachings, meanwhile, seem to have been rooted in the Essene community:

> Simon, then, had been active "for a long time," and his teachings concerning "the Great Power" was acceptable throughout the whole Samaritan people... If Simon himself was a disciple of a previous teacher named Dositheus, then the pre-Christian origins of the movement that came to be identified as Gnosticism would be evident, for Dositheus seems to have been connected at one time with Essenes.[56]

According to Detering, who claims that all of the Pauline letters were fabricated by the Gnostic Marcion (scholars agree Marcion was the first to reference them), Simon represented the *first Christian mission*, which was then brought back down to earth by the more sober Peter:

> It can be inferred that this Simon had also turned to the Gentiles and carried out missionary activity here as well. Even the Pseudo-Clementines could not avoid mentioning Simon's great missionary success; through him even before Peter, many Gentiles were supposedly converted to Christianity.[57]

If Simon's teachings (which are very similar to Marcionite and Valentinian ideas) can be traced back to the Essenes – even if contemporary scholarship only labels them "Gnostic" in their later, second century form – then they preserve the earliest form of Christianity, which was later altered to fit the idea of a suffering, physical Messiah. Noting that St. Paul fits more snugly in the Gnostic tradition than in the orthodoxy which later embraces him, Deterring goes as far as to argue that Paul and Simon were actually the same figure.

Orthodoxy continues to claim that its gospels are earlier – closer in time to the actual life of Jesus Christ and thus authoritative – while maintaining that Gnosticism is a later offshoot because, if there was historical Jesus, *it had to be*. Much more important, however, are the ideas contained within both traditions. The canonic gospels present the unique ideology and values of a Christian community that was dissimilar to its environment by believing in the physical

Christ, and they were chosen for precisely that reason. However, even if they are read literally and seem to describe Jesus the man, there are symbols, motifs and elements in them which stem from the same mystic and philosophical blend of paganism and Judaism which also gave rise to Gnosticism, lending credence to the claim that the story was originally created by those who intended it to be interpreted allegorically.

## Conclusions and Summary

One response to challenges that Jesus wasn't historical is, *there is no evidence that can prove Jesus didn't exist.* Of course this is true, but it is also meaningless: if Jesus did not exist, then why would there be any evidence? *In Harry Potter and the Deathly Hallows,* the inability of evidence to disprove matters of faith is a motif illustrated by Xenophilius Lovegood: when the skeptical Hermione asks how the Resurrection Stone can be real, Xeno's response is short and instructive: "Prove that it is not."[58]

At the same time, it is possible that Jesus *did* exist and left no evidence; we should not doubt a historical founder of Christianity simply because there are no contemporary records of him, and only a handful of later (possibly forged) accounts. However, in searching for the truth, we cannot afford to automatically discount evidence from external traditions that problematize the historical Jesus on the grounds that they fail to edify his actual existence.

As I've demonstrated in this chapter, the danger in trusting the Bible as a historical testimony is that it was written for precisely that purpose. Given the fact that the New Testament, narrative version of Jesus Christ's ministry was written in response to the pre-existing communities and teachers such as Simon, it represents exactly *the idea* of a historical Jesus, which was necessary to secure its own authority, rather than reliable history.

Even if none of the above arguments and evidences for Jesus Christ were convincing, it would still be very acceptable to believe, in the absence of other indicators, that he was a historical person. It can be maintained that there was an oral tradition based on the teachings of Jesus Christ that was later written down in the gospels, which viewed him as a blend of

Messiah and the suffering servant of Isaiah. These texts might have included the immediate expectation of the apocalypse and a connection with Jewish scriptures, and became quickly inundated with pagan elements, leading to the rise of Gnosticism.

Unfortunately, as has long been noted by critical historians, when you begin identifying the specific features that *did not* come from Jesus and taking them away from him, virtually nothing remains. The problem intensifies when you look outside of Judaism and compare Jesus to older mythological and religious traditions. This is true especially of his central features: his resurrection and ascension, miracles and teachings, forgiveness of sins, relationship to God and role in creation as the Logos or Word. Is the evidence for the historical Jesus strong enough to save him from this unraveling process? The short answer is *no* – in fact, it points in the other direction: that Jesus may have originally been a literary metaphor and religious symbol, which became historicized deliberately for a specific agenda.

The goal of the previous chapters has been to establish the basis of the controversy surrounding the historical Jesus, analyze the relevant modern assumptions and pre-established beliefs about the subject, and re-examine critical evidence in the debate. At this stage, if nothing else, we can say that the question of Jesus Christ's true nature remains an enigma which traditionally cited evidence and Christian accounts of history fail to explain. In the absence of evidence supporting the idea of a historical Jesus Christ, the *historicity* of Jesus Christ itself cannot be used to differentiate him from other mythological traditions (including the modern myth of Harry Potter); hence when we discover a parallel between Jesus Christ and earlier mythology and literature so precise that it is unlikely to be coincidental, we must assume it has been assimilated into the literary tradition surrounding Jesus rather than recording a factual, historical occurrence. Identifying the literary, mythological Jesus from the gospels, it will be easier to compare this figure to Harry Potter – one literary figure to another.

To this end, in the following chapter I will give descriptions of the major deities and mythical figures that have been compared to Jesus Christ, using ancient testimonies and Christian sources. Special attention will be paid to the timeline so that priority can be established.

## CHAPTER FOUR

# Going Pagan: The Forgotten Prefigures of Christ

*"The very thing which is now called the Christian religion existed among the ancients also, nor was it wanting from the inception of the human race until the coming of Christ in the flesh, at which point the true religion which was already in existence began to be called Christian."*
*–St. Augustine, 464AD.*

AT TRINITY COLLEGE IN DUBLIN THERE is a medieval manuscript called the Book of Leinster which was compiled around 1160. In it we meet the Irish mythological hero, Cúchulainn, known for his terrifying battle frenzy or *ríastrad*, which turns him into an unrecognizable monster. Cúchulainn's violent rage could only be soothed by women and cold water:

> He sets off on a foray and kills the three sons of Nechtan Scéne, who had boasted they had killed more Ulstermen than there were Ulstermen still living. He returns to Emain Macha in his battle frenzy, and the Ulstermen are afraid he will slaughter them all. Conchobar's wife Mugain leads out the women of Emain, and they bare their

breasts to him. He averts his eyes, and the Ulstermen wrestle him into a barrel of cold water, which explodes from the heat of his body. They put him in a second barrel, which boils, and a third, which warms to a pleasant temperature.[1]

Fans of Marvel Comic's *The Incredible Hulk* might have already noticed the similarities between Cúchulainn and Dr. Bruce Banner's alter ego. The parallels are fascinating and demand the question, are the similarities purely coincidental? Given the difference in geography and time, we might assume so. On the other hand, the story of Leinster may have remained for centuries in the "collective unconscious," or even been passed down from mothers to sons as a bedtime story, before unconsciously popping up as the big green monster. However, if it could be shown that one of the creators of the Marvel character was Irish or had studied Irish myths of that time period, and was most likely familiar with the story of Leinster, then of course we could make a pretty strong argument that *The Incredible Hulk* was a deliberate re-telling of the myth for a more modern audience.

A similar situation develops when we look at the parallels between Jesus Christ and Harry Potter. Harry came almost 2,000 years after Jesus, and since J.K. Rowling grew up in a Christian society, we might charge her with borrowing biblical or Christian imagery (and in fact, she's admitted as much).

But what if these same symbols could also be applied to even earlier figures? Osiris, for example, or Gilgamesh, who we know came about 2,000 years before Jesus. The problem, of course, is that while Harry Potter or The Incredible Hulk are obviously fictional characters, Jesus Christ is assumed to be historical – which makes direct comparisons all the more challenging.

Given a parallel so precise that it is unlikely to be coincidental, in two literary traditions from civilizations that were known to have been in contact with each other, originality should be given to the historically earlier instance. If it can be demonstrated that the gospel writers were already familiar with stories that parallel the gospel accounts of Jesus Christ from contemporary mythologies (such as Attis, Orpheus, Mithras, Osiris, Tammuz, Adonis, Dionysus, or Asclepius), it is very likely that Christianity adapted or assimilated portions of these mythologies into their own literary creations. This idea is not at all challenged by academics today, who, as we have seen, agree that in order to discover what was unique about Christianity (and thus might have come from a historical founder), we must first identify what was obviously borrowed or included.

However, at the same time, conservative biblical scholars or Christian apologists have been careful to refute claims of similarity that can weaken the supremacy and historical validity of Jesus Christ. This defensive position is somewhat justified, as Christ-Myth researchers have sometimes taken unfounded, sweeping liberties and minimized all differences in order to fit their theories. Nevertheless, these criticisms are usually leveled against *the idea* of similarity, rather than any particular similarities, and are invariably founded on the same set of (flawed) arguments.

The first is simply the reiteration of the historical Jesus. Taking support from the academia's continued pursuit of a historical founder for Christianity, potential similarities (when used to question the Jesus of history) are immediately repudiated because "no serious scholar doubts the historical Jesus." However, this merely ignores the otherwise very troubling evidence, and is no improvement from Justin Martyr's original argument dealing with the same similarities: Jesus was real, while all other instances (of crucified saviors) were symbolic, and thus not equal. The only explanation ever put forward by Christians as to *why* pagan mythology and earlier saviors are so similar to the later, actual, life of Jesus is Justin's concept of "Diabolical Mimicry," which blames the similarities on wicked demons who were commissioned by Satan to spread similar stories throughout the world in a sort of pre-emptive attack against Christianity:

> But those who hand down the myths which the poets have made, adduce no proof to the youths who learn them; and we proceed to demonstrate that they have been uttered by the influence of the wicked demons, to deceive and lead astray the human race. For having heard it proclaimed through the prophets that the Christ was to come, and that the ungodly among men were to be punished by fire, they put forward many to be called sons of Jupiter, under the impression that they would be able to produce in men the idea that the things which

were said with regard to Christ were mere marvelous tales, like the things which were said by the poets. (Justin Martyr, *First Apology*, LIV)

C.S. Lewis' later acceptance of pagan Christs is virtually the same, although rather than blaming them on Satan, he sees it as only natural that *God* would create these mythical parallels, which were then actually and historically fulfilled. The only possible way to explain the similarities between Jesus and earlier figures not rooted in faith, however, is that the gospel writers copied from other sources – a natural, common and exceedingly probable solution.

The second tactic of modern apologists is to claim that no such similarities exist at all, and that they are all fabrications of modernity. To this end, they take any specific comparison and demonstrate the ways in which the apparent similarity is actually completely different – or else they undermine the research of the scholar making the claims. Although it is true that a great deal of the early arguments from similarity used poor translations or texts which are now no longer available, we know already from early sources, both Christian and pagan, that Jesus Christ was similar to other gods and that this *was recognized at the time*. These similarities caused controversy and discord between Christians and pagans for several centuries – as Frazer points out, for example, using the following example of Attis:

> In point of fact it appears from the testimony of an anonymous Christian, who wrote in the fourth century of our era, that Christians and pagans alike were struck by the remarkable coincidences between the death and resurrection of their respective deities, and that the coincidence formed a theme of bitter controversy between the adherents of the rival religions, the pagans contending that the resurrection of Christ was a spurious imitation of the resurrection of Attis, and the Christians asserting with equal warmth that the resurrection of Attis was a diabolical counterfeit of the resurrection of Christ. In these unseemly bickerings the heathen took what to a superficial observer might seem strong ground by arguing that their god was the older and therefore presumably the original, not the counterfeit, since as a general rule an original is older than its copy. This feeble argument the Christian easily rebutted. They admitted,

indeed, that in point of time Christ was the junior deity, but they triumphantly demonstrated his real seniority by falling back on the subtlety of Satan, who on so important an occasion had surpassed himself by inverting the usual order of nature.[2]

Notice how, even as late as the fourth century, when the similarities between rival faiths continued to be a source of conflict, Christians still relied on Diabolical Mimicry rather claim historical priority.

Finally, critics argue that the Jews (and following them, the Christians), who were so careful to abstain from pagan worship of any kind (for example, choosing to be martyred rather than worshiping false idols) would never have adopted obviously pagan religious features. Therefore any potential similarities *must* be coincidental, because the opposite is unthinkable. This argument ignores the fact that, even if choosing to refuse them, the Jews would have already been familiar with most of these mythological figures, making their later acceptance of Jesus Christ all the more difficult. On the other hand, despite their restrictions and prohibitions, there are numerous examples of the Jewish people accepting and adopting pagan customs.

In Ezekiel, Yahweh points out the women of Israel mourning the death of Tammuz at the temple gates, the men prostrating before the rising sun in the inner court of the Temple of Yahweh, and the worshipping of carved idols of "every kind of reptile and repulsive animal" (Ezekiel 8:10-16). In Genesis, Rachel steals her father's idols, hides them in her camel cushion, and pretends she was "as women are from time to time" so that he wouldn't find them (Genesis 31:46). The Israelites, after leaving Egypt, made a golden calf to worship (Exodus 32). While it's true that The Old Testament is a collection of prohibitions against idolatry, this is likely due to the fact that the Jewish people were otherwise quick to assimilate into their environments and abandon their iconoclastic religion.

In the syncretism and convergence of cultures brought about by the Greek and Roman empires, we find several Jewish writers who were fully at home in pagan society, interpreted the scriptures metaphorically, and found no conflict between their faith and the beliefs of contemporary philosophers or mystery religions. Philo of Alexandria, to give one example, used allegory to fuse and harmonize Stoic philosophy with Jewish exegesis.

Having knowledge that a controversy over the physical nature of Jesus Christ existed in the earliest days of Christianity, testimony of a conflict based around similarities in rival traditions, and examples of Jews worshipping idols or blending their native religion with paganism, we are well justified in looking for the similarities which were so obvious to those more familiar with the original pagan and Christian sources. Although some parallels will be obvious, others need may need elucidation. For example, Gilgamesh's plant of immortality gets eaten by a snake, and Osiris's phallus gets eaten by a fish; taken literally, there is not enough similarity here to argue for a relationship. But if these myths are understood according to their symbolic meaning, then the precise details are less important than the theme (the loss of immortality).

As for the dating, it will be shown conclusively that central ideas shared between paganism and Christianity predate Jesus Christ by several centuries, if not millennia. The order of these ideas will be presented in this chapter, as far as possible, from earliest to latest. This way we can see, not only that certain elements extend quite far back in time, but also how they evolved and mutated into diverse cultural manifestations. Keep in mind that some of these stories were used to justify religious ritual and practice for thousands of years; and that such practices found in one historical period cannot be assumed to have existed during a different period. At the same time, basic features of these traditions, despite minor differences in practice, are likely to be homogenous. While some of these figures are almost definitely historical, and others completely mythological, the line is often blurred: even the most extremely fictional characters were thought by ancient cultures to have once been historical rulers or kings, while the very historical figures are so wrapped up in mythology it is almost impossible to see them clearly. The following list is by no means exhaustive, but simply represents the most interesting and relevant figures to the present study.

## Gilgamesh

As was pointed out earlier, the epic of Gilgamesh is not only one of the oldest recorded stories known to man, but was also familiar to Israel and may have been rewritten into the Old Testament. It should come as no surprise that elements from the epic of Gilgamesh might have crept into several other literary traditions.

It is likely that the story of Gilgamesh was used as a framework for religious rites or cult practices, as copies have been found in temples; copying the text may have been part of the training process for temple-astrologers.[3] According to Sumerian cosmology, when Ea had created man, he mixed the blood of a god (who was slaughtered for the purpose) in with the clay, so that humans would have a divine spirit. However, the blood was not the best material: "In one tradition, at least, he was the leader of the rebels, who had instigated a mutiny."[4] Therefore men were made part divine, but also flawed and wayward. This theme (humanity receiving the divine spirit from a rebellious god who receives punishment) is found in several later traditions. Prometheus, for example, steals fire from the gods to give to humans. Interestingly the link could also be made to the character of Satan, who gives humanity the tree of knowledge so that they may become "like gods" and is then tormented by God for his transgression.

If Gilgamesh ever existed as an actual king (as tradition maintains), he would have flourished around 2750BC.[5] According to the myth, Gilgamesh was a tyrant whose mother was a goddess. He was a cruel ruler, forcing his people into labor and freely exercising his kingly right to sleep with girls on their wedding day. The people prayed to the gods to make a rival for Gilgamesh, and they created Enkidu – a creature that was half bull, half human. Enkidu was an idyllic spirit, living in harmony with nature. Gilgamesh ordered the harlot Shamhat to seduce him, which would weaken him by alienating him from nature. They coupled for seven days and seven nights. In language reminiscent of the biblical garden story, Enkidu finds himself a "changed but wiser creature."[6] Shamhat brings him to society, but he has trouble eating bread, drinking out of glasses, or wearing clothes. (Could Gilgamesh also be the root of the modern Tarzan story?) Enkidu challenges Gilgamesh and they fight, but recognize each other's greatness and decide, rather than destroy each other, to work together and practice heroic virtue.

Thus begins a series of their adventures and conquests. First, they destroy the dragon (or ogre) Humbaba in the cedar forest, preferring fame to security, a dedication that may call Achilles or Beowulf to mind. In the next episode, Gilgamesh dresses so attractively that the goddess Ishtar (Ianna) wants to marry him, but he refuses her. In retribution, she asks permission from the great father god Anu to have the "Bull of Heaven" at her disposal to slay Gilgamesh. At first he says no, but she (as a goddess of the underworld) threatens to bring up all the dead so that they outnumber and consume the living. Anu relents and gives her the bull, however, Gilgamesh and Enkidu overpower and butcher it. Enkidu cuts off the leg of the bull and throws it at Ishtar as a terrible insult. Ishtar, after mourning the death of the bull, has the gods convene to decide on a punishment – they choose to kill Enkidu. Gilgamesh tries to bring him back to life in vain. Enkidu's death instills in him a terrible fear of death, and so he begins a quest for immortality.

Only one man he knew of had ever been immortal – the Babylonian Noah named Utnapishtim (or Atrahasis), who, along with his wife, became immortal after the flood. Therefore, Gilgamesh determines to seek him out. First, he travels to the edge of the ocean that surrounds the world, where he encounters the wise Shiduri; she tells him he must find Ur-shanabi, the ferryman of Utnapishtim. Ur-shanabi takes him to Utnapishtim's enchanted realm, and Gilgamesh hears the flood story. The gods had decided to destroy mankind, but one god, Ea, was friendly with Utnapishtim and determined to save him. Speaking to him indirectly (Utnapishtim was told to go into a reed hut first), Ea told him to disregard his possessions and construct an ark according to exact specifications, and to gather the seed of all living creatures, his wife, adequate supplies and a crew. After the flood, Utnapishtim and his wife became immortal.

They tell Gilgamesh to stay awake for seven days to see if he is worthy of becoming immortal as well, but he fails the test. Next, they groom him and give him a magical garment that won't get dirty, and prepare him for his return journey. Utnapishtim's wife discloses a secret mystery of the gods – a plant at the bottom of the sea that gives immortality – so he puts rocks on his feet and goes down to get it. Unfortunately he decides to save the plant for later and a snake eats it. Although he loses physical immortality, later versions of the story have Gilgamesh become a deified ruler of the shades in the underworld, and "give verdicts" or judge the dead.[7]

The Gilgamesh myth almost certainly influenced the Old Testament, hence certain themes were bound to be included in the gospel stories of Jesus as well. A few key motifs will prove constructive: the creation of humanity from a fallen god; the quest for immortality in order to rescue or be with a loved one; a plant of immortality that is lost due to the meddling serpent; the slaying of the bull of heaven. These themes will be explored in more detail.

## Dionysus

Despite obvious similarities between Dionysus and Jesus Christ, like wedding wine miracles and Jesus' statements about being "The one *true* vine," these two figures may seem poles apart: Jesus the meek and humble savior, and Dionysus the ecstatic, sexually active founder of wild, drunken revelry. However on closer examination, there are themes that run between the literary traditions of both figures that are closely tied. While it cannot be claimed that Jesus is nothing more than a pagan god of wine, parallels do exist and were easily identified by both believers and critics of the early Christian movement. These similarities have also been noted by modern researchers:

> Dionysus, like Jesus, was son of the divine ruler of the world and a mortal mother, appeared in human form among mortals, was killed and restored to life. Early Christian writers, aware of the similarity between Christianity and mystery-cult, claim that the latter is a diabolical imitation of the former (Seaford, *Dionysus*).[8]

> The correspondences between Christianity and the other mystery religions of antiquity are perhaps more startling than the differences. Orpheus and Christ share attributes in the early centuries of our era; and of all the major ancient deities, Dionysus has the most in common with the figure of Christ (Morford and Lenardon, *Classical Mythology*).[9]

Dionysus was born from a mortal woman, Semele, Daughter of the King of Thebes, and Zeus, the Father of the Gods. Hera, Zeus's jealous wife, planted seeds of doubt in the young mother's mind, and Semele demanded that Zeus come down and take responsibility. However, as no mortal can stand the sight of Zeus without dying, she was burnt up by his firebolts. Zeus rescued the child and sewed him up in his thigh until he was ready to be born.

In another version of the story, which ties Dionysus even more closely to his sacred mysteries, Dionysus was son of Zeus and Persephone, queen of the underworld. The jealous Hera this time sent the Titans to rip the child to pieces by distracting it with toys and mirrors. After they'd dismembered him, the Titans ate all the pieces – except the heart, which was saved. Zeus destroyed the Titans with lightning, and it was out of their ashes that humanity was created. The heart was used to impregnate Semele, who gave birth to Dionysus again. In either version of the story, Dionysus was "twice born" – a title that would later be used frequently in conjunction with his role in the sacred mysteries; initiates of which were said to be "born again." This story has been interpreted as the founding myth for many ancient spiritual traditions, in particular Orphism: it explains why sin or evil came into the world, and how humans are special in all of creation. As Guthrie explains, "Our nature therefore is twofold, born of Titans, wicked sons of earth, but there is in us something of a heavenly nature too, since there went to our making fragments of the body of Dionysus, son of Olympian Zeus, on whom the Titans had made their impious feast."[10] Morford and Lenardon in *Classical Mythology* reflect:

> Surely this is one of the most significant myths in terms of the philosophy and religious dogma that it provides. By it human beings are endowed with a dual nature - a body gross and evil (since we are sprung from the Titans) and a soul that is pure and divine (for after all the Titans had devoured the god). Thus basic religious concepts (which lie at the root of all mystery religions) are accounted for: sin, immortality, resurrection, life after death, reward, and punishment.[11]

On a deeper level, Dionysus was identified as a powerful force that governed and controlled the universe. He was not only the "divine spark" inside of humanity – he was also the beacon for ethical and moral action, as well as the gateway to eternal salvation. This is the standard reading of Dionysus as attested by the following passages:

> Dionysus can free us, wherefore we call him "liberator," Dionysus the immortal, the resurrected, of whose nature there is yet a small part in each and every one of us. Knowing all this, what other aim can we have in life but to purge away as far as possible the Titanic element in us and exalt and cherish the Dionysiac?[12]

> As son and heir of the cosmic deity, Zeus, Dionysus is also a creative deity, but creative through thought, as it were. He produces the idea of the world, and his knowledge sustains it in all its reality.[13]

> In this way, the Orphic Bible provided the divine authority for belief in an immortal soul; the necessity for keeping this soul pure despite the contamination and degradation of the body; the concept of a kind

of original sin; the transmigration of the soul to an afterlife of reward or punishment; and finally, after various stages of purification, an apotheosis, a union with the divine spirit in the realms of the upper aether.[14]

Despite his divinity, Dionysus lived among humans "not as a god but in disguise as a man";[15] and was somehow closer to humanity than any other deity. Stories of his life on earth, notably *The Bacchae* by Euripides (which premiered at the Theatre of Dionysus in 406BC), make it clear that Dionysus' true power was only recognized by his closest followers. Like Jesus, Dionysus freely allows himself to be captured and persecuted by his enemies, before finally revealing himself in his glory:

> Apparently powerless submission (in the Homeric Hymn to the pirates, in Bacchae to King Pentheus) is transformed into its opposite by epiphany, an emotive transformation that is in some respects comparable to the release of Paul and Silas in the Acts of the Apostles. Chased away or imprisoned by mere mortals, but comes back in triumph: associated with victory.[16]

The Bacchae's description of Dionysus submitting to his captors is eerily similar to the same motif in the Christian tradition. When the guard delivers him to Pentheus, he says:

> Pentheus, here we are, having hunted the quarry you sent us after, and our efforts have not been unsuccessful. But we found this wild beast tame – he did not attempt to flee, but gave me his hands willingly; he did not even turn pale, but kept the flush of wine in his cheeks. With a smile he bade me tie him up and lead him away and waited for me, thus making my task easy. (*Bacchae* 434-442)

Dionysus goes through a trial of sorts, where he refuses to answer Pentheus' questions directly, and instead antagonizes the ruler. Then he is put in prison, at which point there is an earthquake. Pentheus grabs a sword and rushes in, but Dionysus greets him calmly and promises he will not try to escape. This episode, although of course very different from that of Jesus, who is crucified, is remarkably similar to Acts of the Apostles 16:25-9. When Paul and Silas are imprisoned, singing to their god in the darkness, there is an earthquake. The doors open and the chains fall away from the prisoners. The jailor seizes a sword, and runs in to find that Paul and the prisoners are still there. Seaford concludes that the author of Acts borrowed directly from the *Bacchae*:

> These similarities are too numerous to be coincidental. How are we to explain them? One possibility is that they derive from knowledge of the Bacchae. The Bacchae was indeed well known at this period: for instance, we hear of it being recited in Corinth in the first century AD…Moreover, in one version of the conversion of Saul the lord says to him 'It is hard for you to kick against the goads' (26:14). This expression occurs nowhere else in the New Testament, but it does occur in early Greek literature, notably when Dionysus says to his persecutor Pentheus 'Do not kick against the goads, a mortal against a god' (*Bacchae* 796).[17]

There are other similarities between the life Dionysus and the life of Jesus as well. Dionysus was a wanderer; his cult emphasized mobility. He does not give instructions for building a temple (as does Demeter in the Homeric hymns to Demeter, or Yahweh in the Old Testament). Worship of Dionysus was roofless – outdoors, in a temple under open sky; just like the early Christian practice, which was originally against the setting up of churches or worshiping indoors.

Dionysus is not only associated with but often actually *identified*

with the animals that represent him, mostly the bull; just as he is associated and identified with wine. Dionysian cults ate raw flesh, and Dionysus himself could be called "eater of raw flesh."[18] In the version cited by Frazer, Dionysus tried to evade the attacks of the Titans by changing forms: first a young man, then a lion, horse, and serpent. "Finally, in the form of a bull, he was cut into pieces by the murderous knives of his enemies."[19] Consequently, when we find that followers of Dionysus followed a cultic ritual of dividing up a bull and eating its raw flesh, and drinking wine in thanksgiving and remembrance of their god, it is not a stretch to argue that they believed they were eating the body and blood of their savior in order to reach a spiritual communion:

> When we consider the practice of portraying the god as a bull or with some of the features of the animal, the belief that he appeared in bull form to his worshipers at the sacred rites, and the legend that in bull form he had been torn to pieces, we cannot doubt that in rending and devouring a live bull at this festival the worshipers of Dionysus believed themselves to be killing the god, eating his flesh, and drinking his blood.[20]

Although Dionysus was not crucified, certain aspects of his worship have early Christian parallels. When Dionysus was torn apart by the Titans, a pomegranate tree sprouted from his blood. This is probably the root of the tradition of worshiping Dionysus in the form of a tree:

> Maximus of Tyre writes that 'the peasants honour Dionysus by planting in the field an uncultivated tree-trunk, a rustic statue' (2.1), and according to Plutarch (*Moralia* 675) all Greeks sacrifice to Dionysus as tree god (Dendrites). Pausanias reports that two images of Dionysus at Corinth were made from this very tree: the Delphic oracle had ordered the Corinthians to find the tree and 'worship it equally with god.' (2.2.7)[21]

Likewise, Jesus is celebrated as the *Tree of Life* – a redemptive symbol counteracting the original Tree of Knowledge that led to the fall into sin. Countless churches in Christendom have worshiped relics or magical pendants made of wood purported to be from the original cross. Within early Christian communities, Jesus was even considered to have been hung on a tree rather than crucified. "It was the God of our ancestors who raised up Jesus, whom you executed by hanging on a tree" (Acts, 5:30).

Dionysus was a god of resurrection, and like other figures he descended into Hell and returned:

> It is no accident that Dionysus is linked with Orpheus and Demeter and the message that they preached. He is in his person a resurrection-god; the story is told that he went down into the realm of the dead and brought back his mother, who in this account is usually given the name Thyone.[22]

Dionysus was also considered a great social leveler: in his festivals and ceremonies, there was no distinction given to class or rank. Dionysus "gave the pain-removing delight of wine equally to the wealthy man and to the lesser man" (*Bacchae* 421-3). He was also credited with freedom from prison, releasing slaves, as a liberator, and "in general resolved conflicts between peoples and cities, and created concord and much peace in place of civil conflicts and wars."[23] He was worshiped by everybody equally, all mixed up in a mob; this inclusiveness was a feature which "may not have appealed to some aristocrats."[24]

And then there are the wine miracles. It was Dionysus who brought wine to the aristocratic wedding of Peleus and Thetis; and during a festival at Elis, three pots were put inside the Dionysus temple behind closed doors and miraculously filled with wine – a feat similar to Jesus' later miracle at the wedding in Cana. This act of Jesus, as well as his claim of being the "True Vine" (John 15:1), may have been direct attempts to usurp the powers and influence of Dionysus.

Another similarity emerges if we take theological liberties. Dionysus wanted to lay with the wife of King Oeneus (of Calydon in Aetolia). Oeneus, whose name means "wine man," tactfully withdrew; for this he was rewarded with the gift of the vine, which benefited the whole community. Stories of gods fertilizing the wife of the king and producing a divine prince who becomes a savior/ redeemer are not uncommon; in the epic of Gilgamesh, the tyrant king takes advantage of this principle, assuming the role of the god to have intercourse with brides on their wedding night. When applied to the Christian birth story, it could be argued that Joseph "made way" for God/ the Holy Spirit to impregnate Mary, who produced Jesus, the True Vine.

Dionysus was also important to the Eleusinian and other mysteries as savior, liberator and ruler of the underworld. His name was a magical password of freedom; initiates who underwent mysteries were promised eternal life, and given special gold leaves that acted as passports into the next life. One of these, found at Pelinna in Thessaly and dating to the late fourth century BC, reads "Tell Persephone that Bakchios himself freed you" (Bakchios/ Bacchus is the Roman name for Dionysus).[25] Interestingly, it is probably Dionysus' role as ruler of the underworld and keeper of the dead that has been transfigured into the modern conception of Satan: Dionysus, as Bacchus, the bull or "the horned one" ruling over the underworld may have inspired the later Christian conception of the horned ruler of the underworld.

According to the doctrine of these mysteries (referred to in Plato), the soul is "imprisoned" in the body for an ancient crime or guilt, symbolized by the Titans' murder of Dionysus (*Cratylus* 400c; *Phaedo* 62b). Humans, by being made from the remains of the Titans, have inherited this guilt; but have also been given the gift of the Dionysian element, which, if cultivated, can result in eternal life:

The 5th century Neoplatonist philosopher Proclus regarded Plato as following Orphic myths and interpreting mystic doctrine. In this interpretation, according to Proclus, the dismemberment of Dionysus means that body and soul are divided into many bodies and souls, whereas the undivided heart of Dionysos, from which Athena recomposed his body, is cosmic mind of intellect (nous). In Neoplatonist philosophy nous is undivided; it comprehends in one act of intelligence all intelligible things; and it is merged with but superior to the soul.[26]

There is no doubt that Dionysus, including his critical role in afterlife beliefs, came before Jesus. His name first appears on clay tablets from the Greek bronze age 3000 years ago.[27] Poetry from the 6th century BC claims that Dionysus gave wine as "joy and burden"[28] and the *Bacchae*, published in 405 BC, was an increasingly popular and well-known piece of literature. Although Jesus is certainly much more than any of these similarities, it is impossible to make the claim that early Christians were unaware of Dionysus, whose public processions were large, loud and involved the entire community:

> When Christianity was establishing itself in the ancient Mediterranean world, the cult of Dionysus was its most geographically widespread and deeply rooted rival. And so the Christian church, while enclosing the revolutionary ethics of its gospels within the necessity of social control, was influenced by Dionysiac cult as well as opposing it.[29]

In fact, according to 2 Maccabees 6.7, the Jews themselves were compelled under Seleucid King Antiochus IV (175-164BC) to wear ivy wreaths and walk in procession in honor of Dionysus, an act which may have had lasting consequences: "Tacitus writes that various features of Jewish cult – the music of pipes and drums, ivy crowns, and the golden vine at the temple – give rise to the view that the Jews worship Liber Pater (Dionysus), the conqueror of the East."[30]

How do we explain the similarities? There are really only two possibilities: either Jesus, aware of Dionysus, set himself up purposely to steal his rival's spotlight, or early Christian writers included these stories and motifs into the gospel story to make their savior more competitive.

# Pythagoras

Pythagoras is one of the most intriguing and mysterious figures in ancient history. Although today known mostly by his mathematical legacy, he was much more than a philosopher or mathematician – he was also the founder of a very secretive spiritual cult with serious political influence, focusing on initiation of the worthy, purification, and salvation.

Born around 570BC, Pythagoras emigrated to Croton in Southern Italy, and there founded a movement that was a blend of politics and mysticism. "Without a doubt, Pythagoras aimed for a viewpoint of the divine, and the opinions he expressed were taken by his followers as sacred revelations."[31]Although it is difficult to separate the man from the myth, there are striking parallels between Jesus and Pythagoras; most likely due to the extensive influence Pythagoreanism seems to have had on the Greco-Roman world through other mystery cults and schools of philosophy, especially Orphism and Platonism.

It is said that when Pythagoras arrived in Croton, he first appeared to the fishermen on the outskirts of the city and performed a miraculous sign; he told them exactly how many fish were in their nets, and he was right (they counted). News of the miracle spread into city and prepared the way for him.[32] In the gospels of Luke and John, Jesus performs a similar miracle, although instead of counting the fish, he causes the fisherman to catch a great quantity. In Luke, this happens at the beginning of his ministry (5:1-11); in John, it occurs after Jesus had resurrected. Interestingly, we are even given the precise number of fish caught: "Simon Peter went aboard and dragged the net ashore, full of big fish, one hundred and fifty-three of them" (John 21:1-14).

Although we are not given the exact number of fish in the Pythagorean story, the Pythagoreans regarded 153 as a sacred number due to its use in a mathematical ratio called "the measure of the fish," which produces the mystical symbol of the *Vesica Pisces* – the intersection of two circles which yields a fish-like shape. It is unlikely that the Christian use of this number is accidental.

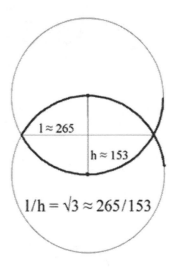

Pythagoreans believed (much like Orphics and modern day Buddhists) in reincarnation, or a wheel of rebirth. They were vegetarians and tried to cultivate purity. Although the soul was immortal, it had to be freed from the contaminating influences of the body. Only a "lover of wisdom" leading the best of lives could escape the prison of the body at the moment of death and break free of the cycle.

Tradition holds that Pythagoras gained his mystical knowledge by spending seven years in the underworld or land of the dead. Diogenes Laertius records the claim of Hieronymus, who said "that when he descended to the shades below, he saw the soul of Hesiod bound to a brazen pillar, and gnashing its teeth; and that of Homer suspended from a tree, and snakes around it, as a punishment for the things that they had said of the Gods."[33] Laertius also mentions how Austophon says in his *Pythagorean*:

> He said that when he did descend below
> Among the shades in Hell, he there beheld
> All men who e'er had died; and there he saw,
> That the Pythagoreans differ'd much
> From all the rest; for that with them alone
> Did Pluto deign to eat, much honouring
> Their pious habits. (Diogenes Laertius, XX)

There is also the story told by Hermippus, about how when Pythagoras returned from the underworld, he was considered a God:

> Pythagoras came up again after a certain time, lean, and reduced to a skeleton; and that he came into the public assembly, and said that he had arrived from the shades below, and then he recited to them all that had happened during his absence. And they, being charmed by what he told them, wept and lamented, and believed that Pythagoras was a divine being; so that they even entrusted their wives to him, as likely to learn some good from him; and that they too were called Pythagoreans. And this is the story of Hermippus. (Diogenes Laertius, XXI)

According to legend, in a past life Pythagoras had been a son of Hermes named Aethalides. Hermes promised him any gift (except immortality), and Aethalides/Pythagoras wished to remember everything, even after death. Thus, Pythagoras remembered all of his previous lives. While staying at Argos, for example, he saw a shield from the spoils of Troy nailed up to the wall. He began to weep, claiming that the shield had been his in a last life when his name was Euphobus and that he had used it at the battle of Troy. He even offered proof: his previous name, Euphobus, was written on the *inside*. They took the shield down from the wall and found the name written as he had claimed.[34] In another story, he recognizes the reincarnation of an old friend in a stray dog:

> And once, they say, when he passed by a dog which was being maltreated, he pitied the animal and said these words: "Stop! Don't

beat him! For he is the soul of a friend whom I recognized straight away when I heard his voice."[35]

Pythagoras believed that the entire universe was musical: each planet made a certain vibrational frequency as it passed through the heavens, and everything on earth could be assigned to one of these seven frequencies: there are 7 notes on a scale, 7 colors of the rainbow, and 7 primary organs of the body:

> According to a legend told by Iambliochos, when Pythagoras heard the different sound made by hammers in a forge, he realized that tones can be expressed in quantitative relationships, and hence in numerical values and geometrical measures. Using stringed instruments, he then discovered the connection between vibration frequencies and pitch. The whole world, according to Pythagoras' theory, consisted of harmony and number.[36]

This life, Pythagoras claimed, was a sentence for a sin or evil done at the mythical level in pre-history. Therefore, we should do our time well and get out quickly, rather than avoiding our punishments and stretching the sentence out longer. Earth was not meant to be enjoyed: "Do not assist a man in laying a burden down; for it is not proper to be the cause of not laboring (also translated as 'idleness' or 'lack of effort'); but assist him in taking it up."[37] Christianity has parallels in its monasticism, valuation of the poor, the weak and the suffering, and ascetic traditions. There are also passages like the following:

> Then, speaking to all, he said, "if anyone wants to be a follower of mine, let him renounce himself and take up his cross every day and follow me. Anyone who wants to save his life will lose it; but anyone who loses his life for my sake, will save it. What benefit is it to anyone to win the whole world and forfeit or lose his very self." (Luke 9:23-26)

The life of a Pythagorean was "governed by strict rules and routines that covered a wide range of issues, everything from dietary restrictions to purification rites to religious taboos to the observance of decorous behavior, not to mention a host of magical practices."[38] These pedantic rules inspired a constantly introspective lifestyle:

> Tradition does mention, though, a great number of taboos and prescriptions, such as 'Do not wear a ring', 'Do not step over a broom', 'don't use cedar, laurel, myrtle, cypress or oak to cleanse your body or clean your teeth: they are for honouring the gods'. The observance of all these rules must have made the life of the Pythagorean an extremely self-conscious one, in which a moment of carelessness could be fatal.[39]

Although the similarities between the actual life of Pythagoras and Jesus may be limited, it is interesting to notice the parallels between the two movements each figure left behind. As we shall see, it was the bureaucratic organization of the Christian movement, more than the originality of its beliefs or practices, which really ensured its survival; this organization may have had its roots in Pythagoreanism. As Professor Konstantine Boudouris of the University of Athens reports, the Pythagorean communities were "unions of people, the members of which had accepted certain principles and doctrines, and who lived, thought, and acted *collectively*, and whose acts were dictated or related to the beliefs that they had accepted."[40] The chief characteristic of the Pythagorean movement, however was *secrecy* – with underground political motivations:

> While the overall tone of Pythagoras' teaching appears concerned with morality, virtue, and religious piety, the mission of the secret group

seems to have been the infiltration and takeover of the government. Thus, it functioned as a political conspiracy on the one hand, while on the other projecting the outward appearance of a bona fide political association.[41]

The speeches ascribed to Pythagoras that have been handed down to us are nothing particularly special: be good, honor your elders, refrain from evil, etc. There was certainly more to the movement than his words of wisdom (although there may have been much that was lost). The *power* of the movement was in its initiations and secrecy. Membership was extremely selective, and the initiation process not for the faint of heart. There was first a series of tests for candidates, followed by a background check involving the applicant's personal life, relationships and behavior: "Did he talk too much or laugh on the wrong occasions? How did he get along with other students? What, for example, made him happy or sad?"[42] Finally there was a physical examination. If he passed these preliminaries, he was sent away for three years and totally ignored, but secretly watched (not unlike Tyler Durton's modern day initiation cult rendition in *Fight Club*).

If they were admitted, candidates had to turn over all of their belongings – money, properties and income – to a special board of trustees,[43] and for the first 5 years, they took a vow of silence. If they were later rejected from the higher levels of initiation, they had their investments returned in double but were treated as if they were dead by members. Likewise, in the earliest periods of Christianity, such socialist practices were also the rule, and strictly enforced. Luke has Jesus caution, "None of you can be my disciple without giving up all that he owns" (Luke 14:33), and according to the Acts of the Apostles, "And all who shared the faith owned everything in common; they sold their goods and possessions and distributed the proceeds among themselves according to what each one needed" (Acts 2:44). Acts also relates the curious incident of Ananias and Sapphira; new converts to Christianity who secretly held back some of their earnings rather than sharing it with the Church. Their transgression was punished by a miraculous execution – they fell down dead when confronted by Peter.

Like the Pythagorean cult, the early church had "administrators" who were responsible for maintaining the wealth and finances of the community. This feature of early Christianity didn't last (later converts were allowed to keep their property), but its presence and inclusion into the Bible suggests external influences. Although Judaism, especially during the decades surrounding the destruction of the temple in Jerusalem, did have socialistic sects where Christianity may have found this feature, these sects were themselves more similar to Pythagoreanism than to traditional Judaic worship.

According to Josephus, the Essenic communities shared all of their property and wealth communally, had no personal possessions, did not sacrifice animals, and focused on cleansings and purity. After a three year probation, newly joining members would take an oath that included the commitment to practice piety towards "the Deity" and righteousness towards humanity, to maintain a pure life to abstain from criminal and immoral activities, to transmit their rules uncorrupted and to preserve the books of the Essenes and the names of the Angels (*The Wars of the Jews*, 2.137–142). They also believed in the immortality of the soul and that they would receive their souls back after death (*Antiquities of the Jews*, 18.18, *The Wars of the Jews*. 2. 153–158).

Another source of commonality is the theme of secrecy, with truth being revealed only to an inner group.

> The notion that Pythagoras founded a movement whose mission was the "education and enlightenment of the masses" is wonderfully romantic, yet the very sources who have sought to convey this impression have also perservered old sayings that paint a very different picture.[44]

The eventual fall of Pythagoreanism may have been due to the contradiction inherent in a selective, spiritual minority ruling the alienated majority. Likewise, although Jesus Christ is often heralded for his democratic inclusion of all people, there are passages in the Bible which make it clear that not everybody would make it into the kingdom, but only the worthy, and characterize the Christian cult as a small, non-inclusive group of separatists: "So the last shall be first, and the first last: for many be called, but few chosen" (Matthew 20:16). Moreover, Jesus frequently speaks in riddles and parables, which he later explains only to his inner group of disciples. Although in theory a community of brothers, it should not be forgotten that Christianity was managed by a select authoritarian group that demanded absolute allegiance and complete surrender of personal property, and which quickly grew in wealth and power.

Finally, like Christians, Pythagoreans were taught to fight against sin and lawlessness. They even had a custom of confessing each day's sins:

> As soon as they got up in the morning, members were required to disclose to one another a detailed account of the activities and events of the previous day. Supposedly, this exercise had a twofold aim: to train a person's memory and to teach him to assess his conduct, in order to, as Diodorus says, "gain knowledge and judgment in all matters."[45]

Some of these lifestyle choices, beliefs and practices would become fairly common in the centuries before and after the coming of Jesus Christ; mostly in various mystery cults and religions. Their inclusion into Christianity is not surprising, and yet proved problematic for the early church, who constantly needed to differentiate themselves somehow from other groups who believed very similar things and practiced similar rituals and habits.

The powerful figure of Pythagoras would grow to supernatural proportions; as we have seen, he was believed to have been born of a God (Hermes, in a previous life descended into the underworld, and taught specific instructions about surviving after death. In the religious-political system that he created, Christianity had a ready template for its own organization.

# Orpheus

Orpheus is the figure credited with a new type of spirituality which began to permeate Greece in around the 6th century BC. He is chiefly considered a prophet, magician, astrologer and musician. The movement known as Orphism, as well as various pieces of poetry known as "Orphica" are ascribed to him. Even in antiquity, Orpheus was regarded as the founder of mystery religions; the first to reveal to men the meaning of rites of initiation. He is chiefly regarded as a human figure – a prophet of Dionysus – however his story is so blended with mythology that it is impossible to say whether or not he ever truly existed. According to Jan Bremmer in *The Rise and Fall of the Afterlife*, Orpheus was a mythological figure created as a mouthpiece for certain developing ideas resulting from the blending of Pythagoreanism and Bacchic ideologies: "Orphism was a product of Pythagorean influence on Bacchic mysteries in the first quarter of the fifth century... but Pythagoras belongs to history, and Orpheus to myth."[46] For other scholars, Orpheus was the prophet who turned the Dionysian spirituality into an organized way of living:

> From the fourth century BC, the killing of Dionysus by the Titans made it possible to explain the state of man, thrown into the world, and was at the origin of the way of life invented by Orpheus for the salvation of the individual soul.[47]

His father was Apollo (or Oeagrus, a Thracian river god) and his mother was Calliope, the muse of epic poetry. His magic power was his perfection of music – with his song and lyre he allured the trees, the savage animals, and even the insensate rocks to follow him (Ovid, *Metamorphoses* XI). The power of Orpheus' music has its roots in the Pythagorean belief that the universe is made up of vibrations like a musical chord: different notes produced the different states of matter. Plants, animals, metals and gemstones were in harmony with the frequencies produced by the planets and could be used in a sort of sympathetic magic:

> Orpheus plays the same instrument as his father Apollo, symbolizing the music of the seven planets and the universal laws of septenary manifestation whose knowledge gives magical power over all created things. Orpheus could charm beasts, plants and even the denizens

of the Underworld, i.e. he understood the laws of sympathy and harmony that link every level of creation, and was able to put them to use.[48]

His music allowed him to perform miraculous feats; for example, when he sailed with Jason and the Argonauts, Orpheus muted out the Sirens' seductive call with his own music, and, according to some accounts, also calmed the guardian dragon to sleep so that Jason could retrieve the Golden Fleece.[49] The most famous story about Orpheus, however, is his descent into the Underworld to save his wife, Eurydice (also known as Agriope).

While she was escaping from Aristaeus (son of Apollo), Eurydice fell into a nest of vipers and was bitten on the heel. Orpheus mourned her with a song that was so touching that all the gods and nymphs wept. At their insistence, he traveled to the Underworld to try to save her. He used his music to soften the hearts of Persephone and Hades as well as Charon, the boatman of the river Styx, and Cerberus, the three-headed dog who guards the gates. In fact, everybody in Hell ceased momentarily from their constant torment to listen to the beautiful music. Persephone and Hades allowed him to retrieve Eurydice from the dead, but on one condition: she was to follow behind him and he must refrain from turning around and checking on her. But he was so anxious that he turned around too early, and she disappeared forever. This motif is similar to many other stories in world literature, including the Genesis episode of Lot and his wife.

Orpheus finally met his death at the hands of Thracian Maenads for failing to honor Dionysus (apparently, at the end of his life Orpheus became monotheistic and worshiped only Apollo). In another version, the Ciconian women, also Dionysus' followers, were angry at him for refusing their advances (he'd forsworn women after the death of Eurydice) and threw sticks and stones at him. At first, his beautiful music stopped the projectiles like a magic shield, but the enraged women then tore him apart – just like Pentheus in *The Bacchae*, and also reminiscent of Dionysus' first death at the hands of the Titans. The Muses gathered up his pieces and buried them beneath Mount Olympus. His head floated to the island of Lesbos, where it prophesied until it was silenced by Apollo.

Orphism, a religious movement that emerged around 600BC, claims to have at its core the revelations given by the head of Orpheus in the cave of Lesbos, *after it had been detached from his body*. These records – known as the Orphica – are a collection of hymns and poetry.

Orphism developed an elaborate cosmogony (a theory explaining the creation of the universe) based on the mythical death of Dionysus. As we have seen, the killing and eating of Dionysus by the Titans, and Zeus's subsequent destruction of the Titans (from whose ashes rose the human race), gave humanity a dual nature: both Dionysiac (divine and good) and Titan (earthly and evil):

> Orphic belief and ritual existed in some form in the fifth century BC, being referred to by Herodotus and Euripides and others. It is a question therefore of how much of the belief and ritual concerning Dionysus goes back to that time – a time when Dionysus was one of the chief gods of every Greek city, worshipped at seasonal festivals with elaborate public rites and with another kind of belief, the local myths pertaining to each festival. Perhaps unexpectedly, it is archaeology which in recent decades has contributed striking details of Orphic belief and ritual: they draw us especially to this matter of Dionysus. The Derveni papyrus, recovered from a funeral pyre in Thessaly, contains a truncated commentary by a ritual adept upon an Orphic creation story dated to c. 500BC or even the sixth century.[50]

Through initiation into the Orphic mysteries, and by living an ascetic life of abstention from meat, wine and sexual activity, individuals sought to suppress their earthly natures and cultivate their divine, Dionysian, selves. Full liberation of the soul could be achieved only through a cycle of incarnations. Orpheus' descent into and return from the underworld gave him unique knowledge and wisdom of the afterlife; hence his followers believed he could act as an intermediary with the forces below:

> The secrets of Hades were in his possession. He could tell his followers what the fate of their souls would be, and how they should behave to make it the best possible. He had shown himself capable of melting the hearts of the powers below, and might be expected to intercede again on their own behalf if they lived the pure life to his precepts. That was the important thing. The reason which once took him there was secondary.[51]

Orphism seems to have had a missionary basis, and spread rapidly. Plato mentions traveling priests, from 400BC or earlier, selling spells and initiation rites into the Orphic way of life. Initiates were taught to control their passions, have respect for all life and refrain from eating meat (because of their belief in transmigration). The object was to free their souls from the cycle of rebirth. Once freed, they could ascend up to "ultimate bliss on the Isles of the Blessed or in the realm of the starry ether."[52] Jan Bremmer claims that the Orphic reservation of an especially desirable afterlife only for initiates, or worthy persons, later influenced Christian ideas concerning the afterlife:

> It is in the fifth century, then, in Orphic-Pythagorean milieus that the contours of the later Christian distinction between heaven and hell first become visible.[53]

In Orphic teachings, "man is suddenly promoted to the climax of creation. Moreover, we can observe that the diversity of the Greek pantheon has been reduced to a virtually monotheistic rule by Zeus, although Dionysus, whose position in the normative Greek pantheon was more 'eccentric', is also indispensable."[54] Orphics dressed in white to demonstrate their aspirations to purity, and followed strict rules of propriety. Free will and personal responsibility were also essential and important parts of the Orphic code.[55]

What distinguished Orpheus from other pagan heroes was his meekness and humility, traits that today are usually believed to have been unique to Jesus Christ:

> The influence of Orpheus was always on the side of civilization and the arts of peace. In personal character he is never a hero in the modern sense. His outstanding quality is gentleness amounting at times to softness.[56]

Although Orpheus cannot be said to have resurrected or come back from the dead (at least not since the first time he did it, when rescuing Eurydice), we do have the curious prophecies of his disembodied talking head, which gave the bulk of his teachings after he'd been violently murdered. Strikingly, Christianity has its own version of a miraculous talking head. Herod's stepdaughter, Salome, is said in Matthew 14:8 and Mark 6:25 to have asked for John the Baptist's head on a platter; the presentation of this head often appears in art. In medieval times it was rumored that The Knights Templar had possession of the talking head of St. John, and multiple records from the Inquisition in the early 1300s make reference to some form of head being worshiped by the Knights.

Guthrie suggests that Orpheus' magical pacification of animals and the forces of nature were the inspiration of Jesus' similar power:

> The common representation of him sitting playing his lyre surrounded by beasts wild and tame who are lulled into amity by his music suggests naturally the picture of the lion and the lamb lying down together.[57]

In fact, many early Christians seemed only too ready to make this identification themselves; the motif of Orpheus playing his lyre has been found intermingled with other symbolism in Christian catacombs, as noted by Littleton in *Gods, Goddesses and Mythology*:

> As an allegory, the pagan story even found its way into early Christian iconography. In the catacombs of Jerusalem, for example, Jesus was

depicted in the guise of Orpheus with the lyre. In some later Christian tombs, Orpheus is shown delivering the Sermon on the Mount or acting as "the Good Shepherd."[58]

This is less surprising when we consider that the Old Testament already had a musical shepherd of its own:

> It was easy to see in the characteristic picture of Orpheus not only a symbol of the Good Shepherd of the Christians (and we remember the Orphic bukoloi), but also parallels to the lore of the Old Testament. It too had, in the person of David, its magical musician playing among sheep and the wild beasts of the wilderness, and the resemblance did not pass unnoticed.[59]

A final bit of interesting trivia is Orpheus' personal antagonism towards women, and their resentment of it leading to his violent death, which was used to justify sexist cultural practices. The ritual of tattooing among Thracian women, for example, was said to be the punishment inflicted on them by their husbands for the murder of Orpheus.[60] Thus, we have women being blamed and punished for a mythological event; not unlike Christianity's subordination of women – "the weaker sex" – for Eve's fall and the temptation of Adam.

Orpheus, a meek and humble bringer of peace, founded a mystery cult of spiritual initiation aimed at eternal salvation based on ritual purity, moral behavior and self-control, after he'd suffered a violent death at the hands of his enemies. He descended into Hell and returned, had unrivalled magical powers, and promised salvation to his followers. It's no wonder that early Christians identified him with Jesus Christ.

## Asclepius

It is perhaps telling that Asclepius is so little known in modern society. While most people are familiar with other Greek and Roman gods – Athena, Zeus, Aphrodite – and Christ myth theorists talk passionately about the similarities between Mithras, Attis, Osiris and other dying and resurrecting gods, the name "Asclepius" has almost completely disappeared outside of academic references. And yet, Asclepius was the largest and most persevering challenge to early Christianity:

> The correspondence between Christianity and the other mystery religions of antiquity are perhaps more startling than the differences. Orpheus and Christ share attributes in the early centuries of our era; and of all the major ancient deities, Dionysus has most in common with the figure of Christ. It was the son of Apollo, however, Asclepius, the kindly healer and miracle worker, who posed the greatest threat to early Christianity.[61]

As we have seen, the claim of Christ's historical nature, above all else, was crucial for distinguishing him from the beliefs of the pagans. All apparent similarities between Jesus and pagan gods could be explained away with diabolical mimicry and the assertion that, while other gods were mythological symbols, Jesus was a real human being. However, apart from the tenacity of his followers, the *proof* behind Jesus Christ's ministry – the signs he gave that he was who he claimed to be – were his miracles; notably, his miraculous healings. Jesus restored sight to the blind, he raised the dead, he cured the sick, he cleansed lepers, and he healed paralytics. These healings are reported in the gospels as signs of his divinity; they are the proof that Jesus was the son of God.

However, long before the Christian movement, Asclepius was universally known as the expert of medicine and healing. And he wasn't considered just a myth: Asclepius was believed to have been a real man, who died a real death, but then came back. Whether "resurrected" or "ascended into heaven," after death he was (reportedly) physically present in his temples. Asclepius was widely believed to provide actual, physical healings, which were directly experienced by many people. He was a living god, prayed to, worshiped, and intimately familiar to every Greek and Roman citizen of the pagan world.

His mother was Coronis, daughter of Phelgyas in Thessaly, (or Arsinoe, daughter of Leucipuus) and his father was Apollo. Apollo loved Coronis, but her father made her marry another man. Apollo cursed the raven who brought the tidings – made it black instead of white – and killed Coronis. Her father placed her on a funeral pyre, but as she was burning Apollo recovered the baby from her womb and brought it to Chiron, the Centaur, by whom the baby was raised and taught the arts of healing. Asclepius became such a great surgeon that he even gained the power to raise the dead – a power for which Zeus struck him down with a lightning bolt:

> And having become a surgeon, and carried the art to a great pitch, he not only prevented some from dying, but even raised up the dead; for he received from Athena the blood that flowed from the veins of the Gorgon, and while he used the blood that flowed from her left side for the bane of mankind, he used the blood that flowed from her right side for salvation, and by that means he raised the dead. But

Zeus, fearing the men might acquire the healing art from him and so come to the rescue of each other, smote him with a thunderbolt. Angry on that account, Apollo slew the Cyclops who had fashioned the thunderbolt for Zeus.[62]

After his death he ascended into heaven (was placed in the stars) and thus became an immortal god. It was said that he was born as a man, died a mortal death and was resurrected.[63]

In another version of the story, Asclepius was the son of Phlegys (who came to Peloponnesus) and Apollo; she bore the child, but exposed him on a mountain. A goat gave him milk, a watchdog of the herd guarded him, and a goatherd found him. Still later, Priscus, contemporary of Cicero, says he was born of uncertain parents, exposed, nourished by a dog, found by some hunters, and turned over to Chiron for medical training. He lived at Epidaurus, but was from Messenian. Cicero claims he was buried at Cynosura.[64] These increasingly detailed reports are the result of an attempt to classify or catalog mythology into a rational account of history. Whether or not Asclepius actually lived as a historical person remains unclear.

At any rate, Asclepius proved an extremely popular and powerful deity in the classical era. Pindar has Apollo give his approval for the worship of his son, citing the fact that Asclepius restores sight to the blind, makes the lame get up and walk, and raises the dead:

> If, then, the son of Coronis accomplished anything meet for a god; if he restored to the blind the sight which had slipped away from their eyes; if he bade the dead return to life; if, making the lame swift of foot, he commanded them to go home rejoicing, then let him be enriched with our due admiration, too; if he was in high repute among some of the most feeble, let him, too, be praised as most nobly going about the task of his medical skill. Yes let him not dishonor the "understand thyself."[65]

The story of Asclepius was known at least five centuries before Christianity. In Aeshylus' play, *Agamemnon* (458BC), it is clear that Asclepius was chiefly known for his ability to raise the dead, and his subsequent punishment: "But man's dark blood, once it hath flowed to the earth in death, who by chanting spells shall call it back? Even him who possessed the skill to raise from the dead – did not Zeus put a stop to him as a precaution?" (1019-24).

Homer sang of Asclepius as one of the fighters before Troy (T135), and according to Plato, Socrates' last words were "Crito, we owe a cock to Asclepius. Pay it and do not neglect it" (*Phaedo*, 118). These references show just how integral Asclepius was to the ancient world. Although the meaning of Socrates' last words remains unclear, it may have something to do with Asclepius' role as protector and guardian of the dead. Asclepius' symbol was a snake climbing a pole; it continues to be used by many modern health organizations.

The temples of Asclepius served as hospitals in ancient times. Priests went through rigorous medical training. The sick or injured would come for incubation or a "sleeping-cure." While they slept they would receive the god's instructions in dream – or sometimes even experience some kind of psychic surgery, where they experienced the god cutting them open. When they woke up, if they were not already miraculously cured, the priests would interpret the dream and prescribe a remedy. The effects of these cures are corroborated by the hundreds of ex-voto offerings that were left at temple sites by the healed:

> They were of terracotta, marble, bronze, silver or even gold, depending on the means of the faithful whose prayers had been granted, but chiefly of clay, the majority of the clientele of the island in the Tiber being of humble estate. There were feet, hands, breasts, intestines, viscera in an open torso, genital organs, eyes, ears, mouths... Above

all, it was necessary to demonstrate gratitude by way of an inscribed tablet bearing the account of the miraculous treatment.[66]

These very detailed descriptions of prescriptions and healings were further supported with the claim that the healing took place in the presence of a crowd and that the healed publicly gave thanks for the cure.

Asclepius was unlike the other pagan gods, whose stories were full of indiscretions and selfish acts; there was nothing in the Asclepius myth that was in the least reminiscent of the divine legends ascribed to the other deities such as thieving, wenching or dealing deceitfully:

> Granted that the tradition is fragmentary, that stories may have been current which are not preserved, there can have been no stories of love affairs or of dissension, tales amoral in tone or character. Otherwise it would be incomprehensible that the Christian polemic, eager as it was to find fault with the outrageous behavior of the pagan gods, does not refer to any derogatory incident in the life of Asclepius, the most dangerous enemy of Christ.[67]

Moreover, Asclepius was unique in offering a more personal, humane relationship to the divine. Since the 5th century BC, philosophers had been arguing that true gods should be free from envy or malice, and were seeking an individual relationship with the divine rather than collective worship.

> There was a craving for a personal relationship to the deity, and the belief in divine providence progressed steadily. In such a world it was natural that Asclepius found favor, for if any god was interested in the private needs of men, in their most personal affairs, if any god showed providence, it was Asclepius.[68]

Asclepius only healed the pure of heart and mind. He healed the poor and he did it for free, out of love and kindness. Images of Asclepius show him as youthful and bearded. He "radiates dignity mixed with compassion; eyes turned upward looking saintly and benign. Curly locks falling over the back and down to the eyebrows."[69] He was fond of children.

The similarities between Asclepius and Jesus Christ did not go unnoticed. Justin Martyr cites Asclepius' healing miracles, and argued that the resurrection of Jesus was no different from Asclepius dying but being raised to heaven:

> And when we say also that the Word, who is the first-birth of God, Jesus Christ, our teacher, was produced without sexual union, and that He was crucified and died, and rose again, and ascended into heaven, we propound nothing new and different from what you believe regarding those whom you esteem sons of Jupiter... Asclepius, who, though he was a great healer, was struck by a thunderbolt, and ascended to heaven. (*First Apology*, 21:1-2)

> When we say that He (Jesus) made well the lame and the paralytic and those who were feeble from birth and that he resurrected the dead, we shall seem to be mentioning deeds similar to and even identical with those which were said to have been performed by Asclepius. (*First Apology*, 22:6)

Asclepius was also, like Jesus, given the power to cast out demons, as is mentioned by the apologist Lactantius in his *Divine Institutions*:

> Behold, someone excited by the impulse of the demon is out of his senses, raves, is mad: let us lead him into the temple of Jupiter Optimus Maximus; or since Jupiter knows not how to cure men, into the fane of Asclepius or Apollo. Let the priest of either, in the name of his god, command the wicked spirit to come out of the man.[70]

Likewise, in the apocryphal work *The Acts of Pilate*, possibly written in the 4th century AD, when Jesus is accused of being "a sorcerer, and by Beelzebub the prince of the devils he casteth out devils, and they are all subject unto him," Pilate responds, "It is not possible to cast out devils in the name of an impure spirit but rather in the name of the god Asclepius" (*Acts of Pilate*).

Asclepius was given power over the elements, as testified by a passage from Aristides (530BC-468BC) which prefigures the calming of the seas miracle which Jesus will later perform: "Now I have heard some people saying that, when they were at sea and in the midst of a storm, the god appeared to them and stretched forth his hand."[71] He was even regarded as a muse for inspired writings, as testified by Libanius:

> 'And he not without the aid of the gods' says Homer, 'nor do you (Acacias) write these words without the influence of Asclepius, for manifestly he joined with you in the writing. It is, of course, fitting for him, as the son of Apollo, to have some of the cultural talent of his father and to apportion it to whomever he desires. How then would it be possible for him not to assist you in these discourses concerning himself?[72]

His role as healer was sometimes expanded into a universal force – Asclepius could thus be considered a ruling principle that kept the universe itself in order and governed all things. According to Aristides, Asclepius was "the one who guides and rules the universe, the savior of the whole and the guardian of the immortals."[73] Julianus says "shall I now go on to tell you how Helius took thought for the health and safety of all by begetting Asclepius to be the savior of the whole world?"[74]

Later, the Neoplatonists expanded this idea. Asclepius was the soul of the world, who held creation together and kept the universe healthy and young.[75] At the same time, despite this supernatural role, Asclepius always remained a humble healer. Scholar Emma J. Edelstein gives the following overview of the similarities between Jesus Christ and the Roman god of healing:

> Christ did not perform heroic or worldly exploits; he fought no battles; he concerned himself solely with assisting those who were in need of succor. So did Asclepius. Christ, like Asclepius, was sent into

the world as a helper of men. Christ's life on earth was blameless, as was that of Asclepius. Christ in his love of men invited his patients to come to him, or else he wandered about to meet them. This, too, could be said of Asclepius. All in all, it is not astonishing that Apologists and Church Fathers had a hard stand in their fight against Asclepius, in proving the superiority of Jesus, if moral reasoning alone was to be relied upon. The nature of the godhead of the two saviors was indisputably identical: both were man-gods. Son of God and mortal woman, the story of Christ's birth in many ways resembled the birth saga of divine Asclepius. God died... through god had risen to heaven, immortal on account of virtue. Human and divine, Asclepius was called a 'terrestrial and intelligible' god.[76]

According to Diogenes Laertius, Phoebus gave to mortals Asclepius and Plato, the one to save their souls, the other to save their bodies. Jesus will become both; however, could the stories, healings, philosophy and world view of Jesus Christ have emerged spontaneously and fully developed without the centuries of competing traditions? When the apostles preached that a man in Jerusalem had healed the sick, raised the dead, resurrected and ascended into heaven, would these claims have astounded anyone already familiar with the many miracles of Asclepius?

# Osiris

Osiris was the Egyptian god of the dead, and also a vegetation and resurrection god. Although the story of Osiris is already told in the *Pyramid Texts* of ancient Egypt (2400BC), his popularity exploded when his cult (or rather, the cult of Isis, which included him and his son Horus) was imported into the Roman empire. The main story of Osiris, which features his death and resurrection, as well as the magical healing powers of Isis and the birth of their son, Horus, is as follows:

Osiris was the great benefactor of humanity; he gave humankind laws, the institution of marriage, civil organization, taught them agriculture, and how to worship the gods. "He conquered the nations everywhere, but not with weapons, only music and eloquence."[77] He ruled the land in peace with his consort (wife/sister) Isis. However, his brother Seth (in earlier versions Typhon), was filled with envy and malice, and decided to kill him. Knowing that Osiris was more powerful, Seth designed a clever trap: he made a beautiful chest out of wood, exactly the size of Osiris, and promised it as a gift to whomever it fit. Everybody tried, but nobody could fit in the box. Finally, Osiris tried; but as soon as he lay down inside, Seth with his companions closed the lid, nailed it shut and threw the chest in the Nile river. Isis wept and mourned, tearing her hair and beating her breast. Dressed in black, with shorn hair, she wandered up and down the banks of the Nile, searching in vain for the body of Osiris. The chest had come to rest on the bank of the river, and the power inside was so great that a large tree blossomed; the chest became part of the tree trunk, which was then used as a column in a palace. Isis discovered the truth, and with a wave of her magic wand, split open the column, revealing the wooden coffin. She took the body of Osiris and hid it in a swamp. But Seth found it (as he was out hunting a wild boar) and tore it into 14 pieces. Isis in her magnificent power found the pieces and put them together again, with the exception of the phallus, which was eaten by a fish. She raised Osiris from the dead, at least enough to impregnate her, and he became the ruler of the underworld. Isis then fled with her infant son Horus into hiding, in fear of Seth. However, when Horus grows up and is strong enough, he will return to defeat Seth and avenge the death of his father. According to Witt, "On this founding myth was built a robust system of Egyptian religious belief and ritual, which included the suffering and burial of Osiris, the mourning of Isis, the birth of the divine child, and then the exuberant celebration of his return."[78] German professor of Egyptology Jan Assman explains these rituals further:

> The rejoicing of the triumph of Horus is the precise counterpart of the mourning over the death of Osiris. Both are extreme and all encompassing. Just as the death plunges the entire world into the depths of despair, so the triumph transports it into the heights of rapture. The two emotions belong together as a pair at the beginning and the end of the story that transpires between them. The entire land participated in the story in an annual cycle of festivals, and all who took part in them experienced them.[79]

Osiris is undoubtedly a vegetation god, sometimes associated with corn or grain, but he could also be a solar deity, "bringing light and food especially to those Yonder, the denizens of the netherworld, as he makes his nocturnal journey through their midst in his boat."[80]

When he was called "the Great Green" he was the life-giving fresh water of the river and under this aspect even the salt water of the sea. Manifested in the grain he was the "Bread of Life," and as with other gods of Egypt he could be addressed as a bisexual being: "You are Father and Mother of men. They live from your breath and eat of the flesh of your body."[81]

At the same time, as ruler of the underworld, he was "the resident king of the dead, true of heart and voice, watching with an eye that was never at rest over the rewards of those who came into his realm."[82] The story of his resurrection had been used for millennia to justify the potential for life after death:

> Osiris was the dying and rising god, the mythic precedent and guarantee that one could say to the deceased king, and later to every person, "Stand up!" The fact that he had risen invested these words with meaning. As is well known, this role of Osiris has led to his being classified with a series of "dying and rising" vegetation gods from western Asia: Tammuz, Attis, Adonis. This might be true to a certain extent. Without doubt, Osiris had a relationship with the agricultural cycle and other processes of death and rebirth in nature.[83]

According to Frazer, Egyptians were sometimes entombed with life-size effigies of Osiris, which were hallowed out. Water, dirt and barley seed would then be sealed inside a water tight compartment, which would "live forever":

> In laying their dead in the grave they committed them to his keeping who could raise them from the dust to life eternal, even as he caused the seed to spring from the ground. Of that faith the corn-stuffed effigies of Osiris found in Egyptian tombs furnish an eloquent and unequivocal testimony. They were at once an emblem and an instrument of resurrection.[84]

The annual commemoration of the Osiris story was an enormous cultural event; it retraced the passion, death and resurrection of the god, and was celebrated even in the Roman capital (the Egyptian cult was established in Rome around 50BC). The Iseum of Pompeii was decorated with two paintings of the passion of Osiris.[85] According to Witt, Isis would discover she was pregnant on the 3rd of October, and rose up the new god Horus in an egg. The search for Osiris' body lasted until the 3rd of November, followed by the embalmment of the body. The mummified body was entombed on the 21st December, and two days later, on the 23rd, Isis would bring forth her child, "23 December being in the Egyptian Calendar the date of the simultaneous burial and rebirth of the Sun God. Of cardinal importance for the chronology of the whole tale is the winter solstice."[86] The precise dates are difficult to determine, as Egypt used a shifting calendar. Dowden argues that the mourning period lasted three days:

> For three days his dismemberment at the hands of his enemy Seth or Typhon is mourned; then he is found by Isis and reassembled... This is the experience which is shared in some way by those who have been initiated into the secrets of the religion, maybe the Melanephoroi ('wearers of black') whom inscriptions mention: it is a death and resurrection, despair and new hope story.[87]

Osiris had his own mysteries, and followers of the Egyptian cult believed that they could, like Osiris, find eternal life after death. He was called "The Good Shepherd" and is always shown with the Crook and Flail; shepherd's tools that became symbols of leadership carried by the pharaohs. Gordon claims that the idea of an afterlife, as either a reward or punishment based on the merits of each individual, is unique to Egypt:

> Egyptian religion developed a kind of Passion Play concerning Osiris, the god of the dead, showing his suffering, death, and revival. Each dead person was identified with Osiris on the assumption that the deceased would undergo, but emerge triumphant like Osiris from, a trial full of vicissitudes to qualify for life eternal... This fully developed concept of personal judgment, whereby each man enters paradise if his character and life on earth warrant it, appears quite remarkable when we consider that centuries later there was still no such idea in Mesopotamia or Israel.[88]

Assman stresses the mourning of Osiris' suffering, noting that followers practiced castration:

> In the innermost part of their temples they buried an idol of Osiris: This they annually mourned, they shaved their heads, they beat their breast, tore their members, etc., in order to bewail the pitiful fate of their king... the defenders of this mourning and those funerals give a physical explanation: the seed, they say, is Osiris, the earth Isis, the heat Typhon. And because the fruit is ripe as a result of the heat, it is collected for the living of men and thus separated from earth's company, and when winter comes it will be sowed into the earth in what they interpret as the death and burial of Osiris. But the earth will become pregnant and bring forth new fruits."[89]

Osiris' son, Horus (known as Harpocrates by the Greeks), an infant god described in the *Pyramid Texts* as "the young one with his finger in his mouth," was a favorite figure of paganism in the time of Christ.[90] Even as a young child, he was given absolute power. "He shall rule over this earth... He will be your master, this god who is but an embryo."[91]

The birth story of Horus (the massacre of infants, retreat into hiding, triumphant return), is very similar to that of Jesus. Horus was reborn every year on January 6th [92] – the date on which the birthday of Jesus was celebrated for centuries until 354AD, when the bishop of Rome ruled in favor of December 25th. Some statues of Isis with the baby Horus in her lap are nearly indistinguishable from those of Mary and Jesus and were accidentally worshipped in Christian churches for centuries.

When the Egyptian cult was introduced to Greece and Rome, Horus became identified with Apollo, Heracles, Eros (god of love) and the sun:

> The Beloved and indeed Only Begotten Son of the Father, the Omnipotent Child, he has under his control the circuit of the solar disk and so assumes the lotus which itself is the emblem of the rising Sun.[93]

Demonstrating the trend towards religious synthesis, Horus assimilated the roles and symbols of other gods. In the depictions of Horus found in Pompeii, "He can don the wings of Eros, anticipating the angel-iconography of Christianity, and in his left hand carry the cornucopia of Bacchus. He possesses the quiver of Apollo and the fawnskin of Dionysus."[94] When Horus grows up, he defeats the dragon/crocodile Seth in a magnificent battle. This battle almost certainly influenced Christian iconography:

> In the period during which Christianity was establishing itself as a world religion the figure of Horus/Harpocrates in conjunction with that of a crocodile typified the triumph of good over evil, exactly the same as the victory over the dragon by the saintly combatants Michael and George... Moreover, the dragon was *pyrrhous* in color: and Plutarch thrice applies the same epithet to the complexion of Seth-Typhon.[95]

It was Isis, however, as great mother-goddess, who was the most powerful of the trilogy. Isis gives Horus his powers, and it was Isis who restored life to Osiris. She was a gifted healer – priests of her temples had to study six branches of medical science: anatomy, pathology, surgery, pharmacology, ophthalmology and gynaecology.[96]

> She was the great sorceress. The art of medicine was hers. Horus, the child born weak, is named 'son of an enchantress'. It is to Isis the divine sorceress that the great god Re is forced to reveal the secret of his name. Her magical nature renders her potentially hermaphrodite. So she is not bound by the normal law of sex. She can resuscitate the dead Osiris and by spells obtain the gift of a son. We learn that she discovered health giving drugs and simples as well as the elixir of life. Like Apollo and Asclepius she was an expert in making men well when they betook themselves to her temples, where after incubation they could look forward in hope to gain a cure. Skilful as healer and discoverer of the mysteries of birth, life and death, she was the lady who saved. She resurrected. The gates of Hell, besides salvation, were in her hands.[97]

Isiac temples held mysteries of redemption involving "living water," challenging initiation rites, and obedience:

> Certainly, Isis gives her children the sure hope of eternal salvation: but in return she demands from them unquestioning, even blind obedience, just as she subjects them to the most grueling tests before they reach their haven of rest.[98]

She had the power to control "demons" (elements) and "nature" (astrology).[99] She loved sinners; according to Lucius, in Apuleius' *The Golden Ass*, "Thou doest always bestow thy dear love on wretched men in their mishaps."[100] She also made her mysteries available to rich and poor alike, "not just to the affluent citizen who made his fortune in shipping but even to the man of lowly birth and the down-trodden slave."[101] One inscription to her, found at the temple of Neith at Sais, reads "I am all that has been, and is, and shall be, and my robe has never yet been uncovered by mortal men."[102] Like Horus and Osiris, Isis increasingly usurped the roles, symbols and powers of other gods; she became all things to all people:

> After this with her untold wealth of titles she could take the one that pleased her best. She could assume the eagle of Zeus and the dolphin of Poseidon, the lyre of Apollo and tongs of Hephaestus, the wand of Hermes, the thyrsus of Bacchus and the club of Heracles.[103]

The similarities between the Egyptian cult and Christianity are many: the entire birth story, as well as the Christian iconography of the infant Jesus; the triumph of good over evil; the death and resurrection; the "Great Virgin" and "Mother of God (Isis was called both before the Christian era). Most importantly the emotional catharsis involved, which is also to be found in most other mystery traditions, in mourning the death and then celebrating the return of the deity. Some researchers claim that the Egyptian myth is unique because it has two generations:

> If we are somewhat reminded of the sorrow of Good Friday and the joy of Easter Sunday, it should again be stressed that in the myth of Osiris, we are dealing with two generations. The god who triumphs is a different one from the god who is killed.[104]

However, Horus grows up to become Osiris every year, and makes a new Horus; if you combine Horus and Osiris together into one figure, you'd create a figure much like Jesus Christ. Of course, the *story* is very different: the details of Jesus' life and personality so clearly presented in the gospels make him dissimilar to the Egyptian myth. But we must ask, what is most relevant to the figure of Jesus Christ – the historical details that make him an ordinary man, or his death and resurrection, role in salvation, and divinity?

# Tammuz (Adonis)

Tammuz (Sumerian *Dumuzi*) was the consort of Ishtar. He is mentioned, already in the Epic of Gilgamesh, as a suffering lover of the goddess, a shepherd beloved and scapegoat of the netherworld. When Ishtar tries to become Gilgamesh's lover, he points out that her past lovers have not fared well. "Dumuzi, the lover of your youth, year upon year, to lamenting you doomed him."[105] When Gilgamesh is mourning the death of Enkidu, he presents a carnelian flute for "Dumuzi, shepherd beloved of Ishtar," so that he may welcome his friend and walk at his side.[106] Thus Dumuzi, who was considered a historical king that entered into sexual union with the goddess, was also viewed as a suffering god in his own right; moreover he was at least in some sense a keeper of the underworld and influential in the afterlife. The great age of this cult is attested by the Uruk Vase of the outgoing fourth millennium BC, which depicts the central event of the rite of the sacred marriage.[107]

His demise is tied to the story of Ianna's descent into the underworld. The reason she gives for entering the underworld is to attend her brother-in-law's funeral rites (Gugalana, the Bull of Heaven which had just been killed by Gilgamesh and Enkidu). After she decides to go down into the Great Below, she leaves instructions for her rescue in case she does not return. (Incidentally, the Underworld or the Great Below is, for gods who reside above in heaven, actually the earth.) As she descends, she is required to remove one of her seven layers of clothing at each of the seven gates, until she stood before Ereshkigal, queen of the underworld, naked and humble. Ereshkigal "fixed the eye of death" upon her and she was turned into a corpse, and hung from a hook on the wall like a piece of rotting meat.

After three days and three nights, her servant Ninshubar, following instructions, tried to persuade the gods to save her. Only one, Enki, agreed to help. He fashioned two sexless creatures from the dirt under the fingernails of the gods, and gave them the food and water of life to sprinkle on Ianna's corpse. She returned to life, and Ereshkigal agreed to release her, but she had to provide another in her place. When she came back to heaven she found Dumuzi enjoying himself in her absence (on her throne or under a tree), rather than mourning for her, and "fixed the eye of death" upon him. The demons took him down to Hell; however his sister loved him so much she wanted to go in his place.

So, Dumuzi spends half of the year in the underworld, while his sister spends the other half. During the time that Dumuzi is in the underworld, his lover Ianna misses him; this infertile time is fall and winter. When Dumuzi returns from the underworld and he is with Ianna, their love fills the world with life, causing spring and summer. The poetry of their love is graphic – but also reminiscent of the biblical Song of Songs:

> *My untilled land lies fallow.*
> *As for me, Inanna,*
> *Who will plow my vulva!*
> *Who will plow my high field!*
> *Who will plow my wet ground!*

> *Great Lady, the king will plow your vulva.*
> *I, Dumuzi the King, will plow your vulva.*

> *Make your milk sweet and thick, my bridegroom.*
> *My shepherd, I will drink your fresh milk.*

*Wild bull, Dumuzi, make your milk sweet and thick.*
*I will drink your fresh milk.*
*Let the milk of the goat flow in my sheepfold.*
*Fill my holy churn with honey cheese.*

The cult of Dumuzi is primarily a (tragic) romance – a story of betrothment and sexual awakening, but also mourning as the groom dies:

> The cult comprises both the happy celebrations of the marriage of the god with Ianna (who originally, it seems, was the goddess of the communal storehouse) and bitter laments when he dies as the dry heat of summer yellows the pastures and lambing, calving, and milking come to an end.[108]

This story is similar to the myth of Demeter and Persephone; both explain the coming of winter through a goddess grieving for a lost loved one, who then returns. At the same time, Dumuzi was revived by Ianna after death (as his sister was allowed to take his place for half of each year), and so he is also a returning vegetation god.

The cult rituals for Dumuzi began with laments sung as a sacred cedar tree was cut down in the compound of the temple Eanna in Uruk. The rite closed with a triumphant procession that followed the god downstream. According to Jacobson, Dumuzi could represent the sap lying dormant in the rushes and trees during the dry season but reviving, to the profound relief and joy of the orchardman, with the river's rise.[109]

The mourning of Tammuz was a widespread annual ritual, which even appears in the Bible. Yahweh, giving Ezekiel a tour of the idolatry being practiced by the Israelites, points out the women sitting by the entrance to the north gate of the Temple of Yahweh, weeping for Tammuz. "Son of man, do you see that?" he says, "You will see even more loathsome things than that" (Ezek. 8:14).

Much later, in Greek communities, Tammuz was called *Adonis* and considered a consort of Aphrodite (Roman Venus). The cult of Adonis existed in Sappho and Lesbos as early as 600BC. As Adonis is a mutation or evolved form of Tammuz, in a different cultural setting, the two figures are not exactly the same.

> The cult of Aphrodite's paramour Adonis held a special appeal for Greek women, combining the erotic adoration of a beautiful youth with the emotional catharsis of lamentation for his death. The Adonis cult was an early import from the Levant, probably via Cyprus, but while many of the outward forms remained the same, its cultural context and significance changed. Adonis was modeled upon Tammuz, the consort of Ishtar whose death was annually lamented by women, and his name is a direct borrowing of the West Semitic *adon,* Lord.[110]

There are multiple versions of Adonis' birth story, but the commonly accepted version is that Aphrodite urged Myrrha to commit incest with her father, Theias. Myrrha slept with her father in the darkness, until he used an oil lamp to learn the truth and chased after her with a knife. Aphrodite turned Myrrha into a myrrh tree, out of which Adonis was born (either when Theias shot an arrow in the tree, or when a boar tore off the bark with its tusks). He was such a beautiful baby that Aphrodite locked him in a trunk and gave him to Persephone – queen of the underworld

– for safe keeping; however Persephone was so enthralled by him that she refused to return him. Finally Zeus decided that he would be shared – six months with Aphrodite, who later seduced him, and six months with Persephone.[111]

Adonis met his death by a wild boar. According to Ovid in *The Metamorphoses*, Aphrodite (Roman Venus), who'd been pricked by Eros' arrow of love, specifically warned him to be careful and stay away from wild beasts:

> The wild and large are much too wild for you;
> My dear, remember that sweet Venus loves you,
> And if you walk in danger, so does she.
> Nature has armed her monsters to destroy you –
> Even your valour would be grief to me.
> (Ovid, *Metamorphoses* X)

But the young Adonis ignored her warning (due to "pride and manliness") and headed off into the wood with his hunting dogs, where he woke the great boar who pierced his white loins with a powerful thrust. Adonis bled to death.

Although the cult of Tammuz "enjoyed near-universal recognition in Mesopotamia and his festival was so important that a Babylonian month was named after him,"[112] worship of Adonis, while popular, rarely gained state sponsorship. It was viewed as a foreign cult; moreover Adonis was mostly mourned by women, in rituals not tied to a sanctuary, temple or sacred space:

> Women sit by the gate weeping for Tammuz, or they offer incense to Baal on roof-tops and plant pleasant plants. These are the very features of the Adonis cult: a cult confined to women which is celebrated on flat roof-tops on which sherds sown with quickly germinating green

salading are placed, Adonis gardens... the climax is loud lamentation for the dead god.[113]

To perform the Adonia, which took place in late summer, women ascended to the roof, where they sang dirges, cried out in grief, and beat their breasts. Greek poetess Sappho mentions that the women tore their garments, a standard sign of mourning:

O Forest-maidens, smite on the breast,
Rend ye the delicate-woven vest!
Let the wail ring wild and high:
'Ah for Adonis!' cry.[114]

Other features of Adonis' ritual belong to the cult in Classical Athens. A few days before the Adonia, garden herbs and cereals were sown in broken pots. These tender young plants were brought to the rooftops during the festival, to be withered in the hot sun emblems of the youthful Adonis' death. Another custom involved the laying out of Adonis dolls for burial.[115]

Frazer notes the similarity between the Eastern Orthodox Church and the cult of Adonis; the tradition is much the same even today. They bring out an effigy of the dead Jesus and parade it through town, mourning. They bury it, fast all day, and then at midnight on Saturday, cry 'Christ is risen!' – "and at once the whole town bursts into an uproar of joy, which finds vent in shrieks and shouts, in the endless discharge of carronades and muskets, and the explosion of fire-works of every sort."[116] The fast is broken and people enjoy the Easter lamb and wine. Frazer concludes that the Christian celebration of Easter was modeled on the earlier ritual concerning Adonis:

When we reflect how often the Church has skillfully contrived to plant the seeds of the new faith the old stock of paganism, we may surmise that the Easter celebration of the dead and risen Christ was grafted upon a similar celebration of the dead and risen Adonis, which, as we have seen reason to believe, was celebrated in Syria in the same season.[117]

Some researchers have denied the claim that Adonis' resurrection was celebrated; the focus always seems to be on the mourning of his death rather than the celebration of his revival. However, Frazer may have had the cult of Attis in mind, which was very similar to that of Adonis, and did stress, not only the death, but the *return* of the god. Incidentally, it may be noted that Adonis, like "Christ," is a title meaning *lord*, rather than a specific name; even Yahweh in the Old Testament is called Adonis.

## Attis

Attis was the consort or lover of the Phrygian mother goddess, Cybele, whose cult, although ancient, was introduced into Rome around 200BC. The addition of Attis into this cult, however, may have occurred later; the first literary reference to Attis is a poem by Catullus (84-54BC). The worship of Attis was primarily an annual celebration of his suffering, death and rebirth (linking him to Osiris and Tammuz), but with notable differences – for example, its emphasis on castration.

Cybele rejected Zeus as a lover, but he spilled his seed on her while she was sleeping and she gave birth to Agdistis – a wild demon that was so fearful the gods cut off his testicles to render him powerless. From the blood grew an almond tree. Nana, daughter of the river god Sangarius, took an almond to her breast (or ate the fruit) from this tree and nine months later gave birth to Attis; hence he was miraculously born, half divine.

According to the Phrygian story Attis was extremely handsome and his grandmother Cybele desired him. Having no idea about his divine nature or his grandmother's desires, he fell in love with the beautiful daughter of the king of Pessinus and wished to marry her. Cybele was so jealous that she caused him to become crazy. He ran through the mountains and castrated himself (and so died) at the foot of a pine tree. From his blood grew the first violets. The tree took Attis' spirit, and his flesh would have decayed if Zeus had not helped Cybele bring him back to life. In another version Zeus, angry at the Lydians for worshipping Attis and The Mother, sends a wild boar that killed him and destroyed the Lydian Crops. In still another version, Attis was killed accidentally by a poorly thrown spear during a boar hunt. Frazer notes that bulls sacrificed during rituals were bled to death with a consecrated spear – which may have its roots in this myth, tying the death of Attis to the cleansing blood of the bull.

In works of art, Attis is represented as a shepherd with flute and staff, sometimes near or under a tree. The cult of Attis and Cybele became extremely popular in Greek and Roman society, and a public festival, commemorating the death and rebirth of Attis, was the first of its kind to be celebrated in Rome:

> Noteworthy variations distinguish the versions of the legend, but from the time of Claudius (AD 41-54) Romans took part in March in a kind of 'holy week' whose rites conveyed the myth of Attis, a god who died and came to life again each year; it was the first of its kind in the liturgy of the Urbs. The methods may have evolved before becoming fixed in the Antonine period, but its highlights were celebrated as early as the first century.[118]

The "Passion" of Attis began on the 15th of March with a procession of reed bearers. On the 22nd, a pine tree was cut, and a ram sacrificed on the stump. The tree was wrapped in wool, like the corpse of Attis had been, and carried to the sanctuary; usually an effigy (like a doll) of the god Attis was fixed to the top. The tree was laid to rest in the Temple of Cybele. The 24th was a day of mourning and fasting, but "after a night of doleful lamentation, on 25 March, the joy of the Hilaria erupted, celebrating the revived Attis. In the imperial period it became the great springtime festival enlivened by a kind of carnival."[119] Attis' followers embraced the suffering of Attis on the 24th, through acts of self-mutilation or even castration:

> The next day was one of vociferous mourning, and on the day following, the 'day of blood', the Mother's worshippers would whip themselves and some of them, carried away by ecstacy, would perform the irreversible act. With the dawn of 25 March came the day of rejoicing for some – convalescence for others – as Attis' resurrection was celebrated.[120]

Such public displays of self-violence, while not common to imperial cults, were preserved in Christianity. The Bible contains many passages recommending physical suffering or suffering with Christ:

> As Christ has undergone bodily suffering, you too should arm yourselves with the same conviction, that anyone who has undergone bodily suffering has broken with sin, because for the rest of life on earth that person is ruled not by human passions but only by the will of God (1 Peter 4:1)

In fact, the closest public rituals in the world today to the ancient cult of Attis are probably the Good Friday celebrations of the Philippines; where, in a bloody display of faith, followers of Jesus flog themselves as punishment for the sins they've committed during the year. Some even choose to be crucified, enduring the pain that Christ met on the cross.

Besides the public ceremony, Attis had his own mystery cult involving secret rituals with mystical meaning. One of the central rites was the *Taurobolium*, or baptism in the blood of a bull. The great Basilica of St. Peter on Vatican Hill is founded on a site of Cybele worship, which had included a Taurobolium – a place to slaughter the bull and use its blood in purifying rituals. Initiates who underwent the somewhat gruesome process of the Taurobolium were said to have been "born again":

> Its hot reeking blood poured in torrents through the apertures, and was received with devout eagerness by the worshipper on every part of his person and garments, till he emerged from the pit, drenched, dripping, and scarlet from head to foot, to receive the homage, nay the adoration, of his fellows as one who had been born again to eternal life and had washed away his sins in the blood of the bull.[121]

It is worthwhile to keep in mind that blood sacrifice for the forgiveness of sins or to attract favors from the gods was an integral part of not only pagan, but also Judaic spirituality: "For the soul of the flesh is in the blood and I have assigned it for you upon the altar to provide atonement for your souls; for it is the blood that atones for the soul" (Leviticus 17:11). Although this passage from Leviticus was used by Christian theologians to justify the need for Christ's saving blood, and the Jews themselves were strictly prohibited from *consuming* blood themselves, innumerable animals (bulls and rams) were nevertheless sacrificed at the Temple in Jerusalem up until it was destroyed in 70AD. (Most of the animals were eaten by worshipers or priests; only some were burnt offerings wholly consumed by fire.)

Christian symbolism of Jesus as the Lamb of God, who gave his blood so that we may be washed in the blood of the Lamb (Revelation, 7:12), is far more similar to the Attic ritual of being washed in the blood of the bull than it is to the Judaic tradition. Jews were commanded to spill the blood on the ground, but keep separate from it – they would have found the idea of bathing in it barbarous. Of course, Christianity's use of the lamb (rather than the bull) is most likely due to the theology of Jesus as the Paschal lamb of Judaic tradition; however this may also have had an economic basis. New converts of the other mysteries, who couldn't afford to buy a (very expensive) bull, could elect to buy a ram instead, or even a lesser animal. "Poorer people made do with a criobolium, in which a ram was killed, and were 'washed in the blood of the Lamb.'"[122] However, it seems Christianity, which had no temple and consisted mostly of poorer segments of society, early began interpreting Christ's death symbolically and not requiring an actual sacrifice. (At the same time, the doctrine of transubstantiation, in which the Eucharist wine is believed to become the *actual* blood of Jesus Christ, Lamb of God, testifies to the fact that symbolic blood alone is not totally acceptable.)

Initiates from the mysteries of Attis would need to recite certain magical formulas or creeds: "I ate from the tympanon, I drank from the cymbal, I carried the composite vessel (kernos), I slipped under the bedcurtain."[123] Followers abstained from pork because a boar killed their god. The most zealous of Attic priests, the Galli, even became eunuchs by castrating themselves – a sacrifice said to have been made also by Origin, one of the first great Christian apologists, and not alien to the Christian tradition: "There are eunuchs born so by their mother's womb, there are eunuchs made so by human agency and there are eunuchs who made themselves so for the sake of the kingdom of heaven. Let anyone accept this who can" (Matthew 19:12).

The castrated priests of Cybele would speak in falsetto and wear bright women's clothing. According to some legends, Cybele resurrected Attis as a woman. One can't help but wonder whether there is a connection between Attis worship and the Dionysiac story of the Bacchae, in which Dionysus makes Pentheus dress up as a woman, before approaching the maenads (who then rip him into pieces while he's sitting on top of a pine tree).

A god that dies, is mourned, and celebrated after three days as having risen from the dead; a god whose initiates can be washed in blood and freed from sin – these similarities to Christianity seem more than coincidental:

> Like Christianity, the cult of Cybele promises immortality and resurrection. In both cases this promise came as a result of an act of sacrifice and death... Moreover Attis as a shepherd occupies a favourite Christian image of Christ as the good shepherd. Further parallels also seem to have existed: the pine tree of Attis, for example, was seen as a parallel to the cross of Christ.[124]

There was also rivalry in ritual. The climax of the celebration of Attis' resurrection, The *Hilaria*, fell on the 25th of March, the date the early Church had settled on for Christ's resurrection. (Today Easter is celebrated on the first Sunday after the Paschal Full Moon, which falls between the 22nd and the 25th.) According to A.T. Fear:

> Once again the closeness of the dates and the fact that the metroac festival of resurrection would fall on the day of Christ's execution both threw down a psychological challenge in itself and may well have undercut the Christian celebration of the resurrection of Christ in the public mind.[125]

A few scholars argue that the definitive features of the Attis cult arose late – in the third or fourth century AD – as a response to the threat of Christianity. And while this may be true, the fact remains that features of the worship of Jesus Christ were adopted from customs of this cult that are still in use today. For example, the ritual of cutting down a Christmas tree (evergreen pine), decorating it and placing an angel on the top, seems far more Attic than anything found in the Bible.

Although the debate is unsettled, it is unlikely that Jesus came first: The Holy Week of Attis was already a State Ceremony by

41-54AD; moreover, Cybele had been worshiped by Romans for centuries, (she was adopted into Roman religion in 204BC after being credited with an exceptional harvest). Also, the numerous clay ex-votos depicting Attis (many of which are datable to the second century BC) unearthed during excavations prove that the god had already reached the ordinary populace long before the appearance of Jesus.[126]

In order to distinguish Attis from Jesus, critics have argued that stories about Attis nowhere explicitly mention any kind of salvation or afterlife prospects, and argue that Attis may have offered some benefit *in this life;* although what possible benefit could be great enough for followers to castrate themselves, they don't care to guess. They have also argued that Attis was not actually resurrected, at least not until much after the spread of Christianity. While it is true that hard documents proving the existence of such beliefs have not survived, it would require a leap of faith rather than an educated guess to conclude that followers of Attis mourned, mutilated themselves, and then celebrated a story about Attis' death and return – especially in a society where other similar figures did clearly offer afterlife rewards – without themselves hoping for some form of salvation. We also know that the cult of Attis was a mystery cult, which did not openly reveal its central doctrines; and so we should assume that a hidden central doctrine of salvation did exist.

For our purposes it is enough to note that the cult of Attis was already a robust spiritual organization in the founding period of Christianity, which proved to be a serious threat to the early church. Ancient Christian reactions to the cult demonstrate that the similarities were recognized by the church early on. While mystery religions in general were not the focus of Christian polemic, Attis and Cybele appear to have been a favorite target for the invective of Christian writers. Some have seen the attack going back to the earliest days of Christianity, and interpret the Whore of Babylon of Revelation 17.3-6 as a veiled depiction of Cybele.[127]

While the brutal, bloody and ecstatic worship of Attis may seem at odds with modern Christianity, we must not ignore the fact that Christianity – to an outsider – might have appeared just as strange and violent. As Joscelyn Godwin in *Mystery Religions in the Ancient World* points out:

> And if generations of Christians believed that Jesus died on the cross as the only means to pacify his father's anger at mankind, it was no more absurd for the devotees of Attis and Cybele to worship a jealous goddess and her mutilated son.[128]

Like Attis, Jesus was sometimes referred to as hung on a tree (Acts, 5:30), and the mournful Easter processions of some modern Christian communities, carrying the bloody, crucified Christ through the streets to place in the Church until his resurrection, are hardly dissimilar to the same practices performed by the Attic cult. Likewise, the modern celebration of Christmas, with its candles, trees and gifts, may have roots in the Attic story.

## Mithras

Mithras was originally an Indo-Iranian sun god – his name is found in both the Vedas and the Avesta (Hindu and Persian sacred texts), in which he is a light or solar deity, and second to the chief god Ahura Mazda. The inscriptions of the Achaemenidae (seventh to fourth century BC) assign him "a much higher place, naming him immediately after Ahura Mazda and associating him with the goddess Anaitis (Anahata), whose name sometimes precedes his own. Mithras is the god of light, Anaitis the goddess of water."[129] He became associated with Chaldean astrology and worship of Marduk, and finally came into contact with the Western world through Alexander's conquests. Mithraism spread rapidly through the entire Roman Empire and reached its zenith during the third century.

Predominantly a cult of soldiers, stress was laid on brotherhood, fellowship, bravery, cleanliness, and fidelity. Mithraism was also a mystery religion, and demanded a very rigorous initiation process. According to Pseudo-Nonnus, an early 6th century author of a commentary on Gregory of Nazianzen's first four orations, fasting was first imposed upon the neophytes for a period of about fifty days. If this was successfully endured, for two days they were exposed to extreme heat, then again plunged into snow for twenty days.[130] The severity of the discipline was gradually increased: there was also immersion in water, passing through fire, solitude and fasting in the wilderness, and numerous other tests. Participation in the rites of Mithras was not allowed to anyone who had not passed through all the grades and proved himself pure and disciplined.[131]

Pictures of Mithras show him being born out of a rock, often surrounded by the twelve signs of the zodiac. He was also symbolized as a lion. A major motif, found in the central location of places of worship, was the image of Mithras standing over a bull, slitting its throat with a sword. Although this led some early researchers to conclude that Mithraism revolved around the Taurobolium (the practice of slaughtering a live bull and drinking or bathing in its blood), there was no physical space for such a procedure in the Mithraea. It is unlikely that this act was any more than a symbolic, commemorative allegory, and "seldom if ever would the initiate be sprinkled with the blood of a slain bull."[132]

According to Plutarch, Zoroaster taught (500 years before the Trojan war) that Mithras was the mediator between two divine beings, the god Horomazes (Ormuzd) and the daemon Areimanios (Ahriman).[133] As a mystery cult, Mithraism had at its core secret spiritual doctrines. Researchers have speculated that Mithraics believed, through certain ritualistic processes, that they could achieve immortality.

After baptism into the Mysteries of Mithras, the initiate was marked on the forehead with the sign of the cross. (The cross was already a magical religious symbol as a pictograph of the sun; the cross formed by the elliptic and the celestial equator was one of the signs of Mithras.) There were seven levels of initiation – each level was tied to a metal, color and planet. A criticism of Christianity by the philosopher Celsus, which has been recorded by Origen, is that this "ladder" (which represented the soul's passage through the heavens) is the same ladder that Jacob saw in the Old Testament, with angels going up and down. "These things are obscurely hinted at in the accounts of the Persians, and especially in the mysteries of Mithras, which are celebrated amongst them." Celsus demonstrates some of the complexity of this system:

> The first gate they assign to Saturn, indicating by the 'lead' the slowness of this star; the second to Venus, comparing her to the splendour and softness of tin; the third to Jupiter, being firm and solid; the fourth to Mercury, for both Mercury and iron are fit to endure all things, and are money-making and laborious; the fifth to Mars, because, being composed of a mixture of metals, it is varied and unequal; the sixth, of silver, to the Moon; the seventh, of gold, to the Sun, - thus imitating the different colours of the two latter. (qtd. in Origen, *Contra Celsum*, 5.22)

According to Origen, Celsus also demonstrates the musical reasons and explanations of these levels; no doubt tied to the Orphic/Pythagorean belief in the harmony of the spheres.

Unfortunately, Mithraic written texts and studies on Mithraicism (such as the many volumes on Mithras written by Eubulus, as recorded by Jerome) have been destroyed. What remains are the symbolic and graphical representations found in the cave-like Mithraic grottos, and the unflattering criticisms of Christian apologists. What is clear, however, is that Mithraism and Christianity had a lot in common. Godwin points out a few of the more remarkable similarities:

> He is one of the gods, lower than Ahura Mazda (the Supreme Deity of Light of the Persians) but higher than the visible Sun. He is creator and orderer of the universe, hence a manifestation of the creative Logos or Word. Seeing mankind afflicted by Ahriman, the cosmic power of darkness, he incarnated on earth. His birth on 25 December was witnessed by shepherds. After many deeds he held a last supper with his disciples and returned to heaven. At the end of the world he will come again to judge resurrected mankind and after the last battle, victorious over evil, he will lead the chosen ones through a river of fire to blessed immortality. It is possible to prepare oneself for this event during life by devotion to him, and to attain a degree of communion with him through the sacramental means of initiation.[134]

Although it is impossible to prove that the last supper of Mithras is like the communal meal experienced by the Christians, the following passage from Justin Martyr makes it likely:

> For the apostles, in the memoirs composed by them, which are called Gospels, have thus delivered unto us what was enjoined upon them; that Jesus took bread, and when He had given thanks, said, "This do ye in remembrance of Me, this is My body;" and that, after the same manner, having taken the cup and given thanks, He said, "This is My blood;" and gave it to them alone. Which the wicked devils have imitated in the mysteries of Mithras, commanding the same thing to be done. For, that bread and a cup of water are placed with certain incantations in the mystic rites of one who is being initiated, you either know or can learn. (*First Apology*, 65-67)

M.J. Vermaseren, in his 1963 book *Mithras, The Secret God* has Mithras say, "He who will not eat of my body, nor drink of my blood so that he may be one with me and I with him, shall not be saved";[135] however, this passage has been questioned and may actually belong to Zarathustra in an older Persian or Zarathustrian text. A fragment found in a Mithraic site reads, "You have saved us too by shedding the external blood,"[136] but this is probably about Mithras killing the bull. Like Dionysus and others, Mithras was sometimes himself identified with the bull, so this could theoretically indicate a self-sacrifice. Another early church father, Tertullian, (c.160-c.220AD) draws a more detailed comparison in his *Prescription Against Heretics*, which includes baptism, the forgiveness of sins, the resurrection, and hints at forgotten Christian rituals:

> The question will arise, By whom is to be interpreted the sense of the passages which make for heresies? By the devil, of course, to whom pertain those wiles which pervert the truth, and who, by the mystic rites of his idols, vies even with the essential portions of the sacraments of God. He, too, baptizes some - that is, his own believers and faithful followers; he promises the putting away of sins by a layer (of his own); and if my memory still serves me, Mithras there, (in the kingdom of Satan) sets his marks on the foreheads of his soldiers; celebrates also the oblation of bread, and introduces an image of a resurrection, and before a sword wreathes a crown. What also must we say to (Satan's) limiting his chief priest to a single marriage? He, too, has his virgins; he, too, has his proficients in continence. (Ch. 40)

Modern apologists argue that the features Mithraism shared with Christianity did not develop until late in the Christian era; however, Celsus seems to have been one of the first to analyze the similarities between Christianity and the Persian cult, which proves that Mithraism was already very well formed in the 2nd century, while the somewhat floundering Christianity as yet could not agree on central doctrines. Furthermore, certain Mithraic principles, such as the transmigration of souls, vegetarianism, communal meals (that may have involved eating the body and blood of the god), the passage of the soul through the seven planets, the musical theory behind this harmonic arrangement, can all be traced back to earlier groups such as the Orphics or Pythagoreans. The same can be said of the central motif of Mithraism, the killing of a sacrificial bull, which is a motif found in several other mystery cults, even going as far back as Gilgamesh, and almost certainly has an astronomical origin.

Thus, we could conclude (as Charles François Dupuis did in 1798) that since early Christian apologists both confirm and fail to explain the similarities between Jesus and Mithras, the similarities must exist; and since practices found in Mithraism are older, Christianity must have borrowed from Mithras:

> Of course, Tertullian calls again the Devil to his assistance, in order to explain away so complete a resemblance. But as there is not the slightest difficulty, without the intervention of the Devil, to perceive, that whenever two religions resemble each other so completely, the oldest must be the mother and the youngest the daughter, we shall conclude, that since the worship of Mithras is infinitely older than that of Christ, and its ceremonies a great deal anterior to those of the Christians, that therefore the Christians are incontestably either sectarians or plagiarists of the religion of the Magi.[137]

While it is impossible to deny the claim that Mithrasists *may have* borrowed from Christianity, this claim seems unlikely and is based on poor logic. Bremmer, for example, in *The Rise and Fall of the Afterlife*, argues that the success of Christianity also influenced other religions either to revalue their belief in the resurrection (i.e. Zoroastrians) or to copy the belief (Mithraism, Attis). "Success stimulates imitation – not only in economics, but also in the market of symbolic goods."[138]

While the statement "success stimulates imitation" may be true, Christianity was not particularly successful during the formative period of Mithraism. In fact, Christianity was a persecuted sect, always at odds not only with the ruling classes, but also with philosophers, Gnostics, and mystery cults. Why would Mithraism have needed to borrow from Christianity when the elements shared between them were common to other organizations which did clearly predate them both?

Fearful of the identification of Mithraism with Christianity, elaborate efforts have been made to distinguish between the two. Consider the following passage found in the *Catholic Encyclopedia*:

> Christ was an historical personage, recently born in a well-known town of Judea, and crucified under a Roman governor, whose name figured in the ordinary official lists. Mithras was an abstraction, a personification not even of the sun but of the diffused daylight; his incarnation, if such it may be called, was supposed to have happened before the creation of the human race, before all history. The small Mithraic congregations were like Masonic lodges for a few and for men only and even those mostly of one class, the military; a religion that excludes the greater half of the human race bears no comparison to the religion of Christ. Mithraism was all comprehensive and tolerant of every other cult, the Pater Patrum himself was an adept in a number of other religions; Christianity was essentially exclusive, condemning every other religion in the world, alone and unique in its majesty.[139]

Basically a summary of Mithraic scholarly conclusions, this passage argues first that Christ was historical, while Mithras was not; a distinguishing feature which this book will take great lengths to refute. Second, that Mithraism excluded women, while ignoring the blatant misogynist practices of the church and continuing refusal of women into the priesthood; and third, the "exclusivity" of Christianity, which has always been its most dangerous and destructive feature. Absolutely, Christian exclusivity and condemnation of all other religions made it unique; the same intolerance continues to be an integral feature of many forms of Christianity today. This feature should not, however, be used to demonstrate the superiority of Christianity over more inclusive traditions.

If Mithraism did borrow, then it borrowed and thrived; it also borrowed within decades and became a fully independent, complicated organization replete with rituals and allegorical meaning. If nothing else, we can say that the cult of Mithras was a challenging contemporary movement of Christianity. An illuminating anecdote from the Christian historian Socrates (305-438) illustrates the climate. According to him, when Emperor Constantius turned over a formerly pagan temple to the Christians, in the process of cleaning it they found the bones and skulls of human beings, which they claimed had been sacrificed to Mithras (in some kind of magical divination practice). We have no way to check the truth of this statement; it is equally likely that they had raided a sacred burial ground. In fact the language used, "were said to have..." sounds a lot like rumor. Christians, who had been persecuted, marginalized and, even more hurtfully, ignored, by the pagans for centuries, were excited to be given the upper hand and quickly used the opportunity to furnish *proof* against the heathens:

> In the process of clearing it, an adytum of vast depth was discovered which unveiled the nature of their heathenish rites: for there were found there the skulls of many persons of all ages, who were said to have been immolated for the purpose of divination by the inspection of entrails, when the pagans performed these and such like magic arts whereby they enchanted the souls of men. (*Ecclesiastical History*, Book III, Chap. 2)

Demonstrating the righteousness, immaturity, lack of propriety and respect for tradition which made them disliked by their contemporaries, the Christians took all the bones and skulls and ran around town showing them off. The pagans were furious, and killed many Christians in retaliation:

> On discovering these abominations in the adytum of the Mithreum, (the Christians) went forth eagerly to expose them to the view and

execration of all; and therefore carried the skulls throughout the city, in a kind of triumphal procession, for the inspection of the people. When the pagans of Alexandria beheld this, unable to bear the insulting character of the act, they became so exasperated, that they assailed the Christians with whatever weapon chanced to come to hand, in their fury destroying numbers of them in a variety of ways: some they killed with the sword, others with clubs and stones; some they strangled with ropes, others they crucified, purposely inflicting this last kind of death in contempt of the cross of Christ: most of them they wounded; and as it generally happens in such a case, neither friends nor relatives were spared, but friends, brothers, parents, and children imbrued their hands in each other's blood. (Book III, Chap. 2)

This story is, of course, written to vindicate and justify the Christians while demonizing the barbarism of the pagans; however we can learn much more from it. Although Christianity had been made the legal religion, and was growing in property, riches and political power, it was still unpopular. Moreover, the majority of the citizens of Alexandria weren't willing to bear insult to the god Mithras (or perhaps having the remains of their loved ones exhumed).

A final point of interest is the relationship between Mithras and the archangel Michael. After Christianity became the official religion of the Roman Empire, Michael became the patron saint of soldiers; immediately usurping the role of Mithras. Mithraea were converted into shrines for Michael (for instance, the sacred cavern at Monte Gargano in Apulia, refounded in 493); and many such shrines still have bull imagery. Michael is always depicted standing over Satan or the Dragon, winged and with a sword and shield – much like Mithras, and exactly like Perseus, who was the highest grade of initiation.

Michael is the field commander of the army of god. In Catholic tradition, it is Michael who defeated Satan and Michael who will come back to defeat the antichrist at the end of times. Michael was also a great healer – founding healing springs and sites of medicine; taking over the traditional medicinal authority of Asclepius.

It is unlikely the soldiers of the Roman empire would have been satisfied with Jesus. (Indeed, how are any soldiers to be satisfied with Jesus' ethical advice to "turn the other cheek" and his Old Testament commandment of "Thou shall not kill"?) The inclusion of St. Michael was crucial for the success of Christianity, because it allowed Mithras worship to continue under another name. This should not be seen as the superiority of Christianity or the insignificance of Mithraism – rather it is a testament to the strength and popularity of the "god of the rock."

## Conclusions and Summary

As I mentioned before, I am not trying to make the argument that these gods are exactly the same thing as Jesus Christ. Of course they are not – they are each unique cultural manifestations and syntheses of older traditions. However, a number of them share very precise similarities. Moreover, the ritual practices of many of these gods, (a communal meal, baptism, fasting or asceticism, and the ideas they held about their gods' divine natures and saving roles), show common ground.

The growth of the Roman Empire witnessed an unprecedented level of religious tolerance and syncretism: that the majority of these figures did adapt and assimilate each other's distinguishing features is widely agreed by scholars. Many of them were routinely interpreted as being merely translations, different in title only. Initiates of one cult could (and did) also join several others. Family altars were filled with diverse gods. At the same time, there was an academic pursuit of a better, philosophical god – a ruling power or wisdom; the order behind the universe.

Set in this background, as a human, Jewish prophet in Palestine, we would expect Jesus Christ to have very little similarity to these other mythological figures. But in fact, we have seen that the opposite is true. It is impossible that the human Jesus would have been unaware of or unfamiliar with the stories of these other deities; and if we rule out that either God or Satan planted these similarities for some ulterior motive, or that Jesus Christ was a fraud who deliberately copied other traditions, then we can only be left with the conclusion that Christian writers assimilated elements from paganism into the Christian mythos.

While some features of Christianity definitely come from Jewish tradition, there are other features (such as eating the body and blood of the god), which are completely alien to Judaism. The idea of a historical Jesus has been preserved mainly by differentiating him from these pagan influences, based on the claim that he *is* historical, and by trying to tie him exclusively into the Jewish tradition. However, the pagan influences on Christianity cannot be ignored. It may be easy to conclude that Jewish theological and prophetic literature, plus the ritual practices of salvation mystery cults, were added on to the tradition left by a historical Jesus and quickly overwhelmed him. However, since the earliest accounts of Christianity do not point to a historical Jesus, and since many early Christians believed that Jesus did not come in the flesh at all, this theory lacks credibility.

This is not to say that Jesus is just the same as or identical to other figures of mythology; indeed, Jesus would be something entirely new simply by virtue of his being an assimilation of the best features of each. Jesus is the culmination and combination of all other religious traditions of his time: while Orphism had a human prophet (Orpheus) and a divine god (Dionysus), in two separate stories, Jesus became both human and divine – prophet and god – in a mysterious, impossible Truth that was beyond all sense or logic. Without any attempt to make the story coherent, Jesus was given every feature, every power, every moving anecdote, parable and saying found in rival literature.

Yet divergent ideologies in what became orthodox Christianity really were unique. The novelty factor of Christianity derives from its unusual claim that Jesus had recently been a historical figure and had physically risen from the dead. Indeed, it was the resurrection of the flesh, and Christians' stubborn insistence on it, that proved most difficult for their contemporaries to accept.

# PART TWO

## Tracing the Roots
## the Christian Mythos

1943, C.S. Lewis made the seemingly convincing argument (which is still used today as a staple of Christian rhetoric) that Jesus could not have been a "great moral teacher." Instead, he was either a lunatic, a liar or what he claimed to be – the Son of God:

> A man who was merely a man and said the sort of things Jesus said would not be a great moral teacher. He would either be a lunatic – on the level with a man who says he is a poached egg – or he would be the devil of hell. You must take your choice. Either this was, and is, the Son of God or else a madman or something worse. You can shut Him up for a fool or you can fall at His feet and call Him Lord and God. But let us not come with any patronizing nonsense about His being a great human teacher. He has not left that open to us.[1]

The logic of this argument falls apart when we don't take the Bible literally, and consider the alternative that the gospel writers may have written a great many things about Jesus Christ that have no historical basis. Moreover, even Lewis could not deny the fact of Jesus' similarities to other pagan mythological figures, which he claims actually motivated his conversion to Christianity:

> If my religion is erroneous then occurrences of similar motifs in pagan stories are, of course, instances of the same, or a similar error. But if my

religion is true, then these stories may well be a preparatio evangelica, a divine hinting in poetic and ritual form at the same central truth which was later focused and (so to speak) historicised in the Incarnation. To me, who first approached Christianity from a delighted interest in, and reverence for, the best pagan imagination, who loved Balder before Christ and Plato before St. Augustine, the anthropological argument against Christianity has never been formidable. On the contrary, I could not believe Christianity if I were forced to say that there were a thousand religions in the world of which 999 were pure nonsense and the thousandth (fortunately) true. My conversion, very largely, depended on recognizing Christianity as the completion, the actualization, the entelechy, of something that had never been wholly absent from the mind of man.[2]

I can understand how, as a spiritually minded individual, Lewis came to understand Jesus Christ as the culmination of world literature and the natural religious inclination of mankind. And in at least some sense – *he is*. However, at the same time, Lewis' modern inversion of the Diabolical Mimicry argument over-simplifies. For one, it ignores the probability that the gospel writers copied or borrowed from other contemporary traditions – something which is infinitely more likely and easier to explain than a God who revealed the full Truth of His intentions only once, to one small group, while teasing everyone else with a message 99% similar but only mythical. It also ignores the early church controversy over the historical Jesus, the deliberately constructed and falsified history of apostolic tradition, and the violent conflict with and destruction of the pagan traditions which Jesus is "the completion" of.

Most importantly, Lewis takes for granted that Jesus Christ's miraculous physical resurrection and bodily ascension into heaven is a "myth become fact" – that unlike other pagan deities, Jesus Christ alone *actually* rose from the dead. This conviction, although supported not by historical evidence, logic or reason (and in fact counter-intuitive – even "impossible"), continues to be used in nearly all scholarly works which distinguish Jesus from his parallels. The following passage from Burkert's *Ancient Mystery Cults* demonstrates how deeply this faith can color research conclusions:

The Frazerian construct of a general "Oriental" vegetation god who periodically dies and rises from the dead has been discredited by more recent scholarship. There is no evidence for a resurrection of Attis; even Osiris remains with the dead; and if Persephone returns to this world every year, a joyous event for gods and men, the initiates do not follow her. There is a dimension of death and rebirth in all the mystery initiations, but the concept of rebirth or resurrection is anything but explicit. On the other hand, tales of suffering gods, who may die and still come back, are not confined to institutional mysteries.[3]

Burkert claims that "there is no evidence" for the resurrection of Attis or Osiris (as opposed to the presumed evidence that Jesus actually rose from the dead) and that Persephone's followers are not resurrected (as opposed to Christians, who will be). These assumptions are the result of Christianity's fascination with the flesh; it is true that the distinguishing characteristic of Jesus, according to his earliest followers, was his physical incarnation and fleshly resurrection – which guarantees also a resurrection of the flesh for his followers. It is the inherent absurdity and foulness of this idea which made the Christians so unpopular in their day; and facing criticism on this one doctrine, Christian theology expanded and focused peculiarly on Jesus the man, come in the flesh. This was, however, a *theological necessity* rather than a historical certainty.

The purpose of Part One was to explore whether the similarities between Jesus Christ and Harry Potter can be swept aside by appealing to the fact of Jesus' historicity; now we find that they cannot. I have shown that the claim that Jesus was historical has been protested against from the early days of Christianity, noting also that his similarity to pagan saviors, as well as his physical birth, death and resurrection, have caused the major points of controversy. I've also demonstrated that many of the earliest Christian communities and teachers had no consistent beliefs about the historical Jesus, and that the historical events in the gospels were always meant to be taken on faith rather than evidence. Moreover it appears that Paul's Jesus was, like the Jesus of the Gnostics, a spiritual metaphor for personal enlightenment rather than a recently crucified savior; and that this tradition (preached by Simon) may have predated the tradition later recorded in the gospels.

Does this *prove* that Jesus wasn't historical? Not at all. Even though most of the words in the gospels are probably not his, even though he may not have performed the miraculous deeds ascribed to him, and even though historical references to him are not unquestioned, there is no way to prove that there was not a historical figure that sparked the legend. However – for our present study – the historical figure of Jesus is not important. We are interested in the literary Jesus, the image of popular culture that people recognize, as found in the Bible. This Jesus is a composite of various mythological traditions and preserves many ancient symbols; although modern readers enjoy the story and take the moral lessons without knowledge of the esoteric values of those symbols.

In this sense, the Harry Potter books are the Bible of modern times. They interest children (and adults) in reading, they offer a comprehensive story full of issues of morality, guilt, sacrifice, friendship, and they depict a fight between good and evil where eventually good triumphs. They also teach the importance of Love and Faith. More specifically, they employ the powerful emotional device of catharsis as the hero dies, but then comes back triumphantly; of the rise of a hero fulfilling prophecy; and of magical healings and displays.

If nothing else, I have proven that there is the *possibility* that Jesus may not have been historical (or more precisely, that his chief traits are due to Christianity's inclusion of mythical literature), that the evidence surrounding the growth of the early church does not lead us infallibly to a historical founder, and that therefore Jesus Christ and Harry Potter might both be literary creations, which drew on the various mystical and spiritual traditions before them to present readers of their times with an engaging story.

Now that we've created space for the possibility of Jesus as a literary character, we can proceed to the more satisfying investigation of alternative, perhaps more fitting, theories about how the story of Jesus came about. Many researchers focus on the similarities between Christianity and paganism but fail to delve into what for me is one of the most exciting facets of this topic: where the common features came from, and what they actually mean. In the next several chapters we'll explore the symbols of the lion, the snake, the Ankh or Cross, the sheep, the death and resurrection, and argue that they were developed in response to astronomical observations, which later evolved into a mystical spirituality that included ideas of a suffering savior who promised eternal life.

## CHAPTER FIVE

# Jesus, the Lion King: Astrological Foundations and the Journey of the Sun

*"I am the light of the world; anyone who follows me will not be walking in the dark, but will have the light of life." –John 8:12*

IN THE FIRST SECTION OF THIS BOOK I challenged the traditional view of Jesus Christ, the historical figure, by noting the early historical debate over the physicality of his life and deeds. I've also tried to meet common criticisms and evidences that have been used to support the notion of a historical Jesus, and demonstrated that central themes in Christian folklore and practice relating to Jesus Christ are very similar to various older pagan deities, which may lead the impartial reader to the conclusion that Christianity extensively modeled on earlier organizations, customs and beliefs.

While all of this is necessary to even broach the topic, it does not go far enough. Enormous questions remain unanswered. Where did the shared symbols come from in the first place? Why didn't Christianity choose completely different symbols? Why did vastly diverse cultures often maintain central motifs in the story of their mythical heroes: the miraculous childhood, the escape from an evil ruler, growing up in the wilderness, symbolized by a lion and fighting against a serpent, coming of age to avenge his father, being captured, tortured, and put to death before rising up and defeating his enemies?

If the communities who worshiped these similar gods gave their saviors a new name, altered rituals, and even changed the allegorical meaning of their customs, why did the biographical events of the story stay so rigorously exact? And why can we find traces of this same story from Asia to South America?

The answer, as we will explore in this chapter, is that the commonalities in the stories come from a very ancient drama, which humans have been watching play out in the skies since the dawn of time – it is the annual story of the sun's passage through the heavens.

In modern society astrology is sometimes considered a fringe pseudo-science about as believable as the tooth fairy. However, humanity's earliest spiritual sentiments were developed from watching the changing skies, and expressed through astrological symbols. Stories about the constellations and the moving planets developed into tales of gods and goddesses, which later became world religions. Understanding ancient conceptions of astrology helps us to decode many mythological and religious traditions. For the present study it is important to recognize that for the original myth-makers, these symbols and astronomical occurrences were observed with religious devotion. As New Testament Professor Clinton Arnold makes clear:

> There can be no doubt about the existence of astrological beliefs in the first century. As with magic, astrology became an increasingly dominant spiritual force after the collapse of classical Greek religion in the fifth and fourth centuries B.C. An awareness of the movements of the stars was believed to give one the key to unlocking the mysterious outworking of fate. In popular belief, the stars and planets were thought to bear a close association with angelic intermediaries. This opened up the possibility of altering one's fate through manipulating the astral "powers." In this respect, astrology is closely connected with magic which sought to harness and utilize the power of these so-called deities. Helios (sun) and Selene (moon), the planets, and the twelve animal-type images in the heavens (the zodiac) were regarded

as most powerful. The rays of the sun and moon were also thought of as spirits, demons, or angels.[1]

While I will not claim that Jesus Christ is *just* a sun myth or solar deity, I hope to demonstrate that certain symbols and motifs found in Christianity can only be fully explained after exploring this ancient tale of the sun's journey. I will also establish that at least some early Christian communities associated Jesus with the sun (or previous solar deities) and deliberately incorporated astrological symbolism into their texts, rituals and practices.

In order to deepen our understanding of and exploration into the literature of Jesus Christ, this chapter will provide the astronomical background to humanity's oldest religious symbols and motifs, illustrate how the planets and constellations became anthropomorphized into gods and heroes, and affirm that certain elements found in Christianity can only be situated within the tradition of astronomical observation.

# Astrology in Ancient Times

It should come as no surprise that Greeks and Romans thought of the planets as gods – the names we use for them today are the Roman names given to these deities. In the massive space of the sky, these celestial orbs are distinctive in having autonomous movements and actions. Unlike the great masses of stars, which appear to move together as the earth turns, the planets alone have their own unique trajectory; giving the impression that they are free to move as they like or have some urgent business to attend to. The various hues, size and speed of these planets inspired their humanistic features.

**Mercury**
Messenger of the gods with winged feet; the fastest moving planet

**Venus**
Goddess of love and beauty; the brightest planet

**Mars**
God of war and bloodshed; the planet with a distinctive red hue

**Jupiter**
King of the gods; the largest planet

**Saturn**
Oldest god, ruler of time and agriculture; slowest moving planet

There is also Neptune, god of the sea and Pluto, god of the underworld – but these planets are modern discoveries and were named using appropriate figures from mythology. Finally there is the Sun, whose life giving energy is the benefactor of all life on earth, and the Moon, whose cooling nocturnal influence reflects the sun's light when he is away.

As ancient astronomers studied the skies, they found that the planets trace the same path annually. Every year, they pass through the same constellations, rise and fall on the same spots of the horizon, and routinely run into each other in small groups – easily leading people to wonder what they were up to.

Over the years, people began telling stories that explained their behavior and also allowed priests to forecast events and keep track of time. Elaborate myths were constructed, in considerable detail, chronicling the events, conflicts, reunions and challenges that the "gods" faced in their journeys.

At the same time, constellations were made by grouping nearby stars into recognizable figures, patterns and shapes, and held together in the tapestry of folklore. Great deeds and events, it was believed, merited "eternal life." Hence, heroes and their accompanying items or companions were said to have "ascended into heaven" – or been preserved eternally in the night sky.

Different cultures would adapt existing myths to create their own cultural heroes, redefining existing constellations. The sign of Ophiuchus "the snake bearer" for example, which for a brief time was considered the 13th zodiac sign between Scorpio and Sagittarius, was originally viewed by the Sumerians as their god

Enki. Later, Egyptians viewed him as Imhotep and the Greeks as Aesclepius. These diverse figures shared many of the same qualities, such as healing powers, and were all associated with the snake. (This sign made international news in January, 2011 after professor Parke Kunkle of the Minnesota Planetarium Society upset the world by claiming that all modern zodiac signs are wrong and need updating).

According to legend, both Imhotep and Aesclepius began their lives as mortals, accomplished great feats of healing and technological invention, and ascended into heaven (were immortalized by the gods as constellations).

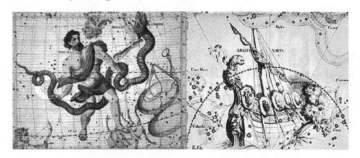

Likewise, the heroic journey of Jason and the Argonauts, who sailed through many hardships to bring back the Golden Fleece, was commemorated by preserving their vessel in the stars – right, as it should be, on the horizon of the ocean:

> More southern stars were visible to the ancient sailors of the Mediterranean than are visible today. Low on their horizon, in spring skies, there appeared the apparition of a great ship. This ship sailed ever westward skimming along the southern horizon. The ancient Greeks said it was Argo Navis, the ship sailed by Jason and his Argonauts in search of the Golden Fleece.[2]

The story of Perseus, Andromeda and Pegasus is also written in the stars; the three constellations spin around the night sky as the sea beast Cetus raises its monstrous head out of the ocean (the head of this constellation, more modernly viewed as a whale, rises above the horizon while its body remains out of sight). Cassiopeia, Andromeda's proud mother, sits sternly in her throne above the drama.

In today's night sky you can also find Lyra, the Lyre of Orpheus; and Crater, the cup of Dionysus – which later was interpreted as the Holy Grail. In the middle ages "Christianized" star maps were made reinterpreting these symbols into the current mythos.

All of these legends were considered to have begun with a real historical event; even in ancient times scholars attempted to attribute the myths to real kings or heroes (human figures) of the past. But let's not forget that for earlier civilizations, these were *living stories* with miraculous implications: the "proof" that they were true lay in the stars. The constellations were a record of humanity's greatest deeds and interactions with supernatural characters, and promised the possibility of eternal reward and glory for those who suffer or persevere in their pursuit of greatness.

And they were not simply bedtime stories; these planet-gods were the main objects of worship in ancient times. According to Iamblichus (c. AD 250-325) Egyptians believed in nothing else:

> Egyptians know of no other gods "but the planets and those stars that fill up the zodiac... and Robust Princes, as they call them." Eusebius says "that the very arcane theology of the Egyptians, deified nothing but stars and planets, and acknowledge no incorporeal principle or demiurgick reason as the cause of this universe, but only the visible sun... see now what is become of this arcane theology of the Egyptians, that defies nothing but senseless matter or dead inanimate bodies."[3]

It was also believed that the stars and planets had a physical connection and interaction with humanity. Understanding the heavens was seen as a kind of esoteric wisdom that could give users special powers: since the planets and stars influenced the affairs of men, understanding these subtle influences gave one control over them. Assman writes:

> A major part of the Egyptians' astronomical knowledge served specifically to measure time, especially the lunar month, whose beginning rested on observation, not calculation, as well as the hours, whose length varied – for day and night, from sunrise to sunset and sunset to sunrise, were always each divided into twelve segments of equal length. Above all, however, this knowledge was related to the course of the sun, which was conceived of as a journey through the sky and the netherworld and described down to the last detail. The oldest and most widely used Book of the Netherworld enumerates the 900 deities and beings who come nightly into contact with the sun god, precisely specifies the length of each of the distances he covers in one hour (eg 745 miles) and cites verbatim the words he exchanges with those in the netherworld. All this elaborate store of knowledge, so oddly compounded of observations, speculations, and mythological interpretations, had a cultic function.[4]

## The Sun Myth

For many early cultures, the sun was seen as the source of all life; an idea which, although scientifically precise, is often taken for granted today. According to an ancient Egyptian hymn which scholars have compared with Psalm 104 of the Old Testament, death comes when the sun sets or "hides its face":

> The world becomes on your hand, as you made them; when you dawn, they live, when you set, they die; you yourself are lifetime, one lives by you. (Akhenaten's hymn 111-114)

> Thou hidest thy face: they are troubled; thou takest away thy breath: they die and return to their dust; Thou sendest forth thy breath: they are created and thou renewest the face of the earth. (Psalm 104)

Of all the stories told about constellations and planets, the most important was the epic struggle of the sun with the forces of darkness. Each year, the sun defeated his enemies in the spring, rose to power and strength in the summer, and was overcome by darkness again in the fall. In the winter he was at his weakest, but people knew that somehow he would come back and save the world again.

The sun was usually depicted as male and had a female counterpart, the moon. Many cultures saw them as lovers, or sometimes twins, separated tragically and trapped in the cycle of time. The relationship between these two, the delicate balance, created and maintained the world. During solar eclipses, the pair were re-united, and their encounters generated life on earth.

One of the earliest written characters, found in pre-historic cave paintings, is the solar cross. The equilateral cross meant many things to early cultures, but at the earliest it was a probably a pictograph for the sun's rays. It is often found by a full circle, or a crescent, which stood for the moon. The solar cross is a composition of these two symbols. Another is the Egyptian Ankh.

Granted, these symbols have meant many things to many people. I will not suggest that people who use these symbols today are still worshiping the sun. At the same time, it is vital to notice how human spirituality developed and the astrological roots of the symbols used today.

In the fall of every year, the sun gets weaker and weaker. The seasons change, the crops die, and the ground freezes. Then in the spring, the sun comes back and saves life as we know it. This celestial struggle was elaborated with constellation folklore. The sun's enemy, the dark winter, was symbolized by a snake. This is because of the constellation Hydra, the primordial sea-serpent, which at one point spread all the way across the night sky and even today remains the largest constellation. With night came the Hydra chasing the sun away, and in the morning the sun returned to defeat the Hydra. It is a never-ending battle, being re-enacted even today. Thus, the serpent became a symbol of night, and was also considered the ruler of winter and darkness. In some cultures it represented evil; in others esoteric wisdom or knowledge.

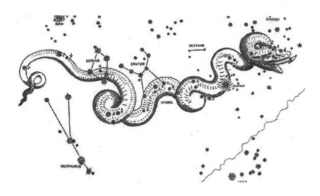

Cultural myths about heroes defeating monstrous snakes stem from the sun's conflict with darkness and winter, represented by the Hydra. Babylonian sun god Gizdhubar fought the dragon as Tiamat (as did Gilgamesh), Apollo slew the Python, and Zeus killed the Typhon. Even Yahweh in the Old Testament was given credit with defeating an ancient sea serpent, the Leviathan, although this story was probably taken from descriptions about Baal killing the serpent Lotan in Northern Canaan.

The story becomes a romance when we add in the figure of the moon. The moon was the sun's lover, lost or trapped in darkness, guarded over by the Hydra. The sun was always trying to find and rescue her. There are numerous versions of this story in mythology – a young hero has to enter into "the kingdom of death," or hell, or Somewhere Really Dangerous, and kill a big snake of some kind to save his love. The sun is usually defeated or killed before his journey is through, but escapes or resurrects in order to win the final battle.

Another important constellation is Leo, the Lion. Leo is the constellation of the sun; the constellation that the sun is exalted in (the sun is in Leo in the middle of summer, when it is strongest). For this reason, while winter and darkness are represented by a snake, summer, light and the sun are represented by a lion. As snakes slither underground, the sun is flying over our heads in the sky; his "kingdom of light" is above us, while the "kingdom of darkness" is below. This is why the personified sun is usually depicted with wings of some kind: a magical flying horse (Perseus saving Andromeda, above left), wings on his hat or feet (Hermes, Mercury), or a flying chariot (Appollo) so that he can get around more conveniently. In other versions, wings are presented in the form of a pet bird or winged sidekick. In the picture of Hercules killing the Hydra, (above right), he is shown both with a lion's head mask and wings, just like the Griffin – a lion with the wings and the beak of an eagle – which is also a sun symbol.

Myths about the moon are sometimes blended with stories about the constellation Virgo, which is right next to Hydra and comes into the sky at the same time as it does. Virgo is the 2nd largest constellation, only a little smaller than Hydra, and the constellation was worshiped as a great goddess. Due to their close positions, myths about her always involved Hydra. Hydra is also a feminine constellation (the masculine form would be Hydrus), and sometimes these two great constellation were merged to create a larger symbol of night; a creature with the tail of a serpent and the upper body of a woman.

Meanwhile, the constellation Leo immediately precedes Virgo in the night sky and seems to be escorting her past the treachery of Hydra. This is why, invariably, mythological sun saviors slay great serpents to save virtuous maidens. Their weapon of choice is almost always a sword, probably because it takes the same shape as a cross; the oldest known symbol of the sun.

Hydra, Leo and Virgo, shown together in a star map by Andreas Cellarius, c. 1660AD

As we have seen, certain constellations (Leo, Virgo, Hydra) were often featured in the sun myth. However there were others. The most important were the 12 signs of the zodiac. The zodiac signs are the constellations of stars that mark the sun's path and have been used for at least 6,000 years to keep track of time. The Western zodiac signs are often seen in churches, catacombs, and Greco-Roman temples.

The zodiac refers to the signs that lie behind the sun's apparent path. Each month, the sun is passing in front of 1 of the 12 signs. It is from the word "Zodiac" – which literally means *circle of animals* – that we get the modern word "zoo."

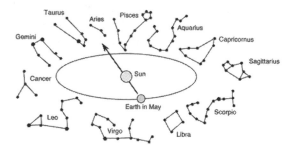

Stories about the sun often include zodiac animals in the course of the hero's quest; as the sun carved its path through the twelve zodiac signs, the hero would encounter or challenge the symbols which represented each sign. Krishna, for example, was chased by a snake and kills both a bull and a lion.

In Ovid's *Phaethon*, the Greek sun god Helios promises his mortal son a gift, because he feels guilty for never spending time with him. The boy begs for a chance to drive his father's golden chariot, which races across the sky bringing light to the world. Helios, knowing that only he can control the powerful horses, tries to dissuade his son.

> Are you fancying that there are all sorts of wonders up there, cities full of Gods and beautiful things? Nothing of the kind. You will have to pass beasts, fierce beasts of prey, and they are all that you will see. The Bull, the Lion, the Scorpion, and the great Crab, and all will try to harm you. (Ovid, *Metamorphoses II, Phaethon*)

Hercules, often portrayed wearing a lion skin, is most famous for his twelve labors, which correlate to the twelve signs of the zodiac (although the specific acts seem to refer only to summer and fall constellations).

1. Slay the Nemean Lion and bring back its skin
2. Slay the Lernaean Hydra
3. Capture the Ceryneian Hind
4. Capture the Erymanthian Boar
5. Clean the Augean stables in one day
6. Slay the Stymphalian Birds
7. Capture the Cretan Bull
8. Steal the Mares of Diomedes
9. Obtain the Girdle of Hippolyte
10. Obtain the Cows of Geryon
11. Steal the Apples of the Hesperides
12. Capture Cerberus

Many other figures face similar challenges. These constellations "come out" or are more visible in the dark winter months. The boar that killed Attis and Adonis (Osiris was also dismembered by Seth under a wild boar), and which Hercules must also capture is Khrysaor, son of Medusa, who often took the shape of a winged boar and presided over the summer months (the harvest season). Vegetation gods die or are cut down under this month, due to the harvest. You can still find this tusked, charging boar constellation in modern star maps. Taurus, the bull is visible in September and October along the eastern horizon, but the most favorable time to observe Taurus in the night sky is during the months of December and January. Heroes associated with the sun like Mithras, Dionysus, and Gilgamesh overcame or destroyed the bull, symbolically ending winter.

## Birth of the Sun

Although the great triumph of the sun was during the spring, there are four turning points which held monumental significance for ancient cultures. These points are related to the apparent path the sun travels, called the ecliptic, and the line of the equator projected into space, or the celestial equator. If you imagine that the earth stands still, the sun seems to go around the earth following a set path. Astronomers would calculate dates by looking at the constellations behind this line, and so marking it on star charts and world maps was a common practice. This is the ecliptic.

The celestial equator is equally important. If the equator were projected into space, it would cross the ecliptic in two places. These spots are exactly the points where the transitions between spring and fall occur. During the spring equinox, the sun crosses the equator heading north, making the days longer than the nights. During the fall equinox, the sun crosses going south, making the days shorter than the nights.

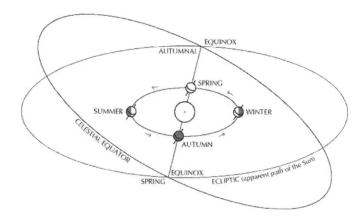

In the winter, less and less light from the sun reaches the earth, causing cool weather. The sun is at its farthest away (south) from the celestial equator. Due to the earth's tilt, the sun will appear to "stand still" here for three days before heading north again. This takes place on December 21st, the winter solstice. The opposite occurs six months later during the summer solstice on June 21st. The sun has reached its farthest point north of the celestial equator, and after a brief pause, begins moving south.

Sites of megalithic stone structures such as Stonehenge in England or the older L-Imnajdrasite in Malta (c. 3000BC) are oriented astronomically, aligned with the rising sun during solstices and equinoxes. In 1998 scientists discovered the huge stones slabs of Nabta in the Sahara desert of Egypt, which have been dated to around 4000BC, making them the oldest astronomical megaliths in the world. These sites demonstrate that the sun's movements were noted and deemed considerably important even in prehistory. Although the sun doesn't actually move, it is possible to mark the changing seasons based on where it rises or sets on the horizon. This is how megalithic structures function: a little hole is drilled marking the spot of the horizon where the sun will rise on one specific day of the year. Imagine this point on the horizon like a giant pendulum. Every day, it will move a little to the left or right, approaching one of the solstices. When it reaches the end of its path, it has to "slow down" and go back the other way. It will be seen on the same spot of the horizon for three days, before beginning to move in the opposite direction. On December 22nd, the winter solstice, (midnight of the 21st), the sun appears to stop moving. Early civilizations mythologized this event as a "death" of the sun – darkness had triumphed. But only three days later, at midnight on December 24th, the sun appeared to begin moving again. This was a "birth" of the new sun (and also a "resurrection" of the old sun), which would someday challenge the rulers of darkness and re-create the kingdom of light. This victory comes on the spring equinox, when light returns to triumph over darkness.

The astronomical alignment of ancient monuments show that December 25th was marked as a special day for thousands of years before the advent of Christianity. In the face of a long winter, it was celebrated as a time for hope in the eventual return of life and light. That December 25th was originally a pagan holiday is generally well known, but not everyone realizes that it was a birthday celebration for the infant sun. On December 24th, the priests waited for a sign that the sun had returned, so that they could announce the birth of a divine child. The sign the priests saw was probably the star Sirius, one of the brightest stars in the winter sky, which rises just before dawn. Edward Carpenter confirms this in *Pagan and Christian Creeds*:

> The coming of Sirius therefore to the Meridian at midnight became the sign and assurance of the sun having reached the very lowest point of his course, and therefore having arrived at the moment of his re-birth.[5]

If this name sounds familiar, you might recall that "Sirius" is also the name of Harry Potter's godfather. As Hans Andréa from *Harry Potter for Seekers* notes:

> When Jesus was born, a star appeared in the east. When Harry was born, Sirius became his God-Father. Both boys had a star rise at their birth. He who understands the language of symbols will see that these two things are identical![6]

People in those days believed that every night, the sun rested in a vast subterranean cave before rising again in the East. Therefore this "birth" of the sun was pictured underground, in a cave, or sometimes a manger. Late to the birth were three wise men following a star. Many traditions have called the three stars of Orion's belt the "kings" or "magi." They form a direct line to Sirius and appear to follow him straight to the birthplace of the sun. Try to find them early on Christmas morning – they'll be the brightest stars you see.

## The Wicked Ruler

Although the sun had been born, winter was just beginning. On December 22nd, the winter solstice marks the moment when Saturn, the slow moving king of winter, assumes his thrown, for a three month rule of tyranny, cold and darkness. (The 22nd is the beginning of Capricorn. Just as Leo's ruling planet is the sun,

Capricorn's ruling planet is Saturn.)

Saturn, or in Greek, Chronos, was the father of time – from him we get words like "Chronology." In the picture below, Saturn is seen with his symbol, the scythe, and with a dragon biting its own tail; the symbol for infinity. The inevitable consequence of time, of course, is death. The modern day Grim Reaper, usually shown holding an hourglass or a lantern, is based on images of Saturn.

In the Greek version of the myth, Chronos began to eat all of his children after hearing a prophecy from Uranus that one of his children would overthrow him. After losing five children, his wife Rhea saved the 6th, Zeus, by feeding Chronos a stone wrapped in blankets. Zeus grew up in exile but came back in strength to challenge his father.

This event – the threat from an evil tyrant and escape of the infant hero – became a common literary motif; one especially shared by sun gods. Just three days after Saturn comes to power on December 22nd, the baby sun (who is predestined to overthrow his rule) is born on the 25th. Saturn gets nervous and "eats all his babies," or "orders a massacre of infants." Mythical stories that employ this attribute include Dionysus, Hercules, and even Moses. The infant son, however, is smuggled away safely, usually by his mother. This incident also begins the sun's travels: he is always moving, and generally going "up" and "down."

The sun grows up in exile, becoming stronger all the time. After Saturn has lost his power, the sun will return to challenge the ruler of winter and overthrow his kingdom. This happens on the spring equinox, when the day becomes longer than the night. The sun has been victorious, at least until the fall equinox, when darkness comes to power again. On December 22nd, the sun dies, is buried for three days, and "resurrects." Like the birth, this is depicted underground, or in a tomb. Of course, there are many variations: sometimes he descends into Hades for three days, sometimes he sleeps, sometimes he is imprisoned, and sometimes people just *think* he's dead. The clue is the length of time (3 days) and the date near one of the solstices or equinoxes.

Sun myth features are apparent in some of the stories we explored earlier. For example in the Egyptian version of the myth which was popular throughout the Roman Empire in the first two centuries AD, the moon goddess was Isis, while Osiris and Horus were both aspects of the sun. Isis was considered a "virgin" because her consort is also her son; originally she needs to somehow get pregnant by herself. Later, she gives birth to Horus on December 25th (although as we saw the 23rd might have been used much earlier) and he grew up to become Osiris, his mother's lover. At this time Isis' brother Set was in power. Set was a figure of darkness, and in later traditions became identified with Typhon, the giant serpent. Set killed Osiris and scattered his body parts down the banks of the Nile.

Set wanted to kill the child Horus also, fearing that he would someday usurp his throne. Luckily, Isis was warned in time to flee and conceal the child. At the Spring Equinox, while Horus was returning to defeat darkness, Osiris had already died and needed to be resurrected. Isis collected all of Osiris' body parts (except the penis, which was eaten by a fish) and brought him back to life. At the same time, Horus grew into manhood and defeated Set to avenge his father, freeing Isis from Set's tyranny. Horus took his father's place, and became Osiris. He and Isis would give birth to a new Horus the next year, restarting the cycle.

# The Lion King

It may seem very foreign to give human characteristics to the sun, but you are far more familiar with this story than you know. This is because for centuries, and increasingly in the past few decades, modern stories have revolved around solar mythology. (This is mostly because our greatest story-tellers, from Disney to Lewis to Tolkien, have been well-versed in classical studies). As mentioned previously, the sun rules the zodiac sign of Leo, the Lion. The yellow color of this animal, as well as his flowing mane, have made it an ideal symbol for the sun – although the real reason is that the sun is considered to be at the peak of its "rule" during the hot summer months of July and August, when the sun crosses the constellation Leo. Historical and mythological figures, in order to elevate them to a divine status, were often affiliated with lions for this reason. Modern-day heroes and popular re-tellings of classical literature sometimes include the same symbols: the lion for goodness and light and the snake for evil and darkness. In fact, the easiest way to spot a sun-myth is to look for snakes and lions. Because the sun flew through the sky, he was given wings, a winged chariot, or a flying companion that symbolized his dominion over the air.

Many figures in contemporary literature, including J.K. Rowling's Harry Potter, continue to act out the ancient motif. Harry is marked as a sun god by his placement in Gryffindor, whose emblem is a lion (or rather, a Griffin – a winged lion). He also has his characteristic mark, the lightning bolt on his forehead; the symbol of Zeus. He can fly, with a broomstick, and is also sometimes helped by Dumbledore's phoenix. Like the sun, an evil power threatens him at birth and he is hidden away in obscurity. He battles the basilisk, an enormous snake, with a magical sword, in order to save the lost maiden, Ginny. Eventually he will defeat Lord Voldemort and end the threat of darkness altogether – although he has to pay for it with his own life.

If you saw the 2004 movie *Alexander* by Warner Brothers, you probably remember that Alexander's mother, played by actress Angelina Jolie, kept poisonous snakes around her, and the young Alexander was surrounded with snakes as a child. But did you notice that Alexander's helmet is a lion? Or the scene when, to be even more explicit, he is wearing an actual lion's head? Alexander is also accompanied by a pet eagle, and seems to have some psychic connection with it. Alexander strays farther away from his kingdom, where he is strong, and grows weaker and weaker until his own followers betray him.

The newest *Peter Pan* movie (2003, live action version) is also full of sun symbolism. In the beginning of the movie, "Never Never Land" is frozen in a deep winter and the pirates' ship is stuck in ice. Spring hits fast and hard, and the ice melts, letting the pirates know that Pan (the sun) has come back. Peter can also fly, of course, and instead of a phoenix is accompanied by Tink, a winged fairy. Peter battles Hook with a sword to save Wendy from the pirates, so she can be mother to the boys. And although the giant alligator is Hook's enemy, the creature is an effective representation of Hydra, the water serpent. There is also a significant scene, where the weather gets nasty because Peter is sad over Tink's death. The pirates think Pan is dead, and that they have won, only to have him reappear triumphantly.

In the first Narnia movie (2005), based on the original chronicles by C.S. Lewis, Aslan is an obvious sun-savior who has to battle with the queen of winter to restore life and spring to Narnia. He meekly allows himself to be captured and tortured only to be instantly resurrected and continue the fight. Although many Christians consider Narnia to be a wholesome family movie, and Aslan to be a portrayal of Christ, all of the ideas in Narnia stem from the sun myth, which predates Christianity by thousands of years. (Lewis' contemporary, Tolkien, criticized Narnia for being an "irritating blend of different cultural traditions."[7])

The "discovery" of Aslan's resurrection in *The Lion, the Witch and the Wardrobe* is actually the discovery of the empty rock where Aslan's body had been – which is shown with the rising sun directly behind it; the rising sun is used as an allegory for the resurrection of Aslan (and, for those who wish to further interpret, for the resurrection of Jesus). However, in fact the converse may be true – that Jesus' resurrection has always been a symbol of the rising sun.

When the sun reaches his highest point on the summer solstice, he is depicted as the king of kings, seated on a throne and wearing a purple robe and a crown of golden rays. At the time when these stories developed, the summer solstice was actually in the sign of Leo. The sun could easily be identified as a "lion king."

Not surprisingly, Disney's animated motion picture "The Lion King" (1994) captures the sun myth surprisingly well. Simba can't fly himself, but he is always near his winged chaperone, the toucan Zazu. In the first five minutes, we are inundated with sun references. The infant king is anointed with the juice of a fruit that has been lifted up to the sun, the clouds part and a single beam of sunlight illuminates the child. The catchy opening song mentions "the sun rolling high in a sapphire sky." Some viewers have argued that the Lion King plot is based on Shakespeare's *Hamlet*, but Shakespeare most likely drew his ideas from Greek stories like Oedipus, whose tale also includes sun symbolism.

While Simba is still young and dreaming of being ruler, ("I just can't wait to be king"), there is a quip about the king of kings having so little hair. Some sun gods, when they reached maturity, were shown with long flowing hair to symbolize their strong rays of light, and short hair when they were newborn or weak. This is the reason that Samson, a biblical sun figure, was defeated by the winter goddess Delilah when she cut off all his hair. This is also why, when Aslan had his mane cut off by his enemies, it instantly grew back once he resurrected. A fourth century writer records an Egyptian ritual with a similar motif:

> In their desire to make a dedication specifically to the Sun himself the Egyptians have fashioned a figure whose head is shaven except for the hair remaining on the right side. The retention of these hairs teaches that in our world the Sun is never covered up. The hair which has been removed bears witness through the roots which stay that even when we do not see this heavenly body it still possesses the property of coming forth again like hair.' (Macrobius, end of 4th century AD)[8]

Soon after, Mufusa tells Simba, "A king's time as ruler rises and falls like the sun. Someday, the sun will set on my time here and will rise with you as the new king." Mufusa's brother, Scar, is the ruler of death, or winter. He's in league with evil hyenas, and plots with them in a fiery cave full of dancing skeletons. Scar succeeds in killing Mufasa, but Simba escapes into exile. The whole land falls into darkness and shadow when Scar takes over, but Simba grows up quickly outside of the kingdom. Simba runs into Nana, who thinks he's back from the dead, and they have a brief spring love affair. (The sun and moon are necessarily lovers, in order for the new sun to be born each year). Simba is still struggling with the death of his father, but Rafiki the monkey-priest tells him, "He's alive, and I'll show him to you. You are your father. You are the same. He lies in you."

Simba journeys home through the wilderness landscape that had once flourished under his father's rule. The land is destroyed now and everyone is starving, on the brink of death. When Simba returns, they assume he is Mufasa back from the dead. There is a battle between Scar and Simba, now exactly the same size and strength. They exchange blows, and finally Simba grows a little bigger and wins. This fight demonstrates the spring equinox, when the hours of sunlight struggle with and then surpass the hours of darkness. "It is time," says Rafiki. A cooling rain falls as the new king climbs majestically up to his place of power on the throne. A skull is washed away, signifying the end of winter, and the earth springs to life again. At the end of the movie, Simba and Nana have a new child and repeat the cycle.

You may have heard of another lion king, Jesus of Nazareth, also called the "Lion of Judah" and the "King of Jews." Jesus has many symbols, one of which is the white dove; and, feathers or no, he has no trouble defying gravity. Like the sun, Jesus had to hide from an evil ruler soon after his birth, because King Herod heard a prophecy concerning a future king. Jesus refers to himself as the light of the world, and his enemy, Satan, is represented by the symbol of the serpent. Jesus comes to save his love, the Holy Mother Church (the earth-bound communities of those faithful to Jesus are always collectively feminine). He uses the symbol of an upright cross, which looks just like a sword, to defeat his enemies.

The question now is to explore how deeply these symbols go in the story of Jesus, and whether they came from the sun myth either unconsciously or deliberately. If inclusions were accidental, or later additions, then we should be able to take them away from the figure of Jesus Christ without any ill-effect; without changing the basic core structure of Christian belief. However, we will see that astrological symbolism permeates the gospel story in such a way that it is unlikely to be coincidental, and also impossible to extricate it from "the real Jesus."

## The Jesus Zodiac

Before King Herod tried to find and kill the infant Christ, who was smuggled safely into Egypt, a Pharaoh tried to kill the infant Moses, who also survived. Both returned to triumph over their adversaries. Before either of them came Horus and many others, all based on the sun myth. In the most recent adaptation of this story, the infant Harry Potter survived an attack from his enemy Voldemort, went into hiding, and likewise came back to challenge his would-be murderer.

Only two of the four biblical gospels even include a birth story, and there are few scholars today who would deny that they were copied wholesale from pagan mythology. However, there is much more to say about Jesus than his miraculous birth. In this section, I'll explain how the biographical details in the gospel account of Jesus Christ may be based on observations of the sun, and how specific symbols identified with the Christian movement like the crucifixion, the lamb and the fish also came from astrology.

What follows is an "astrological exegesis" of the life and ministry of Jesus. It may sound far-fetched at first; however the fact that the gospel story presents us with the exact figures, numbers, motifs and animals needed to construct this interpretation is, in itself, extremely telling. Moreover, as we will see, the interpretation of Jesus' ministry as symbolizing the annual journey of the sun was confirmed and approved of by some very early Christian writers.

After the infant sun ran away from the powerful ruler (Saturn), we hear nothing about him until he is grown into adulthood. Jesus also leaps from a child to a 30 year old man in the gospels, apparently because there is nothing worth mentioning during the early part of his life. Many authors have written about where Jesus might have spent these years, failing to appreciate the nature of mythological literature. When specific numbers are used in mythology, they are rarely random; instead they help preserve astronomical trivia and are a way of passing on wisdom to those who could decode their meaning. In the sun myth, the number 30 has an astrological significance.

There are 360 degrees in the zodiac wheel, giving each of the 12 signs exactly 30 degrees (each section is called a Semisextile). Saturn's reign is finished at the end of Capricorn, which means that after 30 degrees, the sun can come out of hiding. For a real man, 30 years is a long time, but for the sun myth, the number 30 only represents the degrees of Capricorn and is just 1/12th of the distance the sun will have to go. This is the reason why the first 30 years of the sun savior are only the very beginning of the story.

By the end of January, the sun has escaped the persecution of Saturn, but he is still weak and the weather is cold. Climbing up to the celestial equator, and defeating his enemies by crossing over it and ending winter, will be his final struggle and challenge. This process is often tied to the number forty, which like the years of the sun's age, has an astrological significance. The winter solstice in the sign of Capricorn lies 16 degrees below the celestial equator.

The spring equinox in the sign of Aries, where the sun will triumph over darkness, is 24 degrees above the celestial equator. Starting from his birth in Capricorn, the sun must climb a total of 40 degrees (16+24=40) before he escapes from the clutches of winter. According to Malik H. Jabbar in *The Astrological Foundation of the Christ Myth*:

> This term forty represents the struggle of the sun in the wilderness, climbing toward salvation. With Israel, it was forty years in the wilderness, and with Noah, it was forty days of torrential rain, but regardless, the symbolism is the same; the plight of the young sun in the valley of Amenta, the Nether World, fighting his way to cross the forsaken territory between the zodiacal sign of the winter solstice and the spring equinox.[9]

Jesus begins his ministry by spending forty days in the desert being tested by the devil. Like the sun, he then passes through Aquarius, the Water Bearer (baptism by St. John, portrayed with flowing hair and a jug of water) and Pisces, the Fish (calling his first fishermen disciples to become "fishers of men") before he can be exalted at the spring equinox in the beginning of Aries, the Ram (as the crucified lamb of God.) After climbing these forty degrees, the sun is finally strong enough to defeat the darkness that has plagued him since birth. The length of days and nights on the spring equinox are exactly equal, but after the long battle that marks this day, the sun will be the victor. Crossing the celestial equator on the spring equinox was seen as the sun's definitive triumph over evil, but it was also viewed as a kind of perpetual suffering.

Every year the sun had to face the same enemies, suffer defeat, and fight to regain his kingdom. Many myths illustrate the idea of the sun leading a life of toil for mankind, who brought light and life to the world at great personal cost. Tragic figures like Sisyphus, who was forced to push a boulder up a hill and then let it roll back again for eternity, or Prometheus, bound to a rock so his liver could be eaten every day, may represent the perpetual toil of the sun. Although climbing over the celestial equator is just one piece of the sun's never-ending torment, it became a symbol for his great sacrifice.

As we already know from Justin Martyr, Jesus was not the first to be crucified; many sun saviors met their deaths on a cross of some kind, or else were hung from trees or nailed to boulders. (Osiris was locked in a coffin that got stuck inside the trunk of a tree that was later used as a temple pillar.) While these grim endings may appear dissimilar, drawings or representations of these saviors usually show them in an X or cross-shaped position.

The argument can be made that the motif of "crucifixion" comes from astronomy. The ecliptic, or path of the sun, crosses over the celestial equator at an angle, making the shape of an X. Plato, in his dialog, "Timaeus," said that when the Creator of the universe first formed the cosmos, He shaped its substance in the form of the letter X: the intersection between the sun's apparent path and the celestial equator.[10]

The massive event of critical importance, signifying the triumph of the sun and the end of winter, takes place on this cross. Many heroes met their fate with this cross, including the Greek King Sixion and St. Andrew, underscoring their divine status.

Here someone might interject that Jesus was crucified on a vertical cross, like the one worn by modern Christians; but there is no evidence for this. More likely, Romans would have used a T-bar shaped cross because they were easier to build. However, Jesus Christ may not have been crucified any more than Dionysus was actually ripped apart and eaten by his followers. The vertical cross is a spiritual symbol referring to a specific restorative salvation, not a historical fact.

The sun continues upwards until he reaches his northern-most peak at the beginning of summer. The summer solstice is the height of the sun's glory and the beginning of his reign, but he has also reached the end of his path and will begin to regress. He may warn that his enemies will overthrow him, or that he has to leave but will return again. On the fall equinox, when the night is again longer than the day, the sun is weakened, captured, and taunted.

Just as the sun had to wait thirty degrees after his birth before beginning his mission, he also has to go through the last thirty degrees that lead to his death. After passing through the twelve signs, he is delivered to his death at the beginning of Capricorn by the sign Sagittarius. For each degree that Sagittarius gains, the sun is closer to his death, leading to the idea of a betrayer who gets paid off to lure the sun to his death. In the gospels this is Judas, who sold Jesus to his enemies for thirty pieces of silver. Some scholars contend that Judas represented the sign of Scorpio, who is lord of the fall equinox. In this case, Judas leads Christ to his enemies at the beginning of the fall season, where he is tormented and afflicted for three months until his death at the hands of Sagittarius on the winter solstice. (Matthew relates the number thirty to the Worthless Shepherd of Zecharaiah 11:12-13, in an attempt to fulfill Jewish prophecy.)

When the sun reaches the winter solstice and holds still for three days, he has died and been buried in the tomb or cave where he began. He will remain in the underworld, in the land of the dead, or in the tomb, for three days, until he begins his return. While maintaining the three-day hiatus, some versions of the sun myth placed the death and resurrection together in the spring in order to tie it into the great victory reached when the sun crosses over the celestial equator.

## The Lamb of God

Besides the lion, the animal most often associated with Jesus is the lamb. The choice of this animal, along with nearly all other Christian symbolism, comes from constellation mythology. As the sun passes through the twelve zodiac signs, the four signs that govern the four cardinal events in the sun's journey are the most significant. Of supreme importance is the sign under which the sun crosses the celestial equator on the spring equinox. Astrological ages are named after this sign. For example, today we are somewhere at the end of the age of Pisces, because Pisces is the sign behind the sun when it crosses its midway point in the spring. Due to a slight imbalance in the earth's wobble, these four signs change roughly every 2,200 years, in a gradual process called the precession of the equinoxes. It takes an entire 26,000 years for all twelve signs of the zodiac to pass behind the place where the sun crosses the celestial equator during the spring equinox. Every 72 years we slip backwards 1 degree of the zodiac, meaning that soon we will be entering the age of Aquarius.

Before the present age of Pisces was the age of Aries from about 2400BC to 200BC, and before that was the age of Taurus from 4600BC to 2400BC. During that period, the spring equinox was in Taurus, the summer solstice in Leo, the winter solstice in Aquarius, and the fall equinox in Scorpio. Although Scorpio is today represented by the Scorpion, that part of the sky used to be represented by another constellation, the Eagle or Phoenix. The symbols that represent these signs – the Lion, Eagle, Bull and Man – are often found in religious and mythological texts that were developed during the age of Taurus.

### Age of Taurus, 4600BC - 2400BC

Fall Equinox: Scorpio                    Summer Solstice: Leo

Winter Solstice: Aquarius              Spring Equinox: Taurus

There are several references to these four animals in the Old Testament, which were later copied into the New Testament book of Revelation.

The first living creature was like a lion, the second like a bull, the third living creature had a human face, and the fourth living creature was like a flying eagle. (Revelation 4:7)

These four symbols, which represented the four seasons and the four elements (fire, earth, water, air), were later assigned to four specific apostles whose names were given to the four books of the gospels.

Matthew = Human
Mark = Lion
Luke = Ox
John = Eagle

These animals are often put into the corners of religious iconography to represent "the whole world." Among other things they correlate to the four houses at Hogwarts, the four children of Narnia, the four horsemen of the apocalypse, and the four suits of a deck of poker cards. The same four animals are shown in the esoteric Tarot tradition of A.E. Waite, a mystic who developed illustrations for his Tarot deck based on the writings of 19th century occultist, Eliphas Levi. In the "Wheel of Fortune" card, the Bull, Eagle, Man and Lion surround a wheel, which is ruled over by another lion with a sword that represents the sun controlling the universe. The dog-headed man is the constellation Orion, who has ties to the Egyptian god Osiris. The three stars of Orion's belt point to and follow the bright star Sirius, which is found in Canis Major, or the "big dog" constellation. The snake is Hydra, which appears to chase Orion around the world. Early Christian art uses many of the same motifs.

During the age of Taurus, bulls were sacred animals that figured prominently in religious worship and mythology. Sumerians regarded a bull as the bringer of spring, and the bull cult of Minoan Crete arose during this time. For Egyptians this was the period of Montu, the Bull, and it was also the time of the biblical golden calf. Taurus is a feminine earth sign, ruled over by the planet Venus, and goddess-centered religions flourished during this period. The ancient megaliths on the island of Malta for example are fertility goddess temples which were built and used doing the age of Taurus. When the sun rose in Taurus during the spring equinox, the bull became a symbol for the sun and shared his fate. Both were crucified on the celestial cross, sacrificing themselves to renew the earth. The blood of the bull became a sacrificial atonement for sins.

Later, this motif would be transformed into many bull-slaying deities like Mithras, whose great victory during the spring equinox depended on him defeating or passing through the bull. Mithras was often depicted driving his sword deep into a bull, clenching it like a massive lever, surrounded by the zodiac wheel. It is possible that besides representing the sun meeting the celestial cross under the sign of Taurus, Mithras was also seen as the divine force causing the precession of the equinoxes. His great act of slaying the bull would then also include ending the age of Taurus and rotating the zodiac wheel into the next sign. This is the view taken by Professor Religion David Ulansey in an article on the Mithraic Mysteries published by *Scientific American*:

> By killing the bull – causing the precession of the equinoxes – Mithras was in effect moving the entire universe. A god capable of performing such a tremendous deed would be eminently deserving of worship. Furthermore, the ability to move the cosmos would be seen as endowing Mithras with other powers as well, such as the ability to overcome the forces of fate residing in the stars and to guarantee the soul a safe passage through the planetary spheres after death.[11]

Mithras slew the bull with a sword, and it was this symbol, identical to an upright cross, that his followers imprinted on the round buns they used for their communion. To further clarify matters, sometimes the sword symbol was combined with an X shaped figure to show the cross of the celestial equator and ecliptic.

Symbolically, the act of slaying a bull with a sword is identical to crucifying it on a cross.

The astrological symbolism in Mithraism has been noted by several scholars. According to Burkert, "one literary text explains the killing of the bull in astrological terms as the sun passing through the sign of Taurus. This is the 'esoteric philosophy' of these mysteries, the author says, admitting that this is not the accepted meaning, but at the same time claiming that it comes from insiders of the cult."[12] Dowden affirms this view:

> Mithras, as he kills the bull, usually looks up and away – apparently to the sun-god with whom he is closely associated and for whom, maybe, he performs this vital feat: the sun is, after all, in the constellation Taurus ('Bull') in spring as life begins again.[13]

The age of Taurus was followed by the age of Aries, the Ram. Most of the symbols used in bull cults were adapted to reflect this shift. The lamb became a holy animal, identified with the sun and his celestial triumph. Like the bull, it died on the cross with the sun, and was considered a restorative offering. In ancient Egypt, lambs were sacred during this period, and sacrificed to the sun during the spring equinox. Linked to the sun's resurrection, the lamb was thought to have regenerative powers. In Egypt the lamb-sun god was called Amun, and many enormous temple complexes were built, with exact celestial precision, in honor of him. Pharaohs like Tut-ankh-*Amun* were named after this god to give them supernatural status. Amun, as the sun, is both the ram and the lion at the same time:

> He is the bas of Amun-Re, lord of Karnak, chief of Ipet-Sut, the ram with sublime face, who dwells in Thebes, the great lion who generated by himself, the Great god of the beginning... of whose nose the air comes forth, in order to animate all noses, who rises as sun, in order to illuminate earth.[14]

Many of the psalms in the Old Testament bear uncanny resemblance to Egyptian prayers to Amun, and it is possible that Christians to this day invoke this Egyptian god's name at the end of their prayers by saying "Amen." This word is commonly associated with truth, and used to mean "truly" or "verily." When the Old Testament was translated into English, the word "Amen" became "truth":

> That he who blesseth himself in the earth shall bless himself in the God of truth, and he that sweareth in the earth shall swear by the God of truth, because the former troubles are forgotten, and because they are hid from mine eyes. (Isaiah 65:16)

The Jewish communities spent a long time in Egypt (although even this has been disputed), and some of their religious ideas may have been taken from Egyptian practices. If you replace the original "Amen" in this passage and read it as a name, it can be seen as a psalm to the God of Amun, the lamb-headed sun god of Egypt. Even the concept of Israel in the Old Testament, made up of 12 tribes, shares remarkable similarity with the sun myth. As Mircea Eliade points out, citing from Josephus:

> We find a similar temporal symbolism as part of the cosmological symbolism of the Temple at Jerusalem. According to Flavius Josephus the twelve loaves of bread on the table signified the twelve months of the year and the candelabrum with seventy branches represented the decans (the zodiacal division of the seven planets into tens.) The Temple was the imago mundi; being at the Center of the World, at Jerusalem, it sanctified not only the entire cosmos but also cosmic life is, time.[15]

The founder of the covenant, Abraham, was given a test to prove his obedience to God: he was asked to sacrifice his first and only son Isaac. At the last minute God intervened and provided a ram to use instead. This story may be an astrological myth about how Aries came to be stuck on the celestial cross (Genesis 22:1). In an interesting reversal of the Abraham tale, Yahweh later rescued Israel out of Egypt by killing all of the first-born sons among the Egyptians. Israelites were told to mark their doorways with the blood of a specifically prepared sacrificial lamb, so that Yahweh could take note of which homes to pass over during his ethnic cleansing (Exodus 12:1).

The Passover Lamb became an integral feature of Judaism until the destruction of the temple in Jerusalem; Exodus 12-13 gives careful instructions on how the lamb is to be prepared (roasted, without its head, feet, or inner organs being removed) and eaten (in haste: with your loins girded, your shoes on your feet, and your staff in your hand). Orthodox Christians in Italy and Greece continue to slaughter a lamb every year. Muslims follow similar procedures to prepare lambs for their own festival of sacrifice, Eid-ul-Adha, which is a commemoration of Abraham and Ishmael (in the Islamic version, it was Ishmael who was to be sacrificed).

## Age of Aries, 2400BC - 200BC

Fall Equinox: Libra                              Summer Solstice: Cancer

Winter Solstice: Capricorn                       Spring Equinox: Aries

Early Christians continued this practice, relating the Passover Lamb to Jesus' suffering on the cross, because it was placed on a cross-shaped spit made by the intersection of two sticks:

> The mystery, then, of the lamb which God enjoined to be sacrificed as the passover, was a type of Christ; with whose blood, in proportion to their faith in Him, they anoint their houses, i.e., themselves, who believe on Him... and that lamb which was commanded to be wholly roasted was a symbol of the suffering of the cross which Christ would undergo. For the lamb, which is roasted, is roasted and dressed up in the form of the cross. For one spit is transfixed right through from the lower parts up to the head, and one across the back, to which are attached the legs of the lamb. (Justin Martyr, Dialog with Trypho, 40)

This great wealth of symbolic background was readily available during the foundational periods of Christian history. Jesus would become the sacrificed son, and at the same time the ram God provided to save Isaac. He would also be identified with the sacrificial lamb of Passover. Like the sign of Aries on the ecliptic and the Passover Lamb on the spit, Jesus makes his great restoration on a cross. Like the lamb, his death was a great sacrifice, and his blood washed away sin. The details recorded in the gospels about his crucifixion were written deliberately in order to clearly bring out this identification.

Jesus had to die on the cross, for example, without having any of his bones broken, because God commanded that the Passover Lamb be without blemish or broken bones. However, it is difficult to crucify a man's body to a cross in such a way that the nails support his weight without breaking his bones, and it isn't likely that the Roman soldiers would have been extra careful with Jesus in order to fulfill Jewish prophecy. The gospel writers were more concerned with spiritual allegory than actual circumstances, and took liberties with their version of events.

Early Christian catacombs identify Jesus as the sun god tied to the precession of the equinoxes rather than a historical victim of crucifixion. One of the symbols used was the Chi-Rho, also called the "Monogram of Christ" because it is made up of the first two letters in the Greek word "Christos." It may also have been a solar symbol, and includes the X shaped cross as a symbol of the sun's triumph at the Vernal Equinox.

Instead of a crucified savior, the image of Christ often found in the catacombs is that of the Good Shepherd carrying a lamb over his shoulders, identifying him as a Lamb-God like Amun. Similar statues, along with the good shepherd motif, have been found to predate Christianity by centuries. A contemporary of Jesus, the Gnostic god Abraxas, was drawn with the age of Aries at his head and the age of Pisces at his feet. Some statues, like the one below made in Athens around 570BC, show the Good Shepherd with a calf, a remnant of the age of Taurus.

Jesus became not only the Good Shepherd, but also the sacrificial lamb itself. As the sun, he shared the fate of Aries when it met the celestial cross. His suffering there was an act of restoration, and Christians refer to being washed in the blood of the lamb for the forgiveness of sins, just as Attis' followers were washed in the blood of the bull. After the lamb, the next most popular symbol found in Christian catacombs is the fish – specifically, two fish swimming in opposite directions, or the zodiac glyph of Pisces. Early Christians identified themselves with this sign more than all others, calling each other "little fishes" and using symbols of fish to identify each other. As the mover of the equinoxes, it was Jesus' role to end the Age of Aries and begin the Age of Pisces.

Persian dualism is a faith of the Age of Aries (second-first millennia BC), which is the sign of the Sun's exaltation and Mars' rulership; so Mithras, the solar warrior, is still re-enacting the close of the previous age of Taurus (fourth-third millennia BC) by slaying the cosmic bull. All the Arien leaders are fighters: the ram-horned Moses, Ammon and Mars/Ares himself. Jesus Christ, on the other hand, immolates the age of war in the only way possible: by sacrificing himself as the Ram or Lamb of God. In doing so he ushers in the Age of Pisces (second-first millennia AD), the era which cherishes in its heart an ideal of devotion and love.[16]

Although Christianity has tried to separate itself from its pagan beginnings, some customs have proved difficult to suppress. After nearly 2,000 years, we still use trees and wreaths, and give gifts during the "Dies Natilis Invictus Solis" – the birthday of the unconquered sun. And while many profess to worship the birth of Jesus on December 25th, it is not hard to compare the most popular Christmas icon, Santa Claus, flying around the world in one night on a magical flying sled bringing presents and good cheer, with Sol Invictus and his golden Chariot; or, with his lamp and white beard, as "father time" – a direct descendant of Saturn and Chronos.

Jesus has been so far removed from his roots that identifying him with a pagan sun cult may seem offensive even for non-Christians. For the early church however, it was all too easy to assign qualities of the sun myth to the Jesus story. In fact, at least one of the four gospels included in the Bible's New Testament may have been purposely structured to emulate the sun myth.

## Jesus through the Zodiac

Making these connections between Christianity and astrological symbolism may be intriguing – but is it *true?* How can we prove that it isn't all a big coincidence, or that Christianity didn't just blindly copy symbols from their contemporaries without also importing the esoteric meaning? While Christianity could have borrowed the symbolism and immediately reinterpreted everything as relating to their personal, historical savior and founder, devoid of any astrological associations, it appears that some early Christians deliberately identified Jesus with the sun. Problematically, the gospels themselves, upon which the paradigm and conception of the familiar, personal, human figure of Jesus Christ is based, may have been originally constructed with deliberate astrological associations.

Of the four gospels in the New Testament, Matthew, Mark and Luke largely share the same stories and parables, but the order varies with each one. In Matthew's version of events, the parables and imagery appear to be arranged to match the progression of the sun through the zodiac. The following exegetical exercise is in no way given as proof; this is only a theoretical interpretation. Nevertheless, it is pertinent and interesting. Moreover, given the (already established) likelihood that gospel writers were familiar with similar pagan cults, who were openly associated with solar worship, and given the extent of astrological influence that pervaded Greek and Roman spirituality, it should not be surprising if the gospel writers recognized and expanded upon these parallels.

In Matthew, the parables of Jesus' life are grouped into themes that match either the symbol or the influence of the zodiac signs. The imagery changes with the seasons and completes exactly a one year cycle, from December to December. Either the actual zodiac animal or the traits of the zodiac sign are used to keep the order. In some cases only a hint of the weather gives us an indication of the time of year, as if the author were trying to leave subtle clues. Notice the chronological order of the verse numbers.

**Aquarius, the Water Bearer – Matthew 3:13 (January).** Although modern astrology begins with Aries, the first sign the sun encounters after his birth in Capricorn is Aquarius. This constellation is shown as a solitary figure with long hair, living in the wilderness of winter, pouring water from a vase. Jesus begins his ministry with his baptism at the hands of John, who is often portrayed standing in a river with long hair, pouring water out of a vase. John also lives alone in the wilderness, like Aquarius.

**Pisces, the Fish – Matthew 4:18 (February).** Jesus calls his first disciples. They are fisherman, mending nets and fishing boats. Jesus tells them they will now be fishers of men.

**Aries, the Ram – Matthew 5-11 (March).** Aries is ruled by Mars, the Roman god of aggression and war. Jesus asserts his growing power and gives his first sermon, the Sermon on the Mount. He pities the crowd of people, calling them sheep without a shepherd. Jesus cautions against pride and anger, (both traits of Aries) but also admits that he came not to bring peace, but the sword. Jesus also asks us to look at the birds of the sky and think of the flowers in the field, demonstrating that it is spring.

**Taurus, the Bull – Matthew 11:28 (April).** "Come to me, all you who labor and are overburdened, and I will give you rest. Shoulder my yoke and learn from me, for I am gentle and humble of heart, and will find rest for your souls. Yes, my yoke is easy and my burden light." This curious metaphor is wedged into the story abruptly, and has no parallels in the other gospels, nor anywhere else in the Bible, although it is similar to bull-centered cults like that of Attis and Mithras. Its inclusion at just this point, rather than anywhere else, is necessary to preserve the zodiacal order.

**Gemini, the Twins – Matthew 12:1 (May).** This is a sign of restlessness, communication, and inconsistency. The Pharisees began to plot against Jesus, trying to trap him with loaded questions about Jewish law. Jesus says, "Everyone who is not with me is against me." His disciples pick ears of corn from the stalks, showing it is early summer and the harvest has not yet begun.

**Cancer, the Crab – Matthew 12:25 (June).** Cancer is a water sign and represents domestic life. Jesus uses three parables here. The first is a reference to Jonah and the whale. The next two concern the home and family, both within the influence of Cancer.

**Leo, the Lion – Matthew 13:1 (July).** It is late summer now, and time for the harvest. Jesus speaks about "reaping the rewards of what you sow." His parables are about the sower, the darnel, the mustard seed, and the yeast.

**Virgo, the Virgin – Matthew 13:53 (August).** Virgo is concerned with order, cleanliness and purity. Jesus quarrels with scribes over purity laws, saying, "What goes into the mouth does not make anyone unclean; it is what comes out of the mouth that makes someone unclean." This section also begins a new chapter, called "First Fruits of the Kingdom." The harvest is over and it's time to prepare for winter. Two separate miracles of loaves are here. People are hungry and Jesus produces bread for them.

**Libra, the Scales – Matthew 16:13 (September).** Libra's focus is on equality and justice. Jesus discusses heavenly rewards, rules and laws, judgment and financial matters. Topics include the danger of riches, the reward of renunciation, and the parable of the laborers in the vineyard. The themes of judgment and retribution come up frequently. This is also where Jesus casts the money changers, along with their fancy scales, out of the temple.

**Scorpio, the Scorpion – Matthew 12:18 (October).** This section begins with the story of a barren fig tree. Often used to demonstrate the power of faith, it is also another indication of the season. There is no fruit on the tree because it is fall. Scorpio is the sign of union and marriage, so it is not surprising we find the entire collection of wedding parables here. Jesus talks about the bride, the bridegroom and the wedding chamber. There is a feeling of urgency, as Jesus warns that the end is very near and we must be careful not to be locked out in the cold. He tells us that when he is gone, we need to help those who thirst, are hungry, sick or without clothes. *Winter is coming.*

**Sagittarius, the Archer – Matthew 26:36 (November).** Many sun gods, although crucified, were actually killed on the cross (or under a tree, like Krishna and Attis) by an arrow; symbolically combining the betrayer Sagittarius at the beginning of December with the cross of the celestial equator. Jesus is betrayed by one of the twelve disciples for thirty pieces of silver. When confronted by a group of armed men he asks, "Am I such a bandit that you had to set out to capture me with swords and clubs?" (In John's gospel, Jesus was killed by the soldier who stuck a lance into his side. "Lance" – Greek *belos* or Latin *telum* – can refer to any sharp object such as a spear, sword tip, or arrow.)

**Capricorn, the Goat – Matthew 26:57 (December).** Jesus is scourged, tried and crucified at "Calvary" (from the Latin *Calvaria*; original *Golgotha*) which means "place of the skull." The sun has reached its farthest, weakest point. There is an emphasis on darkness. "From the sixth hour there was darkness all over the land until the ninth hour," showing that it is December 21st, the darkest day of the year. Jesus is buried in a tomb, which is found empty three days later. He has been resurrected, and will come again in power.

Even if we ignore the astrological associations and only look at the seasonal clues, it is clear that the ministry of Jesus in this gospel lasted for one year and ended in December. But why, if Matthew shows his death in winter, do Christians celebrate Easter during the spring? Actually, many early Christians were also confused by this issue; enough of them, in fact, to make church fathers commit the heresy to ink and lasting memory:

> They endeavor, for instance, to demonstrate that passion which, they say, happened in the case of the twelfth Aeon, from this fact, that the passion of the Savior was brought about by the twelfth apostle, and happened in the twelfth month. For they hold that He preached only for one year after His baptism. (Ireneaus, *Against the Heresies*, II, 20)[17]

According to the Pseudo-Clementine Writings Jesus had 12 disciples because the sun has 12 months; while John had 30 chief men symbolizing the days of a lunar month.

> There was one John, a day-baptist, who was also, according to the method of combination, the forerunner of our Lord Jesus; and as the Lord had twelve apostles, bearing the number of the twelve months of the sun, so also he, John, had thirty chief men, fulfilling the monthly reckoning of the moon, in which number was a certain woman called Helena that not even this might be without a dispensational significance. (*Clementine Homilies*, 2.23)[18]

Although people soon began to see Jesus as a human figure, the sun symbolism nevertheless has influenced Christian art since its inception. In dozens of cathedrals across Europe and Africa, the center dome is decorated with a giant zodiac wheel, with Jesus in the center radiating light and his twelve apostles surrounding him in even sections.

The similarities between Jesus and other religions and philosophies of the Greeks and Romans are much more difficult to ignore now that we've discovered that, rather than accidental coincidences, they are intentional astrological symbols. Further, there were at least some Christians who understood the symbols and viewed Jesus Christ in astrological terms. Do the basics of the gospel story come from the same source as the other sun-saviors? It would certainly help to explain a passage in the gospel of Luke that identifies Jesus' herald, John the Baptist, as the prophet of the *rising sun*:

> And you, little child, you shall be called Prophet of the Most High, for you will go before the Lord to prepare a way for him, to give his people knowledge of salvation through the forgiveness of their sins, because of the faithful love of our God in which the rising Sun has come from on high to visit us, to give light to those who live in darkness and shadow dark as death, and to guide our feet into the way of peace. (Luke 1:76)

If constellations and the movements of the sun are the foundation for the biographical framework of the sun myth, how can we explain the similarities between the gospel stories and myths about other sun-saviors? Can we expand the idea of "diabolical mimicry" put forth by the church fathers, and claim that Satan put the sun and the planets in orbit in just such a way as to cast suspicion on the later ministry of Jesus Christ? Is Satan then, the real creator of the universe?

## Conclusions and Summary

Although most people consider sun-worship to be a superstitious and primitive practice, the truth is that we still worship the sun. Sitting your kids down in front of Peter Pan, Narnia or the Lion King is no different from attending a re-enactment of the adventures of Horus or Hercules 2,000 years ago. Harry Potter defeats his enemies with magic spells, and Jesus Christ overcomes his foes with miracles, but the symbolism from both stories comes from an ancient sun myth. Most of the world now takes "Sun Day" off as a day of rest, although the Jewish Sabbath was Saturday. (The practice of closing business on Sunday was enacted by Constantine in 321 AD and forms the basis of subsequent Christian legislation in this area.)

Even if the similarities between Jesus and pagan gods were accidental, how can we reconcile the evidence that many early Christians themselves worshiped Jesus as the sun? As we've seen, besides the many passages found in the Bible, there is also non-biblical evidence that Jesus was originally considered a sun myth by his followers.

If these events in the life of Jesus were taken from solar mythology, was the sun used as a metaphor to enhance Jesus' saving role? Or, conversely, was Jesus the metaphor – establishing a new current of sun-worship among the traditionally exclusivist Jews?

Some modern Christian communities, familiar with Christianity's inclusion of pagan symbolism, simply cut those features out of their worship. December 25th was not Jesus' real birthday, they counter, but that doesn't change his role as spiritual guide and savior. If we let go of the biographical details of the historical Jesus that are similar to solar worship, can we maintain, at the very least, the spiritual image of Jesus? Jesus as the first born, pre-existing son of god; Jesus as the forgiver of sins, as our spiritual comfort and companion; Jesus as the Word of God the creator and sustainer of the universe? To answer this question, we need to dig deeper into the roots of Christianity's spiritual claims and those of external religious traditions so we can see just how tightly they are wound together.

## CHAPTER SIX

# Meeting Satan Again
# for the First Time: Draco
# and the Creation Mythologies

*"And the great dragon was cast out, that old serpent, called the Devil, and Satan, which deceiveth the whole world: he was cast out into the earth, and his angels were cast out with him." –Revelation 12:9*

*"It is possible that mankind is on the threshold of a golden age; but, if so, it will be necessary first to slay the dragon that guards the door, and this dragon is religion." –Bertrand Russell*

IN THE LAST SECTION WE EXAMINED how the basic biographical details of Jesus Christ can be traced to an ancient story about the sun and demonstrated that for some Christians, identifying Jesus as a solar deity was all too easy. However there is much more to Christianity than merely the biographical details of its founder. The role of Jesus Christ is not restricted to his earthly ministry, his parables or his miracles. Jesus is considered in Christian ideology as *God's answer* to all the problems of the world – he is the solution to the problems of evil, suffering and death, which were brought into the world through original sin. For modern Christians, it is

Jesus' role as mediator, his divine son-ship, and his sacrifice for our sins that sum up the real purpose and message of his ministry. Jesus came to be regarded as the pre-existing Son of God, born in flesh; the "new Adam" to counteract the effects of Eve's original trespass; and even the creator and sustainer of the physical world. These are powerful spiritual ideas that cannot be overlooked in our study of Christian history. Where did these complex, philosophical ideas come from – if not from a human founder?

Like the details of the sun myth, however, the spiritual essence of Christian salvation can also be found in many pre-Christian belief systems, and when we explore the roots of these ideologies, we discover that they are also, to an extent, based on astrology. While many researchers have noted the inclusion of Greek or pagan philosophical concepts in the development of Christian theology, the link between these ideas and astronomical knowledge has been almost completely ignored. In this chapter I will assert that most core religious ideologies can be traced back to early responses to astronomical observation – specifically, regarding the constellation Draco.

## Draco, the Dragon

In the biblical story of Genesis (1: 1-31), God created the earth, stars, trees and animals before creating the first humans, Adam and Eve. Everything was made perfectly, according to His plan, and he announced that it was all very good. In the world He created, there was no death and no suffering, which suggests that time and the basic laws of physics hadn't yet been installed. It is only after the snake tempted Eve that the *real* world, with the moving planets and consequential seasons, came into being. This is further demonstrated by the penalties incurred from the fall; they are the characteristics of the natural world. Humanity would be cold and hungry, and there would be pain and death. They were given clothes to protect themselves from the weather and told that they must provide for themselves by the sweat of their brow.

Adam and Eve may have begun as symbols for the sun and moon. It is the moon, like Eve, that falls first into darkness, and it is the sun, like Adam, that follows her. Adam, like the sun, becomes an eternal enemy of the snake, and begins the daily cycle of light and darkness:

> I shall put enmity between you and the woman, and between her offspring and hers; it will bruise your head and you will strike its heel. (Genesis 3:15)

The Christian interpretation of the story of "Original Sin" is that God must be obeyed at all costs, and that the snake is a liar and deceiver. A different viewpoint however, could be that the snake was the real creator of the world as we know it – the world with time, sickness, labor and death. Besides the sudden harshness of life's realities, it seems that Adam and Eve also gained self-consciousness from eating the apple; they became aware that they were naked, and felt fear and shame for the first time. They covered themselves with leaves and hid from God.

Thus, through the meddling of the serpent, Adam and Eve separate from God and each other, while at the same time setting the universe in motion and beginning the cycle of time. The snake represents division, discord, and expansion. While a few Christian fundamentalist groups continue to view the garden story as recorded history, the biblical creation myth is not unique to the Christian tradition. Early explorers to the Middle and Far East were shocked to find ancient relief carvings and paintings of a very similar story, including a man, a woman, a snake and a tree. In fact, creation stories about a man, woman and a snake are nearly universal in world mythology. In contrast with Christianity, several ancient religions (and some modern ones) treated the serpent as a sacred icon. Religious iconography and images portraying serpents or snakes can be found in temples everywhere – from Mexico to Japan to Egypt.

The symbol of the snake was particularly tied to creation stories and was often seen as the lord of both time and of the physical world. To share a few examples: the Fon tribe of West Africa named their sun god Liza, and his twin sister and lover was the moon god Mawu. Together, they created the universe with the help of the cosmic serpent, Da. In Orphic mythology, the world was formed out of the snake-entwined cosmic egg when the creator-god Phanes emerged from it at the beginning of time. In Egypt, the giant serpent Apepi chased the sun god Ra as he traveled across the sky every day.

This does not mean that the snake was always seen as *good*; only that it was a very important spiritual icon. Often, the snake was a symbol for this world, along with its hard realities: sickness, death and the desires of the physical body. Many divine heroes or saviors, therefore, are shown stepping on, clutching or killing snakes, in order to demonstrate their power to transcend the snares of the flesh. This basic symbolism can also be found in Christianity, which personifies Satan as a slithering serpent. Jesus specifically gives his followers the power trample over snakes unharmed (Luke 10:19).

In 2006, Associate Professor Sheila Coulson from the University of Oslo discovered that the San people of Botswana worshiped a python deity around 70,000 years ago, making it by far the world's oldest known ritual.[1]

But where did the symbol of the snake really come from? Why, of all animals, did ancient people give the serpent such a privileged position? And why is it often found in conjunction with stories about the beginning of the physical world and the end of a balanced unity? The constellation Hydra – the ruler of night and darkness – may have had some influence in these stories; after all, Hydra slithered past the earth every night. Fear of the dark, combined with the snake's naturally dangerous venom, could have inspired these mythologies. However there is another serpentine constellation with a much more *central* role – especially with regard to myths of creation. It is the constellation Draco, the Dragon.

In fact, once we appreciate the mechanics of certain astronomical phenomena, this constellation acts as a kind of Rosetta Stone, unlocking spiritual symbols from nearly all the world's religions. Common to all ancient civilizations was the night sky. As we've mentioned, astronomers divided groups of stars into constellations and told stories about the relationships between them, and also of the planets whose independent paths crossed through them. But there is another, much more profound feature formed as the heavens spin (or as we know now, as the earth rotates). This aspect can be picked up today on any camera using long exposure photography.

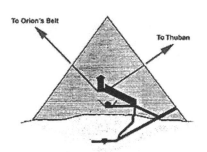 

As the earth turns, the point in the sky that is above the North Pole seems to remain in place, while the other stars revolve around it. This one, immovable spot, this "hole" in the center of the sky, was viewed as the center or birthplace of the universe. Constellations closer to this hole were considered royalty; the kings and queens of heaven. Further, these stars never set, so they were eternal or undying. Those constellations farther away, towards the horizon, are often depicted as creatures and monsters that hide under the land or sea. Among all of those whirling stars and planets, there was one constellation that was in the very epicenter, so close that it must be "guarding" the doors to the immortal realm. Today, the North Pole points roughly towards the star Polaris, but because of the precession of the equinoxes the North Pole changes its orientation. About 4,000 years ago it was pointing at the star Thuban, which is in the tail of the S-shaped constellation Draco. Some astrologers have claimed that the Great Pyramid of Giza is aligned to this star; which is not impossible – Egypt already had astronomical megaliths at Napta.

Draco used to spin around the Celestial North Pole like the hands of a giant clock. Due to its central location, it looked like Draco was actually *causing* the rotation of the other fixed stars. Because of this, Draco was put at the center of ancient star charts, and in mythology, given the role of creating the cosmos and time. Since Draco was at the center of the birthplace of the universe, it was assumed that the universe must have been made by her, through her or of her (like Hydra, Draco is usually feminine).

With this in mind, it's easy to read mythological stories as *direct references* to Draco. In the Babylonian creation story (*The Epic of Creation*, Tablet IV) Marduk conquered the great serpent Tiamat, cut her in half, and stuck her in heaven with a bolt. The world was created out of her pieces. This epic probably influenced the very similar Dionysian version. Mircea Eliade would later compare the story of Tiamat to the Old Testament version of creation, where the Hebrew God also battles a primordial serpent before creating the world:

> The dragon must be conquered and cut up into pieces by the gods so that the cosmos may come to birth. It was from the body of the marine monster Tiamat that Marduk fashioned the world. Yahweh created the universe after his victory over the primordial monster Rahab.[2]

In the Indian *Rig Veda* (IV, 17, 9) Soma or Indra "struck the Snake in his lair," and his lightning bolt "cut off his head" (I, 52, 10).[3] In the Greek myth about Draco, Minerva the Goddess of Wisdom seized the great dragon by its tail and hurled it from the Earth. As the dragon sailed away into the void of Heaven, it started to spin and got itself twisted up in knots. The dragon struck the dome of the stars and became tangled in the rotation of the heavens. Before it had time to undo all the knots in its body, the dragon froze because it was so close to the Celestial North Pole, where it is always very cold. In India, in order to produce a liquid of immortality, the gods wound the snake Visiku around a mountain and began to spin him, gods at the tail, and demons at the head. They spun until venom began to pour downwards towards the earth out of his mouth. To save the world from destruction, Siva drank the poison. The venom became a sea of milk, and produced many things, including the world. This story is remarkably similar to the account in the biblical book of Revelation:

> As soon as the dragon found himself hurdled down to the earth, he sprang in pursuit of the woman, the mother of the male child, but she was given a pair of the great eagle's wings to fly away from the serpent into the desert, to the place where she was to be looked after for a time, two times and half a time. So the serpent vomited water from his mouth, like a river, after the woman, to sweep her away in the current, but the earth came to her rescue; it opened its mouth and swallowed the river spewed from the dragon's mouth. (Revelation 12:1)

The common inspiration for these stories, rather than some nebulous psychological tendency (as claimed by the 20th century mythologists) is the constellation Draco, "turning the heavens" from his position above the North Pole.

The spinning Draco may also have been the inspiration for two of humanity's oldest spiritual symbols: the swastika and the yin-yang. Draco completes a full revolution every 24 hours, which, given its shape, would appear as a cross with its arms bent at right angles if depicted in 8-hour increments. A spiritual symbol since pre-history, the equal armed cross with arms at right angles is still considered a holy icon by Hindus, Jainists and Buddhists. In Hinduism, the right-hand (clockwise) swastika is a symbol of the sun and the god Vishnu, while the left-hand (counterclockwise) swastika represents Kali and magic. The Buddhist swastika is almost always clockwise, while the swastika adopted by the Nazis (many of whom had occult interests) is counterclockwise. The swastika symbolizes prosperity and well-being, but also represents the wheel of time. In Chinese star maps, such as the one found on this ancient Chinese tortoise shell (below right), the center symbol is indistinguishable from Draco (below left).

Before compasses, finding north at night would have been nearly impossible without the fixed stars over the North Pole. In thousands of jade carvings found throughout China, Draco is presented in the center of a small disk, with the constellations spinning around him. Sometimes there is a hole in the center of these discs, which are always decorated with dragons. These objects, referred to as "Bi" disks, may have been used for navigational purposes – by placing Thuban or Draco in the hole, you would be able to find north. According to researcher Shu-P'Ing Teng:

> It is found that these objects testify to early stages of development of cosmological concepts that remained important in Chinese culture

during the Warring States and Han periods: the notion of a covering sky (*gaitian*) that revolves around a central axis, the cycle of the Ten Suns, and the use of an early form of the carpenter's square. These objects were handled by shamans who were the religious leaders of Liangzhu society and the transmitters of cosmological knowledge.[4]

The Bi disks also had a cultic function: from Neolithic times they were buried with the dead as a holy symbols, accompanying the dead into the afterworld or "sky."[5] This would make sense if these early communities, like other cultures, viewed Draco as the center of the universe and believed in the possibility of immortality.

In the most rudimentary jade carvings, Draco is depicted as a simple S-shaped line in the center of a circle; an image that is probably the origin of the modern yin-yang symbol. Although the connection between Draco and the yin-yang symbol has been almost completely lost, it can be re-established by consideration of the relevant mythology. Most people know that the yin and yang represent forces of positive and negative energy, which balance each other and sustain the universe – but an older myth gives the same role to the serpent. In Chinese, *yin* literally means "moon." The dark patch, with the white sphere inside, represents the full moon (often portrayed as a woman with a snake's body). *Yang*, on the other hand, literally means "sun," and is represented by a Tiger (similar to the Western sun-symbol, the lion). Together, they formed the body of Draco; the sun became a symbol for the dragon's head while the moon became a symbol for the tail. It is the separation of these two energies, and the interplay between them, that generates and sustains the universe – known in the East as the "Tao."

This is not a balance or a harmony: it is an active, constantly moving relationship. The polarities both attract and repel each other, like two sides of a magnet. This is why Draco is always spinning, or "chasing its tail" – he has been divided and is trying to get back together. His head (male) keeps trying to catch up to his tail (female).

As Draco spun the cosmos, causing the seasons, the constellation Hydra circled around the world, bringing night and darkness. Another snake symbol, possibly a combination of these two serpentine constellations, is the Ouroboros, a Greek word meaning "tail swallower." Found from China to Egypt and even depicted by the Maya, Inca and Hopi tribes, the Ouroboros is a universal symbol of the cycle of time, and the universe. (Incidentally, the Ouroboros may also be linked to the Milky Way; it is possible to see, at its center, the image of a snake biting its tail.)

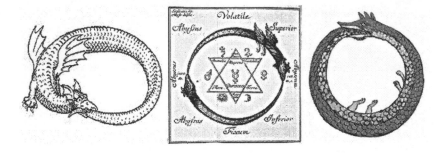

You may have noticed that in the Bi disks or turtle shell above, Draco the dragon is shown surrounded by one or several phoenixes. The rotating pair of dragon/phoenix is common in Asian illustrations, displaying the polar opposites of the yin-yang. Fusing these two together into the Ouroboros is how we get the symbol of a *winged* dragon, sometimes shown with a beak as well. This combination of bird/snake is common in many cultures and has esoteric significance, as we will see.

# The World Tree

Now that we've come to recognize Draco's role in constellation mythology, we are prepared to understand another powerful symbol. Looking at the spinning heavens and the one fixed spot, it was natural to imagine that there was an invisible connection or bridge between the center of the sky and some sacred place on earth. This connection was often visualized as a tree, binding or bridging the cosmos, with its roots deep in the earth and its branches reaching towards heaven. With Draco among its leaves, the tree represents the downward movement of creation and the "fall" of mankind. It is also, however, the ladder back to the center, and the pathway towards salvation.

Incidentally, if this symbolism seems vaguely familiar, perhaps, like many of us, you once played the board game "Snakes and Ladders" as a child. Not surprisingly, the game originated in India, where it was played as early as the 16th century as a tool to teach children about the ethics and the consequences of virtue and vice.[6]

Christian tradition would later associate Jesus Christ with the "Tree of Life" from Genesis 3:22, however the use of the tree as a spiritual symbol is not limited to Christianity. Many other deities are associated with a sacred tree, including Attis, Dionysus, Buddha and Krishna.

This imaginary tree grew from the "navel of world," and often had a snake guarding its precious fruit (as in the Garden of Eden or the myth of Hercules and the Golden Apples of Hesperides). It could also represent, for example, Jacob's vision of the ladder (Gen. 28:11–19), or even the cross of Jesus' crucifixion. As Joseph Campbell points out, this relationship between a holy site on earth and the immovable spot in the heavens, guarded by Draco, is central to several world religions. This is not only due to the creation stories; many religious saviors will later complete their definitive act of salvation-redemption or enlightenment on a sacred spot on, in, or under a holy tree:

> This is the most important single moment in Oriental mythology a counterpart of the Crucifixion of the West. The Buddha beneath the Tree of Enlightenment (the Bo Tree) and Christ on Holy Rood (the Tree of Redemption) are analogous figures, incorporating an archetypal World Savior, World Tree motif, which is of immemorial antiquity... The Immovable Spot and Mount Calvary are images of the World Navel, or World Axis.[7]

William Blake, "Jacob's Ladder"    Alchemical ladder    The World Tree

Campbell also notes an important detail in the following passage: the hero himself is not just associated with this spot – as an incarnation of god, the hero actually *is* the tree or ladder; a personification of this divine bridge:

> The torrent pours from an invisible source, the point of entry being the center of the symbolic circle of the universe, the Immovable Spot of the Buddha Legend, around which the world may be said to revolve. Beneath this spot is the earth-supporting head of the cosmic serpent, the dragon, symbolical of the waters of the abyss, which are the divine life energy and substance of the demiurge, the world-generative aspect of immortal being. The tree of life, i.e., the universe itself, grows from this point. It is rooted in the supporting darkness; the golden sun bird perches on its peak; a spring, the inexhaustible well, bubbles at its foot. Or the figure may be that of a cosmic mountain, with the city of the gods, like a lotus of light, upon its summit, and in its hollow the cities of the damons, illuminated by precious stones. Again, the figure may be that of the cosmic man or woman, (for example the Buddha himself, or the dancing Hindu Goddess Kali) seated or standing on

this spot, or even fixed to the tree (Attis, Jesus, Wotan); for the hero as the incarnation of God is himself the navel of the world, the umbilical point through which the energies of eternity break into time. Thus the World Navel is the symbol of the continuous creation: the mystery of the maintenance of the world through that continuous miracle of vivification which wells within all things.[8]

As mentioned above, this magical place in the center of the world, if not a tree, could also be symbolized as a mountain – for example Mt. Olympus, home of the gods. According to Mircea Eliade in *The Sacred and the Profane,*

> Since the sacred mountain is an axis mundi connecting earth with heaven, it in a sense touches heaven and hence marks the highest point in the world; consequently the territory that surrounds it, and that constitutes "our world," is held to be the highest among countries. This is stated in Hebrew tradition: Palestine, being the highest land, was not submerged by the Flood. According to Islamic tradition, the highest place on earth is the kā'abfula, because "the Pole Star bears witness that it faces the center of Heaven." For Christians, it is Golgatha, which is on the summit of the cosmic mountain. All these beliefs express the same feeling, which is profoundly religious: "our world is holy ground *because it is the place nearest heaven,* because from here, from our abode, it is possible to reach heaven; hence our world is a high place."[9]

This point on earth connecting to the center of heaven (Thuban, in the tail of Draco) could also be imagined as the *navel* of the world, through which the world was born.

> Hebrew tradition is still more explicit: 'The Most Holy One created the world like an embryo. As the embryo grows from the navel, so God began to create the world by the navel and from there it spread out in all directions.' And since the 'navel of the earth,' the Center of the World, is the Holy Land, the Yoma affirms that 'the world was created beginning with Zion.' Rabbi ben Gorion said of the rock of Jerusalem: 'it is called the Foundation Stone of the Earth, that is, the navel of the Earth, because it is from here that the whole Earth unfolded.'[10]

A related symbol, common in many spiritual traditions (and which can also be traced back to Draco's central, rotating position) is the image of a snake or serpent winding up a pole or tree. This is basically just a 3D image of the symbols we've already examined. Given the concepts of an immovable spot, a world tree, and the serpentine constellation, this was a natural step for early illustrators.

The symbol of a snake spinning around a pole demonstrates the unfolding cosmos and the principles of expansion and retraction: the cosmos is a continuous cycle, but it is not truly eternal. Everything unfolded at one time out of a single point, and everything will return to that point again. This is both ancient conjecture and modern science; in principle it is identical to the Big Bang theory. Most likely coincidence, but fascinating nonetheless, is the fact that scientists suggested recently (in an article titled "Astronomer's say Draco's glow is the beginning of time") that the original Big Bang – the beginning of our universe – *actually took place* near the constellation Draco. This claim was based on the glow left from the universe's earliest stars, which first formed in the area of Draco.[11]

Of the hundreds of murals and paintings depicting the biblical story of the fall, nearly all of them show the snake winding up the Tree of Knowledge. In most of them, the "snake" is depicted as a woman with a serpent's tail – more like the tail of Draco than the modern day, masculine Satan. Eastern religions use the identical symbol to decorate their temples; usually with dragons winding up the front pillars. These dragons may also represent the cosmic wheel, or karma.

The division of the polarities and the expansion of matter into the universe (which Draco was given credit for in some form) was the beginning of life as we know it. However, it also brought the consequences of time, including pain, sickness and death. Draco was up there spinning the seasons and the years like a conductor.

Struggling to find meaning in a life that was – as Thomas Hobbes put it, "solitary, poor, nasty, brutish, and short" – humanity began dreaming of a perfect, eternal place, where it was always spring and never winter. Evil, it was decided, must have come into the world by accident, through some grave error. The purpose of life must be to somehow rejoin the polarities, uniting the head and tail of the serpent, and climb back up the world tree to the eternal place from which we came. The different methods utilized for this spiritual experience defined what would later become the world's religions.

As people yearned for immortality, the serpent was regarded as the enemy of goodness and the lord of evil. He represented the inevitable beast of time and the earthly passions that led men into death. In Persia, Draco was called Ashdehj, the Man-eating Serpent, and Arabian astronomers referred to it as the Poisonous Dragon.

In the west, with its tradition of great heroes, the idea arose of a savior who would slay the beast, end time, and bring everyone into an eternal kingdom. Sun gods no longer slayed dragons in order to end winter; they now fought them as symbols of darkness in general. The literal battle between light and dark became a symbolic battle between good and evil. Despite the shift, the symbols and language used in the story have continued to this day. As pointed out earlier, this includes modern heroes such as Harry Potter, whose school nemesis is fittingly named *Draco* Malfoy.

An Egyptian depiction of killing the serpent. The snake is in the shape of the letter Omega, the last letter in the Greek alphabet, and may refer to ending time.

## Suffering Saviors

As these stories matured, they developed into more robust spiritual philosophies. Rather than one "end of all time" – the dissolution of all things and return to original unity – people began to believe in a personal afterlife. This idea was based on the concept of an individual soul; a divine spark that had somehow been given to each human being in the beginning of time. Explanations for this idea vary: in some myths, as we have seen, the divine spark comes from a dragon or criminal deity (divine, but with evil attributes) that gets cut up and divided, or spews his divine substance down into the world.

In the Babylonian version, Marduk (the sun god) combats Tiamat who had revolted against the divine order, and creates the universe from Tiamat's dismembered body. After that episode, it was resolved that mankind should be created, as servants.[12] However, man needed to be made with divine blood; a blood sacrifice was required. No deity was willing to make this sacrifice, so Marduk chose Kingu, Tiamat's chief ally, as punishment for aiding Tiamat in his revolt:

> Marduk needed materials with which to create man, and it was decided that a guilty god would have to give up his life to provide them. Kingu was chosen because he had incited and helped Tiamat in her revolt. He was put to death and his blood was used for creating man. Thus man was created out of divine stuff, albeit from a rebellious god.[13]

A reenactment of this conflict was recited during the Babylonian new year.[14] It was celebrated as a story of thanksgiving – for without Kingu's (unwilling) sacrifice, we would not be partly divine. This is a story about human existence, and not yet about spiritual resurrection or afterlife. Yet the basic components are already there: a guilty character that was chosen as sacrifice, whose blood gave mankind the divine spark, but which also came with sin and the element of evil (for Kingu was, in effect, a criminal). Later, this idea will evolve into the idea of a suffering figure, who willingly or unwillingly gets sacrificed, with the same results (endowing humanity with the divine spark). Dionysus is a prime example; his story demonstrates how a sinless figure – he was only a child at the time – could be murdered, cut into pieces (eaten by Titans or swallowed by the elements), and give mankind an element of divinity. As we've seen, this concept would allow worshippers of Dionysus to later believe in an eternal life.

The "suffering savior" – who undergoes torment so that humans have the possibility of eternal life through the divine seed or spark of the savior's fallen half or companion – was often identified with the sun god. The sun toils every year, is "crucified" or battles a beast in the spring, and is finally victorious, instituting his kingdom of light. Over time, this kingdom began to be imagined as an eternal victory rather than a summer period; at the end of time the sun would reign forever, in a place of great prosperity.

Through the sun, we are given a spark of the divine. This "soul" was a piece of the sun's former glory, and could return to it at the end of time – if we knew the way. In the Egyptian Teachings of Ani, we read "the god of this land is the sun in heaven. He gives his *bas* in millions of forms." One translation of *ba* could be life-energy. This energy was shared throughout mankind and divided into their individual souls. People are not only "created by" – instead they "have life in":

> You made the heavens remote to rise in it to see all that you created, you being alone, but there being millions of lives in you (for you) to make them live. (Shorter Hymn)[15]

> By praising this god as "ba" rather than with his usual name, the hymn refers to god as the ba of the world, the vital principle of the cosmos which gives life to the cosmos in the same way that the human ba ("soul") gives life to the individual human being.[16]

Hence, the sun is not only a god, but also the divine principle in mankind. In his *Oration upon the Sovereign Sun*, Julianus later applies the same symbolism to Asclepius:

> And since he (the Sun) fills the whole of our life with fair order, he begets Asclepius in the world, though he has him by his side even before the beginning of the world.[17]

In other accounts, this divine light was stolen for us by a hero or demigod, who was punished for this offense. At any rate, the symbolism remains the same: a figure, associated with the sun, gifted humanity a piece of the divine light when the world was created, through some action which caused him great personal suffering. Through this precious gift we were given the keys to the kingdom and a chance at immortality.

This gift came with a great cost, a burden that the sun bore alone, and savior figures that developed out of the sun myth underwent some sort of painful and bloody sacrifice for the good of mankind. References to Tammuz, for example, characterize him as an atoning offering for sin, and describe his death as "suspensus lingo"; hung on a tree or crucified.

> Trust, ye saints, your Lord restored,
> Trust ye in your risen Lord
> For the pains which Tammuz endured
> Our salvation have procured. (Ctesias, Persika)[18]

Prometheus brought "fire" to humanity, and was punished for it by Zeus. Prometheus was to be chained to a rock, and have an eagle prey upon his liver everyday for eternity. At night, he would be made whole, so that the eagle could continue the torture the next day. His blood is called "atoning" by the Greek tragedian Aeschylus (c. 524/525 BC):

> Lo! streaming from the fatal tree
> His all atoning blood,
> Is this the Infinite?—Yes, 'tis he,
> Prometheus, and a god!
> Well might the sun in darkness hide,
> And veil his glories in,
> When God the great Prometheus, died
> For man the creature's sin. (Aeschylus)

That Prometheus was depicted as "crucified" in antiquity we know from Lucian. Thomas Medwin, author of the 1832 preface of the English translation of Aeschylus' *Prometheus Bound*, expresses that "This idea of a self-devoting divinity has been mysteriously inculcated in many religions, as a confused foreboding of the true; here, however, it appears in a most alarming contrast with the consolations of revelation."[19] Interestingly, Milton relied heavily on *Prometheus Bound* when writing his *Paradise Lost,* leading the

Romantic poets Keats, Shelley and Byron to view Milton's character of Satan as a tragic hero. Although Christian tradition considers Satan as the enemy, the motifs (rebellion, forbidden fruit, spinning snake, eternal punishment) certainly connect him to this branch of mythology. He could thus be seen as a parallel to Kingu, the divine rebel who was sacrificed to create humanity, and the fruit would represent the divine spark, or "knowledge of good and evil."

The characters in these stories are depicted in a paralysis, or eternal torture, which is represented as being tied to a tree, nailed to a rock, or divided into pieces. It is, in part, linked to the same eternal torture endured on the cross of the equinoxes. The sacrifice in the sky was necessary to maintain time and life but the idea was expanded to include salvation even after death. However, it can also be traced back to Draco: half of the serpent is stuck to the fixed point in the heavens, while the other half spins around, spewing its insides (the divine material) down into creation.

# The "Sun" of God

As early philosophers began to ponder the meaning of life and the origins of the universe, they developed a more abstract version of this story. The spark of divine life, they reasoned, must have been accomplished as the world was being created. This inspired cosmological considerations such as "What is at the center of the universe?", "Why is there something rather than nothing?" or "Is existence one, or many?" In the following reconstruction of the creation of the universe, I am attempting to generalize what I believe to be a nearly universal cosmology in ancient times. Although these questions are still debated by today's greatest scientific minds, this simplified account should be enough to support the aims of the present research. That my version is very close to what ancient philosophers actually believed will be supported later with textual evidence.

What follows is a theoretical description of how the "Sun God" became "The Son of God." Unfortunately a clear, linear outline of this historical development is not possible; the best I can do is explain the philosophy of the Son of God and prove that this idea was associated with the various sun-gods. The Son of God is also directly related with the concept of Draco discussed earlier: he is the sun, the head of the serpent that gets divided and cut up, generating the world and specifically, endowing mankind with consciousness.

Although philosophers have debated the qualities of the origin of the universe for thousands of years, most agree that it contained some variation of three ingredients: matter, void, and will. These qualities are similar to what modern scientists posit may have existed before the Big Bang. Another way of describing them would be something to play with, the space to play in, and something that likes to play.

Theists have argued that the "will" quality must be God but this isn't necessary. It may be the nature of that certain quality to create, and it could do so unintentionally and unconsciously. The "will" quality just refers to the idea of a first mover; that there must be a reason why, in the beginning, anything happened at all.

The Father and his copy, the Son, separated by the snake-ring of eternity. Ph.O. Runge, 1803

This is the way I like to think of it: picture a toddler playing with building blocks. He makes one thing, and then two, and then three and soon the possibilities are endless. The more building blocks he makes, the more options he has. He isn't trying to build anything; he just likes to play with the blocks. If the toddler continues to play with the blocks for eternity, eventually every possibility, even the least likely, will come up. So let's imagine that that one day he succeeds in creating *an exact copy of himself*. Looking at his creation is like looking into a mirror, and for the first time, he becomes self-conscious. He and his creation are identical in every way except that one was first, and the other was second. For this reason Egyptians and later Greek philosophers referred to the first as Father, and the second as Son.

The toddler is no longer alone in the room. There are two children creating now, and out of the new relationship, they will produce a third. Many cultures describe the ultimate reality in terms of a three-personed god, or trinity. In nearly every version except Christianity, the third person of this trinity is feminine. She is both the consort of the father and the mother of the son. Generally, (and counter-intuitively), the son is the second person of the trinity, while the mother is a result of the relationship between the Father and Son.

The second person of the trinity, first born Son of God, is now in effect standing between two perfect copies of himself, or two mirrors. Have you ever been inside a department store and had a mirror on either side of you? You can look into one mirror and see yourself, but also see yourself in the mirror behind you. In fact, you can see yourself repeated in both mirrors, getting smaller and smaller, without end.

This is how philosophers pictured the creation of the universe – mirrors and reflections were already considered magical objects. Due to the positions of these three self-aware creative forces, the Son was divided and the self-consciousness he had developed after seeing his own reflection was split into billions of little pieces. As the light divided and became smaller, it slipped through the cracks of matter and grew into complicated forms.

We are already familiar with how the story of Dionysus' dismemberment was used to explain how humanity received a piece of the divine light and hence a chance at immortality. In some versions of the story, however, Dionysus was torn apart after having first been distracted by a *mirror*. Plato later used this symbolism to develop his own theory of the "fall of the soul." As Godwin relates:

> Dionysus' fascination by a looking-glass, followed by his temporary death, represents the fate of the human soul which, according to Platonic doctrine, looks down from its home in the heavens and sees its reflection in the deceptive surface of the material world. Allured like Narcissus by the beauty of his own image, it tries to grasp or follow the evanescent vision, and in the effort it tumbles down into the miry toils of a life that is death to the soul.[20]

Dionysus was Son of Zeus, Father of the Greek gods. His Egyptian counterpart – Horus, son/sun of Osiris – likewise was perceived as dividing himself (although as we've seen in later versions it is Osiris that gets dismembered). In a nineteenth century (BC) Hymn to Amun Re, this identification is made clear:

> Hail, the One who makes himself into millions, whose length and breadth are limitless! Horus of the east, the rising one whose radiance illuminates, the light that is more luminous than the gods.[21]

Strictly speaking, this may simply affirm the fact that all life comes from the sun; that every living being receives its energy from the sun is a scientific fact. Egyptians began to interpret Horus, as the Son of God, as a divine being divided into the individual souls of mankind. These souls were viewed as little pockets of consciousness that forgot who they were and became trapped in physical bodies. Picture them like diamonds scattered in the mud. All of those pieces became immediately buried in the depth of matter, swallowed up by the expanding power of the serpent, which represents the functioning universe.

The idea that heaven is somewhere up above comes from the idea that heavier matter sinks and gets farther away from the source. The serpent had begun the cycle of time, and the divided Son became many separate conscious beings. This story was used to describe how the "image and likeness" of God found a home in corporeal bodies, and how the fallen piece of divinity gave humanity a hope for immortality.

This was a mystic truth long before it was conscientiously and deliberately written down. Plato was one of the first writers to speak of it openly:

> According to Plato in the *Phaedrus*, the soul is of one nature, whether it belong to men or gods, and exists at first in the highest region of heaven. But not all souls are perfect, and some cannot stay at that height. These fall, until they come into contact with what is solid (corporeal), and are then forced to take to themselves material bodies to inhabit. The whole, formed of soul and body, is what we call an animal, and the familiar distinction between mortal and immortal is really the distinction between these souls which have become attached to bodies and those which have remained in heaven uncontaminated by matter.[22]

This view of an eternal soul inhabiting physical bodies only for a brief while before leaving them behind was popular in mystery traditions such as Orphism. It is also found in the *Bhagavad Gita*, an important text in the history of literature and philosophy which may have been written in the first century AD. The teacher of the work is Krishna, who is revered by Hindus as a manifestation of God.

> Only the bodies, of which this eternal, imperishable, incomprehensible Self is the indweller, are said to have an end. (Bhagavad Gita, 2:18)

In the same work, Krishna also claims, "I am the Self, seated in the hearts of all creatures. I am the beginning, the middle, and the end of all beings" (Bhagavad Gita, 10:20). The similarity between Jesus' claim in Revelation 1:8 is striking: "I am the Alpha and the Omega – the beginning and the end; I am the one who is, who always was, and who is still to come." Greece and India had been in contact with each other at least since the time of Alexander the Great, and there is a good chance that, if not directly influential, these two statements were developed based on shared sources.

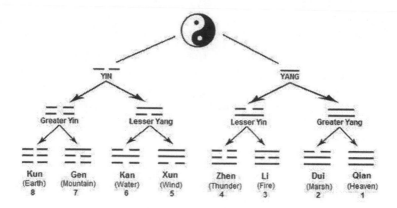

The concept of the unity at the core and beginning of the universe which then expands numerically to create everything is also found in Eastern cultures. In oriental religions, as we've seen, the creative force which spontaneously uses void and matter to generate the physical universe is called the Tao:

> The Tao begot one.
> One begot two.
> Two begot three.
> And three begot the ten thousand things.
> (*Tao Te Ching*, 42)

Although it is argued that Taoism is not exactly a religion (it has no definite statements about God or the afterlife) Taoism does appear to share the idea of a soul that is eternal and separate from the body:

> Being at one with the Tao is eternal.
> And though the body dies,
> the Tao will never pass away.
> (*Tao Te Ching*, 16)

Around the 6th century BC a Greek philosopher from the Ephesian school named Heraclitus associated the ultimate unity, and specifically the 2nd person or Son with the Greek word *Logos*.

He described the Logos as a kind of divine logic that created and sustained the universe, in language that is almost identical with Eastern concepts of the Tao (although, like many of the pre-Socratic philosophers, he claims he was educated by priests in Egypt – thus he probably had the Egyptian *ba* in mind). Rather than yin and yang, Heraclitus called the two forces of the universe Love and Strife, and declared that even though they were in constant flux, there was an order behind everything.

Heraclitus taught that the Logos was a common truth; a voice of wisdom inherent in every person. Equating the Logos with fire, he saw this wisdom as a kind of divine spark. He complains, however, that most people do not even recognize that it is there:

> Men have no comprehension of the Logos, as I've described it, just as much after they hear about it as they did before they heard about it. Even though all things occur according to the Logos, men seem to have no experience whatsoever, even when they experience the words and deeds which I use to explain physics, of how the Logos applies to each thing, and what it is.[23]

The Logos is a mysterious, unknown force, a piece of divine energy that resides inside us. It is the fire that Prometheus stole from the gods and brought to humanity. Philo of Alexandria later equated the Logos with the sun. Almost all of the resurrecting sun-saviors, including Mithras and Osiris, were identified as the 2nd person in the trinity as well as with the concept of the Logos. Certain Christian communities borrowed terms from this philosophical tradition to clarify the cosmic nature of their own savior, Jesus Christ. The gospel of John in particular relies heavily on the concept of Logos, which is usually translated into English as "The Word":

> In the beginning was the Word: the Word was with God, and the Word was God. He was with God in the beginning, through him all things came into being, not one thing came into being except through him. (John 1:1)

Consequently, Jesus became not only a sacrificial offering, crucified on the cross of heaven, but also a super transcendent, eternal force. He was a pre-existent quality of the Father that created and sustained the universe, and also came into the physical world. Nevertheless, identical with Heraclitus' Logos, Jesus as the Word was not recognized:

> The Word was the real light that gives light to everyone, he was coming into the world. He was in the world that had come into being through him, and the world did not recognize him. He came to his own and his own people did not accept him. (John 1:9)

What is important to remember here, is that the concepts related to the Logos (Son of God, 2$^{nd}$ person of the trinity, life force) are a package of philosophical ideas which predate Christianity by centuries. In particular, it seems that this role was championed by Jesus' contemporary Asclepius. According to Proclus (Platonic Rem Publicam, I), "he who causes everything to act according to nature is Asclepius who keeps the universe from falling sick or growing old, and the elements from relaxing their indestructible bonds.[24]

Further, Ascelpius was begot by God (the sun god Helius) specifically for this healing role. Julianus says "shall I now go on to tell you how Helius took thought for the health and safety of all by begetting Asclepius to be the savior of the whole world?"[25] Other gods took on the same features. The Egyptian god Thoth (who was openly associated with Ascelpius) likewise became the Word of God, the Logos by whom all things were created[26].

This advanced cosmology was paired with earlier mythological symbolism, and in many ways replaced the older (astrological) view of a spinning serpent. Instead of Draco being cut up and his essence spilt upon the earth, the focus was shifted unto a savior figure, stretched between heaven and earth, divided into millions of pieces: providing through his suffering the souls of mankind. This figure was fixed or associated with the "World Tree" – the imaginary bridge between a holy site on earth and the fixed spot in heaven – and often with the serpent Draco as well.

This was not just a one-time sacrifice: as long as there is time, the Son continues to be divided or split. Through this division and fall of the Logos, we have the unique characteristics of humanity. However, the Son is caught in a constant, crucifying recurrence. This was seen as a great sacrifice for both the God and His only

Son:

> For God so loved the world, that he gave his only begotten Son, that whosoever believeth on him should not perish, but have everlasting life. (John 3:16)

Similarly, Prometheus, who brought fire to mankind, was chained to a rock and tortured. Krishna and Attis died at the base of a tree, pierced by arrows. Dionysus was ripped apart by his followers so that they could have life by eating his flesh. In the Egyptian story, Osiris was butchered into little pieces (after first being buried in a tree). Heraclitus, developing into a mythological figure himself, was reportedly torn apart by dried dung.

The motif can also be found in the Christian tradition. In First Corinthians, for example, St. Paul is chastising the community for dissensions and factions among them. He asks:

> Has Christ been split up? Was it Paul that was crucified for you, or was it in Paul's name that you were baptised? (1 Cor. 1.13)

A mainstream reading of this text translates the first line as "Is Christ divided?" or "Has Christ been divided?" The answer, it is implied, is "No, and neither should you be." However, other translations have treated this sentence as an assertion: *"Christ is divided."* Although difficult to place in the Christian tradition, Jesus' crucifixion as the division of the Son of God is certainly more akin to the common understanding of the era. It also helps us situate Paul's many statements about having life or existing *in* Jesus.

Biblical passages referring to soldiers casting lots for the garments of Jesus may also carry this meaning (the dividing up of Christ) although they were probably written in order to fulfill the "prophecy" from Psalms 22 "They divide My garments among them, And for My clothing they cast lots" (Psalms 22, 13-18).

As previously mentioned, saviors who were identified with the Son were hung or killed on or under a tree – the symbol for the transition between unity and division. Sometimes this tree took the shape of the celestial cross identifying it with the toil of the sun, but it was also depicted as a vertical cross like the sword of

Mithras. The cross shape could also symbolize, as it does for the falling souls in the Platonic version, the "cross of matter"; the intersection of the four elements. When the Son came in contact with the material world, he was divided into pieces, which became stuck in earthly bodies; hence these figures could be described as "crucified" – or nailed to the crux of matter. Like the Logos, Jesus was considered the Son of God who was divided on the cross of matter, and through this atoning sacrifice offers us eternal life. This is the reading provided by Godwin:

> Out of compassion and truly divine love they may descend to this and other earths to take on the burden of a human body. For such beings, physical incarnation is a veritable crucifixion: a nailing of their divinity to the fourfold cross of the elements. This is the esoteric meaning of Christ's love for us, and of his symbolic death on the cross.[27]

Symbolically, the cross was often used to demonstrate the expansion or contraction of the universe. The horizontal bar of the cross shows the divided universe, while the vertical bar shows the path from heaven to earth. When the horizontal bar is placed up high, like the cross used by Christians, it is closer to the source and represents the process of going back up to the original unity, or the One.

An inverted cross represents the process of falling down and expanding. This may be why Christian tradition calls the inverted cross "St. Peter's cross." It was said that he chose to be crucified upside down out of respect for Christ, however there is a symbolic meaning: Catholic tradition maintains that Peter was singled out by Jesus to be the rock upon which the church was founded, and even given a new name to complete this transformation. While Jesus symbolizes the higher power of the Logos and is represented by an upright cross Peter represents humanity – the fallen Logos – and so his symbol is an inverted cross.

The image of a snake on the tree or cross represents the expanded universe, the fall of the Logos into the world, and also the path of redemption through reunification. It is this tree that snares Eve in the garden. The image of a man on a cross or under a tree, meanwhile, shows the divided Logos stuck in matter. This is the suffering that the Son of God endured for the sake of humanity, in order to render our salvation.

Blake, 1794          Cross of St. Peter, with keys          A. Eleazar, 1760

Going back again to the constellation Draco, we can now appreciate the symbolism fully. Draco is the combined set of polarities. It is the man who gets divided (sun) as the head of the dragon, and the woman (moon) who is collectively the divine sparks on earth. Hence, romance mythologies tell of the separation of lovers, their eternal torment as they are divided, and their hope for an eventual reconciliation. At the same time, Draco is the monster that guards the path to immortality and must be slain; or conversely the tainted sacrifice that gives both divinity and sin to humanity.

All of these features can be found in the most commonly accepted version of Draco's arrival in the heavens: that Draco was the serpent killed by Cadmus. Cadmus was the brother of Europa, who was carried off to Crete by Jupiter in the form of a bull (Taurus). Cadmus was ordered by his father to go in search of his sister, and told he couldn't return unless he brought Europa back with him. "Cadmus wandered over the whole world: for who can lay hands on what Jove has stolen away? Driven to avoid his native country and his father's wrath, he made a pilgrimage to Apollo's oracle, and begged him to say what land he should dwell in" (Ovid, *Metamorphoses* III 9-11). Later, Cadmus would conquer the serpent of Mars, "a creature with a wonderful golden crest; fire flashed from its eyes, its body was all puffed up from poison, and from its mouth, set with a triple row of teeth, flickered a three-forked tongue" (*Metamorphoses* III 31-34). Cadmus planted the teeth of the monster in the ground, and from them sprung the first people (of Thebes).

# Conclusion and Summary

In the last two chapters I've tried to demonstrate how astronomical observations were developed into stories, which became first myth, and then religion. These stories matured, developed and changed, taking on new forms with each new culture that they came into contact with. Reading the texts literally, it can sometimes be difficult to perceive the shared origins, like the constellation Draco or the movement of the sun through the zodiac. However, the inclusion of common elements and astrological symbols support the theory that religious iconography has not freed itself from its astrological beginning.

Looking again at Adam and Eve, we are now able to interpret the story's hermeneutical meaning. The myth is already used to show how sin and suffering came into the world: humanity was divided from God through the meddling of the serpent and the waywardness of the female. Adam represents the sun, the head of the dragon, while Eve represents the moon. After the fall (of Draco's tail into the world), they must toil and travel without end. Hidden a little deeper in the story is the idea that Eve represents humanity, the fallen half of the divided Logos, which was divided as the $2^{nd}$ person of the trinity fell into matter.

Although the biblical symbolism is rarely interpreted this way, Jesus (as the Son of God) was actually crucified as soon as Eve took the apple. This is why, like Prometheus, his suffering is seen as a perpetual, atoning event. In order to reverse the process and recreate the original unity, the head and tail of Draco must be rejoined.

This union of the universal Logos with the fallen light of God has been the purpose and aim of many secret societies, as well as the theological backbone of most religious traditions. Spiritually, each person was believed to have a piece of the divine light inside them. Today, many hikers carry a mirror with them so that in case they get lost in the woods, they can signal for help; likewise, spiritual communities believed that if we took care of our mirror, polished it, and aimed it in the right direction, the Son would see the bright reflection and come down to collect the spark in us. Symbolically, the reunion of polarities and the establishment of the undivided One can been illustrated by the masculine head of the snake biting its own tail, as in the Ouroboros. It can also been demonstrated by joining the sun and the moon, stylized as human figures, in conjugal love.

An alchemical woodcut from the "Rosarium Philosophorum."
The sun and moon symbols are provided to identify the lovers.

The evolution of these ideologies is not hard to follow once you know what to look for. Due to the constellation Draco, we have stories about a snake or dragon, fixed in the center of the sky, that generates the universe. The separation of the dragon's head and tail represents the interaction between the masculine (active) and feminine (passive) principles of "love and strife" or "yin and yang." Later, rather than two halves of the snake, the head and tail were seen as independent entities. The masculine head remains stuck: tortured or crucified on the world tree, in the space between the immovable spot and the holy ground on earth. The feminine tail, meanwhile, is lost or cast down to earth; hence we have stories of a fallen or lost goddess. This basic symbolism has been the basis for many myths and fairy tales, as we will explore in the next chapter.

## CHAPTER SEVEN

# Jesus the Handsome Prince: Reuniting with the Higher Self

*"Let him kiss me with the kisses of his mouth, for your love is better than wine. Your oils have a pleasing fragrance. Your name is like purified oil. Therefore the maidens love you. Draw me after you and let us run together!" –Song of Songs 1:2*

WHILE THE SON IS HANGING on the cross of matter, tormented by his desire to be unified with himself, the individual sparks are often shown as promiscuous or lost women, sunk deep in the illusion of the world. In many creation stories, the woman leads the way into matter and the man follows her, just as Eve "tempted" Adam into sin. Because the pathway between unity and the expanded universe was symbolized by a tree, in mythology the original fall and separation of polarities can be represented by a woman who runs through the woods or turns into a tree, demonstrating that she has fallen into the material world.

In the myth of Daphne and Apollo, for example, mischievous god of love Cupid struck moon-goddess Daphne with an arrow that made her scorn all men, and then shot the sun god Apollo with another arrow to make him fall in love with Daphne. Apollo chased after Daphne, and she ran away from him, deeper and deeper into the woods. Eventually she was turned into a tree, and Apollo vowed to stay at her side, making the tree his holy symbol.

In another Greek myth, Psyche, which means "soul," was so beautiful that the gods got jealous. As a punishment, she was told she had to marry a monster, but would never be allowed to see his face. Although she was initially happy with her mysterious lover, her curiosity was so great that one day she lit a lamp to take a peek at her husband.

She was thrilled to find out that her husband was actually the handsome god Eros, which means "love." But as soon as Eros woke up and saw that Psyche had broken the rules, he ran away. Psyche wandered away through the forest, lost in misery and grief. Like the Logos and his consort, when Psyche and Eros are divided and recognize each other clearly, they can no longer be together. Psyche had to perform a number of challenging tasks in order to be reunited with her husband.

The symbol of a dragon, representing the snares of the flesh or the physical world, was also used to illustrate the separation, then reunion of these lovers. Hence, the archetypal story of a flying hero who slays a dragon and rescues a princess (for example Perseus and Andromeda), taking her away with him, can also demonstrate the release of the fallen soul and reunion with the higher self. The same symbolism may fit the story of Theseus, who rescued Ariadne from the Minotaur. In the following passage, Godwin associates Ariadne with the soul, but places her true resolution only after Theseus later abandons her and she is discovered by Dionysus:

> The soul is Ariadne, the sleeping beauty abandoned by her human lover Theseus (the physical body) and swept off her feet by love of a god. Borne on Dionysus' tiger-drawn quadriga, she ascends with him to the sound of maenadic music – the music of the spheres – to her proper realm, and his.[1]

In still other stories, the hero loses a lover or wife to death, and has to descend into the underworld in order to bring her back with him (Orpheus and Eurydice, etc). Note also that the gender roles in the stories can often be reversed; for example it is Isis who finds and collects the pieces of Osiris' body.

Of course this may be an overgeneralization: not every myth should be interpreted strictly in this manner, and many have other cultural or historical meanings. Still, it is relevant to understand that Greek and Roman myths were usually intimately tied with ethical and spiritual teachings, and intended to hide esoteric truths. The myth of Demeter and Persephone, for example, which is often taken as a simplistic vegetation story describing the changing seasons, was also the foundational myth of the Eleusinian mysteries – the most important spiritual tradition of ancient times, beginning as early as 1500BC and lasting nearly 2000 years:

> Sir James Frazer rightly saw in the central myth of the Eleusinian Mysteries an allegory of the vegetation cycle, in which Persephone is the power of fertility which disappears underground in winter and returns with the spring; but like all exoteric commentators he was blind to other meanings, without which the ancients would scarcely have taken the Mysteries as seriously as they indubitably did. The stolen goddess represents the soul, alternatively descending at birth for 'half a year' in the underworld of bodily existence, and returning at death to the familiar and fruitful fields of her true home.[2]

Although it is difficult to know exactly what the mystery schools taught or believed in, it would be careless not to assume a deeper significance behind their rites or symbols.

# The "Wisdom" of God

In Greek speaking communities that actually used the word Logos as the name for the Son of God, his consort was called Sophia. In one version of her story, Sophia was a goddess who became attracted to a great light in heaven. She tried to get closer but ran into a barrier and fell backwards unconscious, deep into darkness. When she woke up, she was stuck at the very heaviest level of reality. An early Christian (Gnostic) work that tries to explain the nature of this figure is called the *Sophia of Jesus Christ*:

> And his consort is the Great Sophia, who from the first was destined in him for union by Self-begotten Father, from Immortal Man, who

appeared as First and divinity and kingdom, for the Father, who is called "Man, Self-Father," revealed this.[3]

However, it must be noted that the *Logos* and the *Sophia* were often used interchangeably; one is the masculine form, and one the feminine – but they capture pretty much the same idea. Sophia could be a great goddess coming down to rescue the masculine, suffering man; or the Logos could be a masculine figure rescuing the fallen feminine.

> The highest of these (angels or powers in god), subsuming all the others, Philo called the Logos: the principle of reason and order through which God makes the universe. The Wisdom Literature had already separated this concept as Chokmah, the Divine Wisdom; the Gnostics knew it in Philo's day as Sophia; St John the Evangelist was to identify it with the Christ.[4]

Sophia, in English, means "Wisdom." In the Old Testament it is through her that God created the world. In fact, she is the pervasive theme underlying the Old Testament, and she even has a book devoted to her. The Logos and Sophia represent dualistic forces that create the physical universe through their separation. The Logos is the Son that gets divided, and the Sophia is the resulting flood of light into matter, which activates and sustains the universe. The book of Wisdom describes her in an identical role as the Logos, showing that the lines between the two were often blurred.

> For Wisdom is quicker to move than any motion; she is so pure, she pervades and permeates all things. She is a breath of the power of God, pure emanation of the glory of the Almighty; so nothing impure can find its way into her. For she is a reflection of the eternal light, untarnished mirror of God's active power, and image of his goodness. (Wisdom 7:24)

In matriarchal (or gender-tolerant) religions, Sophia could actually be the great goddess of the trinity, the mother of the Logos.

> In the Graeco-Roman world 'wisdom' (Sophia) became a very popular term among both pagan and Judeo-Christian theologians. For Plutarch, Isis herself was both 'wise' and 'philosophic'. Sophia was one of the key words in the heretical Gnosticism which Catholicism strongly attacked and in which Isis was at work. An Isiac priestess at

Athens bore the name, probably in religion. A very important bridge between paganism and Christianity was the speculative system of the Hellenizing Jew Philo of Alexandria and in it the cornerstone was 'Holy Wisdom' (Hagia Sophia), Mother of the divine Logos, rightly identified with Isis, Isis-sophia could be thought to produce Harpocrates as the Logos.[5]

This form of "Wisdom" was threatening to Christianity's patriarchal, all-masculine trinity. In Christian symbolism, however, the divine feminine is often preserved as either Mary, *mother of god*, or a mysteriously feminine Holy Spirit. In Christian art, Mary often fills the role of Sophia as the third person of the Trinity. In this picture, taken from the Portland Grotto in Oregon, Mary is caught between the Father and the Son and descends down into matter.

At her feet are two angels, a male and a female: the divided polarities. Around her head are the 12 stars of the zodiac which trap her in the world of time. She looks longingly up at the crown which is held out for her until she is ready to receive it. Notice the similarity between the much older Babylonian depiction of creation.

Sophia has fallen down into the physical world and is trapped here. In the myth, the Logos came down to save her, humbling himself by coming down into the flesh, and brought her back up to the highest heavens:

> The Word became flesh, he lived among us, and we saw his glory, the glory that he has from the Father, as the only Son of the Father, full of grace and truth. (John 1:14)

## Snow White and the Seven Dwarves

This same motif has been preserved in the popular fairy tale of Snow White. In the story, a young girl spends her days dreaming of a charming prince until her life is threatened by the evil queen. (Like the story of Psyche, it is her beauty that gets her into trouble). She runs away through the forest and is found by seven dwarves, who bring her home. She cleans up their house and takes care of them, but the evil queen finds her and gives her a poisonous apple. She falls into a deep sleep and is placed in the middle of the forest and watched over by the seven dwarves. When the handsome prince does come, she is awakened by his kiss and they live happily ever after.

The story of Snow White makes much symbolic use of mirrors, and also re-introduces the symbol of the apple, the same tempting fruit that caused Eve to fall from the garden (at least in some translations: the Latin plural for both evil and apple is *malum*, which led to the identification). The apple is often used in mythology to symbolize the seed of creation.

When you cut an apple in half horizontally, the pattern of the seeds makes a star or pentacle. Like the tree and the cross, the pentacle or five-pointed star is a symbol representing the transition between unity and disunity. As demonstrated in Dan Brown's *The DaVinci Code*, the primal symbols for man and woman are both triangles, one pointed up and the other pointed down.

Together, the two triangles form a magical symbol, the Seal or Star of Soloman – which represents the unified universe, like the yin-yang symbol. While the six-pointed star symbolizes balance and completion, a five-pointed star shows movement. The pentacle has 4 points for the 4 elements, wind, water, fire and air, with a 5 point for spirit. Pointed upwards it is a holy symbol, aimed at restitution, but pointed downwards it becomes a symbol of evil – sometimes exaggerated with the image of the demon "Baphomet," which can be formed from an inverted pentacle. Strictly speaking, there is nothing satanic about the physical world, other than the obvious drawbacks of sickness and death – but the process of dividing and separating was seen as sullying the pure, clean original substance. This is like smashing a diamond into pieces; you end up with equal amounts of diamond, but the little pieces are worthless.

While an upside down pentacle acts like a funnel, pointing things downward away from the center, a right side up pentacle shows the process of unification and of all things returning to the source. In a remarkable coincidence, in fractal geometry the transition from stability to chaos and vice versa is also marked by this fruit: the heart-shaped figure which arises during this transformation is known by scientists as the Mandelbrot *Apple*.

The number of dwarves in the Snow White story is also significant. Many religions continue to teach the ancient idea that when the world was created, it was divided into seven different layers. The seven known planets – Mercury, Venus, Mars, Earth, Jupiter, Saturn and the Sun and Moon – were seen as seven heavens which asserted influence over our seven vital organs. There are also seven notes leading through an octave, and schools like the Pythagoreans believed that each planet vibrated to the frequency of a certain note, generating the "music" or harmony of the universe. Octaves were seen as the fulfillment of the beginning and the end, thus eight was a number of perfection and completion.

This is not simply mythological creativity; after all, pure white light can be divided into seven colors of the spectrum, and science recognizes that each color is caused by light's wavelength or frequency:

> Color is the result of the vibratory activity of atoms of matter or matter in motion. As the frequency increases, the vibrations become shorter and more rapid, the color changes, each change in color being due to a change in the rate of vibration.[6]

Spiritual imagery often refers to God as pure, radiant light. In order to create the physical universe, this light had to be divided into the seven colors of the spectrum. Each layer of reality has one color and one frequency, and in order to restore unity, all the colors have to be combined back into pure white light. Perhaps this is why, in the book of Genesis, God chose the rainbow as the symbol of his relationship with all living things:

> I have set my rainbow in the clouds, and it will be the sign of the covenant between me and the earth. (Gen. 9.13)

There is hardly a more fitting symbol of the relationship between God (the one, pure light) and the physical world (the division of the light into seven colors and frequencies) than the rainbow.

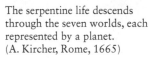

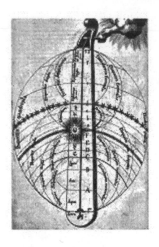

The serpentine life descends
through the seven worlds, each
represented by a planet.
(A. Kircher, Rome, 1665)

The "great musician"
tightens the strings of the
universe. Each element and
and planet makes a note on
the scale.

In Chinese legend, it is the goddess Nuwa who was credited with creating mankind out of clay on the seventh day. She is pictured as a woman with a snake's body, sometimes shown with her brother/consort Fuxi. Her great act was restoring the sky with seven different colored stones (and the legs of a giant tortoise), which became the rainbow; or other versions, using her long body to fill a hole in the sky, stopping a great flood. Obviously, this myth shares much in common with the constellation myths about Draco or Hydra.

When Nuwa is shown with Fuxi, they are usually depicted with a set-square and a compass – architectural tools – to demonstrate their role in creation. These tools have also been added to artistic renditions of Jesus or God for the same purpose, and today remain the official symbols of Freemasonry.

It is also possible that Yahweh, like Nuwa, was originally a feminine serpent goddess, and the two may share a common mythological root. Yahweh's highest class of angels, which surround him always singing "Holy, holy, holy" is even called the Seraphim, or literally, "fiery serpents."

## Reuniting the divided polarities

Central to the depictions of a "fallen soul" or spirit was the possibility of somehow escaping from the feeble body, with its change and decay, and connecting to the original pure light or being, which is eternal. This is the Kingdom of Heaven, or the Happily Ever After. It is represented, symbolically, by any conjunction of opposites; the yin-yang, bird-snake, head-tail or man-woman. It can also be represented by joining a cross or square (the four straight lines representing the four directions or elements) with a circle – the perfect, unbroken geometrical shape suggesting unity. In the Christian iconographic tradition, Jesus is usually shown standing on a square platform with a circle behind him, demonstrating his role in the great restoration as the bridge between heaven and earth.

The Egyptian symbol of the Ankh was later
adopted by the Egypt-based Coptic church

This relationship was symbolized in Egypt by the Ankh. Adding
a circle on top of the cross joins the symbols for heaven and earth
together, showing that the path to salvation begins with linking our
earthly, divided selves back to the eternal divinity. The symbol of
the Ankh was the key of Osiris, who ushered souls into the afterlife.
Each soul would first be weighed, and if it was lighter than a specific
feather, Osiris would lead it into heaven. If the soul was too heavy, it
would be consumed by Set, the devourer. It is interesting to note the
importance of *weight*. Thinking "scientifically," the soul was likened
to a balloon or lantern. Just as it would be impossible for a balloon
to fly if it were full of sand, the soul could not ascend to heaven if it
were attached to the weight of the body; but the soul free from the
body's lusts and desires was like a balloon filled with air.

In one Gnostic salvation story, the Logos had to descend through
the seven heavens and save Sophia from the dragon of corporeality,
or the physical body. This story is probably a remnant from Ianna's
descent into the underworld, where for each of the Seven Gates she
had to remove one of her seven garments. Mythologically, this can
also be demonstrated by a young hero who slays a snake or dragon
to rescue a young maiden. Moreover, the dragon often had seven
heads, representing the seven heavens.

Perseus is a good example. He found Andromeda bound to a
rock, and rescued her from the sea monster on the condition that
she became his wife. Perseus is also famous for slaying Medusa,
the serpent-haired Gorgon. Medusa was the fallen woman, cursed
because of her beauty, living in the wilderness. Her hair was
transformed into many snakes; the desires of our bodies which turn
men to stone, or trap them in death. The power to turn people to
stone was also given to the ice queen in Narnia, who was based on
pagan mythology and represents similar concepts.

Hercules slayed the seven-headed Hydra, by cutting off its
heads and burying the last one alive; this is not dissimilar to the

story of Cadmus. The Leviathon, which was killed by Yahweh at the beginning of time, also had several heads, as recorded in Psalm 74 of the Old Testament. Significantly, Yahweh used the pieces of the Leviathon to "feed the people inhabiting the wilderness"; perhaps originally this was intended to explain how humanity acquired the divine (but flawed) element:

> Yet God is my King of old, Working salvation in the midst of the earth. Thou didst divide the sea by thy strength: Thou brakest the heads of the sea-monsters in the waters. Thou brakest the heads of leviathan in pieces; Thou gavest him to be food to the people inhabiting the wilderness. (Psalm 74:12-14)

The seven-headed beast is already a feature in Ugaritic mythology; Ba'al Hadaad fights it by the name of Lotan. More modern examples included Harry Potter rescuing Ginny from the basilisk, and even Nintendo's Mario saving the Princess from the fire-breathing dragon in the dungeon. Ironically, the Christian story of St. George the dragon slayer, which has been memorialized in hundreds of paintings and sculptures and is sometimes believed to represent how Christianity defeated paganism and Devil-worship, actually *preserves* pagan mythology and is identical to stories like Perseus and Andromeda.

Another modern example (with a twist) is Disney's *The Little Mermaid* (1989). The first official mermaid was Atargatis, worshipped by the Babylonians as early as 8000BC and depicted as half fish. In Medieval times mermaids were used as symbols embodying the lure of fleshy pleasures to be shunned by the God-fearing.[7] In the Disney movie, Ariel represents the lost feminine, who dreams of being reunited with her handsome prince. The Sea Monster is Ursula; an octopus with many serpentine appendages. Instead of a garden of stone statues, she has a garden of writhing, green polyps – which all used to be merpeople before Ursula tempted them into captivity. Ursula is finally defeated by Eric (the prince), who saves Ariel and brings her up into his kingdom above the water.

The symbolic elements in these stories focus on a hero or savior, who will come down to save humanity. Other versions, more popular among Eastern religions (especially most forms of Buddhism), view unity or the One as a passive force or energy. It is up to us to get back to the source – which requires mastery over our physical drives, caused by the illusion of the physical world, or *maya*. That is, by controlling our passions we can break out of the cycle of reincarnation. Again, these ideas are very similar to, for example, the Orphic conception of transmigration; it is possible that mystery religions inwardly interpreted their symbols along the same lines as their Eastern counterparts. Buddhism (which appeared in India around 600BC) may have been inspired by the early Egyptian or Greek cults, or at least by common roots.

If you're familiar with yoga or meditation, you've probably heard of the unconscious, libidinal force called Kundalini, which literally means "coiling." In the classical literature of Hatha Yoga, Kundalini is described as a coiled serpent at the base of the spine. Through fasting and meditation, it is thought that we can elevate this energy up through the spine and unite it with a universal spirit located at the top of our heads. As this dormant, feminine energy unfolds, it unlocks the seven chakras of our spiritual body, which each have their own color of the spectrum as well as a unique vibration or note in the octave. After the seven chakras within our body have been opened, we can activate the Crown chakra, and find unification with the God-head:

> In this way, the divine mother Shakti, in the form of Kundalini, can find union with her beloved, the supreme Shiva, who resides in eternal bliss at the top of the skull. Thus one can move beyond the elements and achieve the non-dual consciousness that brings liberation from the ever-changing world of illusion.[8]

  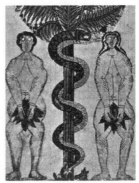

Like the biblical garden story, the tale of Buddha's enlightenment is always associated with the snake and a special tree. Pictures show him sitting under the Bo-tree, or tree of wisdom, with a halo around his head similar to illustrations of Attis or Krishna. Statues of the Buddha often display him sitting on the coils of a giant seven headed cobra, which weaves directly up his spine and hovers over his head (this is especially true for "Muchalinda" statues of the 12th century Khmer region). Buddhist tradition teaches that just before the Buddha attained enlightenment, a cobra wrapped around his body seven times. After he was enlightened, he danced around the tree for seven days.

Images from the mystical tradition of the Jewish Kabbalah show remarkable similarity to the Eastern idea of Kundalini. The tradition of the Kabbalah centers on the Tree of Life, a symbolic spiritual path to purification. Through devotion, meditation and spiritual rituals, Kabbalists try to climb the Tree of Life like a spiritual ladder, unlocking key points in the body. In some cases the symbol of a snake is even used to show the correct procession through the points. Leonora Leet, author of *The Universal Kabbalah*, confirms:

> Fallen man, driven out of the Garden in a condition that identifies him with the snake, must now climb the Tree of Life internally, through the initiatic practices of kabbalistic meditation.[9]

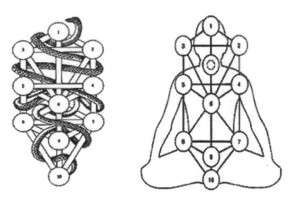

Mystics refer to the chakras as seven seals or locks that must be opened by increasing or tuning the vibration or planetary resonance. This can be compared to descriptions in the book of

Revelation, in which the Lamb of God (usually associated with Jesus) must open or break seven seals in order to end the world; a system which, as has been pointed out, is similar to Harry Potter's quest to find and destroy Voldemort's seven horcruxes. When the seven seals are broken, the chakras open, the heavens unify, and the physical world ends, leaving only the perfect, blinding white light of the original unity. One of the main disagreements between world religions is whether this "Nirvana" (to use the Buddhist term) can be achieved in this life immediately, or will come at the end of time.

While Sophia and the flesh were represented by a snake, the higher universal spirit was usually depicted by either an owl, for wisdom; a dove, for purity; or an eagle, for power. Just like the Ankh, symbols that joined the bird and snake together signify the unification of the soul with the universal spirit. Many sun figures are associated with a bird and a snake, alluding to their intermediary role between heaven and earth. Other figures are shown with a snake wrapping up around their legs and a bird over their heads. In Egypt, the lower kingdom (the body) was represented by a cobra, and the upper kingdom (the spirit) was represented by a vulture. The cobra and the vulture were both worn on the Pharaoh's crown, to show his power over life and death.

Alchemists often used the symbol of a two headed hermaphrodite to represent the combined sun-moon dichotomy. In the pictures above (right and left), the male side is holding a bird to symbolize the spirit, and the female is holding a cup containing three snakes to symbolize the physical world of the flesh. Under their feet is the crescent moon or dragon, symbol of the fallen woman and the lower regions of matter. Near them is a tree with six branches on either side. The two must climb up separately before reaching the final, seventh branch, and then join together in the eternal unity symbolized by the sun. In the center picture this takes place inside the cosmic egg. The seven planents are represented and the man and women hold the set-square and compass. Mercury is the planet at the center, which is the planet most often associated with mystic rituals or esotericism.

The Caduceus, the mystical symbol carried by Hermes (or his Roman counterpart, Mercury) is another ancient symbol that uses the bird-snake symbol. According to legend it was given to him by the sun god Apollo. The symbol appeared early in Babylonia and is related to other serpent symbols of fertility, wisdom and healing. It is stylistically similar to the staff of Acsculpius, which portrays simply a snake climbing up a pole.

Today, many modern medical groups, Medcorp for example, use the Caduceus in their emblems. Others, including the World Health Organization, use the staff of Asclepius. Both symbols use the ascending snake to represent healing and spiritual growth, and in both symbols the snakes often cross the pole at seven points.

## Meeting Satan Again for the First Time

With the virtual disappearance of the fallen feminine aspect of this myth in Christianity (it is preserved in the mother-consort figure of the two Marys, but difficult to identify), many of these esoteric symbols became fixed onto the tradition of Lucifer, the Devil.

Stories about Satan, the enemy of God ruler of the world and darkness, adopted much symbolism from the feminine lower regions of the divided Draco. The fallen woman was identified with the constellation Virgo, trapped at the side of Hydra, the sea serpent. She was also linked to Aphrodite or the planet Venus, because she represented earthly comforts and physical love. Stories about a great goddess who fell into the material world because of her beauty are common in mythology, and the biblical tale about Satan being a beautiful angel, cast out of heaven because of his pride, may also have its roots in the division of the Logos:

> You were the model of perfection, full of wisdom and perfect in beauty... Your heart became proud on account of your beauty, and you corrupted your wisdom because of your splendor. (Ezekiel 28:10 - 17)

Although Satan today is nearly always masculine, his two nicknames, "The Morning Star" and "Lucifer," (light bringer) were titles assigned to the planet Venus because it came in the morning just before the sun rose. As we've seen, most early renditions of the fall of mankind show a snake with a woman's head wrapped around the tree of knowledge. Rather than a specific mastermind ruling the underworld, Satan is a composite character whose images reflect the process of expansion and separation. We can see this more clearly by contrasting two of the cards from Waite's Tarot deck.

The Devil is crowned by an inverted pentacle, which seems to cut his horns in two and then curve down – demonstrating both the separation, and the downward expansion, of the polar energies. In case we missed the point, his head is also an inverted triangle, and he is even pointing a torch downwards to signify the fall of the Logos, or divine spark. The male and female are separate, naked and in chains, signifying their bondage to their physical desires. They are also horned and tailed (governed by their animal senses), and gazing downwards. While not necessarily evil, the fleeting lusts and desires of the flesh blind the soul from seeing its true purpose, and threaten its eventual homecoming. When we fulfill them, we are giving into the animal side of us, letting it have control. When the body dies, the light may be lost forever. In order to gain eternal life (it was believed), we have to free ourselves from the body and return to the light.

The Lovers card, on the other hand, demonstrates the restoration. There is a large triangle (the mountain) in the middle of the card pointing up. The woman represents the fallen Sophia. She is next to a snake in a tree. The man on the right has his own tree – but it is almost barren. There are exactly 12 leaves, hinting that, until the restoration, he is still stuck beneath the 12 zodiac signs, and subject to time and death. They are both looking up at the large welcoming angel and dazzling sun.

The Alchemist's Sun-Logos, symbolized by the Lion, is the unification of all polarities. In the mystical symbol to the left, the snake signifies the physical world, with its divided polarities, represented by the sun and the moon. The tail is in the figure eight of eternity, showing the continuity of time. When the polarities are rejoined, time will end with an eternal summer, or the kingdom of the lion.

An elaboration of the cross is the anchor symbol. This ancient magical icon is a representation of the created universe. Pictures of anchors are more common in early Christian art and architecture than crosses. The anchor shows the trinity (the top point is sometimes a loop, to show the eternal unity), the descent, and the two polarities that are divided. Many anchor symbols are drawn with either a snake or a rope winding up it to show the process back up to the top.

If you look again at the Lovers card above you will see that if you combined the two trees, the entire picture forms an anchor. This symbolism is also common in Christian iconography; you can see it in the painting from the Oregon Grotto. By overlaying the anchor symbol on this painting (below left) we can see how precisely the scene was laid out. The other picture (below right) is an alchemical illustration depicting the anchor as a kind of fishing hook, cast back up to the cross from the heart of the world. It also incorporates symbols of bird and snakes, as well as the roots of the World Tree.

## Conclusion and Summary

Although most of the discussion above has relied on liberal interpretation, I believe that these symbols hold specific mystical meaning that was recognized by early spiritual traditions, which gradually set up forms of spiritual education to pass on this experiential wisdom. To cheat death and achieve immortality, mystics and philosophers tried to unite the divided polarities in their own lifetimes. The male had to seek out and rejoin the female; the sun had to catch up with the moon.

In the West, myths were created about gallant knights who would go out and slay dragons. Hercules, for example has to defeat the dragon Ladon in the garden of Hesperides to seize the golden apples (an interesting reversal of Adam and Eve's "seduction" by the serpent). In the East, the dragon represented our spiritual energy, winding upwards to be reunited with the universal Tao or Shakti. What is common to these various traditions is the idea of balancing energies, which will someday be reunited.

Some communities founded schools based around a series of initiation ceremonies and rituals aimed at taming the serpent and reuniting the fallen soul with its universal counterpart. Participation often required preparation and sacrifice. The event could be a one time, life-changing experience, or an incremental set of steps that led an initiate into a fuller understanding of truth. At higher levels – when the initiate was spiritually ready for it – certain stories or symbols became revealed in a new and unexpected way. The higher levels had to remain absolutely silent about what they'd learned so that they would not interfere with the progress of the newer initiates. This led to strict oaths of secrecy; hence they were called "Mystery" schools. These schools kept few written materials and had no encyclopedia of beliefs, so it is difficult to know with certainty what each one practiced or what its members believed in. However, based on the commonality of symbols and using what evidence is available to us, a fairly comprehensive view of the mysteries is possible.

A common element of these schools was the belief in the fallen spark (or soul) that must return through the seven layers of the universe before reuniting with the universal Logos. In the next chapter, I will explore some of the early beliefs of these schools and prove that Christianity, from its earliest stages, was one of them.

# PART THREE
## The Accidental History

The first two sections of this book have attempted to demonstrate that much of the symbolism and motifs in the Bible were appropriated by early Christian writers from external sources and added into the story of Jesus Christ. The material provided so far, however, while noteworthy and significant, may still be dismissed as speculative research or inference by those who refuse to believe that Jesus Christ was *only* literary.

Are there enough similarities, interesting bits of historical trivia and common features between Christianity and other various pre-existing religions to make the claim that Jesus was purely mythological? Maybe – but large holes remain. If this book ended here, some readers might conclude, "Well that's certainly inventive, but it's not convincing. *Where's the proof?*"

As the formidable modern defender of the historical Jesus J.P. Holding, author of *Shattering the Christ Myth* (2008), writes in his online essay "Did The Greek God of Wine Influence Christian Beliefs":

> What more needs be said? The Christ-Dionysus parallel has very little to commend it. What few exist are based on universal conceptions and themes. Moreover, to make his argument persuasive, the claimant must explain how and why a group of Palestinian Jews borrowed the theology and teachings of a foreign cult and founded a new religion based upon them. He must also explain why the parallels between the doctrine taught by Jesus and that of contemporary Judaism were so similar, not to mention why the early Christians initially maintained

the trappings of Jewish religious observation (Temple attendance, circumcision, etc.)[1]

In order to finish the investigation into the literary Jesus, therefore, we must address these and other historical issues. Even if the symbols and motifs were similar, and Christianity did borrow from paganism, that doesn't mean that they interpreted the symbols in the same way. They could have borrowed the nuts and bolts but applied specific, innovative Christian interpretations without relying on paganism. Therefore, we have to show that Christians *did* interpret, in the beginning, their savior and his ministry in identical terms; i.e. as spiritual allegory rather than historical fact. We will also need respond to the objection that Jews would never have become involved in pagan mystery cults or idolatry. More importantly, we have to demonstrate how the story of Jesus was created, for what reason, and by whom. We will do this in Chapter Eight.

There is no denying that from early on, many Christians did believe in Jesus as a historical person – passionately enough to die for him. Why would they believe he was historical if he wasn't? Where did they get this idea from? If, as we've seen, there were competing ideas about Jesus, which was first (the original), and which was an offshoot or "heresy"? In Chapter Nine, we establish that the idea of the historical Jesus came late, was seen by the original church leaders as a mistaken offshoot, and was properly reprimanded. Further, we will discover exactly how, why and when this "mistake" came about.

Finally, even if Christianity was somehow a grievous error or mistake, how could it have grown so strong so quickly? How could it have eradicated virtually all other forms of beliefs – surpassing (either by assimilating or destroying) various other forms of religious and spiritual practice? In Chapter Ten, we give strong historical evidence for the non-spiritual conditions that fueled the spread of Christianity.

## CHAPTER EIGHT

# Abracadabra:
# The Magical Name and the
# Creation of the Jewish Mysteries

*"Jesus said to the 12 apostles: 'You have been given the mystery of the Kingdom of God, but to those, the ones outside, everything is given in parables, so that seeing, they may see and not perceive, and hearing, they may hear but not understand.'" –Mark 4:11*

THE PURPOSE OF THIS CHAPTER will be to demonstrate that Christianity was originally a mystery religion; that it had distinct layers of meaning; and that only the higher level initiates were given the full understanding of their faith. This understanding of early Christianity will be crucial in explaining the communicative decay that finally led to the uniquely Christian revolution of viewing the divine Logos as a historical person.

In order to accomplish this task, it must be shown that the concept of such a religious organization was already widely understood and practiced, that the worship of the other Jesus-like savior figures was conducted in a similar manner, and that, although diverse, these organizations shared some basic features and rites. We must also show why the Jews, who so scrupulously avoided pagan idolatry, would have been interested in a Jewish version of the Greek mystery cult tradition, as well as demonstrate convincingly *how* and *why* such a novel combination of religious traditions was achieved.

## What is a "Mystery Religion"?

In brief, a mystery religion is a religion that keeps its inner teachings secret – even from its own members. This *Arcanum* or "secret wisdom" is divulged to initiates step-by-step, only after they've gone through certain ceremonies or achieved an elevated level of understanding. The ancient Greek term μυστήρια (mysteria) actually means "initiation"; which gives the above passage from the gospel of Mark a new implication: You who have been initiated can understand the *meaning* of the parables. Nearly all early Christian texts refer to the "mysteries" of God or receiving the "mysteries" of Jesus. Later, this word will be translated into Latin as *sacrament* – a word still used by the Church to explain rituals of mysterious power.

The ancient mysteries represented a kind of esoteric initiation based in part upon the reenactment of a (usually tragic) story of a suffering god, which promised members a deeper understanding of the universe and their role in it. This was the standard religious structure for many kinds of spiritual organizations in the Greek and Roman empires. It was related especially in conjunction with mythic figures who exemplified death and rebirth in some way, such as Dionysus, Osiris, Tammuz, Orpheus, Mithras, Asclepius or Attis. The Eleusinian Mysteries are believed to have been established around 1500BC, and might have eastern origins – although similarities between the Isiac mysteries of Egypt have led scholars to suggest a shared link:

> The reception of the wandering goddess, her power that can be used either for good or evil, the child in the fire, danger and salvation: these form an impressive and characteristic complex and not just a superficial parallel. This would suggest that some Egyptian influence on the Eleusinian cult or at least on Eleusisian mythology right at

the beginning of the sixth century, in a context of practical 'healing magic.'[1]

In fact, although Western philosophy attributes its birth to the early "Naturalist Philosophers" of Greece, these same philosophers admit to having gained their wisdom in Egypt, where they had become initiates of the mysteries. It is likely that what we know as "Greek philosophy" was really just an attempt to describe the cosmology of these mysteries in rational terms.

In the 5th century AD, Proclus, head of the Neoplatonic school of Athens, wrote a brief history of Geometry known as the Eudemian Summary, claiming that the tradition of seeking knowledge from Egyptian mysteries began with Thales:

> Thales was the first to go to Egypt and bring back to Greece this study [geometry]; he himself discovered many propositions, and disclosed the underlying principles of many others to his successors, in some cases his method being more general, in others more empirical. (Proclus, *Commentary on Euclid*)[2]

Thales later recommended the mysteries of Egypt to Pythagoras, as recorded by Iamblichus, who wrote a history of Pythagoras and his followers called *On the Pythagorean Life*. Born in the third century AD and student of Porphyry, Iamblichus portrays Pythagoras as a spiritual seeker, becoming initiated into various mystery cults in order to gain wisdom. It is worth quoting in full:

> Then he sailed on to Sidon, aware that it was his birthplace, and correctly supposing that crossing to Egypt would be easier from there. In Sidon he met the descendants of Mochos the natural philosopher and prophet [who was believed to have originated Atomism], and the other Phoenician hierophants [priest and keeper of sacred mysteries], and as initiated in all the rites peculiar to Byblos, Tyre and other districts of Syria. He did not, as one might unthinkingly suppose, undergo this experience from superstition, but far more from a passionate desire for knowledge, and as a precaution lest something worth learning should elude him by being kept secret in the mysteries or rituals of the gods. Besides, he had learnt that the Syrian rites were offshoots of those of Egypt, and hoped to share, in Egypt, in mysteries of purer form, more beautiful and more divine. Awestruck, as his teacher Thales had promised, he crossed without delay to Egypt.

From there [Egypt] he visited all the sanctuaries, making detailed investigations with the utmost zeal. The priests and the prophets he met responded with admiration and affection, and he learned from them most diligently all that they had to teach. He neglected no doctrine valued in his time, no man renowned for understanding, no rite honored in any region, no place where he expected to find some wonder. So he visited all the priests, profited from each one particular wisdom. He spent twenty-two years in the sacred places of Egypt, studying astronomy and geometry, and being initiated - but not just on impulse or as the occasion offered - into all the rites of the gods, until he was captured by the expedition of Kampyses and taken to Babylon. There he spent time with the Magi, to their mutual rejoicing, learning what was holy among them, acquiring perfect knowledge of the worship of the gods and reaching the heights of their mathematics and music and other disciplines. He spent twelve more years with them, and returned to Samos, aged by now about fifty-six.[3]

Although not strictly historical, this passage testifies to the importance and relevance of the mysteries in the third century AD, as well as the fierce competition between them. Pythagoras and his followers could claim to have *the best*, most complete form of the mysteries precisely because – according to Iamblichus – he'd already become a member of all the others.

Perhaps in the beginning only those with the dedication, perseverance and intelligence were admitted into the higher mysteries. However, when these ancient practices were assimilated into the cosmopolitan societies of Greco-Roman civilization, teachers or entrepreneurs opened their own schools and actively recruited members. These schools were usually centered around highly charismatic leaders or mythical saviors, who were attributed with miraculous powers. As membership became a sign of status, some schools began charging steep fees, and may have become entertainment for high society clubs rather than genuine havens for wisdom.

At the zenith of the phenomenon, the basic format of the mystery organization was copied again and again, based on ever-evolving spiritual promises in response to the increasingly competitive environment. It is estimated that in Athens alone there were over 600 mystery schools. Unfortunately, much of what we know about the mysteries was preserved via condemnation or criticism from external sources. Due to the secretive nature of the mysteries, we may never know exactly what was taught at the highest levels. However, we can piece together something about these groups from the clues they left. The following list comprises a basic sketch.

- ★ Code of Silence
- ★ Hieros Logos (Sacred Story)
- ★ Hierarchy of Initiation
- ★ Brotherhood
- ★ Ritual death and rebirth
- ★ Identification with God
- ★ Ethics
- ★ Afterlife

I will briefly expand each point before continuing.

## Code of Silence

A key (in fact, the defining) characteristic of the mysteries was their secrecy, which also makes academic research into the mysteries difficult. The Eleusinian Mysteries of Demeter were so integral to Greek culture that the Law of Athens made it illegal to reveal the secret proceedings experienced by initiates. According to Godwin:

> Silence was maintained with such admirable strictness in antiquity that the inquisitive researcher can discover very little of what went on in the rituals of these religions. The only things that were committed to writing were those which might be generally published; of the rest, memory was the best vault and silence the best guardian. But the most eloquent language of the Mysteries is not verbal but symbolic. Symbols elude the limiting precision of words, a precision which pins the ideas like butterflies to a single plane, while they should be free to flutter up and down all the levels of being and of meaning.[4]

There are two basic reasons that the mysteries evolved a code of silence. The first is mystical: the "Truth" of the universe was seen as inherently a mystery; it was beyond all human comprehension and expression. As soon as you try to speak about it, you contaminate it. All that can be done is to try to hint towards it, in parable or myth.

To protect its doctrine from external critique and to safeguard the spiritual progress of its own initiates, the central truths of the cult had to be kept hidden. The following passage by the 4th century Neoplatonist philosopher Macrobius describes how only the "elite" could interpret the true meaning of the mystery stories.

> Plain and naked exposition of herself is repugnant to nature... she wishes her secrets to be treated by myth. Thus the mysteries themselves are hidden in the tunnels of figurative expression, so that not even to initiates the nature of such realities may present herself naked, but only an elite may know about the real secret, through the interpretation furnished by wisdom, while the rest may be content to venerate the mystery, defended by those figurative expressions against banality. (Macrobius S. sc. 1.2.17f)[5]

Many traditions were divided into "Higher" and "Lesser" mysteries; for the higher initiates, the stories were spiritual metaphors to be interpreted. For everyone else, the very obscurity and complexity in the stories gave them a vestige of sacred power, which made them venerable and holy. The perplexing and enigmatic nature of the parables was designed to protect the truth, and command respect from the crowd. Demetrius explains:

> What is surmised (but not overtly expressed) is more frightening... What is clear and manifest is easily despised, like naked men. Therefore the mysteries too are expressed in the form of allegory, in order to arouse consternation and dread, just as they are performed in darkness and at night. (Demetrius Eloc. 101)[6]

Acknowledging this dimension of participation-by-exclusion, the mysteries were used in some cultures as a political tool to control the masses while justifying the ruling classes. Clement of Alexandria imparts that the mysteries of Egypt were mainly reserved for those in authority:

> The Egyptians do not reveal their Religious Mysteries promiscuously to all, nor communicate the knowledge of divine things to the Profane, but only to those who are to succeed in the kingdom, and to such of the Priests as are judged most fitly qualified for the same, upon account both of their birth and education. (Origen, *Contra Celsum*, 1.12)[7]

The second reason for the secrecy is more practical. The mysteries were, like most other religious organizations, at least in some sense *business enterprises*. That is, they traded rites of initiation for sacrifices and donations, without which they could not operate. Hence, having their sacred secrets leaked could destroy them. Powerful or rare mysteries not commonly available could command a higher price than others. Plato remarks, for example, that myths such as the suffering of Kronos should only be told to those who make a big sacrifice in advance, not just those who offer a pig, as at Eleusis (Plato, Republic 377).[8]

Hungarian scholar Károly Kerenyi, one of the founders of modern studies in Greek mythology, remarks that this distinction was inherent to the Greek language:

> Of course, there could be different degrees of secrecy in connection with cults of like content. The Greek language itself draws a distinction between the *arrheton*, the ineffable secret, and the *aporrheton*, that which was kept secret under a law of silence.[9]

In both cases, the obvious question is "how do you communicate the *incommunicable?*" This is perhaps the foundational question behind the evolution of the mysteries.

## Hieros Logos (Sacred Story)

The mysteries were organized around a sacred story or foundation myth. These were almost always tales of suffering gods who in some sense died and were reborn; they involve a process of first mourning the loss, and then celebrating the return of their savior. These stories may have originally been vegetative myths that were reappropriated, and were reenacted either publicly in grand processions or privately in initiation ceremonies. Burkert relates:

> It has long been held that mystery myths are of a particular type, that of the "suffering god." The appropriate Greek word is pathea, "sufferings," and this, connected with rituals of grief, mourning, and a nocturnal setting, is the proper content of mysteria already in Herodotus. We do find the abduction of Persephone, and indeed the death of Dionysus, Attis, and Osiris. There is a sequence of mourning followed by joy in the mysteries, whether those of Eleusis, Meter, or Isis. The grief of Demeter ends with the return of Persephone, and

"The festival ends with exaltation and the brandishing of torches"; at the festival of Mater Magna, the *dies sanguinis* is followed by the Hilaria, the day of joy; the mourning rituals of Isis end with the finding of Osiris, the water of the Nile: "We have found, we rejoice together."[9]

By suffering, the mystery gods appear much more sympathetic to the problems of existence, more approachable and more intimate with humanity. As Godwin clarifies:

Unlike the gods of Olympus, the Mystery gods have usually suffered pain, loss or death, and this gives them compassion for our own sufferings and joys. Osiris, Orpheus, Hercules, Christ, Dionysus, Attis and Adonis were all slain and resurrected.[11]

But the foundational myths of the mysteries were not things that had to be "believed in"; a proper experience of these stories (enhanced by ritualistic initiation) would affect a profound psychological change in the participant – which was aided by the emotional underpinnings of the tale. This process may be related to the classical idea of tragedy, the first of which was recognized as an official state cult in Athens in 534BC in honor of Dionysus. Aristotle gives the following definition:

Tragedy, then, is a process of imitating an action which has serious implications, is complete, and possesses magnitude; by means of language which has been made sensuously attractive, with each of its varieties found separately in the parts; enacted by the persons themselves and not presented through narrative; through a course of pity and fear completing the purification (catharsis, sometimes translated "purgation") of such emotions. (Aristotle, *Poetics* VI 2 (1449 b))

The *mystai*, or initiates, had to first witness a story about a tragic figure (this was probably already a well-known cultural myth open to the public). This story was later used in the mysteries as the background that would lead into a mystical experience beyond words.

Is it not true that the mysteries were "unspeakable," *arrheta*, not just in the sense of artificial secrecy utilized to arouse curiosity, but in the sense that what was central and decisive was not accessible to verbalization? There is an "unspeakable sympatheia" of the souls with the rituals, Proclus states, and much older is the well-known pronouncement of Aristotle that those undergoing mysteries (*teloumenoi*) should not "learn" (*mathein*) but should "be affected," "suffer," or "experience" (*pathein*).[12]

Mysteries often incorporated active participation in the therapeutic process of role-play or story telling. Consequently, this *hieros logos* or sacred story nearly always justified the rites and rituals that an initiate would personally have to go through later. It should be noted that the "suffering god" motif does not appear to apply to Mithraism, unless Mithras is associated with the bull, implying a self-sacrifice. Kerenyi explains:

> Without effort on his part, the spectator was transported into what he saw. What he saw and heard was made easy for him and became irresistibly his. He came to believe in it, but this belief was very different from that aroused by the *epopteia*. He entered into other people's sufferings, forgot himself, and – as Aristotle stressed – was purified. "Through pity and terror, tragedy brought purification from all those passions."[13]

## Hierarchy of Initiation

The mysteries attempted to convey a non-rational experience of the divine; truth was not something to be learned, but something to be witnessed. Consequently, initiation involved not a sermon, but a series of grueling physical challenges and experiences designed to shock and awe initiates, perhaps into a kind of sensory overload. These included initial tests or preparations, which could be significantly daunting. At the very least they might include fasting, a vow of silence, ritual bathing, dressing in specific clothing, and sacrifice or donation. A few of the rituals are mentioned in the following passage for the cult of Isis:

> In the cult of Isis the rich symbolism and the conduct at her services must have been carefully mastered by her ministers. From the pages of Apuleius we gain a good picture of Lucius' 'father in god' giving spiritual guidance, possessing the title of the highest Mithraic grade and called Mithras. The priest has to deal with the mysteries of the

faith: the cleansing of the soul by baptism, whereby the initiate gained admission into the sacred band, the seven washings, the soul's death unto sin and rebirth to a better and purer life, the impatient wait in the darkness of the Magaron cell and the worshipper's apotheosis by sanctification in a resurrected Osiris.[14]

Rituals were often listed by initiates as steps *that they'd completed,* which would be understood by fellow initiates who'd experience the same process, but seem like impossible riddles to outsiders.

I approached the frontier of death, I set foot on the threshold of Persephone, I journeyed through all the elements and came back, I saw at midnight the sun, sparkling in white light, I came close to the gods of the upper and the nether world and adored them from near at hand. (Apuleius, *Metamorphoses* 11:23. 6-8)[15]

I ate from the tympanon, I drank from the cymbal, I carried the composite vessel (kernos), I slipped under the bedcurtain.[16]

Although divided loosely into greater and lesser mysteries, initiates could actually face many separate levels of initiation. Each level could include specific rituals, memorization of secret passwords or magic phrases, different props, various garments or accessories, or even a physical mark such as a brand or tattoo. The mysteries of Mithras, for example (which as we saw above may have been blended with the mysteries of Isis) had seven levels, probably representing the seven known planets:

The initiations are more prominent and more sophisticated in these mysteries than anywhere else, since they are multiplied to produce seven grades of initiates: Korax/corvus, the raven; Nymphus, the chrysalis; Stratiotes/miles, the soldier; Leo, the lion, Persa, the Persian; Heliodromus, the sun-runner; and Pater, the father.[17]

After each level they would be awarded a new title as well as some external symbol of their status. An initiate at the highest level ("Father"), wore a red cap, a mantle, a ring, and carried a shepherd's staff – much like today's Pope.

Initiates of Mithras would first be baptized and born again as infants into their new life, and then made to fast and keep a special diet in order to gain control over their bodies. Once their physical drives were in check, they would perform a ritual death, often actually dressing in death rags and being buried or sealed in a tomb. The goal of Mithraism was the unification of the lower self with the Logos, for which they used the name "Perseus", during a ritual called the Wedding Chamber.

Having completed all of the levels, initiates would be marked with a symbol of the organization and allowed to teach. According to Franz Cumont, "This indelible imprint perpetuated the memory of the solemn engagement by which the person under vow contracted to serve in that order of chivalry which Mithraism constituted."[18] At the highest levels was a kind of naturalistic monotheism: initiates would learn that the mythologies of gods and goddesses were pious fictions, which could be interpreted. At the center of the universe, however, remained an invisible and anonymous God which could be experienced:

> By passing the threshold between the lesser and the greater mysteries, the initiate is supposed to abrogate his former beliefs, to recognize their erroneous and fictitious nature, and "to see things as they are." The disillusionment of the initiate is brought about by telling him that the gods are just deified mortals and that there is only one invisible and anonymous God, the ultimate cause and foundation of Being "who originated all by himself, and to him all things owe their being." These phrases are taken from Eusebius and Clement of Alexandria, who both quote an Orphic hymn which Warburton interprets as the words by which the hierophant in the Eleusinian mysteries addressed the initiate.[19]

## Mystical Experience

It is has been asserted, based on ancient testimony, that the mysteries consistently produced spiritual or mystical experiences which required very little preparation, and were almost universally effective. New initiates really did experience something that *transcended* any normal experience they'd ever had; further, people were willing to travel great distances and pay for this experience, year after year. Consequently, several researchers have posited the use of a mind-altering chemical or plant. This view is elaborated in the classic book, *The Road to Eleusis,* which contends that the Claviceps purpurea mushroom was used (in the Eleusinian Mysteries) to induce visions and spiritual experiences. Although inconclusive and not directly related to this study, the following account helps us to understand the mystery experience.

As the authors point out, the experience was a vision whereby the pilgrim became someone who *saw*, or an "epoptes." The archaeological remains of the hall in which this experience took place is considered unsuited for theatrical performances, actors or stage apparatus. Hence, it is claimed, "What was witnessed there was no play by actors, but phasmata, ghostly apparitions, in particular, the spirit of Persephone herself, returned from the dead with her new-born son, conceived in the land of death."[20] According to the authors, this vision was most likely produced by a hallucinogen:

> The Greeks were sophisticated about drama and it is highly unlikely that they could have been duped by some kind of theatrical trick, especially since it is people as intelligent as the poet Pindar and the tragedian Sophocles who have testified to the overwhelming value of what was seen at Eleusis. There were physical symptoms, moreover, that accompanied the vision: fear and a trembling in the limbs, vertigo, nausea, and a cold sweat. Then there came the vision, a sight amidst an aura of brilliant light that suddenly flickered through the darkened chamber. Eyes had never before seen the like, and apart from the formal prohibition against telling of what had happened, the experience itself was incommunicable, for there are no words adequate to the task. Even a poet could only say that he had seen the beginning and the end of life and known that they were one, something given by god. The division between earth and sky melted into a pillar of light. These are the symptomatic reactions not to a drama or ceremony, but to a mystical vision; and since the sight could be offered to thousands of initiates each year dependably upon schedule, it seems obvious that an hallucinogen must have induced it.[21]

These claims are strengthened by the revelation that some rich Athenians began reproducing the experience at home with friends, such as the Athenian aristocrat Alcibiades who was condemned for it in 415BC. "We are confirmed in this conclusion by two further observations: a special potion, as we know, was drunk prior to the visual experience; and secondly, a notorious scandal was uncovered in the classical age, when it was discovered that numerous aristocratic Athenians had begun celebrating the Mystery at home with groups of drunken guests at dinner parties."[22]

The ritual use of such a drug or chemical is thus not outside the realm of possibility, and certainly helps answer some questions about the fundamental experience of the sacred initiations, as well as why the mysteries at Eleusis enjoyed continued success for almost 2,000 years. At the very least, we can conclude that the mysteries were powerful, life-changing events for participants.

### Brotherhood

Membership in a common mystery was an immediate bond between strangers. They could greet each other using secretive riddles and responses they had learned, and many cults probably had a secret handshake as well. Aristides comments on this fellowship as an initiate of the mysteries of Asclepius:

> Neither belonging to a chorus nor sailing together nor having the same teacher is as great a thing as the boon and profit of being a fellow pilgrim to the temple of Asclepius and being initiated into the first of the holy rites by the fairest and most perfect torchbearer and leader of the mysteries, to whom every rule of necessity yields. (Oratio, 23.15-8)[23] (125))

Referring to initiates as a "brotherhood" goes back as far as the early mysteries of Eleusis and was used widely in later mystery organizations:

> The term 'brother,' *adelphos*, is used even at Eleusis for those who receive initiation together. This is remarkable even if it is to be understood more in terms of a clan system than of emotional affection. Plato's Seventh Letter refers to the uncommonly close ties of friendship that develop through hospitality and common participation in the mysteries – those of Eleusis, no doubt – although for the philosopher this kind of friendship lacks the stable basis provided only by philosophy.[24]

This brotherhood was especially useful in the mysteries of Mithras, which became especially popular among the Roman military, and helped support bonds of solidarity between them. It was also sometimes used to establish an alternative sub-society: a "kingdom of god" rather than man.

Pythagoras, for example, after returning from his studies in Egypt, founded an entire community of followers who lived together in a school, owned no possessions, followed strict rules of moral conduct and ate no meat. There were also codes of silence. Time was spent reading, playing music, and studying. He may have based this school on the early Orphic mystery cult, which is considered to be the first proper mystery school based on esoteric wisdom and initiation.

### Ritual Death and Rebirth

The central ritual of the mysteries, it appears, was a symbolic death of the initiate, followed by a rebirth into a new life. This was intimately tied to the conception of the cult's savior as divine intermediary, and the idea of a spiritual soul caught in a physical body. By controlling the body's urges, and symbolically putting the animal body to death, initiates could be reborn "in" the life of their god, so that only their higher, spiritual essence remained. As Burkert mentions of the mysteries of Isis:

> The mysteries of Isis are to be accepted, the priest says, "In the form of voluntary death and salvation by grace." In any event, the day following the night of initiation is reckoned as a new birthday (natalem sacrorum).[25]

Likewise, the password of the Attic mysteries was pronounced in the temple "in order that one who is about to die could be admitted to the interior parts."[26] This death was often a physical reenactment; initiates of Osiris, for example, were wrapped in burial shrouds and physically buried before "resurrecting" into their new life as Horus. A similar theme is found in the rite of the taurobolium:

> In this ritual bull-slaughter, the vital forces of the bull are poured out with the blood over the devotee. Extraordinary power was attributed to this act, and those who had undergone the experience were celebrated as 'eternally reborn.'[27]

Burkert shares a passage from Firmicus Maternus describing a mystery scene in which, after days of lament in the presence of an idol lying on a litter, "light is brought in and a priest anoints the throats of the mourners, saying in a whispering voice: 'Be confident, mystai, since the god has been saved: you too will be saved from your toils.' It is unclear to which cult he is referring, but it is evident that the fate of the initiate is modeled on the fate of the god as represented in myth and ritual, following the peripety from catastrophe to salvation."[28]

It seems the mysteries at Eleusis had a theme of an expiatory sacrifice: even the poorest had to sacrifice a pig to the goddess before they could be initiated. The victim, Socrates explains in Plato's *Republic* (378a), was sacrificed in order that "One might hear what was otherwise forbidden to hear." In other words, the pig was sacrificed because the price to hear the truth was death; the pig paid that price for the initiate. (Jesus, it could be argued, fills a similar role.)

## Identification with God

As suffering, sympathetic figures, the mystery gods were more accessible than the distant gods of Olympus. Believers could form a closer, personal relationship with them rather than one based on fear:

> If one had to single out one paramount feature that distinguished all the Mystery cults from other religions, of their period, it would be that they sought a personal relationship with their gods. Consequently the attitude of their devotees to the gods was one of love rather than of fear or indifferent manipulation.[29]

Mysteries also allow initiates to follow the moral example of their god. Plutarch writes that the sufferings of Isis, as enacted in the mysteries (*teletai*), should be a lesson in piety and a consolation to men and women caught in similar sufferings.[30]

Many groups viewed their saviors as manifestations of the divine Logos, Son of God, and believed that they could act as intermediary to the invisible, eternal God. Moreover, it was believed that in identifying with the sufferings of their savior – such as "dying" and being reborn – they could in effect give themselves over to the divine principle in themselves. As Burkert makes clear, "The identification of the initiate with the fate of his god has been held to be the distinguishing characteristic of ancient mysteries."[31] Initiates in the mysteries of Osiris, for example, would try to become an Osiris:

> Each person had a *ba* (soul) that survived death, left the body, and managed the posthumous journey into the divine realm. Each person became an Osiris and followed the mythic precedent of the god.[32]

Other semi-magical rituals were used to increase this bond: as pointed out previously, the cult of Dionysus already had a sacred meal that represented the body and blood of their god. This ritual can be inferred to have similar meaning in later mysteries, which likewise shared communal meals of mystical importance:

> One such means, not in any way peculiar to Christianity, is holy communion, in which the goal of assimilation to the god on his level is furthered by assimilation of him on this plane. Dionysus was believed to be present, not merely symbolically but actually, in the wine and raw flesh which his devotees consumed.[33]

The divinity was a spirit to be invoked with ritualistic incantations; it could descend into an initiate's body, "possessing" them in a sense.

> Come into me, Hermes, as children come into women's wombs. I know thee, Hermes and thou knowest me: I am thou, and thou art I.[34]

As Assman reasons, "if we understand mysticism as the obliteration of one's identity with the goal of becoming one with the divine, something of this sort seems to occur when a priest declares, in cult or magic, 'It is not I who says this to you, it is the deity... who speaks (through me) to you,' or when spell and rituals promise individuals that their knowledge or recitation or performance will make them into a deity."[35] According to an ancient Egyptian hymn:

> The one who knows this spell
> Will be like the sun god in the east
> The one who executes this pattern
> Is like the Great God himself.[36]

## Ethics

The ethics of the mysteries were mostly designed to control the urges of the physical body, sometimes purposely to weaken its strength, through fasting, meditation, strenuous action or inaction. The body was viewed as a shell or prison, holding the spark of the divine logos. Constantly keeping the baser, animal nature in check would make it easier to free the divine light. Eventually initiates could grow into the image of a god themselves, and become eternal. Assman describes this system in detail, citing Plato's description of Orphism:

> The beginnings of salvation lie within every one of us, since they are identical with the germ of divinity which it is our nature as human beings to possess. Yet it does not follow that everyone is assured of a blessed future simply by reason of his origin. By a life of *adikia* or sinfulness, the divine element may be stifled and the 'Titanic nature' in us brought to the surface (Plato, laws 70IC – Plutarch calls it 'the unreasonable and disorderly and violent part of us (De esu carn 996c)…The state of those who have let this happen is far worse than if they had merely been 'finished and finite clods, untroubled by a spark.' To misuse the divine is to use it to our own damnation. Hence the believer will try to lead the Orphic life, to which we shall come later, and which aims at the exaltation and purification of our Dionysiac nature in order that we may in the end shake off the last trammels of our earthly selves and become actually, what we are now potentially, gods instead of mortals.[37]

The Orphic was an ascetic, that is to say, he believed that the source of evil lay in the body with its appetites and passions, which must therefore be subdued if we are to rise to the heights which it is in us to attain. This is precept, but like all Orphic precept it is based on dogma. The belief behind it is that this present life is for the soul a punishment for previous sin, and the punishment consists precisely in this, that it is fettered to a body. This is for it a calamity, and is compared sometimes to being shut up in a prison, sometimes to being buried in a tomb. This doctrine is mentioned by Plato, and we may be eternally grateful that for once the whim took him to ascribe it, not vaguely and mysteriously to 'the wise', or 'the old and sacred writings', but expressly to the Orphics.[38]

It should be stressed that the final, *interpretive* wisdom of the mysteries is not based on faith, but an inherently rational philosophical doctrine. Ethics are understood, not as the arbitrary commands of a tyrannous God, but as practical methods to experience truths built into the fabric of the natural universe. Thus Plutarch can say of the Egyptians:

> Their sacred rites do not institute anything dissonant to reason, anything fabulous, anything smelling of superstition, but they contain in their recesses certain ethical and useful doctrines or philosophical or historical insights. (Plutarch *On Isis and Osiris* 8.353)[39]

While the mysteries helped a person along in the process, they were not infallible; initiates needed to take responsibility and attempt to lead disciplined lives, in addition to initiation. The conflict between "grace" and "work" was recognized already by Diogenes the Cynic – referring to Eleusis, he asks, "What! Is Pataikion the thief to have a better lot after death than Epaminondas, just because he has been initiated?" (Plutarch, *de aud. Poet.* 21f)

## Afterlife

Cicero wrote that at Eleusis it is shown "how to live in joy, and how to die with better hopes" (Cicero, *De Legibus* 2.36). It should be noted that, although it can be affirmed that the central characters in these rites appeared in some sense to experience death and rebirth, and although philosophies concerning the eternal life of the soul were common and definitely proposed by certain cults (Orpheus, etc.), scholars continue to debate whether the initiates of *all* mysteries believed in or hoped for an afterlife. Although it can be most readily inferred based on common practices, due to the secrecy of mystery organizations, it is difficult to prove. Burkert, taking a conservative position, urges caution:

> In fact, we meet with a paradox: in the perspective of "religions of salvation," concern and doctrines about the soul should be the very center of interest; yet in the evidence there is hardly even a faint indication of this, whether in the mysteries of Eleusis, Dionysus, Meter, Isis, or Mithras. Ancient mysteries were a personal, but not necessarily a spiritual form of religion.[40]

He continues to contend that, although an afterlife doctrine was taught by Pythagoras or Orpheus by at least 600BC and included into their mysteries, it is nevertheless uncertain whether it was a central feature:

> It is all the more remarkable that despite this evidence, which is concentrated in the fifth and fourth centuries, there is nothing to suggest that belief in transmigration was a basic or essential tenet of mysteries practiced.[41]

While there may not be definitive proof that each mystery cult interpreted their symbols in the same way, it would be most unusual if they did not. After all, how could a mystery religion with no doctrine of eternal life hope to compete with those that very clearly did promise it? Sophocles, speaking on the Eleusinian rites, confirms that they were associated with an afterlife:

> Thrice happy are those mortals who see these rites before they depart for Hades; for to them alone is it granted to have true life on the other side. To the rest all there is evil.[42]

The rites of Dionysus and Orpheus (which were often mingled) believed in reincarnation, or "transmigration of souls." These beliefs were not later derivations, but can be found in early forms of both religious traditions:

> The Orphics called this sphere of the visible universe the Circle of Necessity; Buddhists called it the Wheel of Existence. According to both, the soul can take two alternative routes when it leaves the body: it can either remain within the Wheel, in which case it will sooner or later have to incarnate in another human body; or else it can leave the system altogether and attain perpetual liberation from rebirth. Both believe, moreover, in the eventual liberation of all souls.[43]

> The same is true for the Dionysiac mysteries from at least the fifth century BC onward. Scholars have been reluctant to acknowledge this dimension of Dionysiac worship, on the assumption that concern about the afterlife should be seen to have developed in later epochs; but the clearest evidence is of the concentrated right in the classical period, whatever we make of the indication at the end of the Odyssey that a vase of Dionysus is to hold the bones of Achilles and Patroclus. For those who decline the rites, bad things are waiting.[44]

A common metaphor (originally Egyptian) used in the mysteries is the punishment of carrying water forever in a leaky sieve; those that didn't "seal up the holes" in their lifetime couldn't carry the divine light, and would perpetually return until they could remedy the situation. By the first century AD, the ideas of reincarnation and eternal life were relatively common; a few centuries later they would become ubiquitous, as philosophers began to interpret every myth along the same spiritual lines.

> The most important myths from the point of view of the Mystery religions are those that concern the descent and ascent of the soul itself. The inclination of the Neophythagoreans and Neoplatonists was to interpret most myths as such, in their fundamental meaning. Homer's Odyssey, for example, received such treatment from Porphyry, the whole tale being understood as the journey of a man's soul to its true home. Such an attempt to adapt mythology to the purposes of spiritual philosophy is looked down upon by modern philosophers and dismissed as a NeoPlatonic 'phase'.[45]

# Christian Mystery Texts

The mysteries, then, were ancient and fully established spiritual traditions, which grew increasingly varied and diverse with the trend towards syncretism inspired by the Greek and Roman empires. This was the background out of which sprang Christianity. Were the Christians influenced by pagan mysteries? Almost definitely. The gospel writers or early Christian communities could not have been unaware of the mysteries; at least in their enormous public displays, processions and feasts. According to Witt, "There were the public religious dramas such as those of the Phrygian Magna Mater. In the Isiac ritual an emperor like Otho or Commodus might openly take part. There were also the traditional secret *orgia* as a never-failing attraction. Hadrian went through two ceremonies at Eleusis, first an initiation as 'mystes' and then the second degree as 'epoptes'."[46] Due to the continuing success of the mysteries during the formative period of Christianity, when we find parallel rituals, symbols or ideas, even if a connection cannot be proved, it should be assumed.

This is especially the case when Christianity adopts exact mystery language and expressions:

> For the Mediterranean world where Orphic and Eleusinian rites had long flourished the mysteries in later antiquity did not lose their importance. The importance of Hellenistic mysteries for Christianity is evident when we turn to the Pauline interpretation or to the use of the term for the knowledge that only the disciples had, or to what the fathers write about baptism as mysterion or the enlightenment (photismos) and about the creed as a symbolon (a password).[47]

Besides the common use of mystery language, there is also overlap between cultic practices. Frend claims that the rituals of Christianity were also borrowed from the mystery schools:

> The cities of the Roman provinces in Asia Minor were among the centers where the mystery religions flourished most in the first two centuries A.D. It was tempting to ask how much Christianity owed to these; whether, for instance, the Christian's relation to his Savior was not akin to that which united the pagan initiate to the gods of the oriental cults. There was just enough evidence to suggest that, in the rites of Baptism and the Eucharist, the resemblances between Christianity and the mystery religions were influenced by pagan mysteries.[48]

The writings from some Gnostic communities, which were branded as heretical and lost for millennia, clearly fall within the mystery tradition. Many of these texts have re-emerged only this century, quickly changing the traditional understanding of the early church. While it may be debatable whether or not Christianity was *only* a mystery religion or even *originally* a mystery religion, it is indisputable that there were Christian communities who interpreted the story of Jesus Christ as a mystery, and utilized it as such.

Although later weeded out of the Roman Catholic fold, Gnostic communities considered themselves to be the true followers of Christ, and claimed that they had received secret teachings, usually from the apostle Paul:

> The Gnostics were organized like mystery sects... Upon initiation the Gnostic received an entirely new relation to spiritual authority. Each sect had its own baptism ceremony, its passwords, its sacred meal,

its "ceremonies of the Bride Chamber," even its final instructions to the dying, how to outwit the powers the soul would encounter on its upward flight.[49]

A fragment of the *Secret Gospel of Mark*, a Gnostic text claimed to have been rediscovered by Prof. Morton Smith in 1958 at the Mar Saba monastery southeast of Jerusalem, describes Jesus performing initiation rituals. Before the discovery of Gnostic writings, our only knowledge of this text came from a letter written by Church Father Clement of Alexandria (150AD-211AD), which quotes this secret gospel and refers to it as "a more spiritual gospel for the use of those who were being perfected." Perhaps the most important issue confirmed by this letter is the fact that in Clement's time "hierophantic teachings of the Lord" and Gospel texts now lost were still transmitted within the church to a select group of Christians. Clement makes it clear that writers had to be careful not to reveal too much in writing, and that this secret gospel was guarded carefully, to be used only by those initiated into the greater mysteries:

> As for Mark, then, during Peter's stay in Rome he wrote an account of the Lord's doings, not, however, declaring all of them, nor yet hinting at the secret ones, but selecting what he thought most useful for increasing the faith of those who were being instructed. But when Peter died a martyr, Mark came over to Alexandria, bringing both his own notes and those of Peter, from which he transferred to his former books the things suitable to whatever makes for progress toward knowledge. Thus he composed a more spiritual Gospel for the use of those who were being perfected. Nevertheless, he yet did not divulge the things not to be uttered, nor did he write down the hierophantic teaching of the Lord, but to the stories already written he added yet others and, moreover, brought in certain sayings of which he knew the interpretation would, as a mystagogue, lead the hearers into the innermost sanctuary of truth hidden by seven veils. Thus, in sum, he prepared matters, neither grudgingly nor incautiously, in my opinion, and, dying, he left his composition to the church in 1, verso Alexandria, where it even yet is most carefully guarded, being read only to those who are being initiated into the great mysteries.[50]

A passage from this secret gospel actually helps explain the otherwise peculiar appearance of the naked youth that appears in the Garden of Gethsemane at about the time Jesus was finished healing the ear of the servant of the high priest named Malchus. According to Mark 15:51-52 "And there followed him a certain young man, having a linen cloth cast about his naked body; and the young men laid hold on him: and he left the linen cloth, and fled from them naked." The identity of this naked youth has long been a mystery. As one Christian website asks, "Who was this young man? Why was he following Jesus? Why was he naked? Why was he draped in a linen cloth instead of wearing normal clothes? And why was the Holy Spirit so careful to include this unique story in Mark's account of the Gospel? What is the significance of this event?"[51] Fascinatingly, the secret gospel of Mark fills the holes in the story with homoerotic tones:

> And they come into Bethany. And a certain woman whose brother had died was there. And, coming, she prostrated herself before Jesus and says to him, "son of David, have mercy on me." But the disciples rebuked her. And Jesus, being angered, went off with her into the garden where the tomb was, and straightway, going in where the youth was, he stretched forth his hand and raised him, seizing his hand. But the youth, looking upon him, loved him and began to beseech him that he might be with him. And going out of the tomb they came into the house of the youth, for he was rich. And after six days Jesus told him what to do and in the evening the youth comes to him, wearing a linen cloth over his naked body. And he remained with him that night, for Jesus taught him the mystery of the Kingdom of God. And thence, arising, he returned to the other side of the Jordan.[52]

Incidentally, we could argue at this point that the gospels chosen for inclusion in the New Testament were chosen based on the fact that they *do not reveal too much*; that all spiritual revelations and advanced teachings had first been carefully scrubbed out so that initates would need a leader to guide them through the vague and obtuse text.

Another Gnostic text that explicitly refers to the mysteries of Jesus is the Gnostic Gospel of Philip, usually dated to around the 2nd or 3rd century, but reflecting ideas of Valentinus who was a leader in Rome from 138 to 158AD. Philip records that the mysteries of

Jesus included a baptism, a communal meal, and a bridal chamber:

> The Lord did everything in a mystery, a baptism and a chrism and a eucharist and a redemption and a bridal chamber. (GPhil 60)[53]

Although the church has always argued about the nature and number of sacraments, those cited by Philip are roughly the same as those still used by many churches. The chrism is an anointing of oil, marking the initiate's forehead with the cross to make them "christs." It continues today in the form of confirmation. The mystery of the "bridal chamber" refers to a lost mystery aimed at uniting the upper and lower selves; a mystical wedding ritual is recorded in other mysteries as well:

> He who has been anointed has the totality—he has the resurrection, the light, the cross, the Sacred Spirit. The Father bestowed this upon him in the Bridal-Chamber (and) he received. (GPhil 101)

> When Eve was still with Adam, death did not exist. When she was separated from him, death came into being. If he enters again and attains his former self, death will be no more. (GPhil 76)

Today most churches claim that marriage is a sacred institution – although the apostle Paul clearly recommended celibacy over marriage, and priests of most Christian denominations are not even allowed to enter into it. How could the marriage between two people be both a sacrament, sanctified by God, and unacceptable for priests? The answer is that originally, the "sacrament of marriage" referred to the mystery of the bridal chamber, and the fusion between the *Sophia* and the *Logos* inside each person, becoming "one with God" or eternal.

Other passages from Philip speak of light and mirrors, which are common motifs found in other mysteries:

> We are reborn by the Holy Spirit. And we are born by the anointed (Christ) through two things. We are anointed by the Spirit. When we were born we were joined. No one can see himself in the water or in a mirror without light. Nor again can you see by the light without water or a mirror. For this reason it is necessary to baptize with two things – light and water. And light means chrism. (GPhil 67)

We can understand this to mean that the bride and bridegroom (light and water) can be joined to create a mirror, with which to see back up to the original unity:

> Rebirth exists along with an image of rebirth: by means of this image one must be truly reborn. Which image? Resurrection. And image must arise by means of image. By means of this image, the bridal chamber and the image must embark upon the realm of Truth, that is, embark upon the return. (GPhil 59)

The true meaning of the bridal chamber mystery was kept hidden from initiates of the lower levels, who were familiar only with stories and parables attributed to the savior. Secrecy was very important, because if initiates heard the truth before they were spiritually ready, it would be spoiled for them. Only those who *become* a bridegroom (pass through the initiation themselves) can witness the ceremony.

> If a marriage is open to the public, it has become prostitution, and the bride plays the harlot not only when she is impregnated by another man, but even if she slips out of her bedroom and is seen. Let her show herself only to her father and her mother, and to the friend of the bridegroom and the sons of the bridegroom. These are permitted to enter every day into the bridal chamber. But let the others yearn just to listen to her voice and to enjoy her ointment, and let them feed from the crumbs that fall from the table, like the dogs. Bridegrooms and brides belong to the bridal chamber. No one shall be able to see the bridegroom with the bride unless he become such a one. (GPhil 102)

At higher levels, initiates could freely interpret the philosophical implications of the stories, weaving Greek and Jewish thought together freely. Substituting Christ into the role of the Logos, they explain that his role is to repair the separation that happened in the beginning of Genesis:

> If the woman had not separated from the man, she should not die with the man. His separation became the beginning of death. Because of this, Christ came to repair the separation, which was from the beginning, and again unite the two, and to give life to those who died as a result of the separation, and unite them. But the woman is united to her husband in the bridal chamber. Indeed, those who have united

in the bridal chamber will no longer be separated. Thus Eve separated from Adam because it was not in the bridal chamber that she united with him. (GPhil 70)

Just as the sun had a female companion, the moon, and the Logos had a female companion, Sophia, the stories about Jesus also incorporated a woman as his friend and companion:

As for the Wisdom who is called the barren, she is the mother of the angels, and the companion of the Savior, who is also Mary Magdalene. (GPhil 48)

Many texts describe the ecstasy encountered between Mary and Jesus, who represent the Logos and the Sophia as they are fused into one in the bridal chamber. It is no wonder that there are so many books written about the sexual exploits of Jesus and Mary, and even the possibility of their royal offspring – an idea featured most prominently in Dan Brown's *The DaVinci Code*. As long as Jesus is assumed to be historical, Mary can be viewed as his real, physical companion. However, it is obvious that the writer is using them as mystical symbols rather than historical personages. Like Sophia, Mary was sometimes called a whore, as were many consorts of the sun. She was the one who was lost, sullied in matter, trapped and in need of rescue. Significantly, Mary is identified in the Bible as the woman out of whom seven devils were cast. After Mary had her seven demons removed, or ascended past the seven illusionary heavens, she was able to become Christ's partner and lover in the bridal chamber. In an ancient manuscript called the Gospel of Mary Magdalene, Mary was not only Christ's beloved disciple, but also the revealer of secret mysteries:

Peter said to Mary, Sister we know that the Savior loved you more than the rest of woman. Tell us the words of the Savior which you remember which you know, but we do not, nor have we heard them. Mary answered and said, what is hidden from you I will proclaim to you. (Gospel according to Mary Magdalene 5:5-7)[54]

When a certain branch of Christianity later refused the higher mysteries, they viewed this form of Mary as a threat because of the authority it gave to women. The symbol for Sophia, the bride of Christ, was changed from Mary Magdalene into The Holy Mother

Church. Christ was viewed as the head of the Church, and his great sacrifice was undertaken for the sake of this body. The Church, like Sophia, was the collection of individual sparks trapped in the world. Once the meaning of the Wedding Chamber was lost, this relationship between Christ and the Church became a metaphor for human marriages rather than the relationship between the higher and lower selves; yet even in Ephesians it is referred to as a "mystery with great significance," which was being taken out of context:

> Husbands should love their wives, just as Christ loved the Church and sacrificed himself for her to make her holy by washing her in cleansing water with a form of words, so that when he took the Church to himself she would be glorious... This is why a man leaves his mother and father and becomes attached to his wife, and the two become one flesh. This mystery has great significance, but I am applying it to Christ and the Church. (Ephesians 5:25)

As difficult as it might seem, even the crucifixion of Jesus was interpreted as spiritual metaphor rather than historical event, in a feat of astrological exegesis. According to the Old Testament, when Moses came down from the mountain and found his people with the golden calf, he smashed the idol and replaced it with a bronze serpent fixed it to a pole. "And Moses made a serpent of brass, and put it upon a pole, and it came to pass, that if a serpent had bitten any man, when he beheld the serpent of brass, he lived" (Numbers 21:4).

You may well wonder, remembering Asclepius, where Moses acquired his magical healing symbol. However, this image can also be interpreted symbolically. While the bull was a symbol of astrological precession, the snake on the pole represented the soul's ascent to the One. Moses was introducing a new spirituality based on personal transformation rather than celestial observation. Thus, the writer of John's gospel links Jesus' crucifixion to Moses' serpent stick, affirming his unique role as the pathway to spiritual perfection:

> As Moses lifted up the snake in the desert, so the Son of man must be lifted up, that everyone who believes may have eternal life in him. For this is how God loved the world: he gave his only Son, so that everyone who believes in him may not perish but have eternal life. (John 3:14)

This association is later confirmed by Cyril of Jerusalem, who credits Jesus with bestowing mastery over scorpions and snakes:

> According to Job, the dragon Behemoth was in the Waters and received the Jordan into his jaws. Now, since the heads of the dragon must be broken, Jesus, having gone down into the Waters, bound the Strong One, so that we should have the power to walk on scorpions and snakes.[55]

A Gnostic or mystery reading of Jesus' crucifixion would be this: Jesus (the Logos) has fallen into matter, and in this state he appears crucified, or stuck. All of the pieces of him, his body, need to be lifted up and rejoined to the head. The pieces of him were called Sophia, the wisdom of God, and biblical passages state clearly that Jesus crucified *is* Sophia. This identification is obscured by translating Sophia into "Wisdom":

> We are preaching a crucified Christ... who is both the power of God and the wisdom (Sophia) of God. (1 Corinthians 1:22)

Finally, the Sethian Gnostic text "Allogenes," found at Nag Hammadi, lists the spiritual accomplishments of a Christian initiate in the same style as other mysteries:

> Now I am listening to these things [the speech of the "holy powers]. I was filled with revelation... I knew the One who exists in me... I saw the good divine Autogenes and the Saviour who is youthful, the perfect triple Male... I sought the ineffable unknowable God who subsists in stillness and silence and is unknown. (Allogenes, 58-61)[56]

# The Example of Mithras

Part of the problem in comparing Christianity to other mysteries is that it retains a very ancient text, while corresponding texts for other traditions (if ever created) were either lost or destroyed. Moreover, the gospels chosen for the Bible were chosen because they portray a human Jesus, rather than reveal mystery truths (which were not meant to be written down, anyway). In contrast, although a trove of Gnostic gospels was discovered in 1978, much of the secret wisdom of other mystery traditions remains unknown to us. In other words, although we know that certain Gnostic communities did use the story of Christ as an initiation cult, it is difficult to ascertain the details of their "higher mysteries." It is likely, however, that they were comparable to the many other mystery schools of their times. We can therefore look at the symbolism of other mystery traditions, and given what we know about the beliefs of contemporary movements, arrive at an interpretive reading of the symbols. This will be especially profitable when comparing Jesus to Mithras.

Mithraism is well suited to this task because, while little textual evidence remains, the sculpture and portrayals of Mithras are rich with symbolism. Although most of the symbols, rites and beliefs found in Mithraism probably came from earlier traditions, it is possible that Mithraism borrowed features from Christianity. However, whether or not Mithras borrowed is not really important; the similarities between the worship of Christ and Mithras were so startling that they were remarked upon by Christian apologists, as well as criticized by enemies of Christianity. Specific parallels are mentioned. *Who came first* is not at all the issue, because as we've seen, neither of them did. Since early testimony, however, links the practice of Christianity most often with Mithraism, and since we know that Christianity was *used* as a mystery cult, Mithraism can help us reconstruct what the "higher mysteries" of Jesus Christ might have looked like.

### Symbolism in Mithraism

Although there are few written remains of Mithraism, we can tell a lot about how his followers viewed him by looking at the artwork left in their tomb-like temples. The following is a summary based on an interpretation of these symbols.

Mithras was often shown standing on a globe with a cross through it (representing the world and the cross between the elliptic of the sun and the celestial equator), wearing a lion's head mask to identify him with the victorious sun on the spring equinox. Sometimes he was shown with the zodiac circle surrounding him, or else with specific symbols of constellations that also figured prominently in the myth. Many statues give him wings and a snake around his legs, and show him raising a lit torch – like the symbol of the Caduceus. He was seen as the bridge between heaven and earth; the spiraling snake may indicate either the unfolding of the cosmos or the ascent of the soul.

Inside of the cavern-like Mithraic temples (which were built in the image of the cosmos) was a symbolic ladder with seven rungs, opening at "the eighth gate," representing the path of initiation and likewise the afterlife journey of the soul. In the center of each temple was a large image of the tauroctony: Mithras' greatest feat of slaying the bull, ending the age of Taurus.

Although this central mystery of Mithraism appears to have little in common with Christianity, its symbolic meaning can be given esoteric meaning, which equates it with the crucifixion. The symbols of the cross and the sword not only look alike, but they have precisely the same function. Mithras slew the sacred bull, ending the age of Taurus, and this sacrifice somehow cleansed the sins of initiates (this can be inferred from the similar mystery rites of Attis or Dionysus; both of which feature the redemptive powers of the blood of the bull). Jesus slew the sacred lamb, ending the age of Aries, and his followers were cleansed of their sins through its blood. In a fascinating passage, Jesus even says, "Do you think I came to bring peace? I tell you, I came not to bring peace but the sword." The sword Jesus mentions is probably the vertical cross.

There are further parallels. In the Christian tradition, Jesus is crucified between two thieves (Demas and Gestas). According to Luke, one criminal reviles him, but the other recognizes him as the Son of God. Jesus is often portrayed in Christian art as crucified between them; they are designated by their gaze – one looks up, and the other looks down, in expectation of their fate.

Mithraism has a similar motif in the "two torchbearers." According to Godwin:

> Just like the crucifixion, the Mithraic sacrifice takes place between the sun and moon and under the eye of the Father God. The good and bad thieves also have their correspondences in the two torch-bearers Cautes and Cautopates, who have as many meanings as the sacrifice itself. They are at every level reflections of the primal duality of light and darkness, life and death, spirit and matter, etc. Cautopates, with lowered torch, rules the autumn equinox and winter solstice, the barren half of the year; Cautes, with raised torch, is the return of fertility in spring and summer.[57]

Godwin also points out that Mithraism envisioned "two keys, the silver one is the gate of Cancer which leads to the way of ancestors (Pitri-yana) and to reincarnation. The gold one is to the Gate of Capricorn, the Way of the Gods (Deva-yana) which leads beyond the Circle of Necessity, i.e., to release from the round of birth and death."[58] We find these keys also in the Christian tradition: Christ says to Peter, "I will give you the keys of the kingdom of heaven, and whatever you bind on earth shall be bound in heaven, and whatever you loose on earth shall be loosed in heaven" (Matthew 16:18-19).

The keys represented the power to forgive sins and also the power of church authority; they are represented in art as being gold and silver, respectively.

St. Peter with gold and silver key, Rubens

In the base relief *Hercules Crowned* (1671), French sculptor Martin Desjardins captured much of the mystery cult symbolism. At his feet is the defeated dragon. Behind him is his symbol – the lion – hanging on the tree. He's holding a staff (to symbolize the tree or bridge), has wings, and is about to be crowned by his companion goddess – who is holding a small statue (Nike, the Greek goddess of victory) over the world; showing him as king of the world. On the globe is the T or X shape of the zodiac path intersecting the sun's path. These are symbols that any mystery initiate would have understood, and most of them can be applied equally to both Mithras and Jesus.

The image on the right, meanwhile, is a stained glass window depicting Jesus being anointed by Mary. There are no other symbols present; however the symbols do continue in the tradition. "Christ" means anointed, or crowned. Despite refusing authority over the kingdoms of the world when tempted by Satan in the desert, he is nevertheless a king. He is always associated with a lion, and called the Lion of Judea. He is the defeater of Satan, the serpent. He was born in a cave or manger, and surrounded by animals. He is the tree of life, the bridge between heaven and earth, and like Mithras he controls the precession of equinoxes. While Mithras defeated the bull under Taurus, in the time of Jesus, the spring equinox had already progressed into Aries, the lamb. Jesus receives his kingship, Christ-hood or "anointing," at the hands of his consort, Mary Magdalene.

### Rituals of Mithraism

While little is known of the actual ceremony of Mithraism, we have the testimonies of early Christian apologists, who recognized the similarities between Mithraism and Christianity and denounced them as diabolically inspired. The following passages by Justin Martyr and Tertullian mention baptism, communion, chrism (anointing the forehead with oil or a magical seal), "putting away sins," and "producing an image of resurrection":

> For the apostles, in the memoirs composed by them, which are called Gospels, have thus delivered unto us what was enjoined upon them; that Jesus took bread, and when He had given thanks, said, 'This do ye in remembrance of Me, this is My body'; and that, after the same manner, having taken the cup and given thanks, He said, 'This is My blood'; and gave it to them alone. Which the wicked devils have imitated in the mysteries of Mithras, commanding the same thing to be done. For, that bread and a cup of water are placed with certain incantations in the mystic rites of one who is being initiated, you either know or can learn. (Justin Martyr, *First Apology* 60)

Although it has been argued that sharing a communal meal does not make a *Eucharist,* Justin clearly places the meal as an initiatory experience, an integral part of the spiritual process, rather than a normal function of the community. He also does not take the opportunity to distinguish the precise meaning of the communal meal, but rather says that "the same thing" was done in Mithraism.

In the following passage, Tertullian mentions the "putting away of sins by a layer of his own," which may refer to the inner-god or higher-self replacing the lower animal self. An image of the resurrection is also produced – as it was in other mysteries:

> The question will arise, By whom is to be interpreted the sense of the passages which make for heresies? By the devil, of course, to whom pertain those wiles which pervert the truth, and who, by the mystic rites of his idols, vies even with the essential portions of the sacraments of God. He, too, baptizes some – that is, his own believers and faithful followers; he promises the putting away of sins by a layer (of his own); and if my memory still serves me, Mithras there, (in the kingdom of Satan,) sets his marks on the foreheads of his soldiers; celebrates also the oblation of bread, and introduces an image of a resurrection, and before a sword wreathes a crown. (Tertullian, *De praescriptione haereticorum* 40)[59]

Tertullian also mentions a rite of initiation that may have been lost from the Christian tradition, which includes kneeling before a sword and being crowned. It appears to refer to Mithraic martyr-ideology; that Mithraics were to deny human authority, and, if pressed, reject government law in favor of divine law. Another reading may be that Mithraics are expected to eschew worldly possession and power, in favor of a spiritual humility. In either case, although the ritual seems to have been lost to Christianity, both concepts remain in Christian tradition:

> Blush, ye fellow-soldiers of his, henceforth not to be condemned even by him, but by some soldier of Mithras, who, at his initiation in the gloomy cavern, in the camp, it may well be said, of darkness, when at the sword's point a crown is presented to him, as though in mimicry of martyrdom, and thereupon put upon his head, is admonished to resist and cast it off, and, if you like, transfer it to his shoulder, saying that Mithras is his crown. And thenceforth he is never crowned; and he has that for a mark to show who he is, if anywhere he be subjected to trial in respect of his religion; and he is at once believed to be a soldier of Mithras if he throws the crown away – if he say that in his god he has his crown. Let us take note of the devices of the devil, who

is wont to ape some of God's things with no other design than, by the faithfulness of his servants, to put us to shame, and to condemn us. (Tertullian, *De corona*, 15)

Keep in mind that Christians would have no reason at this point to attempt to be more similar to their competitors. These similarities were listed because they were already well known, and hence, they demanded an answer – one that could not be given without invoking the theory of diabolical mimicry. Also, we can point out that Tertullian appears to have great personal knowledge of the mysteries of Mithras; in writing down the secrets of initiation, he is making a bold and "blasphemous" attack against Mithraism. While Christianity today has grown even further away from the mystery cult of Mithras, the similarities recorded between the two allow us to understand more about the mystery practices and initiation rituals of some Christian communities, and hence draw a picture of what the greater mysteries of Jesus Christ may have looked like.

## Was Christianity Originally a Mystery Religion?

Due to the variance between diverse Christian communites, this is a complex question. The answer is "yes" – and also "no." It can be shown that the very earliest practices of Christianity coincided with popular mystery cults on many levels. Church leaders talked about "initiations, passwords, and mysteries" using exactly the same terms as other contemporary mystery religions. But it is the interpretation of Christianity that makes all the difference. It may have been the similarity of Christianity to mystery cults that made it define itself as *different* from them. Everyone who practiced levels of initiation, allegorical interpretation, death and rebirth in this life (as opposed to the bodily resurrection) were basically excluded from orthodoxy. So if one defines Christianity as "those communities of the early church who did not interpret themselves as a mystery," and all other groups of believers in Jesus Christ as Gnostics or heretics, then no, Christianity – by this highly constricted definition – was *not* a mystery. But even that definition would only establish that Christianity was immediately and irrevocably assimilated into the mystery tradition, to the exclusion of any specific details about its alleged historical founder.

What we *can* say is that the passionate story of Jesus Christ – his death and resurrection, his enigmatic parables and inner circle of disciples, the rituals he founded such as Baptism and the Eucharist, as well as the spiritual symbols of his saving role as sacrificial lamb and Logos, Son of God – were *perfectly suited* for the production of a new mystery cult that blended the ancient tradition of Judaism with the Greek mysteries. We can also demonstrate that this ideal foundation was recognized and built upon very early in the Christian tradition. If Jesus was only a historical Jewish rebel, and all of the qualities of a mystery were later added to the kernel of this real, crucified man, then one would expect the original story to be more secular, less phenomenal, less magical. But instead, as Christians have pointed out, Jesus' atoning death, victorious resurrection, and intermediary position between a loving God and his fallen creatures were the *core elements* of the gospel story from the very beginning. Consequently, a more profitable question for us to ask is who created the story, and why. Where did the story of Jesus really come from? There are only a few possible options:

1. Jesus was a historical figure who copied other mystery school traditions in the building of his own cult.

2. Jesus was a historical figure upon which the literature of the mysteries was placed so thoroughly that almost no trace of him can be found.

3. Jesus was originally mystery literature that was mistaken as human by overzealous followers.

The first option is logically and spiritually unsatisfying, and the second option is popular, but not necessary. It is the third option that is most fully justified by historical evidence.

## Pagan Influences in Judaism

Despite the similarities, many Christian apologists and Bible scholars continue to dispute that the mystery traditions have anything to do with Christianity. The thrust of their argument is that it is *impossible* for a Jewish-Pagan synthesis of the mysteries to have arisen, given the Jewish abhorrence for idolatry and the worship of foreign gods. In addition to carefully safeguarding their beliefs from outside influence, Jews had very strict dietary and ritual laws and squeamishness towards raw blood. For these reasons, evangelical pastor Gregory A. Boyd contends that the Jews would never have been attracted to the mystery rituals:

> For instance, to get to the higher level in the Mithras cult, followers had to stand under a bull while it was slain, so they could be bathed in its blood and guts. Then they'd join the others in eating the bull. Now, to suggest that Jews would find anything attractive about this and want to model baptism and communion after this barbaric practice is extremely implausible, which is why most scholars don't go for it.[60]

First of all, although the tauroctony was a prominent motif in Mithraism, it is unlikely that initiates were washed in blood (like Attis) or ate its flesh (like Dionysus); and secondly, taken symbolically, there is no difference between the tauroctony and the Christian claim to have their sins "washed in the blood of the lamb" and the proclamation that the Eucharist is the *actual* body and blood of Jesus Christ – which would have been equally repulsive to Jews.

At any rate, Boyd's argument (which is repeated by the majority of biblical scholars, who as we have seen believe the historical Jesus was entirely Jewish rather than pagan) fails on several points. The first is that it simply does not matter whether the scenario appears likely; a pagan, mystery form of Jesus worship *did exist*. What remains is to explore how it was developed. The second is a logical oversight: the argument assumes that, while rejecting pagan mystery gods such as Mithras, Jews accepted the "more Jewish" story of Jesus Christ. In fact, the Bible is very clear that the Jews refused and persecuted Christianity. Paul and the other apostles were tortured, jailed, and stoned for preaching the story of Jesus Christ, which makes much more sense if he was something the Jews would have hated most: a pagan-Jewish mystery god.

Thirdly, it is historically false to say that Jews didn't participate in pagan culture: many of them did, especially outside of Israel. They practiced Greek philosophy, worshipped foreign gods, and otherwise integrated into pagan life – even though these practices were condemned by the Jewish authorities. As mentioned previously, in the Bible we find the examples of Rachel stealing her father's idols (Genesis 31:19); the episode of the Golden Calf created by Aaron after leaving Egypt (Exodus 32); and the women of Jerusalem mourning Tammuz at the door of the Temple (Ezekiel 8:14-17). Although these episodes stem from an earlier period of history, and although Judaism in the Roman Empire was actually very diverse, it is likely that the strict punishments for idolatry actually belie the Jewish tendency and interest towards worshipping pagan gods.

Many Jews also participated in the cultural synthesis taking place in the "melting-pot" created through the unification of diverse nations under the Greek and Roman empires:

> The majority of members were Greek-speaking, though Hebrew and Aramaic were by no means unknown. The more educated would be deeply influenced by popular versions of Stoic and Platonic philosophy and would possess a smattering acquaintance with the Greek poets, but they would also be intent on adapting that acquaintance to the advantage of Judaism.[61]

This was particularly true in the Egyptian city of Alexandria, founded by Alexander in 332BC. A considerable segment of the population, Jewish communities there had their own district and relative political independence. Alexandria was also a hot-spot for academic study and research, with the largest and most significant library of the ancient world – charged with collecting all the world's knowledge:

> This reformed Judaism developed primarily in Hellenistic Alexandria, where a large colony of Jews throve in easy commerce with people of other races. The Septuagint translation of the scriptures into Greek was made in the last centuries BC to serve those Jews whose first language was no longer Hebrew, and in the same climate of Hellenic

and Egyptian influence some Jewish philosophers sought to reconcile their ancestral faith with the wisdom of other peoples.[62]

There were several Jewish scholars, who – taking advantage of the academic environment – were seized with a passion for comparative literature, and wrote texts attempting to bridge the gap between Greeks and Jews. "From the second century BC onwards the Alexandrian Jews were consciously the mediators of Hellenistic-Jewish culture to the Greek world."[63]

One such scholar was Philo of Alexandria (c.20BC - c.50AD). Philo combined Jewish history and literature with Greek philosophical (and mystery) terms such as the Logos, identification with the divine and ultimate deification:

> As had Plato, so he understood God as existence apprehensible to the human mind as abstract Perfection. Yet God was also the Creator, creating the universe out of Non-being, and stamping upon it the pattern of order and rationality, his own Reason or Logos. The Logos was interpreted in Platonic terms as "the Idea of Ideas," the first begotten Son of God, pattern and mediator of Creation and "Second God." Scripture was the word of the Logos to be understood by the same mystical process as that by which the human mind approached the Logos himself. The Bible, therefore, was to be interpreted allegorically, and the historical aspects, even the religious development of the Jewish people told in its pages, were lost among the spiritual and moral sentiments whereby Philo sought to demonstrate the harmony and rationality of the universe. Ultimately humanity itself was destined for deification, representing harmony and conformity with the Divine.[64]

Professor of Biblical Criticism Robert M. Price, author of *The Incredible Shrinking Son of Man,* points out that Philo was already using all of the titles that would later be appropriated into Christian theology:

> Philo and various Egyptian Gnostic sects experimented with the philosophical demythologizing of myths such as the primordial Son of Man and the Logos. Philo equated the Son of Man, Firstborn of Creation, Word, heavenly High Priest, etc., and considered the Israelite patriarchs, allegorically, as virgin-born incarnations of the Logos. All,

I repeat, all, New Testament Christological titles are found verbatim in Philo.[65]

This movement was not limited to Philo; several books of the Old Testament were actually written not long before and preserve similar concepts:

> The point at which canonical Judaism comes closest to the Mystery religions is in the Wisdom literature of the early centuries BC: Koheleth (Ecclesiastes), Ben Sira (Ecclesiasticus), Chokmah (Wisdom of Solomon), Proverbs, and the Book of Job. Here the Jewish perspective extends over the whole of humanity, dividing mankind not into Jews or Gentiles but rather into the Wise and the Foolish. The piety of the heart is stressed more than obedience to the Mosaic law, and Jehovah is seen as the Lord over the whole earth who has created and ordered all things visible and invisible.[66]

Thus, the gap between contemporary Judaism and the redemptive spirituality of the pagan mystery cults was not really that wide to begin with. Moreover, the monotheism of Judaism was also compatible to the doctrine of the one true god revealed in the mystery cults:

> Based on Spencer and Cudworth, Warburton argues that Jews always had 'greater mysteries.' And Josephus tells Appion that, unlike the Greek mysteries that attained the doctrine of the one only as a secret – the Jews always worshipped the one, everyday: "For those things which the Gentiles keep up for a few days only that is, during those solemnities they call mysteries and initiations, we, with vast delight, and a plenitude of knowledge, which admits of no error, fully enjoy, and perpetually contemplate through the whole course of our lives. If you ask the nature of those things, which in our sacred rites are enjoined and forbidden; I answer, they are simple, and easily understood. The first instruction relates to a deity, and teaches that god contains all things, and is a Being every way perfect and happy: that he is self-existent, and the sole cause of all existence; the beginning, middle, and end of all things, etc."[67]

Since interfaith discussion and religious syntheses between Jewish and Greek cultures were already taking place in Alexandria before the rise of Christianity, the claim that Jews "would not have" participated in the pagan mysteries has no basis.

## Magic, Divination and Names of Power

Another trend relevant for understanding the development of the Jesus story is the widespread use of magic. Cicero, speaking on divination, claimed "I see no race of men, however polished and educated, however brutal and barbarous, which does not believe that warnings of future events are given and may be understood and announced by certain persons."[68]

Famous oracles such those at Delphi were esteemed and consulted by emperors and the state before making weighty decisions in policy, or generals before planning a battle. A formal argument for divination, attributed by Cicero to the Stoics, is a rigorous example of classical logic:

> If there are gods and they do not declare the future to men; then *either* they do not love men; *or* they are ignorant of what is to happen; *or* they think it of no importance to men to know it; *or* they do not think it consistent with their majesty to tell men; *or* the gods themselves are unable to indicate it. But *neither* do they not love men, for they are benefactors and friends to mankind; *nor* are they ignorant of what they themselves appoint and ordain; *nor* is it of no importance to us to know the future – for we shall be more careful if we do; *nor* do they count it alien to their majesty, for there is nothing nobler than kindness; *nor* are they unable to foreknow. *Therefore* no gods, no foretelling; but there are gods; therefore they foretell. Nor if they foretell, do they fail to give us ways to learn what they foretell; nor, if they give us such ways, is there no divination; therefore, there is divination. (*De divination*, i, 38, 82, 83)[69]

Besides divination, another common magical practice consisted in demonology – which meant calling on "daimons" (which were not evil, but rather various kinds of spiritual beings) or gods or goddesses to obtain a desired result. Integral to this practice was the belief that each spirit or god had a secret, magical name. Simply by discovering this name one could have the power to control them; to *force* them to do one's bidding. These magical names were commonly invoked to improve romance, business, or health; aid in legal matters or political conflicts; or seek revenge or justice:

Magicians frequently used special words and phrases typically described as secret. Often the words were understood as special names of gods or angels, names sure to catch the entity's attention; a magician who used them would not fail to gain aid. This does not necessarily represent coercion of the god or angel; although coercion was clearly intended in some cases, in others, we can better understand the use of secret names as forging a stronger bond between the magician and the addressee, as shared possession of secret knowledge typically does.[70]

The true names of the gods were considered to be both powerful and concealed; they were difficult to discover and kept from the public. In an ancient Egyptian hymn, Amun is recorded as a hidden God whose secret name is so powerful, it would wreak havoc even if accidentally uttered:

> Amun, who keeps himself concealed from them, who hides himself from the gods, no one knowing his nature. He is more remote than heaven, he is deeper than the underworld. None of the gods know his true form; his image is not unfolded in books; nothing certain is testified about him. He is too secretive for his majesty to be revealed; he is too great to be inquired after, too powerful to be known. People fall down immediately for fear that his name will be uttered knowingly or unknowingly. There is no god able to call him by it. He is ba-like, hidden of name like his secrecy. (Hymn 200)[71]

This powerful, remote secrecy of God's name is not unknown to the Jewish tradition. The original Tetragammon (YHWH) was originally a name only to be written; it was forbidden to speak it out loud. Some researchers have suggested that this facet of Jewish worship was based on the magical tradition:

> Every taboo has a reason. In ancient times, names had power. If you knew the real name of an entity, you had power over it. Often, an entity had two names, one widely-known and one secret. It is quite possible that in the very early stages, Yahweh was God's secret name and was used to influence or even control Him.[72]

So how can these powerful, secret names be discovered? In one story, Isis tricked the great god Re into giving up his name by making a snake out of his own spit and clay, which bit him. She promised to remove the poison if he revealed his name to her:

> The spell itself, as spoken by 'the great lady, the mistress of the gods', possessed its own efficacy, for by it Isis had acquired the name of the Almighty – his most important talisman – and so had made herself mistress of the earth.[73]

Magical practitioners, likewise, believed that by using the true name of Re, they could, like Isis, conquer the world:

> To know the true name and to utter it aloud was as important for the conjurer in addressing either the disease directly or its agents as it had been for Isis herself in her dealings with Re.[74]

These names grew more and more complex, and became magical formulas or codes, imbued with tremendous power:

> Hear me, lord, whose name is ineffable. The demons, hearing it, are terrified – the name BARBAREICH ARSEMPHEMPHROOTHOU – and because of hearing it the sun, the earth, are overturned; Hades, hearing, is shaken; rivers, sea, lakes, springs, hearing, are frozen; Rocks, hearing it, are split. (Greek magical papyri, no.12, 238-245)[75]

As conjurers and magicians faced increasing competition from new and foreign gods, spells grew in complexity. Rather than relying on just one name, magicians could call out a whole list of names for gods or spirits they wished to command, for example in this common love spell:

> I conjure you by the _____, according to Artemis. Ephesia Grammata – most magical words. Artemis, Hekate, Persephone, and Ereschigal – help seducing an unwilling lover – these goddesses have 'keys to the fort of hades' and therefore authority over the underworld gods and demons.[76]

The Ephesia Grammata (Ephesian words) were a set of usually six words with magical powers and often some alliteration. One version is *aski kataski aasian endasian*. You might be more familiar with the 2nd century "Abracadabra," which was prescribed to malaria sufferers in the form of a triangular amulet by Quintus Serenus Sammonicus, physician to the Roman emperor Caracalla.

```
A - B - R - A - C - A - D - A - B - R - A
A - B - R - A - C - A - D - A - B - R
A - B - R - A - C - A - D - A - B
A - B - R - A - C - A - D - A
A - B - R - A - C - A - D
A - B - R - A - C - A
A - B - R - A - C
A - B - R - A
A - B - R
A - B
A
```

Incidentally, J.K. Rowling claims that the killing curse "Avada Kedavra" used in the Harry Potter series is the original form of Abracadabra. During an audience interview at the Edinburgh Book Festival on 15 April 2004, Rowling explained:

> Does anyone know where avada kedavra came from? It is an ancient spell in Aramaic, and it is the original of abracadabra, which means 'let the thing be destroyed.' Originally, it was used to cure illness and the 'thing' was the illness, but I decided to make it the 'thing' as in the person standing in front of me.[77]

Magical practitioners would seek to heighten their powers by combining these powerful names. A newly "discovered" name could *include* all previous names. Foreign gods would be assimilated or blended together. Magicians and mystics promoting their abilities would claim that they possessed the *greatest* name; their god conquered, surpassed (and yet included) all other gods. This was like spiritual one-stop shopping: you could get anything you needed from one powerful god who could do anything.

The practice of commanding these demons or powers through ritual magic was universal – even (or especially?) among the Jews:

> One aspect of Asia Minor Judaism that stands out in the first century is a lively demonology. It appears that these Jews of the Diaspora utilized a number of magical practices, including a Solomonic magical tradition, to cope with the "powers" in their daily existence.[78]

In turn, the ancient tradition of Judaism gave prestige to the god of the Jews, who was likewise invoked – apparently even by pagan practitioners. "Quickly quickly" was a common magical expression to convey immediacy:

> I conjure you all [i.e. the angels] by the god of Abraham, Isaac, and Jacob, that you obey my authority completely...and give me...favor, influence, victory, and strength before all, small men and great, as well as gladiators, soldiers, civilians, women, girls, boys, and everybody, quickly quickly, because of the power of SABAOTH, the clothing of ELOE, the might of ADONI. (Greek magical papyri, no.35, 15-23)

This Jewish form of magic blended so completely with non-Jewish practices that is difficult to separate the two; indeed, with growing interest in new and foreign gods, there was no reason to separate them:

> Numerous strands of evidence point to the fact that the Judaism of the Hellenistic period had been heavily permeated by contemporary magical beliefs... It is often difficult to decide what is distinctively Jewish magic as opposed to syncretistic pagan magic which invokes Sabaoth or uses other Jewish motifs.[79]

Of particular interest here is an inscribed bowl found in 2008 by divers of Franck Goddio in Alexandria's Eastern Harbour. Dated to the 1st century BC, it is inscribed with the text *DIA CHRHSTOU OGOISTAIS*, which reads something like "Chrest Magus." Despite the media frenzy it caused ("Was Jesus a Witch?" etc.), it seems the term "Chrestos" was already being used in the Greek magical tradition. According to *History Hunters International,* "A certain number of elements lead us to imagine that this bowl was used by a magus to tell the future by evoking gods or the dead, questioning about the content of the vessel."[80] The term may have been attributed to the figure of Jesus to play up his magical abilities, rather than simply being a translation of the Jewish term Messiah:

> If Chrestos is a widely accepted name in Greek onomastics, chrestos or christos is the Greek word that translates the Hebrew mishnah, "messia", "Christ" of goet would refer to Jesus-Christ to legitimise his magic abilities. Transformation of water into wine, multiplication of loafs, miraculous curing, resurrection... The story of Christ must

have been veritable manna for the magician who could find (mythical) precedents to his questions and concerns. To resort to "Christ" to support a magical practice does not mean belonging to the Christian religion.[81]

In the immediate environment surrounding the appearance of the character of Jesus, therefore, we have a philosophical synthesis of Platonism and Judaism in Alexandria, as well as a synthesis of pagan and Judaic demonology and magical practices, most notably at Ephesus (not to mention the heavy influences of Stoic philosophy as mentioned earlier.) These two movements began *before* Jesus Christ and continued for several centuries – both inside and outside what became known as the Christian church:

> Philo and his school, however, had already attempted a synthesis between Platonism and Judaism in Alexandria. The same work was taken up by the Gnostics, especially Basilides and Valentinus and their followers in the second century. It was to be brought to fruition in the interests of orthodoxy by Clement and Origen.[82]

It can be asserted, therefore, that the ideas behind Christianity began before Jesus and were developed after him – without his influence. Thus, while it is possible that Jesus was a unifying literary symbol, it is unlikely that he was a teacher with unique or revolutionary ideas. But if Jesus Christ wasn't a historical *person,* where did he come from? Who created him? How does one go about "creating" a god anyway; and who would worship such a fabrication?

To begin with, keep in mind that every figure from mythology, and even many pseudo-historical figures, had to be created by someone. For example, think about the classical Roman gods of Olympus – their complicated stories, romances, and personalities. Were they real? Are they *based* on historical figures? Who chose their names, and why? It doesn't matter if we can't answer these questions with 100% accuracy; they were figures of the public imagination long before their stories were written down. Although today they may seem obviously fictional, they were believed in and worshipped for many centuries. Simply by the fact that they exist, we can presume that at some point, somebody made them up.

We can perceive the modern figure of Harry Potter more clearly. J.K. Rowling wanted to create a character that would combine English culture and lifestyle, a magical-alchemical tradition, and (as it seems) the core story and values of Christianity. So she chose a name, she described his appearance, she created friends for him, a family, a story, and included into her creation elements from many different traditions. Harry is the literary bond that allows this fictional world to exist, in him and around him.

Now let's turn to a far older story, and ask the question, "Where did Orpheus come from?" This question is less easy to answer. On the one hand, we have a combination of history, myth and legend, and we don't know which versions – if any – are "true." And yet a process for separating history and myth can be undertaken, as Guthrie points out:

> We must not expect to find the legend of Orpheus told as a simple and single story, without variations and without inconsistencies. That would be surprising, if we consider the different people who told it, the variety of the motives which prompted them, the remoteness of the times to which they believed their stories to refer, and the ever-present doubt whether even the basis of those stories, the one-time existence of their hero, is a historical fact or not. Even persons whose existence is incontestable, but whose fortune it has been to fire in some way, religious or otherwise, the imagination of their generation, have frequently in the course of time had a string of quite legendary stories associated with their name. With varying degrees of certainty these can be detached and the historical kernel at their centre laid bare.[83]

Orpheus appears into history as the spokesperson for the Dionysian mysteries. Although it may be possible that his legend began around the "historical kernel" of a real prophet or teacher, academic consensus considers him to be fully mythical:

> Orphism was a product of Pythagorean influence on Bacchic mysteries in the first quarter of the fifth century... but Pythagoras belongs to history, and Orpheus to myth.[84]

If mythical, who created the story of Orpheus – and why? I propose that when Pythagorean ideas were met by Bacchic mystery rites, someone decided to fuse them together. In order to justify and introduce this new creation, a fictitious "giver of laws" was needed. Due to an evolutionary new form of spiritual practice, combining Pythagorean influences and Bacchic mysteries, Orpheus was created as a divine spokesperson. We do not know who did it, and it doesn't matter that we do not know; we have the end result, so it must have happened.

## Serapis, the Created God

We are far luckier with the example of Serapis, an Egyptian-Greek syncretic god *designed* to appeal to the largest possible majority, thereby unifying the empire. Serapis is a historically verified, deliberately planned religious synthesis, commissioned by Ptolemy I (323BC - 283BC). Although deliberately fabricated, Serapis worship remained immensely popular for centuries.

Ptolemy I was a general under Alexander and became ruler of Egypt. In 305/04BC, he took the title of Pharaoh. He is also the ruler who conceived of and constructed the great Alexandrian Library. The kaleidoscope of animal-faced Egyptian gods was frowned upon by many Greeks, and religious differences and variation made it difficult to rule his subjects. So he chose two priests, and commissioned them to craft an Egyptian-Greek religious hybrid.

For this task he chose one Egyptian, Manetho, educated in Egyptian history and born close to a famous shrine of Isis, and one Athenic Greek, linked with the mystery rites of Demeter and Persephone at Eleusis.[85]

Serapis combined Osiris and Horus into one figure. He was also identified with the Apis Bull, a popular Egyptian figure. His mother was the powerful goddess Isis. He came with a human face, as a man, but was also a figure of supernatural proportions:

> My head is the firmament of the heaven, my belly the ocean, my feet constitute the earth, my ears are set in the sky, and my far-seeing eye is the bright light of the sun. (Macrobius, *Saturnalia* I, 20, 17: FRA 597, 39)[86]

Serapis also combined Zeus, ruler of heaven, and Hades, ruler of the underworld, into one, supreme new figure: "One Zeus, one Hades, one Serapis" (Julian, *Orat.* 4, 135: FRA 538). Serapis worship came packaged with his mother-consort Isis. Together they were an unbeatable pair:

> Serapis was deliberately created by the Ptolemaic theologians for export abroad. He had powers of assimilation to the leading gods of Greece and in time won international acceptance. Isis, too, became increasingly cosmopolitan.[87]

Serapis was regarded as a healer, with Isis; usurping the role of Asclepius he became the guardian and savior of all mankind. Moreover, his form of healing was *medicinal*, rather than mystical. Ptolemy I built a temple of Serapis (the Serapeum) adjacent to the Library of Alexandria, where doctors could study medicine and healing arts. The Serapeum seemed to have offered treatments similar to those prescribed by Asclepius, like bathing and incubation:

> Next to the Alexandrian Serapeum was the great university: the cult of Serapis and the establishment of the library and the museum were alike due to Ptolemy I. The Library was to overflow into the temple and the links were to remain unseparable till the final onslaught by the Christians. We know that in the temple there existed 'pastophoria'. There were the quarters of the pastophors whose task was to master the medical texts and all the traditional magical lore of Egypt.[88]

Serapis was also seamlessly adapted into the magical traditions, becoming a supremely powerful magical name – equivalent to 10,000 other names:

> Do this for I am your slave and petitioner and have hymned your valid and holy names, lord, glorious one... of ten thousand names, greatest, nourisher, apportioner, Serapis. (PGM XIII.637ff)[89]

> I call on you, lord, holy, my hymned, greatly honored Serapis; consider my birth and turn me not away, me, (magical words)... who knows your true name and valid names (magical words). I hymn your holy power in musical hymn (magical words). Protect me from all my own astrological destiny; destroy my foul fate; apportion good things for me in my horoscope; increase my life; and may I enjoy good things, for I am your slave. (PGM XIII 619ff)[90]

Worship of Serapis and Isis was supported by the Roman Emperor Hadrian, who encouraged the expansion of Alexandrian religion. Hadrian also built the Pantheon and the Temple of Venus and Rome, as well as several opulent temples in Athens.

In our quest for the *beginning* of the story of Jesus Christ, Serapis gives us a clear example of how a deliberately created religion, harnessing all the best parts of many different traditions, could unite the growing spiritual values of the Roman Empire. If Serapis could be created, and yet still worshipped as a God, could Jesus Christ have also been made as a conscious attempt to dismantle the religious barriers between Rome and its conquered Jewish tributaries?

Surprisingly, the connection between Jesus and Serapis goes much deeper: several ancient testimonies claim that Serapis *was worshipped* by Christians, who used him almost interchangeably with the figure of Jesus Christ!:

> In Egypt those who worship Serapis are Christians and those who call themselves Christ's bishops ('overseers') are addicted to Serapis. Jewish rabbis, Samaritans and Christian priests in Egypt become astrologers and soothsayers. The visiting archbishop is obliged to worship Serapis by some and by others Christ. (Athanasius, *Life of Anthony* 90: FRA 561, 24)[91]

In the Egypt of the time of the emperor Hadrian those who called themselves bishops of Christ are recorded to have devoted their souls to Serapis. The link between the two faiths was the gospel of salvation. (phlegon, Epist. Ap. Vopisc, [Saturnin.], 8: FRA 280, 15)[92]

The "time of Hadrian" was 117AD to 138AD; this is still very early in the history of Christianity. Had the small Jewish movement started by Jesus Christ in Israel moved so quickly and grown so much that Jesus could be *equated* with Serapis – a cosmic Greek-Egyptian synthesis? And how are we to reconcile the fact that Christians themselves were "addicted" to Serapis?

Jesus, it would seem, was the next logical step in Hadrian's campaign; a final evolution of the Egyptian-Greek composite figure of Serapis, which may have been written to assimilate the stubbornly rebellious and violent Jewish people under the fold of a State Religion.

## The Jesus Mysteries

Given the spiritual background (the trend towards syncretism and the need for a universal religion that the entire empire could enjoy) we could have *expected* a Jewish-Greek mystery cult to appear on the spiritual horizon. In the following brief summary, I will show that the historical conditions made the creation of a Greek-Jewish mystery cult inevitable.

Starting from around 230BC, the land of Israel fell under Roman influence. The Roman policy was to conquer, improve public facilities, collect taxes, and have people honor the emperor. While many communities lived peacefully under foreign rule, the Jews believed that Israel was given to them by God and could not be taken from them. They considered themselves a holy people, and thought that they were to stay pure by separating themselves from the world in dress, custom and diet. When Romans began to raise temples and statues to Roman gods in Jerusalem, it presented Jews with a theological problem. They reasoned that either they had forgotten to fulfill their religious duties, and were being punished, or that God was expecting them to fight back against Rome and reclaim their homeland. There were many rebellions during this period, but every uprising against the Romans resulted in heavy losses for the Jews. Taking pieces from their scriptures which spoke of a future prophet or king and weaving them together, they formed a description of a savior figure that would liberate them from Roman rule. They pictured a powerful ruler from Israel's royal dynasty, the line of David, who would unify the country, restore the tribes of Israel, and defeat the Romans in a final holy war. Kings were always anointed on the forehead, so they referred to this messiah as The Christ, which means "the anointed one."

Jews who lived outside of Jerusalem sometimes became less austere in their dress and customs, assimilating into their new surroundings. Some became educated in Greek thought and language, and no doubt came in contact with mystery religions and sun gods through public festivals and holidays. A few may have even become initiates themselves. But even if they didn't, Greek philosophers spoke plainly about concepts like Sophia and Logos, and it would have been impossible not to learn something about them.

Around 2,000 years ago, probably in Alexandria, someone began writing a Jewish version of the Greek mysteries. Maybe someone found in them a pearl of wisdom they wished to share with their people. Or perhaps they felt guilty for allowing themselves to become involved with pagan culture and were trying to justify their actions through a Yahweh-centered version of the Logos myth. Like other mysteries, it would have centered around a passion play of a suffering god, been full of magical ritual, Greek philosophy of Logos and salvation, and Stoic philosophy of brotherly love and ethics. They copied rituals from both Judaism and Mystery cults.

Such a story could easily have been created by an Alexandrian Jew like Philo; but it could also have been crafted by someone like Seneca, who wanted to create a new tragedy play based on a crucified Jewish rebel-king. (Seneca was the author of at least nine tragedies based on historical events, and had a lifelong interest in oriental religions).[93] It might have been a clever money-making scheme, forged by an entrepreneur seeking to attract new initiates with a novel mystery religion. It could even have been – like Serapis – *commissioned* by Roman authorities in an attempt to placate

rebellious territories (this would have been particularly feasible for Hadrian, who was determined to solve the Jewish problem at all costs). Given the spiritual climate, any of these is likely. At any rate, the new, Jewish version of the mysteries offered Diaspora Jews a way to integrate culturally while preserving their own theological heritage. These stories were written by people who had most likely never been to Israel, and like the Egyptians used locations metaphorically to describe the sun's ascent and descent.

A common practice among the Greek mysteries and Jewish mystics was gematria, a system in which every letter had a corresponding number. Using this number substitution code, a name was created for this new Jewish-Greek-Egyptian synthesis with special esoteric significance.

This figure was not only a sacred number, it was also a pictograph of the nature of God. The figure "8" turned on its side becomes the symbol of eternity. Three 8's show the three identical persons of the eternal trinity. The numbers 888 can also be reversed, flipped, and substituted with each other without causing any change in their nature, reflecting the unchanging constancy of God. (This is a modern reading; the glyph "8" was first used by western Ghubar Arabs and the infinity symbol is credited to John Wallis in his 1655 *De sectionibus conicis*.) The principles behind this equation were well known in the first few centuries AD, and the church father Iraneaus, although he doesn't seem to believe it himself, can clearly understand the numbers involved:

This is the name of Jesus; for this name, if you reckon up the numerical value of the letters, amounts to eight hundred and eighty eight. Thus, then, you have a clear statement of their opinion as to the origin of the super celestial Jesus. Wherefore, also, the alphabet of the Greeks contains eight Monads, eight Decads, and eight Hecatads, which present the number eight hundred and eighty-eight, that is, Jesus, who is formed of all the numbers; and on this account He is called Alpha and Omega, indicating his origin from all. (Iraneaus, *Against the Heresies* I, 15.2)[94]

That Jesus was associated with a mystical number should come as no surprise; virtually everyone is aware that "the number of the Beast" is 666. The Book of Revelation clearly points out that this number can be decoded from the text. "Here is wisdom. Let him that hath understanding count the number of the beast: for it is the number of a man; and his number is Six hundred threescore and six" (13:17-18). This number is further connected to the Old Testament, as both 1 Kings 10:14 and 2 Chronicles 9:13 record that Solomon collected 666 talents of gold each year. The number 666 is the number of *man*, or the flesh and the lower self.

In contrast, the number 888 represented the higher, spiritual self or the universal Logos. Hence, this new moniker was truly a divine name; a *magical* name. Jesus was superior to other gods, not because he was different from them, but because he had a *more powerful name*. The magical power of the name of Jesus is clear in many biblical passages:

God has highly exalted him and bestowed on him the name which is above every name, that at the name of Jesus every knee should bow. (Philippians 2:9)

The concept of the Logos, represented by the divine number 888, was combined with the image of the awaited messiah and became the title "Jesus Christ." It was an attempt to bridge Greek salvation philosophy with Jewish religious history, and is a literary construction that does not refer to a historical person. This helps us to understand the often quoted biblical passages which stress that the name of Jesus is unique; that only through Jesus can we be saved. It is not Jesus – the historical man – who held the key

to salvation, but the Logos and his magical name, symbolizing an innate relationship with the original unity:

> I am the Way; I am Truth and Life. No one can come to the Father except through me. (John 13:14)

Early Christian communities were well versed in magic and had no difficulty in using this new magical name. The author of Ephesians lists an expansive collection of spirits and daemons conquered by Jesus Christ, who is "far above every principality, ruling force, power or sovereignty, or any other name that can be named" (Eph. 1:20-1:22). While Serapis was greater than 10,000 names, Jesus became greater than any name that *can* be named. As Arnold notes:

> "Every name that is named" is encompassed in the mighty reign of the Lord Jesus Christ – no conceivable power is outside the dominion of Christ. This particular phrase is loaded with significance for exorcism and magical incantation both in Judaism and the pagan world.[95]

Like other magical names listed above, with power over nature (hearing them, sun and earth are overturned; Hades is shaken; rivers, sea, lakes and springs are frozen; rocks are split) the name of Jesus gives unlimited magical ability: "If you ask anything in My name, I will do it" (John 14:14).

Similar to passages in the Egyptian book of the dead, the secret to immortality in the early church lay in knowing God's true name, almost like a secret password. It was the name Jesus itself, and not just the person or function of Jesus, that held power. Like *abracadabra*, Jesus was a special word, that when pronounced properly could produce marvelous effects – and it was understood as such by early Christians, who tried "pronouncing" the name ritualistically:

> But some itinerant Jewish exorcists too tried pronouncing the name of the Lord Jesus over people who were possessed by evil spirits; they used to say, 'I adjure you by the Jesus whose spokesman is Paul.' (Acts 19:11)

One online article (circulating on many websites including

the Zeitgeist discussion board), makes the claim that gematria was further extended to establish a link between Jesus and the Pythagorean Theorem:

> As a mythological figure he (Jesus) incorporates the most important rule of the sacred geometry used by astronomers to measure and by architects to build: The Pythagorean Theorem. In his name the Gnostics in Alexandria encoded the sacred Pythagorean triangle: 3, 4, 5. The name Jesus Christ is a sacred Gnostic riddle, like that of the Sphinx, which were very popular in the ancient alexandrine and Greek sects to distinguish initiates from non-initiates. Jesus and Christ are two of the three sides of a right triangle, and to solve the riddle you must find the third word, the lost word, that represents gematrically the third side of the triangle. The solution is a pun in itself: a Greek word that means "you have known," put together with the name Jesus Christ, gives the answer: "You have known Jesus Christ." The gematria of Jesus (Ιησουσ) is 888 and the Gematria of Christ (Χριστοσ) is 1480. With those two numbers, applying the Pythagorean theorem, you find the third number: 1184, that corresponds gematrically to a very specific word: "εγνωκατε," that Jesus uses when he is referring to the act of knowing god. The word "εγνωκατε" is used repeatedly in 1 John 2, and is the very verb that gave the name to the famous Alexandrian sect: the Gnostics, from ginosko (ghin-oce'-ko), or "knowing."[96]

Sacred Heart of Jesus.

Although for Greeks this new mystery was just one among hundreds, to some Jews this may have been their first glimpse of the mystery salvation philosophy. The permanence of the soul, in particular, may have been an attractive idea for them, and a community grew up around these stories. These groups taught the Greek mysteries in a Jewish framework, and offered Diaspora Jews the opportunity to become initiates without feeling guilty for abandoning their own culture. They taught the mystery of "Christ in you, the hope and glory" (Col. 1:27), and "the knowledge of God's mystery, which is Christ" (Col 2:2).

Rather than believe the Messiah was a historical figure, they imagined that he was the Logos, who gave mankind internal salvation. Paying taxes and living under Roman law was inconsequential after having been saved by the Logos, and even death held no power over those saved. Instead of depending on external forces to liberate them, initiates believed each person could become their own messiah. Because of this, they called themselves anointed ones, or "Christians."

## Conclusions and Summary

Christianity is a Jewish synthesis of Greek-Egyptian mystery cult tradition. Rather than surprising, the expansion of the popular cult of Serapis (founded in Alexandria) to include Judaism (when the Jews of Alexandria were already creating interpretive, comparative literature) is entirely probable.

Such a synthesis had already happened for Orpheus, and again – deliberately – for Serapis. Syncretism and a movement towards monotheism and one state religion, the popular varieties of mystery cults, and the Jewish practice of magic were already heading towards the creation of a Jewish mystery cult, when political conflict in Jerusalem gave even more motivation to develop a new Jewish-Greek-Egyptian hybrid. Thus, a story (hieros logos) was created based on the suffering mystery gods and the idea of a Jewish Messiah or resistance hero, who was given a magical name with a mathematical significance. In the beginning, he was probably little more than an idea, perhaps a selection of wise sayings, preceded by "Jesus says _____." As the story grew, his followers debated challenging topics such as whether or not to keep Jewish Law. The debate sparked heavy revision, and someone tied Jesus to Old Testament "prophecies." Consequently, a story was created in which the character of Jesus fulfills the law. The rest of the details, rather than staying loyal to a genuine tradition based on apostolic succession, emerged, changed and were reshaped in response to external influences and the needs of individual communities – *including* the idea that Jesus was historical.

This theory explains how there could be so many controversies, disagreements and schisms in the early Christian communities: there was no "Truth" for them to agree on – they were involved in the active production of a faith. There were, however, two defining features of this new Jewish mystery cult that were not only innovative, but proved to be fundamental in its future:

1.  Christianity was a synthesis of the totality of the movements around it, so in a sense, Jesus Christ was *more* than all the others.

2.  Christianity sprung a side-movement which believed in the resurrection of the flesh, and hence the physical resurrection of Jesus himself.

Now that we have a clear theory of how the story of Jesus was created, and that it was *originally* a mystery rather than a history, we can reread the early Christian literature found in the gospels and look for clues as to how this story became mistakenly associated with a historical, recently crucified savior.

## CHAPTER NINE

# Stupid Galatians:
# The Resurrection of the Flesh

*"Having begun in the spirit, can you be so stupid as to end in the flesh? Can all the favors you have received have had no effect – if there really has been no effect?" –Galatians 3:1*

WHEN I LIVED IN MALTA AND was seeking spiritual answers, I stopped into a Baha'i group a couple of times. At one meeting, a woman started speaking excitedly about an ancient manuscript that had recently been discovered in Peru, which revealed nine powerful spiritual insights. Had I heard of it? It was called the "Celestine Prophecy." I *had* heard of it. What's more, I knew that it was written in 1993 by James Redfield, was written in the first person narrative blending psychological research and ancient religious principles, and was a novel – a *fictional* story. Somehow, the original message "there's a new book out about a manuscript found in Peru called the Celestine Prophecy" became "they just found an ancient manuscript in Peru called the Celestine Prophecy." Neither of us had a copy of the book handy, so there was no way I could *prove* that the story was not based on true events. In the end, we agreed to disagree. This is a modern example of how a fictional story, written about a made-up recent event and powerful enough to inspire people to spread the message, could become cut off from the details of its own production and mistaken as history.

In my assertion that Jesus Christ was, like Harry Potter, an original literary synthesis of many diverse myths and traditions, there is one urgent question left to resolve: how a certain group of Christ-followers became separated from the full message, the interpretative spirituality at the higher levels of the mysteries, and began to believe in Jesus Christ as a real, physical human being, recently crucified in Jerusalem. In this chapter, I will demonstrate that a select group of Christians who had not been initiated into the higher mysteries began to develop an independent Christology that focused on the resurrection of the flesh. We will analyze the biblical writings of the apostle Paul, whose letters preserve the exact state of communicative decay that led to the literalist misinterpretation of the Jesus myth, and the rebellion of his communities when he tried to reveal the higher mysteries. Using biblical evidence, we will witness how new converts and initiates began to preach a historical, newly crucified and resurrected Jewish savior – without having heard the full message of the new spiritual movement. Finally, we will see how these communities, who believed in a historical Jesus, developed a doctrine of "resurrection of the flesh" in defense of their beliefs which set them firmly against the spirituality of their times.

## Paul's Mystery Initiations

The Jewish mystery cult, a greater spiritual synthesis than even the mighty and popular Serapis, was immediately successful. It was fueled by both the desires and needs of the Jewish people in the Diaspora, and the lust for a greater and more powerful magical name. It also allowed Jews to integrate more fully into their cosmopolitan pagan environment. But there was an inherent and powerful conflict in this new religious practice. Jesus was the *anathema* of everything the Jews believed in; he was a repugnant, crudely constructed, pagan mystery god dressed up as the Jewish Messiah and appropriating Jewish scripture for his own. Those that accepted him anyway had to resolve pressing questions and practical matters. Was the Law of the Old Testament to be followed, or did Jesus do away with the Law? Should taxes be paid to the Roman Empire – or to the Jewish Temple in Jerusalem? Different leaders arose, offering distinct versions of the Jesus mysteries, in fierce competition for monopoly on this new faith. The form of the Jesus mysteries that survived is an offshoot of the version promoted by Paul, but he was not its first teacher. There were other Jewish-Pagan syntheses that were in many ways similar to the movement that ultimately identified itself under the new name "Jesus."

Tradition tells us, for example, that John the Baptist was the forerunner of Jesus, and the gospels compel Jesus to seek John's approval in the scene of Jesus' baptism. John must have been immensely influential for Jesus to need a link to his tradition. One of the greatest threats to the early church was the Gnostic movement attributed to Simon Magus, who apparently really *was* one of John's disciples. Simon was credited with great magical powers such as levitation; it is said that he proclaimed himself the Messiah.[1] During this period after the destruction of the Second Temple by Rome, Jews were actively seeking a Christ – and many were found or came forward. Jesus' claim to be *the* Christ was not without competitors, such as Simon.

Upon this scene came Paul of Tarsus, who became involved in the new mystery cult using the magical name of Jesus. According to the Acts of the Apostles, Paul was a priest charged with rounding up the Diaspora Jews who were participating in the Jewish Mysteries – but once he started to investigate them, he had a mystical experience of his own on the road to Damascus, converted and became the cult's strongest supporter. This powerful marketing technique continues to be used today in most sales letters, in the claims of an initial critic or skeptic who was overwhelmed in spite of themselves. Perhaps in truth Paul was himself initiated into the mysteries; his experience at Damascus certainly sounds like an initiation experience of the type reported at Eleusis. At any rate, Paul set himself up as a teacher, but in a profound cultural shift, proclaimed himself "apostle to the Gentiles."

Paul produced (or popularized) a divergent form of the Jesus mysteries meant for non-Jews; in a sense, we could say he found a new market for an established product. Jews had always kept themselves and their culture apart from their gentile neighbors, even while living among them, in part because their strict dietary laws and other restrictions made assimilation difficult. Paul claimed, however, that Jesus *cancelled* those laws:

> He has wiped out the record of our debt to the Law, which stood against us; he has destroyed it by nailing it to the cross. (Col. 2:14)

When Paul came with this "Good News" that Jews could now worship a mystery God and quit the tedious prescriptions of the Jewish law, he was received gladly. The Galatians greeted him "as an angel of God, as Christ Jesus" (Gal 4:14):

> Paul transformed the Dispersion. Morality, mysticism, promise of salvation without the Law were what very many of its members wanted to hear.[2]

His new version of the mysteries was popular especially among magical communities who recognized the value in the *name* of Jesus. These were usually fringe towns without a strong Jewish center and with heavy interest in paganism, mysteries or magic. But Paul took his mysteries even further: in a revolutionary stance on cultural identity and politics, he not only proclaimed a new experience for the Jews (the participation in mystery spirituality without limitations from the Law), but also that the Gentiles could now participate in the Jewish Covenant. This offered outsiders something new that could not be found in other mysteries: the personal protection of the powerful and ancient God of Moses. Paul reasoned that Jesus, by destroying the Law of the commandments that previously separated the Jews and Gentiles, brought peace to these two cultures so they could live together without hostility:

> For he is the peace between us, and has made the two into one entity and broken down the barrier which used to keep them apart, by destroying in his own person the hostility, that is, the Law of commandments with its decrees. His purpose in this was, by restoring peace, to create a single New Man out of the two of them, and through the cross, to reconcile them both to God in one Body; in his own person he killed the hostility. He came to bring the good news

of peace to you who were far off and peace to those who were near. Through him, then, we both in the one Spirit have free access to the Father. (Ephesians 2:14-18)

This was a highly political claim. On the one hand, as we've seen, this final form of mystery synthesis was a natural production of the synergetic tendency of the times. From the standpoint of the Roman authority, Paul's message was precisely what was needed to placate the rebelling factions of Jews and offer them a place in the empire. From the Jewish perspective, on the other hand, Paul's claims were scandalously blasphemous; they implied a complete break with Judaism:

> For loyal Jews, Paul was a disaster. He had thrown into the open many of the unresolved tensions within the Dispersion. They were aghast at the consequences... If he was right, Moses was wrong and the promises to Abraham were in vain. If Paul went free, the ideal of Jewish universalism was dead, and the communities of the Dispersion would be prey to discord and schism.[3]

Despite modern attempts to root Christianity firmly in Judaism (and thereby bypass the challenging dilemma of its similarity to the pagan mystery cults), Paul's Christianity was rejected by the Jews – indeed, he was violently persecuted for bringing Christ's "Good News." In his own words, Paul relates:

> Five times at the hands of the Jews I received 40 lashes minus one. Three times I was beaten with rods, once I was stoned, three times I was shipwrecked, I passed a night and a day on the deep; on frequent journeys, in dangers from rivers, dangers from robbers, dangers from my own race, dangers from Gentiles, dangers in the city, dangers in the wilderness, dangers at sea, dangers among false brothers; in toil and hardship, through many sleepless nights, through hunger and thirst, through frequent fastings, through cold and exposure. And apart from these things, there is the daily pressure upon me of my anxiety for all the churches. (2 Corinthians 11:24- 28)

Paul's new mysteries stirred up heated controversy. How were Greeks and Gentiles to be reconciled? What foods could be eaten? Should Gentiles get circumcised? Were they really *equal* to Jews in

God's eyes? How could the Jewish people get rid of the Law – what had previously been the defining feature of their people and culture? Surely *some* of it must be saved? Dissension produced dozens of schisms and parallel movements. As we know today, the group of Christians who eventually gained the upper hand, produced the Bible and became the Roman Catholic Church, disagreed with Paul about the Law – their Jesus, as recorded in Matthew, warns:

> Do not think that I have come to abolish the Law or the Prophets; I have not come to abolish them but to fulfill them. I tell you the truth, until heaven and earth disappear, not the smallest letter, not the least stroke of a pen, will by any means disappear from the Law until everything is accomplished. (Matthew 5:17-18)

The New Testament is arranged to appear chronological: the four gospels (Matthew, Mark, Luke and John) present the story of Jesus' ministry; Acts of the Apostles narrates the adventures of the disciples; and the letters of Paul – written to the growing Christian communities – are included at the end. This arrangement is misleading. The letters of Paul are actually the earliest writings in the New Testament. As such, they record an *earlier* conception of Jesus Christ than the view given in the gospels. This difficulty is often noted and overcome by biblical scholars with the claim that, although crucial in spreading the mystery of Jesus Christ, Paul's gospel is profoundly different from the "original" one that Jesus must have taught, and that the Church was later guided back to the Truth through the power of the Holy Spirit.

Without fidelity to the idea that Church doctrine is infallible, this claim is easily dismissed. Paul's letters make it clear that his "Jesus Christ" is a Jewish version of the Greek mysteries, which have been around for some time. The only difference, he claims, is that it is a mystery religion for Jews, God's chosen people, and is thus superior because it is enhanced by Israel's holy covenant:

> I was made a servant with the responsibility... of completing God's message, the message which was a mystery hidden for generations and centuries and has now been revealed to his holy people. It was God's purpose to reveal to them... the glory of this mystery among the Gentiles; it is Christ among you. (Colossians 1:25)

He was saying, in effect, "The Greeks have used this mystery for years and it works great for them. Now I'm giving it to you, under the name of Christ, so that you can participate as well." Paul was a persuasive missionary. He told the story of Jesus Christ, Son of God, who was crucified and resurrected from the dead. New initiates would be baptized and urged to control their physical desires through fasting and abstinence. Paul would then leave a few initiates in charge and promise to return with further revelations.

The epistles of Paul are notoriously obtuse and contradictory, because he seems to be saying different things in every one. This is because not every community was at the same level in the process of initiation. As a mystery religion, Christianity had several layers of meaning that would be divulged slowly when initiates proved their worth. To the beginners, Paul was careful not to reveal too much; the higher teaching would be wasted on them if they weren't spiritually prepared, and the process could be ruined if rushed. To strengthen their willpower, Paul told them to have faith, to be strict in their habits and diet, and to become masters over their physical bodies. Once members had shown a certain level of spiritual maturity, they would be initiated into the higher mysteries and told that the Christ story was a metaphor for spiritual transformation. These advanced pupils, who believed in developing personal wisdom, or Gnosis, are the communities referred to by historians as Gnostics. To these higher level initiates, Paul left behind the initial steps and skipped ahead to more advanced topics:

> Let us leave behind all the elementary teaching about Christ and go on to its completion, without going over the fundamental doctrines again; the turning away from dead actions, faith in God, the teaching about baptisms and the laying on of hands, about the resurrection of the dead and the eternal judgment. (Hebrews 6)

He could also write freely about the mythical interpretations of the stories he'd shared with them. While in the beginning they had learned that their savior Christ was a man from Palestine, they were now to leave even this idea behind:

> From now onwards, then, we will not consider anyone by human standards: even if we were once on familiar terms with Christ

according to human standards, we do not know him in that way any longer. (2 Corinthians 5:16)

Paul revealed Christ as the Logos and explained his role as divine intermediary. Like other mysteries, Christianity had a "burial ritual" that included a symbolic death (to the old, physical, human self), and a rebirth (to a new life in Christ). Paul reminds the Ephesians that they were "*buried* with him in baptism" (Eph. 2:5-6). It should be obvious to us at this stage that we are dealing with a missing piece of early Christian ritual, which finds no expression in modern day Christianity. Followers of Jesus were expected to be *dead* in Christ, because they had already died in Christ. Many passages refer to Christians as having been, like Jesus, crucified, or having their physical passions crucified, or being crucified to the world. Hence, Jesus' crucifixion was understood metaphorically in Paul's mystery:

We died to sin; how can we live in it any longer? (Romans 6:2)

For you died, and your life is now hidden with Christ in God. (Colossians 3:3)

May I never boast except in the cross of our Lord Jesus Christ, through which the world has been crucified to me, and I to the world. (Galatians 6:14)

After their symbolic initiation into death, they would be "reborn" in Christ, living *in* Christ, or have the animating divine Logos living *through* them. Like the mystery initiates who died, were buried and then reborn into a new life, Paul likewise uses the past tense – members had already experienced a ritual of death and rebirth:

Or don't you know that all of us who were baptized into Christ Jesus were baptized into his death? We were therefore buried with him through baptism into death in order that, just as Christ was raised from the dead through the glory of the Father, we too may live a new life. If we have been united with him like this in his death, we will certainly also be united with him in his resurrection. For we know that our old self was crucified with him so that the body of sin might be done away with, that we should no longer be slaves to sin – because anyone who has died has been freed from sin. Now if we died with Christ, we believe that we will also live with him. For we know that since Christ was raised from the dead, he cannot die again; death no longer has mastery over him. The death he died, he died to sin once for all; but the life he lives, he lives to God In the same way, count yourselves dead to sin but alive to God in Christ Jesus. (Romans 6:3-11)

Incidentally, it should be pointed out that many Jewish communities had already adopted beliefs about a final resurrection at the end of time, like the Egyptians. Paul diverged from this belief, teaching that Jesus is inside you, now – and that the resurrection will happen in *this* life. The same idea can be found in the Gospel of John:

Jesus said to her, "Your brother will rise again." Martha answered, "I know he will rise again in the resurrection at the last day." Jesus said to her, "I am the resurrection and the life. He who believes in me will live, even though he dies; and whoever lives and believes in me will never die. Do you believe this?" (John 11:23-26)

It is not hard to imagine early initiates into the mysteries of Jesus participating in a burial ceremony, where they were actually buried or closed in a tomb, and having their rebirth celebrated as they emerged again into the light. This ritual may have even included a mock-crucifixion or at least an image of the crucifixion. It would have been followed by the ritual of the Wedding Chamber (as described previously by the Gospel of Philip cited above) to unite the Sophia with the Logos, or the Magdalene with the Jesus. After that, initiates would be one with the Logos, or Christ:

I have been crucified with Christ and yet I am alive; yet it is no longer I, but Christ living in me. (Galatians 2:20)

Since, then, you have been raised with Christ, set your hearts on things above, where Christ is seated at the right hand of God (Colossians 3:1)

Do not lie to each other, since you have taken off your old self with its practices and have put on the new self, which is being renewed in knowledge in the image of its Creator. (Colossians 3:9-10)

Paul used unambiguous terms and images, exhibiting a mastery of Greek language and mystery school philosophy. In Second Corinthians, Paul claims that he knew a man in Christ that was "caught up to the third heaven" and another that was "caught up into paradise, and heard unspeakable words, which it is not lawful for a man to utter" (2 Corinthians 12:2-4).

After removing the seven veils of corporeality (hinted at in the story of Jesus casting the seven demons out of Mary), Paul's higher initiates could reflect the light of Godlike living mirrors.

> And all of us, with our unveiled faces like mirror reflecting the glory of the Lord, are being transformed into the image that we reflect in brighter and brighter glory; this is the working of the Lord who is the Spirit. (2 Corinthians 3:16)

Paul was also familiar with the magical traditions, as evidenced by his use of specific magical terminology. According to Witt:

> We do well to remember the widespread influence of Egyptian theological beliefs in their Hellenistic shape when we encounter the Pauline statement that Christ is the 'power' (dynamis) of God and the 'wisdom' (Sophia) of God. Power and wisdom are the very gifts claimed by the mages of the Nile in the wonders they work either through the oral or the manual rite.[4]

Arnold argues convincingly that the letter of Ephesians, written to one of the most knowledgeable magical communities, is full of magical words and formulas that would have made sense to readers there. Paul's formula "breadth, length, height and depth" of Ephesians 3:18 is used in the earlier Greek Magical Papyri. According to Nils Dahl, "Commentators have taken account of the similarity between the magical spells and Eph 3:18 but have not quite known what to do with it."[5]

Although the early stages of the mysteries may have prescribed strict rules of conduct, initiates, after their own rite of resurrection, were theoretically dead to their animal selves. Moral action from then on was supposed to come directly from the Logos within them and be spontaneous. However, eradication of desire through this symbolic death was a continuous process; Paul often had to remind his pupils of the implied morality that came with their elevated status:

> You have stripped off your old behavior with your old self, and you have put on a new self which will progress towards true knowledge the more it is renewed in the image of its creator. (Colossians 3:8)

> All who belong to Christ Jesus have crucified self with all its passions and its desires. Since we are living by the spirit, let our behavior be guided by the Spirit and let us not be conceited or provocative and envious of one another. (Galatians 5:24)

Initiates at the highest level, including Paul, understood that in reality there was no right and wrong, no good and evil, because all opposites were united in the Logos. For these initiates, moral excellence was not found in empty physical posturing, but in natural harmony with the internal spirit. The laws and rules of the early stages had been like training wheels, which had served their purpose and could now be removed:

> If you have really died with Christ to the principles of this world, why do you still let rules dictate you, as though you were still living in the world? "Do not pick up this, do not eat that, do not touch the other," and all about things which perish even while they are being used according to merely human commandments and doctrines! (Colossians 2:20)

The Jewish Law, in Paul's ethics, was rendered meaningless. The important thing, rather than moral codes of external action, was to cultivate an internal state of tranquility. The soul was described as a pool of water that needed to be kept still in order to reflect the image of God (similar to the mystery language of Philip). This peaceful internal state was more important even than specific details of the faith:

> Within yourself, before God, hold on to what you already believe. Blessed is the person whose principles do not condemn his practice. But anyone who eats with qualms of conscious is already condemned, because this eating does not spring from faith and every action that does not spring from faith is sin. (Romans 14:22)

Any action that caused worry, guilt, or internal discord was a sin because it splashed the water of the soul, and God could no longer be seen clearly. Those initiates who could act without rippling the water had total freedom from the strict Jewish dietary laws and moral customs. However, they needed to be careful around the lower level initiates, who had not yet reached this ambivalent attitude towards sin:

> One person may have faith enough to eat any kind of food; another, less strong, will eat only vegetables. Those who feel free to eat freely are not to condemn those who are unwilling to eat freely; nor must the person who does not eat freely pass judgment on those who does... the one who eats freely, eats in honor of the Lord and makes his thanksgiving to God and the one who does not, abstains from eating in the honor of the Lord and makes his thanksgiving to God. (Romans 14:2)

While foreign to the Jewish tradition of obedience to the strict stipulations of conduct found in the Old Testament, Paul's philosophy was essentially no different from that preached by the Stoics, an immensely popular form of spiritual wisdom which had flourished for centuries. Paul's views on marriage, for example, are almost identical to what was taught by Epictetus: "As to pleasure with women, abstain from it as far as you can, before marriage; but if you do indulge in it, do it in the way conformable to custom. Do not, however, be disagreeable to those who take such pleasures, nor apt to rebuke them or to say often that you do not."[6] It was also compatible with the teachings from most other philosophers like Plato, or the higher truths of the mystery schools. In other words, while the *story* of Jesus was Jewish, its *meaning* was entirely pagan.

## Missing the Point

The Greek mysteries were well established in Greek and Roman culture, and most likely had an established network of teachers. The basic initiation process would have been common knowledge to new initiates. Paul's Diaspora Jews, on the other hand, might not have been familiar with the procedures involved in this type of religious system. When Paul came preaching the arrival of the Messiah, they were excited; they *believed* him, and told their friends the good news. After Paul had left, his communities continued to meet and talk about what they had learned. Some of them, believing that they were adequately versed in the faith, assumed leadership roles and began to teach new initiates. However, since they themselves had not yet received the higher mysteries, they taught only the basics and made no mention of further revelations. The Acts of the Apostles gives us an example of one of these teachers, a confident and bold speaker, who created many new disciples of Jesus Christ. He even traveled to spread the good news. And yet, the Acts of the Apostles makes it clear that he did not have the full message:

> An Alexandrian Jew named Apollos now arrived in Ephesus. He was an eloquent man, with sound knowledge of the scriptures, and yet, though he had been given instruction in the way of the Lord and preached with great spiritual fervor and was accurate in all the details he taught about Jesus, he had experienced only the baptism of John. He began to teach fearlessly in the synagogue and, when Priscilla and Aquila heard him, they attached themselves to him and gave him a more detailed instruction about the way. (Acts 18:24)

It is clear in this passage that the early church had two baptisms – a feature missing from most forms of modern Christianity. We can assume that the two baptisms refer to different levels of initiation, the baptism of Jesus being the higher level, which Apollos had not yet received. In the Bible, John the Baptist warns against being satisfied with his baptism, because Jesus would come later with more powerful rituals:

> I baptize you with water, but one more powerful than I will come, the thongs of whose sandals I am not worthy to untie. He will baptize you with the holy spirit and with fire. (Matthew 3:11, Luke 3:16)

Each baptism marked a special initiation into a higher level of Christian spirituality, and involved a complicated ritual of herbs, oils, proper attire, special numbers and magical seals. The following ancient passage from the Coptic Church describes a ceremony of the baptism of fire in great detail:

> Jesus said to his disciples, "Bring me grapevines, so that you may receive the baptism of fire." And the disciples brought him the grapevines. He offered up incense. He sent up juniper berries and myrrh, along with frankincense, mastic, nard, cassia flowers, turpentine, and oil of myrrh. And he also spread a linen cloth on the place of offering, and set upon it a chalice of wine, and set loaves of bread upon it according to the number of the disciples. And he had all of his disciples dress themselves with linen garments, and crowned them with the plant pigeon grass, and put the plant doghead in their mouths. And he had them put the pebble with the seven voices into their two hands, namely 9879. And he put the plant chrysanthemum in their two hands, and put the plant knotgrass under their feet. And he placed them before the incense which he had offered up. And he had them put their feet together. And Jesus came behind the incense which he had offered up and sealed them with this seal.[7]

The Baptism of the Holy Spirit – the Baptism of Fire – later became transformed into the tradition of Pentecost; the Holy Spirit came down and "enlightened" all of the apostles with Wisdom, so that they could go and spread God's word. However, once Christianity divorced itself from metaphorical interpretation, and denied the secretive esoteric wisdom of the higher initiates, it was decided that one baptism was enough. A new creed was written, "We believe in one baptism for the forgiveness of sins." (Some forms of modern Christianity, like Pentecostalism, have revived the idea of a second baptism or baptism by fire).

Who were the women that instructed Apollos about the Way of the Lord? How did they know about the baptism of Jesus while Apollos only knew about the baptism of John? This passage is important, because it demonstrates that in Paul's Christianity (at least according to the author of Acts), women were allowed to teach. This feature of early Christianity remains in later Gnostic communities, but was quickly cut out of what became orthodoxy. While literalist Christians took the Wedding Chamber at face value and assumed women were of lower status than men, Gnostics had no qualms about letting women teach and assume leadership roles. Hence, it appears that there was already a Gnostic community in Ephesus when Apollos stumbled in proclaiming Jesus Christ, and Priscilla and Aquila were leaders in that community. Unfortunately, Apollos apparently spread his limited version of Jesus Christ to a lot of people before he was stopped. Paul faced entire communities who had somehow been cut off from the higher levels of initiation:

> Paul made his way overland as far as Ephesus, where he found a number of disciples. When he asked, "Did you receive the Holy Spirit when you became believers?" They answered, "No, we were never even told there was such thing as a Holy Spirit." He asked, "Then how were you baptized? They replied, "With John's Baptism." Paul said, "John's baptism was a baptism of repentance, but he insisted that the people should believe in the one who was to come after him - namely Jesus." When they heard this, they were baptized in the name of the Lord Jesus. (Acts 19)

Another way to read these passages is to recognize that the author of Acts may have been part of a Jesus-mystery that was profiting from a tradition started by John the Baptist. Perhaps John's mysteries were already popular when a new form of mystery (namely Jesus, who was in effect claiming to be John's successor) was developed. The new mystery could be marketed very easily, professing to be just a further addition to the previous one. Moreover, there is reason to suppose that John the Baptist may have also been at least partly literary, especially concerning mythical elements such as his beheading, which parallels Orpheus' prophetic disembodied head. John may have been teaching an earlier Jewish-mystery based on Orphism even before Jesus was imagined based on Serapis.

At any rate, it is clear in Acts that Paul was facing disciples of his or a similar mystery that had not received the full message of Christianity, and even worse, they didn't even know that there was more to the story. At the same time, due to the ease of communication within the Roman Empire, some of Paul's communities began to interact with each other independently. Followers who had only been taught the lowest levels of the mysteries got wind of other groups doing things differently, even believing in Jesus Christ differently.

It appears that the community of Corinth, for example, received only the basics of the Jesus mysteries, which were, in Paul's own words, "the turning away from dead actions, faith in God, the teaching about baptisms and the laying on of hands, the resurrection of the dead and the eternal judgment" (Hebrews 6). They heard rumors of "secret knowledge" that Paul was revealing to other Christians, and wrote to him demanding answers. Was there really more to the story? And if so, why hadn't they been told? Paul responded that they were not yet ready to hear the higher mysteries, and that by demonstrating their personal rivalries, they had shown that they still were not ready:

> And so, brothers, I was not able to talk to you as spiritual people; I had to talk to you as people living by your natural inclinations, still infants in Christ; I fed you with milk and not solid food, for you were not yet able to take it and even now, you are still not able to, for you are still living by your natural inclinations. As long as there is still jealousy and rivalry among you, that surely means that you are still living by your natural inclinations and by merely human principles. (1 Corinthians 3:1)

Apollos and the community at Ephesus were happy to be instructed in the nuances of the faith, but others were not so cooperative. Paul wasn't sure which communities would still accept his authority, and expressed concerns to his communities about how he would be received during his next visit. He described his fears in such detail it seems clear that he was already experiencing most of them, and becoming frustrated:

> I am afraid that in one way or another, when I come, I may find you different from what I should like you to be, and you may find me what you would not like me to be; so that in one way or the other there will be rivalry, jealousy, bad temper, quarrels, slander, gossip, arrogance, and disorder. (2 Corinthians 12:19)

Trying to restore order, and make sure that the higher mysteries were preserved, Paul may have returned to some of the younger communities and hastily given the "baptism of Jesus" or other rites to initiates who were not yet spiritually ready to receive them. Uncomfortable with the new philosophical view of Christ, or perhaps afraid of making themselves unpopular by refuting an earthly Messiah, some of these initiates reverted back to firmer ground and continued to teach only the basics with which they were familiar. Paul was furious:

> You stupid people in Galatia! After you had a clear picture of Jesus Christ crucified, right in front of your eyes, who has put a spell on you? There is only one thing I should like you to tell me: How was it that you received the Spirit – was it by the practice of the Law, or by believing in some message you heard? Having begun in the spirit, can you be so stupid as to end in the flesh? Can all the favors you have received have had no effect – if there really has been no effect? (Galatians 3:1)

Paul mentions three categories of men in his letters, the spiritual man (pneumatikos), the natural man (psychikos), and the "fleshly" man (sarkikos). Paul criticizes his communities for ending up in the flesh; the lowest category. Only the spiritual man, who has died to the flesh and been resurrected in the spirit, could understand God's mysteries. This is confirmed in John's gospel:

> I tell you the truth, no one can enter the kingdom of God unless he is born of water and the Spirit. Flesh gives birth to flesh, but the Spirit gives birth to spirit. (John 3:5 6)

> But the natural man receiveth not the things of the Spirit of God: for they are foolishness unto him: neither can he know them, because they are spiritually discerned. But he that is spiritual judges all things." (1 Cor. 2:14–15)

In the ancient world, the planets were gods that had influence over the physical body. The pagan mysteries celebrated astrological events as a method to keep track of celestial movements, such as solstices, and related these dates to stories about their savior. In the early levels of the Jewish mysteries, Jesus Christ was introduced as a real person, and initiates may have celebrated these dates in the guise of commemorative events, such as Christmas and

Easter, or continued Jewish customs such as Passover. However, for the initiates who had reached the higher levels and died to their physical bodies, these special dates should have lost their meaning. Some of Paul's communities continued to celebrate these dates even after they had received the full initiation, proving to him that they hadn't really understood his message:

> But formerly, when you did not know God, you were kept in slavery to things which are not really gods at all, whereas now that you have come to recognize God, or rather, be recognized by God, how can you now turn back again to those powerless and bankrupt elements who's slaves you now want to be all over again? You are keeping special days, and months, and seasons and years – I am beginning to be afraid that I may, after all, have wasted my efforts on you. (Galatians 4:8)

It is interesting that the Pauline letters preserved in the Bible were written to communities Paul was unhappy with; these are the communities that became the modern church. Besides constantly reprimanding them for their selfishness, contentiousness and debauchery, Paul was also frustrated by their inability to understand the finer points of his message:

> On this subject we have many things to say, and they are difficult to explain because you have grown so slow at understanding. Indeed, when you should by this time have become masters, you need someone to teach you all over again the elements of the principles of God's sayings; you have gone back to needing milk, and not solid food. (Hebrews 5:11)

The pattern of Paul's initiation was to first tell the stories about Jesus as a man, and later expand those teachings into a transformative spirituality in which the figure of Jesus Christ as an actual person could be discarded. Initiates at higher levels were told to develop Gnosis and use the Logos as a mirror to transform themselves into Christs. They were also told that laws concerning specific moral conduct were no longer necessary, because the Logos living in them would spontaneously seek out the greater good.

For some communities, the philosophical notions of the Logos were impractical, and the "everything is permissible" morality of Paul's ethics was too difficult to enforce. These initiates turned away from Paul, denying his higher mysteries and refusing to accept any interpretation of the original message. They preferred the idea that Jesus was a real man, who said and did real things, and constructed a simple faith based on ritual and moral law. He was the prophesied Messiah who *fulfilled* the Law, they claimed; therefore Jewish traditionalism could be kept. These groups, which considered Christ as a historical person, eventually won supremacy.

When Paul and others criticized them, these communities attempted to defend themselves by providing rational arguments in favor of their misguided beliefs. They developed their own, independent theology, based on Hebrew scripture and a literal reading of sacred texts. Paul complained that his followers were being stolen away from him and his teachings perverted:

> By the grace of God which was given to me I laid the foundations like a trained master builder, and someone else is building on them. (1 Corinthians 3:10)

Some groups even began forging letters from Paul, attempting to justify their beliefs through the authority of his name. Only seven of the fourteen Pauline letters included in the Bible are generally considered authentic by modern scholars. Timothy 1 and 2, along with the letter to Titus, are universally considered forgeries, while Ephesians, Colossians and 2 Thessalonians continue to be disputed. Many of these letters end by affirming that they really are from Paul, and try to use Paul's signature as proof:

> This greeting is in my own hand – PAUL. It is the mark of genuineness in every letter; this is my own writing. (2 Thessalonians 3:17)

While Paul taught that Jesus Christ crucified was the Sophia inside us, and that the kingdom of God was already here and available to us, these rebellious communities began to believe in Jesus as a real man who had recently risen from the dead. They believed Jesus would return at some point in the future to restore the kingdom of God on earth. Using Paul's own name against him, they warned other communities against believing that the kingdom could be accessed immediately:

> About the coming of our Lord Jesus Christ, brothers, and our being gathered to him: please do not be too easily thrown into confusion or alarmed by any manifestation of the Spirit or any statement or any letter claiming to come from us, suggesting that the Day of the Lord has already arrived. (2 Thessalonians 2:1)

Which letters were considered genuine would depend on which ones arrived first. Through this kind of letter, even communities who remained loyal to Paul may have been tricked into refusing his instruction. The forged letters turn away from the ideology of Paul's mysteries and focus on creating a modest and chaste society, based on a literal reading of scripture and strict moral obedience. Unlike Paul, whose close companions and fellow teachers included Priscilla and Aquila, the groups who wrote these letters were uncomfortable with women in roles of authority, and severely limited their function:

> Similarly, women are to wear suitable clothes and to be dressed quietly and modestly, without braided hair or gold and jewelry or expensive clothes; their adornment is to do the good works that are proper for women who claim to be religious. During instruction, a woman should be quiet and respectful. I give no permission for a woman to teach or to have authority over a man. (1 Timothy 2:9)

While Paul had claimed that "there is neither Jew nor Greek, slave nor free, male nor female, for you are all one in Christ Jesus" (Galatians 3:28), these communities taught that slaves should have "unqualified respect for their masters, so that the name of God and our teachings are not brought into disrepute" (1 Timothy 6). Paul's transformative spirituality was meant to liberate the Jews from the Law and dissolve the difference between them and the Gentiles, so that they could blend and participate more fully in pagan culture. For most Jewish communities, however, who until then had survived by keeping to themselves and living their faith through the Law, Paul's theology was impractical. A society where everyone is equal and shares their wealth and possessions with the community is a difficult beast to manage. Communities born in the spirit, eagerly awaiting the coming of Christ, faced urgent challenges of authority, discipline, management of resources, and a consistent doctrine. They tired of ever changing teachers with ever evolving new interpretations, and philosophical discussions and arguments about the details of their faith:

> Have nothing to do with Godless philosophical discussions – they only lead further and further away from true religion. Talk of this kind spreads corruption like gangrene, as in the case of Hymenaeus and Philetus, the men who have gone astray from the truth, claiming that the resurrection has already taken place. They are upsetting some people's faith. (2 Timothy 16-18)

There was the immediate danger of false teachers, who could arrive in a community and shake things up. The "truth," according to these teachers, could not evolve and grow, as it did for Gnostic communities – it had to be static, finished and eternal:

> Anyone who teaches anything different and does not keep to the sound teaching which is that of our Lord Jesus Christ, the doctrine which is in accordance with true religion, is proud and has no understanding, but rather a weakness for questioning everything and arguing about words. All that can come of this is jealousy, contention, abuse and evil mistrust; and unending disputes by people who are depraved in mind and deprived of truth, and imagine that religion is a way to make a profit. (1 Timothy 6:3 – 6:5)

Rather than the eternally inspiring mysteries of God, these communities preferred the establishment of a practical, authoritative set of beliefs. They refused new teachers or variations of their faith, and preferred a simple doctrine that could easily be grasped by anyone, and clear-cut rules of moral conduct. They had, as Paul claimed, *ended up in the flesh*. But, as we will see, their pragmaticism gave them the historical advantage of survival.

## The Promise of the Flesh

*"Many were led astray by reading the allegorical contents of the scriptures literally in the method of the Pharisees and Sadducees."*
*Eusebius, Ecclestical History.*

The more spiritual Gnostics believed in a Jesus Christ that was not restricted to a bodily form (indeed, it was impossible that the Logos could have been tainted by human flesh). Hence, he could continue visiting initiates, in spiritual form, for as long as he liked. Christians who resisted an evolutionary faith needed an authority figure that didn't come from Gnosis but from history. They were terrified of the Jesus that was just a spirit; he could appear to anyone, at anytime, giving new doctrine. As long as Jesus was only an internal spirit, it was impossible to prove which doctrines were true. Jesus *had* to have been fully human, in the flesh, so that the church could claim that Jesus had personally taught a precise message that had been directly transmitted to them in an unbroken succession of apostles; something that the Gnostics regarded as nonsense.

In addition, refusing the idea of a resurrection that had already taken place, these communities spoke of a resurrection at the end of time, when, like Jesus, their physical bodies would be raised from the dead. This belief was most likely influenced by the mysteries of Serapis or other Egyptian cults, who also believed in a resurrection of the flesh. To support these views, they emphasized and expanded a doctrine of the historical, fleshly Jesus and his physical resurrection.

Paul's Gnostic communities were generally educated Greeks or Jews, who could easily see the relationship between Jesus and other mystery faiths. When they wrote stories about Jesus, they would use Greek terms and concepts. They seamlessly blended many philosophical, spiritual, magical and mathematical principles into their writings. They were constantly expanding their literature and believed that inspiration was continuous. For them, the spiritual message was more important than the specific details.

The other Christian communities, which refused to change their initial understanding of the faith and developed a fixation on the flesh, had more trouble expressing themselves. Greek and Roman philosophical movements placed a great emphasis on pure reason, and held that the ultimate truths of the mysteries were not incompatible with logic, science or rational inquiry. The merit of a spiritual system was often how much it made sense. Moreover, most other philosophies and religions of the time believed that the body was a prison – soiled and worthless – from which the soul had to free itself. Plato attributes this belief to Orpheus:

Now some say that the body (soma) is the prison (sema) of the soul, as if it were buried in its present existence; and also because through it the soul makes signs of whatever it has to express, for in this way also they claim that it is rightly named from sema. In my opinion it is the followers of Orpheus who are chiefly responsible for giving it the name, holding that the soul is undergoing punishment for some reason or other, and has this husk about it, like a prison, to keep it from running away. (Plato, *Cratylus*)

Hence the doctrine of transmigration or the wheel of rebirth: you would be born in the flesh again and again, until you were wise enough to break free from it. The idea of a physical resurrection was, for those familiar with the spiritual consensus of the time, difficult to accept:

Yet the most characteristic part of Orphic eschatology, to which this notion on an intermediate stage is closely linked, namely, reincarnation and the wheel of birth, finds no place in orthodox Christianity. It in turn is bound up with the conception of the body as wholly evil, a place of punishment and trial for the soul. The soul cannot be fully purified in one earthly life, and therefore has to be born again in another body; but its final hope is to be rid of the body altogether, since that is the state identified by the Orphics with full purity and full happiness. Incidentally, the Christian talk of the resurrection of the body could not but be repulsive to the holders of such doctrines.[8]

Moreover, the idea of worshipping a god who physically suffers had already been ridiculed by the Greek philosophers:

For another poet, Lucan, yielding to such feelings of sorrow reduces the divine to the merely human: 'Osiris, by your mourning proved a man.' The passion of a dying god, so deeply stirring the hearts of Isiacs and afterwards of Christians, was found to be utterly irrational by one who had been steeped in the traditional philosophy of the Greeks.[9]

The Gnostics and many heretic communities of Jesus Christ tried to make the doctrine of Jesus' crucifixion *reasonable* by claiming that he was not really crucified; that he suffered no pain, or suffered only "in semblance" – but this was not good enough for those hoping for their own physical resurrection. Rather than compromise their beliefs, they clung to the Egyptian idea of an immortal body that would be raised to life, which was rejected by Greeks as barbaric and uncivilized. They justified their belief in the resurrection of the flesh by quoting a handful of passages from the Old Testament, like the following:

> And many of them that sleep in the dust of the earth shall awake, some to everlasting life, and some to shame and everlasting contempt. (Daniel 12.2)

The idea that Jesus could have had a physical body was an abhorrent concept to many. The Logos, the Son of God, was the collection of all of the sparks that existed in every person. His sacrifice and crucifixion were the story of how he became divided and stuck in the world, giving us the opportunity to return to God through him when he would be raised up. The Greeks, Gnostics, and Romans who were familiar with the motifs behind this story would have told the Christians, "You've got it wrong. You've got the basics right, but let us tell you what it *means*."

However, refusing to interpret the story of Jesus Christ or listen to "false prophets" who said that Jesus hadn't been born in the flesh, they began the production of historical evidence to support their beliefs. They met fierce opposition. Paul and his Gnostic communities viewed them as "infants in Christ" and called them "animal men." Greek philosophers were astounded at their simplicity, and the ruling Roman authorities were unnerved by their lack of common sense. Of all of the communities who believed in Jesus Christ, they seemed to be the only ones that declared Jesus was historical rather than spiritual. Letters between these groups generally communicated the same point: beware of what *everyone else* is saying. On the one hand, their beliefs went against centuries of philosophy. According to Plato,

> We must ever maintain a real belief in the ancient and sacred stories, (Orpheus) those which proclaim that our soul is immortal, and has judges, and pays full requital for its deeds, as soon as a man has left his body behind. (Plato, *Seventh Letter*)[10]

On the other hand, there was no historical basis for their claims. They had no help from their scriptures; Jesus promised a resurrection, but *not* of the old body, because the resurrected would be "like angels" (Matthew 22.23-33; Mark 12.18-27; Luke 20.27-40). Even their founder Paul disagreed with them:

> It is the same too with the resurrection of the dead: what is sown is perishable, but what is raised is imperishable; what is sown is contemptible but what is raised is glorious; what is sown is weak, but what is raised is powerful; what is sown is a natural body, and what is raised is a spiritual body. (1 Corinthians 15:43)

> What I am saying, brothers, is that mere human nature cannot inherit the kingdom of God: what is perishable cannot inherit what is imperishable. (1 Corinthians 15:50)

Christians who affirmed the resurrection of the flesh recognized that they were diverging from Paul's original message, and complained that this difference of doctrine was all-too-often pointed out to them. Instead of responding to the criticism, and recognizing that the heretics were closer aligned to Paul's theology, they are merely "annoyed":

> Among the other [truths] proclaimed by the apostle, there is also this one, "That flesh and blood cannot inherit the kingdom of God This is [the passage] which is adduced by all the heretics in support of their folly, with an attempt to annoy us, and to point out that the handiwork of God is not saved. (Irenaeus, *Against the Heresies*, 5:9)

Dismissing Paul and his higher mysteries, these Christians wanted their bodies preserved until some future period when they could reclaim them. The idea was met with contempt. Justin Martyr succeeds in representing the opinion of the opposition, without answering any of the questions raised by them:

> They who maintain the wrong opinion say that there is no resurrection of the flesh; giving as their reason that it is impossible that what is corrupted and dissolved should be restored to the same as it had been. And besides the impossibility, they say that the salvation of the flesh is disadvantageous; and they abuse the flesh, adducing its infirmities,

and declare that it is the cause of our sins, so that if the flesh, say they, rise again, our infirmities also rise with it. By these and such like arguments, they attempt to distract men from the faith. And there are some who maintain that even Jesus Himself appeared only as spiritual, and not in flesh, but presented merely the appearance of flesh: these persons seek to rob the flesh of the promise. (Justin Martyr, *Fragments of "On Resurrection,"* Chapter 2)

In Greek and Roman culture, debates were won through their rational appeal and the speaker's powers of persuasion. As Christians became more outspoken, adamant about the physical death and resurrection of their Lord Jesus, pagans engaged them in a battle of wits. Some philosophers (like Celsus) published whole books to display the inherent absurdity of the new faith. The spirit-saving philosophy of the Logos, which was taught through the mysteries, had developed over thousands of years. The novelty of pinning this philosophy into one historical man required a philosophical dexterity that, unfortunately, these Christians didn't have. Their arguments, though full of zeal, were logically weak, inconsistent, and often missed the point entirely. Many times, when they couldn't answer their opponent's questions, they would resort to character attacks and personal insults. Significantly, the Christians who believed in the physical resurrection of the dead did not point to their own savior as proof, nor did they mention the miraculous raising of Lazarus found in the gospels. They neglected to offer the woman Peter raised to life in Jaffa, or the boy that Paul raised to life at Troas after he'd fallen out of a three-story window, both of which were later recorded in the Acts of the Apostles. When asked to provide even one example of someone who had physically risen from the dead, they couldn't:

Then, as to your denying that the dead are raised – for you say, "Show me even one who has been raised from the dead, that seeing I may believe," – first, what great thing is it if you believe when you have seen the thing done? Then, again, you believe that Hercules, who burned himself, lives; and that Aesculapius, who was struck with lightning, was raised; and do you disbelieve the things that are told you by God? But, suppose I should show you a dead man raised and alive, even this you would disbelieve. (Theophilus, *To Autolycus*, Chapter 13)[11]

Instead, they argue that God, who causes the dying and rebirth of wheat, grain and grass, must also have the power to raise a man from the dead. Theophilus gives the example of a sparrow that swallows a seed, and later leaves the seed in its droppings. If the seed can still produce a tree after such an ordeal, why couldn't God re-animate a dead body?

> Moreover, sometimes also a sparrow or some of the other birds, when in drinking it has swallowed a seed of apple or fig, or something else, has come to some rocky hillock or tomb, and has left the seed in its droppings, and the seed, which was once swallowed, and has passed though so great a heat, now striking root, a tree has grown up. And all these things does the wisdom of God in order to manifest even by these things, that God is able to effect the general resurrection of all men. (Theophilus, *To Autolycus*, 13)[12]

They even attempt to prove the physical resurrection through the example of the planets, which led to the development of the spiritual symbolism in the first place:

> And if you would witness a more wondrous sight, which may prove a resurrection not only of earthly but of heavenly bodies, consider the resurrection of the moon, which occurs monthly; how it wanes, dies, and rises again. (Theophilus, *To Autolycus*, 13)[13]

They offer no eye-witnesses and no physical evidence. The only response ever put forward to defend Christ's physical death and resurrection was, "It is not impossible. It might have happened; and we believe that it did."

One common criticism of the idea that the Logos had a physical incarnation was the impossibility of what is eternal and unchanging lowering itself and becoming mortal while maintaining its divinity. God could not be fully god and fully man any more than white light could remain both white and any other color at the same time. Another point was raised by Celsus, who questioned why God would send his spirit down to one fixed geographical location, rather than allow it to be accessed by the entire human race equally:

Again, if Godlike Jupiter in the comedy, should, on awaking from a lengthened slumber, desire to rescue the human race from evil, why did He send this Spirit of which you speak into one corner (of the earth)? He ought to have breathed it alike into many bodies, and have sent them out into all the world. (Recorded by Origen, *Contra Celsum*, 6:78)

This criticism was repeated about a century later by Porphyry; who wrote a book called *Against the Christians* around 270AD, which was popular until Emperor Theodosius II ordered the burning of every copy that could be found in 448. Frend paraphrases:

Christian doctrine was empty, Christ was not even an extraordinary magician, but on par with Apollonius of Tyana, Zoroaster, or Julian the Chaldean. And if he did descend from heaven to save the human race, why did he not free all men with equal generosity? Why should people be obliged to become Christian in order to be saved?[14]

Porphyry also maintained that "Christians, too, were in error in their belief in the resurrection of the body, and they were blasphemers who showed their contempt for their fellows in their arrogance, credulity, and hopes for the cataclysmic end of the world."[15] The Christians could not compete with the skilled Greek debaters, nor with the Gnostics who also claimed to be disciples of Paul, and could provide no answers to the logical inconsistencies that arose out of their faith. Constantly confronted by rational arguments and logical debates, in which they never seemed to get the upper hand, they began to see reason itself as a threat to their faith and beliefs. The Gospels, which were written in the guise of history in order to transmit spiritual truths (while possibly obscuring real spiritual insight from the unitiated), became a source of information for the wished-for savior that Christians were proclaiming. They took examples from the stories, which were originally meant as mythological narratives, and tried to use them to support their theology of the flesh. (This is a little like trying to prove that Harry Potter physically and historically flew a magical flying car, because it is written down in Rowling's *Chamber of Secrets*.)

Groups that believed in Jesus as a historical being would use scripture to back up their opinions about him. When the scriptures didn't support their views, they would edit them, inserting passages and then quoting those same passages in their arguments. By comparing handwriting and literary style, scholars can identify alterations that have been made to original texts. Some passages in the Bible, which scholars agree were later insertions, add geographical and political details to show that the story actually happened in recent history, and edited the resurrection story to show that Jesus not only lived in the flesh but also rose from the dead in the flesh. Later insertions include post-resurrection passages such as doubting Thomas poking his finger into the wounds of Christ, or of Jesus being hungry and eating fish, or Jesus appearing to such and such number of disciples. They are all attempts to justify the historical Jesus and the physical resurrection.

Once the texts adequately represented the beliefs of the community, they were considered sacred and without error. However, because most of these scriptures were taken straight from the original mysteries of Jesus Christ, they were also full of mystical symbols and formulas that didn't make sense if accepted at face value. One of the first great Bible commenters, Origen, cautions that "The corporal sense or the letter of Scripture must not be adopted, when it would entail anything impossible, absurd, or unworthy of God."[16] Likewise, many rabbis believed that the Old Testament needed careful study, to unravel the spiritual truths *behind* the text. As Moses Maimonides, a Jewish philosopher of the 12th century, later teaches:

> Every time that you find in our books a tale the reality of which seems impossible, a story which is repugnant to both reason and common sense, then be sure that the tale contains a profound allegory veiling a deeply mysterious truth; and the greater the absurdity of the letter, the deeper the wisdom of the spirit.[17]

The Jewish *Zohar* puts it this way: "The narratives of the doctrine are its cloak. The simple look only on the garment, that is upon the narrative of the doctrine; more they know not. The instructed, however, see not merely the cloak, but what the cloak covers."[18] Paul often uses scripture allegorically in this sense. For example, in the letter to the community in Galatia he describes how Abraham's two sons represent the physical and spiritual aspects of our dual natures:

> Scripture says that Abraham had two sons, one by the slave girl and one by the free woman. The son of the slave girl came to be born in the way of human nature; but the son of the free woman came to be born through a promise. There is an allegory here: these women stand for the two covenants. (Galatians 4:22)

Many of the stories in the gospels also have mathematical significance, like the name of Jesus, and use numbers to convey sacred geometrics. Jesus often says things like, "Let those who have ears, hear!" or "Let those who have eyes, see!" alluding to the need to seek a deeper interpretation for his parables. He also chastises his apostles frequently for not understanding the hidden meaning behind his stories. One example is the appearance of Jesus on the shore of Tiberias (John 21:1), after he has been resurrected. He comes to his disciples (who, incidentally, had all abandoned him and returned to fishing), and helps them catch exactly 153 fish. While this number may seem like a supercilious detail – its very lack of significance lending credence to the idea that this miracle really took place — in fact it had a deliberate esoteric meaning.

As mentioned previously, there is a similar story about Pythagoras; and although the exact number of fish that Pythagoras caught has been lost, it may well have been the same figure. The number 153 was a sacred number in Pythagorean communities, a number with special significance. The fish, and the number, are references to a mathematical principle often used in the mysteries called *Vesica Piscis*, or the "measure of the fish."

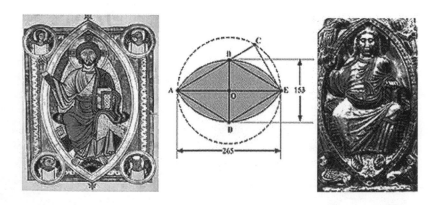

When two equal circles are joined so that the perimeter of one passes the epicenter of the other, it produces a third, intermediate section, which resembles the shape of a fish. This section further contains two equilateral triangles. The mathematical ratio of its width (measured to the endpoints of the body) is nearly 265:153, yielding the number 1.73203, or the square root of 3. This can be confirmed using Euclid's 47th Proposition.

The symbol of the *Vesica Piscis* was used in the mysteries to show the unification of divine principles. Three circles joined this way were used to represent the eternal trinity – Father, Son and Holy Spirit – united in one God. In the mysteries of Ephesus, the Goddess wore this symbol over her genital region, and in the Osiris story, the lost penis was swallowed by a fish, which represented the vulva of Isis. Likewise, in many examples of Christian art, Jesus Christ is proceeding from this symbol, representing his birth from the Goddess.

As we've seen, the fish was also important as an astrological symbol of the coming age. Jesus was the savior linking the old age of Aries with the new age of Pisces, an astrological truth explored in later esoteric or mystical traditions.

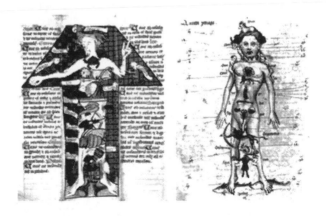

The symbol of the fish was further empowered by making an acronym for Jesus Christ, along with his nature and title, from its Greek letters, ΙΧΘΥΣ (ichthus).

Iesous *Ch*ristos *Th*eou *U*ios *S*oter =*Jesus Christ, Son of God, Savior*

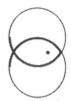
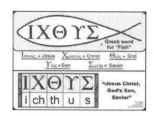

However, having refused allegorical meaning and interpretation, these details were left unexplained, and subsequently lost. Much like the original story, Christianity has maintained the external form of the *Vesica Piscis*, displayed proudly on thousands of posters, bumper stickers, and websites, without retaining any of the symbolic meaning.

Another example of hidden wisdom that has been lost is the mystery of the wedding chamber. According to Hippolytus of Rome (*c.*170 - *c.*236), one the most important 3rd century theologians in the Christian Church, the wedding chamber ritual was reserved only for spiritual initiates:

> For they who obtain their share of the greater Mysteries receive greater portions. For this is the gate of Heaven, and this is the house of God, where the good God alone dwells. And into this gate no unclean man shall enter, no 'man of soul' or carnal. But it is reserved for the spiritual only. And those who go there must cast off their clothes and become bridegrooms, made thoroughly male through the virgin Spirit. For this is the virgin who carries in her womb, and conceives and brings forth a son, not animal (soul), not corporeal (material), but blessed forever more. (Hippolytus, *Refutations of all Heresies*, 5:3)

All "women" (both male and female initiates living according to the flesh) had to be made "thoroughly male" (be reborn into spiritual bodies). This is the esoteric meaning of the Gnostic texts that claim women must be made male in order to enter the kingdom of heaven. However, this understanding is completely lost on modern Christians. Bruce Metzger, professor emeritus at Princeton Theological Seminary, demonstrates how foreign the Gnostic gospels appear to those entrenched in orthodox thinking:

"The Gospel of Thomas ends with a note saying, 'Let Mary go away from us, because women are not worthy of life.' Jesus is quoted as saying, 'Lo, I shall lead her in order to make her a male, so that she too may become a living spirit, resembling you males. For every woman who makes herself male will enter into the kingdom of heaven.'" Metzger's eyebrows shot up as if he were surprised at what he had just uttered. "Now, this is not the Jesus we know from the four canonical gospels," he said emphatically.[19]

Without access to the allegorical meaning, the scriptures became obtuse and difficult, full of contradiction and confusing parables. Church fathers had to keep their flock away from communities who actually knew how to interpret these symbols, and taught that some of scripture's secrets, like the natural world, were meant for only God to know:

> If, therefore, even with respect to creation, there are some things (the knowledge of) which belongs only to God, and others which come within the range of our own knowledge, what ground is there for complaint, if, in regard to those things which we investigate in the Scriptures (which are throughout spiritual), we are able by the grace of God to explain some of them, while we must leave others in the hands of God. (Iraneaus, *Against the Heresies*, 2:8:3).

The very word, "mystery," which used to mean a mystical experience of the divine, began to mean something that was simply forever kept a secret from us, or something that God had chosen not to reveal:

> We should leave things of that nature to God who created us, being most properly assured that the scriptures are indeed perfect, since they were spoken by the Word of God and his Spirit; but we, inasmuch as we are inferior to, and later in existence than, the Word of God and His Spirit, are on that very account destitute of the knowledge of His mysteries. (Iraneaus, *Against the Heresies*, 2:8:2)

The teachers of this form of Christianity, who had all the details but none of the spiritual implications, did not know what to tell their initiates when they came asking questions. Reason began to be viewed as an enemy to the truth, while blind faith in scripture, and a blind eye to anyone teaching different ideas, became the highest virtues:

> You believe because you have seen me. Blessed are those who have not seen me and yet believe. (John 20:27)

Rather than question why their faith had so many critics, they claimed that God had made the gospel sound foolish as a stumbling block to all but the chosen – an idea also presented by Paul in defense of his new mysteries:

> Since in the wisdom of God the world was unable to recognize God through wisdom, it was God's own pleasure to save believers through the folly of the gospel. While the Jews demand miracles and the Greeks look for wisdom, we are preaching a crucified Christ: to the Jews an obstacle they cannot get over, to the Gentiles foolishness. (1 Corinthians 1:21)

In other words, for Paul, wisdom and reason would never satisfy the Greeks, who were acute philosophers, and miracles would never satisfy the Jews, who were experienced in magical traditions. (Did Moses not already prove a greater miracle worker than the Pharaoh's magicians?) In a sense, we could say that Paul was teaching a Zen-like mystical experience that surpassed both rational inquiry and empirical evidence – and he *was*: it was Gnosis, an internal divine wisdom. However, although many pockets of mysticism have popped up in various epochs of the Christian faith, the majority of believers were taught to believe that, despite evidence to the contrary, Jesus Christ was exactly who the Church claimed him to be. This was not faith in God, or in the saving power of Jesus, but only faith in the truth of a historical event. Being "Saved" by Jesus required nothing more than *believing* that this event had actually happened. Being "good" consisted of following Jesus' ethical example and teachings, as well as always *being on guard* against those dangerous advocators of reason who considered such beliefs simplistic.

## Conclusions and Summary

Paul left a legacy of two very different types of Christianity. The Gnostics emphasized the return of the spirit to God, and believed Christ's death was a philosophical truth, necessary for the restoration. They had at least two ritual baptisms and holy seals (water and fire), representing stages of spiritual initiation. Specific actions were not moral in themselves; ethics involved letting the spirit of Jesus live through you and guide your actions. The communities who placed their faith in Christ as a historical reality, and believed that he would come back at the end of time, focused on good works and faith alone. Like the modern church, these communities had just one baptism for the forgiveness of sins, and adopted only one magical seal; the upright cross. If we accept that Paul was the teacher of the mysteries that became the Christian faith, we must realize that the theology inherited from this early period of Christian history, which continues today in most Christian churches, is the repressive theology of Paul's *least favorite* students. Despite these features of Christianity (or perhaps because of them), there was still something so intoxicating about the Christian movement that it quickly became popular among the masses. In the next chapter we will focus on how the most repudiated form of the Jesus movement, whose beliefs initially met with so much opposition, rooted out all the competition and became the controlling power in Europe for over a thousand years.

## CHAPTER TEN

# From Mystery to History: Conflict and Martyrdom

*"Before God and before Christ Jesus who is to be judge of the living and the dead, I charge you, in the name of his appearing and of his kingdom: proclaim the message and, welcome or unwelcome, insist on it."*
*–2 Timothy 4*

CHRISTIANITY'S UNIQUE CLAIMS (the Logos as a historical person and the resurrection of both him and his followers in the flesh) were almost universally mocked by their contemporaries. The fact that this new mystery cult grew from being hated and persecuted to becoming the official religion of the Roman Empire in just a few centuries seems miraculous. In order to dispel the notion that the rise of Christianity can only be explained as divine providence, we need to identify the inherent features, as well as the external conditions, which formed the foundations of its success. Unfortunately a clear, linear history of this transition cannot be provided – as we've seen, the term "Christianity" encompassed many interactive and heterogeneous communities that developed their ideas according to their needs. A deeper understanding of several issues can, however, aid a fuller appreciation of the subsequent triumph of the movement. In this chapter I will identify the main features that secured Christianity's historical conquest.

## Simplicity and Urgency

The story of the conversion of St. Justin Martyr, as told in his *Dialogue with Trypho*, offers us an interesting example of the appeal of early Christianity. Justin was a spiritual seeker looking for the true religion or philosophy that would lead him to God. He first "surrenders himself" to a Stoic, but becomes dissatisfied with his slow progress. He later meets a Pythagorean teacher, but finds his demands for learning and education unreasonable:

> But when my soul was eagerly desirous to hear the peculiar and choice philosophy, I came to a Pythagorean, very celebrated – a man who thought much of his own wisdom. And then, when I had an interview with him, willing to become his hearer and disciple, he said, 'What then? Are you acquainted with music, astronomy, and geometry? Do you expect to perceive any of those things which conduce to a happy life, if you have not been first informed on those points which wean the soul from sensible objects, and render it fitted for objects which appertain to the mind, so that it can contemplate that which is honourable in its essence and that which is good in its essence?' Having commended many of these branches of learning, and telling me that they were necessary, he dismissed me when I confessed to him my ignorance. Accordingly I took it rather impatiently, as was to be expected when I failed in my hope, the more so because I deemed the man had some knowledge; but reflecting again on the space of time during which I would have to linger over those branches of learning, I was not able to endure longer procrastination. (*Dialogue with Trypho,* Chapter 2)[1]

Unwilling to devote a great deal of time and effort to his studies, in defeat he went off to be alone. But then he came across an old man who showed him how Jesus Christ was prophesied in Jewish scripture. He was at first half convinced, and then finally swayed by the martyr's bravery. He became a zealous defender of Christianity, and finally suffered martyrdom himself at Rome under Emperor Marcus Aurelius (between 162 and 168). Although the writings of Justin are extensive philosophical treatises, his conversion was mainly due to the ease of Christianity and the appeal of martyrdom. An interesting dynamic of the text is that Justin, born of pagan parents, interprets Jewish scripture as prophecies of Jesus. Trypho – a Jew whom Justin is trying to convert (who we should assume to be more familiar with the text) – corrects Justin and warns him against taking the Old Testament out of context to refer to a future Messiah, or speaking "monstrous phenomena" by adding mythical elements into the story of Jesus:

> And Trypho answered, "The Scripture has not, 'Behold, the virgin shall conceive, and bear a son,' but, 'Behold, the young woman shall conceive, and bear a son,' and so on, as you quoted. But the whole prophecy refers to Hezekiah, and it is proved that it was fulfilled in him, according to the terms of this prophecy. Moreover, in the fables of those who are called Greeks, it is written that Perseus was begotten of Danae, who was a virgin; he who was called among them Zeus having descended on her in the form of a golden shower. And you ought to feel ashamed when you make assertions similar to theirs, and rather [should] say that this Jesus was born man of men. And if you prove from the Scriptures that He is the Christ, and that on account of having led a life conformed to the law, and perfect, He deserved the honour of being elected to be Christ, [it is well]; but do not venture to tell monstrous phenomena, lest you be convicted of talking foolishly like the Greeks. (Chapter 67)

Trypho's response shows us how most Jews would have greeted the message of the Jewish-Greek Jesus Christ, and the claims that he was prophesied by scripture. It should also be pointed out that Justin's version of Christianity at this point had separated from Jewish Law; circumcision of the flesh was not necessary, only a spiritual "circumcision" of the heart. He even insinuates that God set up circumcision to *mark the Jews* for punishment because they had refused to acknowledge Jesus as Messiah (Chapter 16).

The story of the conversion of Justin shows us that one of the attractions of Christianity was its simplicity. Unlike the obtuse and intellectually challenging philosophies of the times, with ever more levels of Gnosis or understanding, Christianity was truly a universal, "Catholic" faith. Athenagoras, for example, contrasted the "ambiguities and confusions of the philosophers and disciples" with the simple truths expounded by the Christians, which anyone could follow. "With us you will find unlettered people, tradesmen and old women, who cannot express in words the advantages of our creed, demonstrate by acts the value of their principles" (Athenagoras, *Supplication* XI.2).[2]

This simplicity was a powerful tool and motivator; as Athenagoras proclaims, it inspired Christians to *act*, rather than contemplate. This was strengthened by the immediacy inherent in the early movement. Jesus would return like a thief in the night (1 Thessalonians 5:2-4), and Christians were told to prepare and be ready because the world as they knew it was passing away (1 Corinthians 7:31). Believing that Jesus Christ was a radically new kind of savior, Christians were excited to spread the word. Obeying the scriptures and the commands of the church fathers, many gave up their possessions and began actively converting people. Mimicking the gospel stories and following Jesus' instructions, Christians enacted a great number of social services like feeding the poor and taking care of the sick. They gained a reputation for their healing prayers, care of the poor, and selflessness. Emperor Julian, hoping to revive paganism against the spread of Christianity in the mid 300's, notes that this philanthropy greatly advanced the Christian cause:

> (Christianity was) specially advanced through the loving service rendered to strangers and through their care of the burial of the dead. It is a scandal that there is not a single Jew who is a beggar and that the Christians care not only for their own poor but for ours as well; while those who belong to us look in vain for the help we should render them.[3]

New followers were told that they would be saved from death through only a few simple rites, and for publicly pronouncing the name of Jesus. Christian leaders expected very little other than blind faith in the historical figure of Jesus Christ, and as neither wealth nor intellectual prowess were required, the majority of their recruits were poor and uneducated. Paul admits that the Christian message was popular among those who had few merits in the worldly sense:

> Consider, brothers, how you have been called; not many of you are wise by human standards, not many influential, not many from noble families. No, God chose those who by human standards are fools to shame the wise; he chose those who by human standards are weak to shame the strong, those who by human standards are common and contemptible–indeed those who count for nothing–to reduce to nothing all those that do count for something, so that no human being might feel boastful before God. (1 Cor. 1:26)

There was an inherent paradox to the Christian message that strongly conflicted with the pagan values of philosophy and reason. Not only were Christians less educated than their contemporaries – they were *proud* of it: they passionately insisted upon the truth of their message and actively sought out new converts. Cyril of Alexandria admits, "Indeed, the mystery of Christ runs the risk of being disbelieved precisely because it is so incredibly wonderful."[4] Understandably, this made them unpopular with the intellectuals. Celsus characterizes Christianity as a faith of fools, opposed to reason:

> The following are the rules laid down by them. Let no one come to us who has been instructed, or who is wise or prudent (for such qualifications are deemed evil by us); but if there be any ignorant, or unintelligent, or uninstructed, or foolish persons, let them come with confidence. By which words, acknowledging that such individuals are worthy of their God they manifestly show that they desire and are able to gain over only the silly, and the mean, and the stupid, with women and children. (Origen, *Contra Celsum* 3:44)

To fuel the fire of public indignation, Christians refused to offer either evidence or argument in favor of their faith. They could not describe their own rational motives for believing nor answer even basic questions about the savior they claimed was historically crucified. When pressed, they would announce they believed what they believed because it was *true*, and that others should as well. Celsus records that when interrogated, they exclaimed, "Do not examine, but believe!" and, "Your faith will save you!" He also refers to what was assumed to be a common phrase of the early Christian community, "The wisdom of this life is bad, but foolishness is a good thing!" (*Contra Celsum* 1:9).

Salvation no longer required an active, life-long pursuit of the divine but an immediate and absolute forgiveness, based on nothing more than accepting Jesus Christ as savior. As Joel Carmichael points out in *The Birth of Christianity*, "to achieve salvation, an ignoramus need only believe without understanding and obey the authorities."[5]

Consequently, the bulk of their new converts came from the poor and uneducated masses. In Celsus' view (one not disputed by Christian leaders like Paul), "their targets were artisans, slaves, the women and children in major households, and gullible and stupid people, prepared to be taken in by propaganda."[6]

Unfortunately, these were also the people most likely to be taken advantage of by charlatans and false prophets; their disdain for this life and unparalleled generosity made them "easy marks." Lucian records the story of Peregrinus, who apparently had some scheme going with the Christians. Although Lucian was a satirist and under no obligation to be discerning, few historians question these events:

> It is wonderful what celerity they display when some such matter of common interest is afoot. At the shortest notice they will lavish everything. So it is now with Peregrinus. A great deal of money came to him from them on the score of his imprisonment, which he made a rich source of revenue; for the poor wretches have persuaded themselves that they are wholly immortal, and will live forever, wherefore they despise even death and for the most part give themselves up to it with willingness. Moreover, their first lawgiver persuaded them that they are all each others' brothers, when once they are converted and deny the gods of Hellas, and they worship this crucified sophist of theirs and live according to his precepts. Thus they look down on everything alike, and think it all dross, having taken over such teachings with no sure test of their truth (blind faith). If then there comes to them some sham wizard, a man of ingenuity and knowledge of affairs, he gets rich in a very short time, making game of their simple hearts.[7]

It is interesting to compare the story of Peregrinus with the conversion of Justin Martyr; there are parallels, although Peregrinus was apparently more of a scoundrel. Born in the Asiatic side of Hellespont, he left the city under suspicion that he murdered his father. He fell in with some Christians and was soon considered a prophet and synagogue leader; he had a reputation as a "second Socrates." As Lucian mentions, he was treated like royalty by Christians while in prison, but when he got out he quarreled with them, apparently over food laws. He asked for his estate back and was refused. So he moved to Egypt and lived in austerity, flagellating himself and becoming a Cynic. Then he moved to Rome, where he began a campaign of abuse against the authorities until he was expelled by the city prefect. Finally, he moved to Greece and studied philosophy in Athens. At the Olympic games (either in 153 or 157) he was attacked by a mob for his abuse of a wealthy philanthropist. At the games of 161 he announced that he would burn himself to death on a pyre; he carried out the threat three years later, publicly immolating himself after the games of 164.[8]

Obviously, Peregrinus was a forceful personality; today we might call him a publicity hound or label him with an "attention-seeking" disorder. If he had remained Christian, his death would have been considered a martyrdom and he might have been made a saint. As it is, he illustrates some of the profound psychological influences and conflicts in the movements of his time, as well as the sort of individuals who may have been championed by early Christian communities.

## Conflict with Authority and Martyrdom

There is something profoundly inspirational in the stories of martyrs; people so committed to their ideals that they would rather die than give them up, fueled with an unassailable confidence in the righteousness of their cause. And yet, at the same time, how can we fail to make the association between martyrs and political revolutionaries, or even religious terrorists? After all, the tradition of martyrdom comes not only from imitating the passion of Christ, but also from the heroic tradition enshrined in the Maccabean

Wars, whose martyrs believed themselves to be vindicating the justice of the cause against idolatrous oppression.[9] In other words, there is *violence* in martyrdom, which is not simply given by the oppressor, but also inherent in the determination of believers to die for their faith.

Like the Jews, these early Christians obeyed the Second Commandment, which forbids making and worshiping "an idol in the form of anything in heaven above or on earth beneath or in the waters below" (Exodus 20:4, Deuteronomy 5:8). This commandment forbid religious art (as objects of worship) in general, and strict adherence to it was one of the defining characteristics of the early church. (Some early synagogues break this rule; archaeologists were shocked to discover floor mosaics in Israel, but the phenomonen is now taken in stride. Orthodox Jews either don't bow down to the floor in such cases, or first cover the mosaic with a carpet).

For the pagans, everything in life was governed and provided by some demi-god or spirit; the public feasts were ways of thanking the universe for food and drink they had received, for their good health, the fine weather, and blessed fortunes. To withhold gratitude from these forces showed utter audacity, and was seen as taking life for granted. Christians who refused to participate in public feasts and events of thanksgiving to these gods were considered, not only anti-social, but blasphemers, atheists and zealous ingrates. Celsus admonished that they should either respect the positive forces of life, or embrace death without delay:

> They must make their choice between two alternatives. If they refuse to render due service to the gods, and to respect those who are set over this service, let them not come to manhood, or marry wives, or have children, or indeed take any share in the affairs of life; but let them depart hence with all speed, and leave no posterity behind them, that such a race may become extinct from the face of the earth. (Recorded by Origen, *Contra Celsum*, 8:35)

Christians did not merely refuse to pray to these idols, however; they openly attacked all other pagan deities, seeing them as only bits of wood and stone. They quickly gained a reputation for themselves as sacrilegious enemies of the divine powers. Taking pagan myths at face value and interpreting them literally, as they did their own scriptures, Christians accused spiritual mythology of being merely ludicrous fables. They mocked and ridiculed everyone outside of their faith as superstitious fools. It is hard to imagine the public outrage caused by Clement of Alexandria, for example, when he declared that the ancient pagan gods were dead; it would be roughly 1,700 years before Nietzsche would make the same blasphemous statement:

> Poor wretches that ye are, who have filled with unholy jesting the whole compass of your life a life in reality devoid of life! Oh, happier far the beasts than men involved in error! Who live in ignorance as you, but do not counterfeit the truth. There are no tribes of flatterers among them. Fishes have no superstition: the birds worship not a single image; only they look with admiration on heaven, since, deprived as they are of reason, they are unable to know God. So are you not ashamed for living through so many periods of life in impiety, making yourselves more irrational than irrational creatures?... For Zeus is dead, be not distressed, as Leda is dead, and the swan, and the eagle, and the libertine, and the serpent. (Clement, *Exhortation to the Heathen*, 1)[10]

Convinced that they had received a radical new truth that was superior to all others, Christians treated the philosophers and other religious traditions with scorn and derision. They even sullied the sacred mysteries, breaking the strict code secrecy and openly revealing their rituals.

> And now, for it is time, I will prove their orgies to be full of imposture and quackery. And if you have been initiated, you will laugh all the more at these fables of yours which have been held in honor. I publish without reserve what has been involved in secrecy, not ashamed to tell what you are not ashamed to worship. (Clement, *Exhortation to the Heathen*, 2)[11]

According to Celsus (c.170-180), Christians would stand up in the temples, strike an image of Zeus or Apollo, and then proclaim that it was just a "dumb idol" since it had not taken immediate revenge. "Abandon it, become a Christian!" was then shouted.[12]

For these reasons, the Christians were not popular. According to John Holland Smith in *The Death of Classical Paganism*, they were viewed as "the ultimate filth" – a gang of ignorant men and credulous women, who with meetings at night, solemn fasts and inhuman food, made up a hole-in-the-corner, shadow-loving crew, silent in public but clacking away in corners, spitting on gods and laughing at holy things.[13] Misinterpreting their rituals, the pagans declared that the Christians, "in midnight feasts, having murdered a man, ate his flesh like cannibals and drank his blood."[14]

Christians were persecuted as early as 64AD, when they were made scapegoats by Emperor Nero in response to a great fire that destroyed large portions of the city and economically devastated the Roman population. Nero considered Christianity "an evil religion" (prava religio), and not a "legal religion" (religio licita).[15] According to Tacitus, a vast multitude of Christians were convicted, "not so much on the charge of burning the city, as of 'hating the human race.'"[16]

Except for Christianity, Rome was remarkably tolerant and inclusive of foreign gods and diverse religions. Christianity alone stuck out: because of its own intolerance and abuse towards other religious faiths and gods, it could not be tolerated.

Belief in the bodily resurrection allowed Christians to face their own deaths courageously, to the point of reckless living. While everyone else ran away during plagues or natural catastrophes, Christians would stay and tend to the victims. Some even sought out danger, eager for heavenly rewards. Christians became known for their fearlessness and disregard for personal safety. At the same time, they had trouble obeying the law and respecting the proper authorities. Paul often had to remind them to keep out of trouble:

> Everyone is to obey the governing authorities, because there is no authority except from God and so whatever authorities exist have been appointed by God. (Romans 1)

The Roman government asked its citizens to honor the emperor as a god, and offer a small prayer or sacrifice to him. This rule was seldom enforced, unless specific complaints were made, and even then the accused was allowed to make a public offering to clear his name. Many Christian communities saw no difficulty in this, and encouraged their followers keep a low profile:

> I urge then, first of all that petitions, prayers, intercessions and thanksgiving should be offered to everyone, for kings and others in authority, so that we may be able to live peaceful and quiet lives with all devotion and propriety. (1 Timothy 2)

Those Christians who read scripture literally identified Jesus with the jealous god of the Old Testament and saw these offerings as idolatry. They received notoriety for stubbornly refusing to obey the law. When brought to trial, they were asked to worship the emperor and deny Christ. For many, the basis of Christian faith consisted in affirming the name of Christ Jesus, even though they hadn't been taught its mystical significance, and so this request was adamantly refused.

Another aspect of the relationship with authority was whether or not to pay taxes; in Matthew Jesus is specifically asked whether to pay taxes to Rome in order to trick him into taking an anti-establishment position, which could be punished. Instead however, he gives the unclear answer "Render unto Caesar the things which are Caesar's, and unto God the things that are God's" (Matthew 22:21). Many Christians, however, were vocally outspoken against Roman rule, legislation and taxation. They had "died" to this world; hence no authority on earth could govern them.

This resolute independence might be seen as virtuous, especially by Americans – who are the products of a similar rebellion against the authority and taxation of a "foreign" power. But consider for a moment what happened when the southern states decided to throw off the authority of the Union. The Northern States fought against them in the American Civil war, which lasted from 1861 to 1865 and killed as many as 620,000 soldiers. What would happen if tomorrow Texas decided to dust off its 1861 declaration of secession and stop paying federal taxes. Wouldn't the government of America – "the land of freedom" – *force them* to pay up?

Christianity was essentially a poor man's dream of overthrowing society, which lauded the virtues of poverty. By implication, as well as the personal attitude of many Christians, Christianity was opposed to many of the values accepted by the rulers of the Roman Empire and the majority of its inhabitants.[17] As the movement spread through the empire, Christianity was seen by the ruling authorities as a dangerous new offshoot of Judaism, which already had a history of violent rebellion. Even worse, unlike the Jews who kept to themselves and were easy to identify on sight, Christians were an altogether invisible menace. According to an unknown author of the 2nd century:

> Christians are not different because of their country or the language they speak or the way they dress. They do not isolate themselves in their cities nor use a private language; even the life they lead has nothing strange. Their doctrine does not originate from the elaborate disquisitions of intellectuals, nor do they follow, as many do, philosophical systems which are the fruit of human thinking. They live in Greek or in barbarian (foreign) cities, as the case may be, and adapt themselves to local traditions in dress, food and all usage. Yet they testify to a way which, in the opinion of the many, has something extraordinary about it. (*Letter to Diognetus*)[18]

For these reasons, it was persecuted by different emperors throughout the first several centuries of its existence. Suetonius relates, "Capital punishments were inflicted on the Christians, a class of men of a new and harmful superstition (*superstitionis novæ et maleficæ*)." Pliny, Governor of Pontus, after writing his celebrated letter to Emperor Trajan on how to deal with the Christian problem, proceeded to torture two women but "discovered nothing beyond a degenerate and extravagant superstition"(*superstitionem pravam et immodicam*),[19] the contagion of which, he continued, "had spread through villages and country, till the temples were emptied of worshippers."[20]

A consistent charge against Christians was that they were atheists whose neglect of the Graeco-Roman Pantheon could potentially bring about catastrophic acts such as floods, fire, plague or earthquake, which were viewed by the populace as divine retribution. By the time of Tertullian (160-220AD), Christians were so despised by their contemporaries that he could claim:

> If the Tiber reaches the walls, if the Nile does not rise to the fields, if the sky doesn't move or the earth does, if there is famine, if there is plague, the cry is at once "the Christians to the lion!" What, all of them to one lion? (*Apology* 40.2)[21]

Incidentally, similar anti-Christian sentiment exists in modern culture, for many of the same reasons. One contemporary bumper sticker reads *"Too many Christians, not enough lions."*

For their part, although it seems many Christians were able to compromise and escape punishment, those who persisted met their deaths eagerly. This facet was already a feature in Judaism. According to Josephus, "It is an instinct with every Jew, from the day of his birth, to regard them (books of the Law) as the decrees of God, to abide by them, and, if need be, cheerfully to die for them" (*Contra Apionem* II. 32.234.[22]

Likewise, the church fathers taught that the important part of being Christian, virtually the only part, was to proclaim the reality of Christ against critics. They promised initiates immediate rewards in heaven if they faced persecution bravely; much like the spiritual handlers of today's religious terrorists. The Romans, on the other hand, were primarily concerned with maintaining peace and order, and would often make allowances to let Christian go free. Hoping for the esteem and glory of a martyr's death, Christians refused to cooperate. Ignatius, for example, begs his communities not to interfere or try to save him:

> I write to the Churches, and impress on them all, that I shall willingly die for God, unless ye hinder me. I beseech you not to show an unreasonable good-will towards me. Suffer me to become food for the wild beasts, through whose instrumentality it will be granted me to attain to God. I am the wheat of God, and let me be ground by the teeth of the wild beasts, that I may be found the pure bread of Christ. Rather entice the wild beasts, that they may become my tomb, and leave nothing of my body; so that when I have fallen asleep (in death) I may be no trouble to anyone. Then shall I truly be a disciple of Christ, when the world shall not see so much as my body. (Ignatius, *Romans*, Chap. 4)

In 180AD at the town of Scilli near Carthage, seven men and five women were accused before the pro-consul Vigellius Saturninus of being Christians. The spokesman for the group, Speratus, refused to swear by the genius of the emperor, to whom the proconsul required their acquiescence, since he did not recognize the empire of this world. Instead he served the God "that no man has seen" as emperor of kings and of all nations, saying, "If you will calmly lend an ear, I will tell you the mystery of simplicity." Saturninus replied, "I will not lend an ear to you who are about to say evil things about our rites." The proconsul offered a thirty-day reprieve to reconsider, but it was rejected. "In so just an affair, there is no need to consider," said Speratus. When they were beheaded for "persevering in obstinacy," they cried, "Today we are martyrs in heaven: thanks be to God."[23]

This rash disregard for life, a nuisance to the Roman government, was considered the very image of courage to new converts. Passionate novellas were written about the virtues of martyrdom. Several young idealistic women practically threw themselves to the beasts in spite of their family's attempts to reconcile them. These acts agitated the public, and Christianity continued to draw numbers, although almost exclusively from the poorer classes. Church historian Eusebius writes:

> It was then that we observed a most marvelous eagerness and a truly divine power and zeal in those who had placed their faith in the Christ of God. Thus, as soon as sentence was given against the first, some from one quarter and others from another would leap up to the tribunal before the judge and confess themselves Christians; paying no heed when faced with terrors and the varied forms of tortures, but undismayedly and boldly speaking of the piety towards the God of the universe; so that they sang and sent up hymns and thanksgivings to the God of the universe even to the very last breath. (Eusebius VIII.9.4-5)[24]

"Such indeed," reflects Frend, "was the combination of conviction, self-sacrifice, heroism, and obstinacy that was confronting the pagan world."[25] To outsiders, Christians seemed at once heroic and pathetic. Many people asked, "Where is their god, and what good to them was their worship which they preferred beyond their lives?" (Eusebius, *HE* V.1.60).

Even worse, according to their contemporaries, was that they died for a *fable*. They as yet had a vague and unclear idea of the history of their own movement or its founder, Jesus, who – at least in the more supernatural aspects of his ministry – was immediately recognized by pagans as a myth. Trypho, in his conversation with Justin Martyr, admits the common view that Christians "by receiving a worthless rumor, shape a kind of Messiah for themselves and perish for him blindly" (Justin Martyr, *Dialogue with Trypho* 8.4). Eusebius adds that "hostility was rife against those who accepted Jewish Myths at their face value, and made a criminal into a cult-hero" (*Preparation* 1.2 PG 21.28).[26] According to Clare K. Rothschild in her book, *Luke-Acts and the Rhetoric of History,*[27]

> By the first century, legends about Christian origins had multiplied so rapidly that the entire debate was mired in complexity and doubt... The movement was perceived not just as mythical or myth-historical, but as contrary to history – as an elaborate hoax. With sources of anonymous secondary witnesses like the gospel of Mark and Q, the task of formulating a plausible rendition of Christian origins was forbidding.

This was the motivation for Christian writers to use what Rothschild calls "Authenticating Strategies" – the inclusion of specific historical details to support the reliability of the testimony. Moreover, against the claim that their faith was new or strange, apologists would point out prophecies for Jesus in the ancient history of the Jews, or the similarities between Jesus and pagan gods. One early writer, in defense of Christianity against the Greeks, wrote "we do not act as fools, O Greeks, nor utter idle tales, when we announce that God was born in the form of a man... your Aclepius died..."[28] The difference, of course, was slight. While on the one hand Christians believed nothing exceptional, on the other hand their insistence on the physical, actuality of the stories and willingness to *die for them* made them seem both childishly innocent and dangerously depraved.

## Evangelism and Organization

Apart from the passion and zeal of followers, the success of Christianity was also due to the organization and structure of its communities. These were to an extant modeled on Judaism; Diaspora Jews gathered themselves in specific areas and lived mainly amongst themselves, creating their own political infrastructure. Each community was almost self-governing, with its own banks, cemeteries, schools, courts and charities.[29] Furthermore, unlike today, early Judaism made a deliberate, conscious attempt to encourage conversion from Judaism and to justify their beliefs to outsiders. The Gospel of Matthew speaks of the Pharisees, especially, "traversing sea and land to make a single proselyte" (23:15). Frend confirms:

> By the time of Christ, Judaism was the single most vital religious movement in the Greco-Roman world. The focus of loyalty provided by the Temple and by Torah gave its adherents a strength greater than even the sense of an urban civilizing mission among the barbarian peoples that sustained the Greeks in Asia Minor and Syria. So far as worship was concerned, the latter were at a disadvantage when confronted with Judaism that could claim a documented and coherent history of salvation extending back to the beginning of the world. The 'Antiquities of the Jews' and the Septuagint were alike missionary works on a vast scale aimed partly at vindicating to the Greek-speaking world the claim that Judaism as a philosophy and way of life was older and truer than anything the Greeks could offer.[30]

Thus, Christianity already had an established format to follow in regards to building a strong community. In addition, early Christianity placed a great emphasis on both producing large families and indoctrinating children, as well as an aversion to well-established forms of population control such as the exposure of children, homosexuality and prostitution. Hence, according to Burkert, "the *ekklesia* became a self-reproducing type of community that could not be stopped."[31]

Also crucial to the survival of the early church was the development of a body of canonical writings. Confronting the rampant controversies, schisms and diverse beliefs concerning their savior, orthodox Christians (those who believed in a historical Jesus) were eager to settle on one authoritative text, which portrayed Jesus directly in human terms, and could justify the claim of a direct line of unimpeachable knowledge transmitted from a historic founder to his disciples. The Roman church had an interest in maintaining the validity of apostolic tradition and threw its weight on the side of orthodoxy.[32]

From Ignatius of Antioch there was also a trend towards proper authority; no valid Eucharist or service could be held without the bishop's authorization, and there was an exalted view of the episcopate as Christ's high priest.

It should be noted that only those who believed Jesus to be historical sought such stability and authority (or vice-versa, only those seeking stability and authority viewed Christ as historical.) For obvious reasons, the Gnostics and the mysteries had no such need to establish "orthodoxy"; they were seeking truth and spiritual fulfillment rather than political power or authoritarian control. One researcher notes, Gnostics "made no demand for simple or unquestioning faith. They accepted religion as a voyage of discovery, and in this final era of urban prosperity in the ancient world, reflected the fading, tenuous links that bound the educated individual to the age-old Greek spirit of inquiry."[33]

Writing things down could be harmful if the information fell into the hands of those who were not prepared to receive it, and establishing a dogmatic creed or "orthodox" understanding was counter-productive to the establishment of direct, personal wisdom. Many commentators affirm that the Gnostics or pagan mysteries did not have the infrastructure or fixed creeds needed to become a universal movement – although this feature was not necessarily undesirable. Burkert admits that the lack of a set creed or orthodox truth allowed a healthy religious pluralism while encouraging inter-faith tolerance:

> The general lack of organization, solidarity, and coherence in ancient mysteries, which may appear as a deficiency from a Jewish or Christian point of view, is outweighed by some positive aspects with which we may easily sympathize. The absence of religious demarcation and conscious group identity means the absence of any rigid frontiers against competing cults as well as the absence of any concept of heresy, not to mention excommunication. The pagan gods, even the gods of the mysteries, are not jealous of one another, they form, as it were, an open society. If Mithras is somehow a stranger, he still keeps good company with familiar divinities like Helios, Kronos, and Zeus.[34]

The fact that the mysteries did not claim an absolute and sole form of salvation has been seen by modern scholars as the unfortunate key to their eventual demise. Witt, commenting on the mysteries of Isis, claims that Isiacism suffered from the lack of a systematic theology:

> She was ineffectually groping her way towards the impregnable security of a creed that would have said no other gods existed and was seeking to formulate the commandment "Thou shalt have no other gods but me."[35]

Finally, it must not be forgotten that the early church was set up as a kind of commune, in the style of Pythagorean communities. Joining the church meant giving up all property, which was to be managed by a board of leaders for the common good of the community. This was a serious and fundamental aspect of the early church, as demonstrated by the parable in Acts concerning "the fraud of Ananias and Sapphira." Their story is related after the example is given of Joseph/Barnabas, who sold his land and gave all the money, as was expected, to the apostles. Ananias and Sapphira, in contrast, sold their land to join the church but kept back some of the full price. Peter confronts them, saying

> Ananias, how can Satan have so possessed you that you should lie to the Holy Spirit and keep back part of the price of the land? ... You have been lying not to men, but to God. (Acts 5:2-6)

When he heard this Ananias fell down dead. Three hours later when his wife Sapphira comes home, Peter says:

> Why did you and your husband agree to put the Spirit of the Lord to the test? Listen! At the door are the footsteps of those who have buried your husband; they will carry you out, too. Instantly, she dropped dead at his feet... And a great fear came upon the whole church and on all who heard it. (Acts 5:9-11)

The message here is clear: you must give up *everything* to the church. This formula meant that the church authorities soon had a great deal of wealth and power.

The economic basis, depending on the prosperity of the urban upper class who owned lands around the city itself, was too fragile. There was too much imperial estate, too much church land, and too much in the hands of powerful landowners who could defy the city's agents.[36]

As the church later became tax free, and received great gifts of land, the wealth continued to flow upwards into the hands of the wealthy. Emperor Constantine envisioned a world where "the poor can live of the wealth of churches."[37] This set the scene for the feudalism of the middle ages.[38] Soon, the Christians were "too well organized, too widespread, and too numerous to be destroyed."[39]

The orthodox focus on developing authority and enforcing the allegiance and obedience of followers also had doctrinal influences. Unlike Paul's mysteries and their permissible ethics, which varied depending on the spiritual level of every initiate, for a functioning Christian community to survive orthodoxy saw the need for strict, universal rules of conduct – as well as the necessary punishments to enforce them. This further separated them from Paul, the Gnostics and mystery religions, which emphasized a God that was loving, forgiving and kind. In contrast, patristic writers felt that the angry, jealous and violent God of Israel was necessary for discipline. Church father Tertullian ridiculed the heretic teacher Marcion, who rejected the Yahweh of the Old Testament in favor of a merciful, loving and forgiving God. According to Ellerbe, the author of *The Dark Side of Christian History*:

> In orthodox Christian eyes, God must be prone to anger and demand discipline and punishment. Tertullian wrote, 'Now, if [Marcion's God] is susceptible of no feeling of rivalry, or anger, or damage, or no injury, as one who refrains from exercising judicial power, I cannot tell how any system of discipline – and that, too, a plenary one – can be consistent in him. (Tertullian, *Against Marcion*, 1, 26)[40]

Although Christianity has evolved somewhat, and most Christians today would tend to agree with Marcion's more gentle idea of God, there is a paradox in modern Christianity's belief in a loving, merciful God – who condemns sinners to an eternity of punishment – that is not easily resolved. According to New Testament professor Donald A. Carson, for example, God has no choice but to discipline those who break his rules. "If he says it doesn't matter to him, God is no longer a God to be admired. He's either amoral or positively creepy. For him to act in any other way in the face of such blatant defiance would be to reduce God himself."[41] While this may be true, it does not imply the immediate acceptance of *eternal* punishment; an idea that, like Tertullian's angry God, was developed according to the needs of orthodoxy.

Like the mysteries, early Christianity evidently embraced the idea of reincarnation. This is certainly true for later Gnostics – however, it was also taught by the earliest Christian scholars, such as Origen. Like Plato and Orpheus, Origen believed that the human soul existed before it was incarnated into a physical body, and that it would pass from one body to another until it is reunited with God; after which it no longer takes on physical form. He also believed that all souls would eventually return to God. Origen, arguing against Marcion (who taught that salvation was a gift from God which depended on grace alone), taught that since humankind had fallen from God by its own free will, so it must reunite with God through its own volition. While Christ could greatly speed the reconciliation with God, such reconciliation would not take place without effort by the individual. This position was rejected by orthodoxy, insisting that it depended too heavily upon individual self-determination.[42] Further, orthodox Christians thought that the theory of reincarnation minimized the role of Jesus Christ, downplayed the necessity for salvation in this lifetime, and diminished the unique nature of Christ's resurrection:

> A person's salvation, in orthodox eyes, depends not upon self-determination and free will, as Origen's theories suggest, but only upon embracing Jesus Christ. Furthermore, if a person could choose to reunite with god in any one of many lifetimes, then there would be little fear of eternal damnation – and fear was deemed essential by the orthodox. Origen's idea that the soul is separable from the body also seemed to diminish the extraordinary nature of Christ's resurrection. The miracle of Christ's resurrection was understood to offer the possibility of overcoming physical death. If, however, each soul periodically overcomes death by separating from one body and entering into another, then Jesus' feat would not have been unique.[43]

These differences in doctrine were not easily resolved.

## Constantine and a Religion for the Empire

A simultaneous current essential to the triumph of Christianity was the deliberate and continuous attempt by Roman emperors to find a universal "State Religion" that could channel and command the religious yearnings of the empire. This had begun early with the creation of Serapis, and perhaps Hadrian attempted something similar with Jesus. Many emperors saw later deities as various manifestations of sun worship, and tried to forge an all-inclusive form of the Sun God, which could be hailed as Lord of the Roman empire. In 274 Emperor Aurelian built a magnificent temple in Rome in honor of the Sun and established a new college of senators called "priests of the Sun-god." This was to be the universal faith of the empire.[44]

According to Probus (276-82), the unconquered Sun (Helios) was the emperor's companion, and associated with the classical gods: "One Zeus, one Hades, one Helios is Serapis."[45] Many religious practices, which were already similar to sun worship, could easily be included in such a state religion. Christianity was one of the key exceptions, which despite sharing many points of commonality, refused to blend in and kept itself fiercely independent. This was especially challenging to Roman authorities as Christian leaders increased in wealth and power, and commanded the loyalty and obedience of their subjects.

Consequently, on the 23rd of February 303, Emperor Diocletian (most likely prompted by Galerius) initiated a persecution of the Christians. Churches were destroyed and books burned. Christians lost most privileges. Resistance was minimal – most Christians did not martyr, and only one is recorded as refusing to give up his books or church property. However, in some cases, soldiers forced compliance, rather than allow Christians to martyr themselves. In 310 Maximin used a text called the "Acts of Pilate" to discredit Christians on the popular level by teaching children to recite passages in schools.[46] But all of this only confirms what a powerful force Christianity had become.

Then Christianity had a sudden change of fortune under the emperor Constantine. According to legend, while still a general, Constantine had a miraculous dream, wherein he saw a figure of the cross (the Chi-Rho) and was told, "with this, conquer." After he won the battle that made him emperor, he was Christianity's new champion. In 313 he issued the edict of Milan, which granted liberty of worship to all Romans, and restored Christian church property that had been confiscated during earlier persecutions.

Constantine was exposed to Christianity by his mother Helena. As general, however, he had put himself under the protection of the God who was the most popular among his soldiers: Helios Apollo. He allowed himself to be described as the son of Helios Apollo, playing up the sensitivities and religious tendencies of his time. Outward manifestations of the emperor's support for Christianity are few.[47] In public images – on coins for example – he is depicted with his companion, the Sun God. In 321 he ordered Sunday to be kept free for the lord, calling it "the day celebrated by the veneration of the Sun."[48]

Nevertheless, he made himself popular with the masses by protecting Christianity. If any Jew sought to punish apostates (Christians) they would be burned alive – as would proselytes to Judaism. Constantine was probably attracted to Christianity because of its popularity and its monotheism. It was already the religion that seemed to be the most inclusive (being a combination of many other spiritual traditions). By that time it probably also appeared similar to Mithraism, which was popular among his troops. In an effort to unify his empire, Constantine doted on this new faith, and tried to make it easy for his people to convert by tailoring Christianity to pre-existent pagan customs. In an attempt to turn Christianity into the empire's official faith, Constantine changed the face of the Christian movement.

Constantine supported the Church financially, built basilicas, granted privileges to clergy (e.g., exemption from certain taxes), promoted Christians to high ranking offices, returned property confiscated during the Great Persecution of Diocletian, and endowed the church with land and other wealth. Between 324 and 330, Constantine built a new imperial capital at Byzantium (re-named Constantinople, after him). The city employed overtly Christian architecture, contained churches within the city walls (unlike "old" Rome), and had no pagan temples.[49]

Constantine funded these projects by appropriating wealth from the pagans, intending to "to teach his subjects to give up their rites... and to accustom them to despise their temples and the images contained therein." This led to the closure of pagan temples due to a lack of support, with their wealth flowing to the imperial treasure.[50]

In 330 the temple on Vatican Hill, which had been a center for pagan worship of the goddess Cybele for hundreds of years, became the site of the St. Peter's Basilica of Rome. Constantine's own mother traveled to the Holy Land, and after three centuries, claimed to have found the actual cross used in the crucifixion (of course it was under a temple of Aphrodite, which had to be destroyed). According to Theodoret (died c. 457) in his *Ecclesiastical History*, the True Cross also had powers of healing:

> When the empress beheld the place where the Saviour suffered, she immediately ordered the idolatrous temple, which had been there erected, to be destroyed, and the very earth on which it stood to be removed. When the tomb, which had been so long concealed, was discovered, three crosses were seen buried near the Lord's sepulchre. All held it as certain that one of these crosses was that of our Lord Jesus Christ, and that the other two were those of the thieves who were crucified with Him. Yet they could not discern to which of the three the Body of the Lord had been brought nigh, and which had received the outpouring of His precious Blood. But the wise and holy Macarius, the president of the city, resolved this question in the following manner. He caused a lady of rank, who had been long suffering from disease, to be touched by each of the crosses, with earnest prayer, and thus discerned the virtue residing in that of the Saviour. For the instant this cross was brought near the lady, it expelled the sore disease, and made her whole. (*Ecclesiastical History* xvii)

A Christianized account of the Roman Empire, leading to its culmination in the divine ruler of Constantine, was crafted by Church historian Eusebius (who was well-rewarded for his efforts). According to Frend, "In Eusebius of Caesare (the Christians) produced a leader who was not only an immensely hard-working and able propagandist, but a historian in the tradition of Josephus, and a bishop who evolved a political theology that after 325 was to guide Constantine and his successors for centuries to come."[51]

Although today scholars conclude that it is largely erroneous, the traditional account of Church history continues to owe much to Eusebius' fabricated account of the church's foundations. The propaganda of Eusebius re-aligned the entire church as the religion of the empire, supporting and defending the divine role of emperor:

> Eusebius pointed out that the coming on earth of the divine Word coincided exactly with the unification and pacification of the world by Augustus, and the creation of the Roman Empire. Between 311 and 320 Eusebius founded the political philosophy of the Constantinian state, based on the unity of the church and empire under the providence of God.[52]

The fictionized history of Eusebius justified the agressive and at times violent rise of Christianity as the Empire's new religion by portraying Constantine's destruction of paganism as a holy and divine act:

> As to the god of the Cilicians [Asclepius], great was, indeed, the deception of men seemingly wise, with thousands excited over him as if over a savior and physician who now revealed himself to those sleeping (in a temple) and again healed the diseases of those ailing in body; of the souls, though, he was a downright destroyer, drawing them away from the true Savior and leading into godless imposture those who were susceptible to fraud; the emperor (Constantine), therefore, acting fairly, holding the true Savior a jealous god, commanded that this temple, too, be razed to its foundations. At one nod it was stretched out on the ground – the celebrated marvel of the noble philosophers overthrown by the hand of a soldier – and with it (fell) the one lurking there, not a demon or a god, but a kind of deceiver of souls, who had practiced his deceit for a very long time.[53]

Constantine's brutal attack on his traditional culture and religious history was not all that different from the Maoist Cultural Revolution in China; with state sanction, temples were looted for materials to build Christian churches or simply confiscated. Shrines were handed over to people who were dedicated to Christ. The universal freedom of conscience proclaimed at Milan had been abrogated, and the state had become a persecutor once more – only this time in favor of Christian orthodoxy.[54]

## Defining Jesus: the Church Councils

Although Christianity had been given state approval, Constantine soon saw that, as a movement, Christianity was deeply divided among itself in virtually all areas. In order to stifle disagreements and unify the empire under one, simplified religion, Emperor Constantine summoned the first Church Council. In the summer of 325, the bishops of all provinces were summoned to Nicaea (now in modern-day Turkey – a place easily accessible to the majority of delegates) by Emperor Constantine, who presided. Constantine organized the Council along the lines of the Roman Senate. He was present as an observer and did not vote; however it would be misleading to say he was not influential in the proceedings.

One of most popular "heresies" at that time was Arianism, which maintained that Jesus was a created being, and hence, different than God. This was the main threat with which the Councilors had to deal.

### Council of Nicaea (325)

Church tradition maintained that Jesus was the divine Son of God – but how could this be reconciled with strict monotheism? If God is *one*, where does Jesus fit in? These ruminations led a popular presbyter named Arius to conclude that Jesus (as the Logos or Divine Word) could not be exactly equal to God; Jesus was God's first creation, and everything else was created through him. He was "like the father" (*homoios*); as a created being, however, Jesus was not eternal. So, according to Arius, Christ is neither fully god nor truly man. Jesus was human, promoted to divine status. Opposing this position, St. Alexander and Athanasius maintained that Jesus was a divine being in the same way as God the Father: "of the same substance" (*homoousios*); equally divine and co-eternal.

Both sides could use scripture to support their argument and there was no easy way to settle the dispute. As Armstrong points out, "At the beginning of the controversy, there was no orthodox teaching on the nature of Christ and nobody knew whether Athanasius or Arius was right. Discussion raged for over two hundred years."[55] This was the debate that Constantine was determined to settle once and for all at Nicaea. As Eusebius described:

> Constantine himself proceeded through the midst of the assembly, like some heavenly messenger of God, clothed in raiment which glittered as it were with rays of light reflecting the glowing radiance of a purple robe, and adorned with the brilliant splendor of gold and precious stones. (Eusebius, *The Life of the Blessed Emperor Constantine*, Book 3, Chapter 10)

The two sides argued for about two months. Much of the debate hinged on the difference between being "born" or "created" and being "begotten." Arians saw these as essentially the same; followers of Alexander did not.

According to some accounts, debate became so heated that at one point, Arius was slapped in the face by Nicholas of Myra. Nicholas was stripped of his robes and put in chains for the offence, but was later visited by Jesus and Mary, who vindicated him. The St. Nicholas Center (which claims that this is the same St. Nicholas who would later become Santa Claus) gives the following account of this miraculous intervention:

> Nicholas was ashamed and prayed for forgiveness, though he did not waver in his belief. During the night, Jesus and Mary his Mother, appeared, asking, "Why are you in jail?" "Because of my love for you," Nicholas replied. Jesus then gave the Book of the Gospels to Nicholas. Mary gave him an omophorion (a robe), so Nicholas would again be dressed as a bishop. Now at peace, Nicholas studied the Scriptures for the rest of the night. When the jailer came in the morning, he found the chains loose on the floor and Nicholas dressed in bishop's robes, quietly reading the Scriptures. When Constantine was told of this, the emperor asked that Nicholas be freed. Nicholas was then fully reinstated as the Bishop of Myra.[56]

The Council of Nicaea finally agreed with Nicholas' views,

deciding the question against Arius. The primarily resolutions were these:

1. Jesus Christ is described as "God from God, Light from Light, true God from true God," proclaiming his divinity.
2. Jesus Christ is said to be "begotten, not made," asserting his co-eternalness with God
3. Jesus is defined as "from the substance of the Father," in direct opposition to Arianism. Eusebius of Caesarea ascribes the term *homoousios*, or *consubstantial* to Constantine who, on this particular point, may have chosen to exercise his authority.

Incidentally, also established at the Council of Nicaea was the calculation of the date of Easter, a prohibition of self-castration (suggesting that many Christians continued to follow this specifically pagan act), and a ban on kneeling for prayer (penitential prayer was not deemed appropriate for the celebration of the Resurrection).

Although the council solved the immediate concern of Arianism, the definitions did not settle all conflict. Jesus was equal to the Father, but not the same as the father; and yet of the same substance as the Father. Moreover, he comes "from" him but was never made or created (only "begotten"), so he is co-eternal and there is no time he was not. This complex definition did not satisfy everyone.

It was Constantine who demonstrated how a State Religion would be run: everyone who refused to endorse the creed was exiled and excommunicated. The works of Arius were confiscated and burned, and all persons found possessing them would be executed. And yet even this did not stop the controversy.

Nicaea had created a great rift in the church, and there were many who felt that the creed established had flaws. The Council of Antioch (341) was the first of several 4th-century councils that attempted to replace orthodox Nicene theology with a modified Arianism. Attended by the Eastern emperor Constantius II and about 100 Eastern bishops, the council developed four creeds as substitutes for the Nicene, all of them to some degree unorthodox and omitting or rejecting the Nicene statement that Christ was "of one substance" (*homoousios*) with the Father. According to Frend, "the bishops were kept in cramped quarters through a stifling

Italian summer until their morale collapsed. They signed. Christ was 'like the father' (homoios) without any attempt to define how. 'The world,' wrote Jerome some twenty years later, 'awoke with a groan to find itself Arian.'"[57]

## Julian the Apostate (355-363)

The expansion and success of Christianity was momentarily checked by Emperor Flavius Claudius Julianus, a successful general from the Constantinian dynasty (nephew to Constantine I) who ruled Rome after Constantius II. Julian despised Constantine and considered Helena not a saint but a "wicked stepmother."[58]

Julian was a philosopher and hoped to restore the Empire to its classical heritage through a kind of mystical Neoplatonism. According to Julian, there was a single, unknowable supreme being, which emanated a creator-power that was identified with sun – a pure and undefiled and immaterial substance – midway between the created world and the supreme being. He was the giver of life, the creator, the harmony of universe, intelligible in mysticism. In his *Oration upon the Sovereign Sun,* Julian associates this figure with Serapis:

> *One Jove, one Pluto, one Sun is Serapis...* We must conclude that the sovereignty of the Sun and of Jupiter amongst the deities that are objects of intellect is held in common, or rather is one and the same. For this reason Plato seems to me to be right in calling Pluto a *provident* deity. The same god we also name "Serapis," that is "Invisible," clearly because he is the *object of the intellect alone:* up to whom (it is said) that the souls ascend of such as have led the best, and most righteous lives. We must not suppose him (Pluto), the terrible being that Fable describes him; but a mild and benevolent one, who completely frees souls from the trammels of Birth; far from nailing them down to new bodies, and punishing and exacting retribution from souls already released from the body: but on the contrary, he directs them in their upward course, and carries them aloft to the Intelligible World.[59]

Under this benevolent being were local deities; Athena for Greeks, Attis for Phrygians, and Jehova for Jews. The traditional pagan myths could be interpreted as allegories of the single great drama of creation.[60] In 355, Julian restored the Eleusinian mysteries at Athens, and claimed that his ministry would include "honest and reasonable men, intelligent and entirely capable."[61]

Julian was staunchly opposed to Christianity. According to him, not only was Christianity inferior to classical spiritual traditions, it was a deliberate fiction:

> Greeks who had become Christians had not only chosen a culture inferior to their own, which lacked the moral virtue of Hellenism, but a religion that combined the worst features of Hellenism and Judaism in the worship of a pathetic failed revolutionary. Their religion was based on a fabrication, a fiction concocted by evil men. (*Contra Julianum*, PG 76.560C)[62]

Although we cannot be sure of the basis for Julian's claim that Christianity was "a fiction concocted by evil men," it fits the hypothesis that Christianity was, like the cult of Serapis, a deliberate construction – although he might just be referring to the more recent historical fantasy created for it by Eusebius.

In his text *Against the Galileans,* Julian contrasts the jealous, exclusively "particular" (μερικός) Hebraic God with the universal Hellenic gods who do not confine their attentions to small and unimportant portions of the world. "Though it has in it nothing divine," Julian writes, "by making full use of that part of the soul which loves fable and is childish and foolish, it has induced men to believe that the monstrous tale is truth" (*Against the Galileans,* Book 1).[63] In a private letter he continues, "Christians are like a disease, turned aside from the gods to worship corpses and relics" (Julian, Letter XLI.438B).[64]

In spite of his animosity toward Christianity, Julian refused to persecute Christians – they were to be left alone. According to Gregory of Nazianzus, the common people welcomed Julian's reforms (Gregory, *Oration*, IV 75.) Julian was viewed as the "liberator of the Roman world, restorer of temples, re-creator of the common wealth and destroyer of the barbarians."[65] Unruly pagans, seizing the opportunity to right past offences, set upon the Christians. Bishop George in Alexandria was lynched by mob. Julian admonished the Alexandrians, scolding that such behavior was unbecoming to Hellenes, and ordered George's library preserved.

In the *Tolerance Edict* of 362, Julian decreed the reopening of pagan temples, the restitution of confiscated temple properties, and the return of dissident Christian bishops and clergy whom Constantius had exiled, in the cynical belief "that no wild beasts are such enemies to mankind as are most Christians in their deadly hatred of one another" (Ammianus Marcellinus, 22.5.4). The last decree had significant consequences: the Donatists swept in and "reconverted" Catholics. In the summer of 362, with only 21 bishops in Alexandria, Athanasius (back from exile) held an important church council and again pushed the terms "like in all respects" and "of one substance." The revisions were adopted, so after 37 years, the Creed of Nicaea was firmly accepted. For managing to proselytize in favor of Christianity and holding this council, Athanasius was once more exiled as a "bad man."

The rise of Christianity could not be contained for long. With Julian's death on June 26th, 363 in the Battle of Ctesiphon (believing himself a reincarnation of Alexander the Great, he'd not worn any armor), the last formal opposition to Christianity ended. One historian records the tale of a bishop who had appropriated a pillar from the famous shrine of Asclepius in Aegae, Cilicia to build his own temple. Although Julian told him to put it back, it was too heavy for the Greeks to move; therefore they left it and went away. When Julian died, "the bishop again easily lifted it up and restored it to its own place."[66] This story aptly portrays Julian's unsuccessful attempt to halt the progress of Christianity.

Between 375 and 383 Emperor Gratian confiscated temples and abolished privileges for heathen priests. In 380, Christianity was declared the official religion of the empire by Emperor Theodosius I, who forbid heathen religious observances from 379 to 395. By 435, Theodosius II commanded that all temples be destroyed or turned into churches. Emperor Justinian prohibited heathenism on pain of death, and abolished the 900-year-old school of Athens in 529. The ancient temple of Alexandria, with the world's largest collection of academic books and scrolls, was burned to the ground during this period. A few testimonies have been preserved complaining about the rampant destruction and vandalism Christians foisted on their pagan contemporaries. According to one, a public statue was destroyed even though it was not worshiped or sacrificed to (hence it was not illegal); this sort of incident was a common occurrence:

> There was a bronze statue in the city of Beroea – Ascelpius in the form of the beautiful son of Cleinias; and the work of art imitated the work of nature. Of such youthful beauty was it that even those who were able to behold him daily still longed for the sight of it. No one (of the Christians) was so shameless that he would dare to say that sacrifices were offered to this statue. Even such an image as this, O King, perfected as was fitting with great care as well as with bright genius, has been broken to pieces and is gone, and many hands divided up what Phidias' hands had put together. Because of what sacrificial blood? Because of what sacrificial knife? Because of what illegal service to the gods? Just as here, then, although they could mention no sacrifice, still they cut up Alcibiades, or rather Asclepius into many parts, disgracing the city in respect to the statue, in the same way must we believe the matter stands with them in regard to the happenings in the country. (Libanius, *Oratio* XXX, 22-23)[67]

After Julian's failed Hellenistic revival, the restored Christianity focused once more on defining the central aspects of its beliefs. With the final acceptance of the Nicene Creed settling the matter of Christ's divinity, the controversy shifted towards the other end of the spectrum. In what sense was Jesus a human being? Did Jesus have a physical body like ours? Did he have a mind and a soul? Did he sin? These difficulties arose from trying to equate the eternal, divine Jesus (who was of the same substance with the father) with his earthly ministry. In 381, Theodosius I called the second ecumenical council of the church, called the First Council of Constantinople, to resolve these challenges.

### First Council of Constantinople (381)

One of the controversies debated at the First Council of Constantinople concerned Jesus' humanity. A bishop of Laodicea named Apollinaris, who had fought Arianism around 360, was accused of going to another extreme. Counter to the Arian decrees, he proclaimed that Jesus was *fully* God. As a consequence, however, it seemed to him impossible that Jesus could undergo moral development: if Jesus was the same as the father and eternal, then how could he have matured in his ethical wisdom? Therefore, Apollinaris posited a Christ who was human in body and soul, but in whom the human mind had been completely replaced by the Logos.

The problem with this view, according to other church leaders, was that a Christ without a human mind could not truly share in our sufferings, and there is no real possibility of his sinning or being tempted. This kind of Christ was never truly human; and if not human, it was argued, he could not redeem us. The Cappadocian father Gregory of Nazianzus stated, "Only that can be saved (in us) that has been assumed (by Christ)." Thus the full humanity of Jesus Christ had to be affirmed.

Keep in mind that this is now several centuries after the fact, and the church is voting on whether and to what extent Jesus Christ was human based on theological need rather than historical evidence. The choice of what Jesus Christ *had to have been* was made first, and the theological consequences worked out later, no matter how convoluted. Based on these two councils, the Church arrived at a Christ who was fully God (of the same substance of the father; begotten but not made) and also fully human. But how could Jesus' humanity be reconciled with his divinity? Did he have two separate natures? How did that work? These issues soon produced the need for another ecumenical council.

### Council of Ephesus (431)

At the Council of Ephesus, Nestorius, patriarch of Constantinople, was accused of dividing the two natures of Jesus in a way that made the Virgin Mary the mother of Christ, but not of God. Nestorius taught that Jesus had two natures, which were, in a sense, switched on and off at different periods of his life.

According to Nestorius, it was impossible that the Logos, the pre-existent second person of the Trinity, could really suffer; hence, only Jesus' *humanity* suffered in the passion.[68] Likewise, Nestorius claimed that the Logos had not been born of a woman; only Jesus' humanity was born of a woman. He refused to use the title Mother of God (*Theotokos*) – the most beloved title the East could give the virgin mother – for Mary. She is not the mother of God, he said, only of Christ (*Christotokos*).

The leader of the opponents of Nestorius, Cyril of Alexandria accused him of creating not just two natures but two persons of Jesus. Cyril, while acknowledging that Jesus had two natures, argued that they were not separated. According to Cyril, they are like light and heat in a flame: thus it is legitimate to say that "God died" or "Mary gave birth to God," because it was impossible to separate the human and divine natures in Christ. Cyril was the first to use the term "hypostatic union" about the joining of the two natures.

Cyril drew up and presented at Ephesus twelve statements, called "anathemas," condemning Nestorius. After a great deal of political maneuvering, synods and counter-synods, Cyril's views triumphed and won the support of the pope – and the Nestorian party was condemned. The Council declared that Christ had two natures, but only one person, which is divine.

Another issue resolved at this council, which significantly altered the spiritual climate of Christianity while increasing Church authority, was the condemnation of Pelagian heresy. Pelagius (c.354 AD - c.420/440AD) was an ascetic who denied the need for divine aid in performing good works; consequently, he refused the more specific doctrine of original sin as developed by Augustine of Hippo.

While the Peligians taught that each person was completely free to heed the call of God, Augustine claimed that, through the original sin of Adam, we were *born* sinners. According to Augustine (who was reading Jerome's recently translated Latin Vulgate Bible rather than the original Greek), sin was no longer an action that stirred the lake of the soul but a *birth defect*, which we had no way of repairing. No one was capable of redeeming themselves, or of even choosing to break with sin. Humanity was irreparably humbled in sin, and it was only through God's actions that we were saved.

In Pelagius's eyes, reliance upon redemption by Christ should be accompanied by individual responsibility and efforts to do good.[69] The church, however, sided with Augustine: salvation is entirely in God's hands, we are slaves to our flesh and sin and cannot do anything for ourselves – but some of us will be saved through grace. The Pelagian heresy was first condemned at the Council of

Carthage held in 416, and this decision was affirmed at the Council of Ephesus.

### Council of Chalcedon (451)

In an extreme reaction against Nestorianism, another conception of Christ arose wherein Jesus had only one nature, "the Incarnate Word." This has been called Monophysitism, and was at the forefront of the controversy underlying the Council of Chaldedon.

Eutyches, presbyter and archimandrite at Constantinople, declared that Christ was "a fusion of human and divine elements."[70] Although eternal and divine, during the incarnation the Divine Logos was fused together with the Human Jesus. The difficulty is in positing when the incarnation took place: was Jesus born human first? Or did the incarnation take place at the very moment Christ was conceived? If you taught one divine nature in Christ, rather than two, then you invited the belief in a docetic Jesus, a God who walks around with a cloak of humanity. There was also the danger of the Apollinarian concept that Jesus did not have a human mind, but only the body and soul of a human.

Roman Pope "Saint Leo the Great" attacked Eutyches for this "one-nature" belief. The council concluded that Jesus had two natures, which were separate; and yet Jesus Christ was to be regarded as one and the same person. The actual wording is "one and the same Christ, Son, Lord, only begotten, to be acknowledged in two natures, without confusion, without change, without division, without separation." According to Baylor University professor Chris Armstrong, these four "withouts" are referred to as the "four fences of Chalcedon."[71] They can be understood "not as a precise definition of the relationship between the divine and human in Christ, but rather as limits to orthodoxy, beyond which Christians cannot stray and remain in the truth. What lies within those fences is still mysterious!"[72] The definition of Chalcedon is worth sharing in full (capitalized in the original):

> Therefore, following the holy Fathers, we all with one accord teach men to acknowledge one and the same Son, our Lord Jesus Christ, at once complete in Godhead and complete in manhood, truly God

and truly man, consisting also of a reasonable soul and body; of one substance [homoousios] with the Father as regards his Godhead, and at the same time one substance with us as regards his manhood; like us in all respects, apart from sin; as regards his Godhead, begotten of the Father before the ages, but yet as regards his manhood begotten, for us man and for our salvation, of Mary the Virgin, the God-bearer [Theotokos]; one and the same Christ, Son, Lord, Only-begotten, recognized IN TWO NATURES, [en dyo physesin] WITHOUT CONFUSION, [asynchytos] WITHOUT CHANGE, [atreptos] WITHOUT DIVISION, [adiairetos] WITHOUT SEPARATION [anchoristos]; the distinction of natures being in no way annulled by the union, but rather the characteristics of each nature being preserved and coming together to form one person and substance [hypostasis], not as parted or separated into two persons, but one and the same Son and Only-begotten God the Word, Lord Jesus Christ; even as the prophets from earliest times spoke of him, and our Lord Jesus Christ himself taught us, and the creed of the Fathers has handed down to us.[73]

## Continuing Controversies

Still the debates continued. The Council of Constantinople II, in 553, was divided between the Antiochene theology, emphasizing Christ's humanity, and the Alexandrian theology of their opponents, emphasizing Christ's deity. The Council of Constantinople III, in 680, condemned monothelitism (that Christ had a single will), and affirmed that Christ had both a human will and a divine will that functioned in perfect harmony. This is *over 600 years* after the historical Jesus is claimed to have walked the earth, and his followers continue struggling with the basic logistical problems and fundamental philosophical difficulties with their faith in the human-and-divine Christ. Whenever a believer tried to explain the mystery of Jesus, following the nature of Jesus Christ to its rational implications, it was repudiated as a heresy. Concerning the nature of Jesus Christ, going too far in *any direction* would lead to error. The role of the Church councils was to block rational inquiry from upsetting the faithful, by declaring what was to be believed.

The only truth, it was decided, is that which is mysterious and impossible; what cannot be understood but only believed.

Moreover this theology (ignoring the claim of Church infallibility and the guidance of the Holy Spirit) has never relied on who or what Jesus Christ was *originally*. Rather than from one early idea to many, as we would expect a historical founder to produce, in fact the tradition goes from many ideas to one:

### Council of Nicaea II (787): Iconoclasm and Idolatry

One final controversy was settled at the Council of Nicaea II in 787, which is of particular interest; in a sense, its ruling closed the book on the early movement of Christianity and turned it into something vastly different.

As we have seen, one of the most severe differences between Christianity and its pagan surroundings was its refusal to worship idols. The anti-idolatry stance comes from the Old Testament section commonly known as the Ten Commandments. Many people are familiar with an abbreviated form of the second commandment ("idolatry is bad"), but unaware that there is a biblical prohibition against any visual representation of not just God, but *anything*:

> You shall not make for yourself a carved image, or any likeness of anything that is in heaven above, or that is in the earth beneath, or that is in the water under the earth; you shall not bow down to them nor serve them. For I, the LORD your God, am a jealous God, visiting the iniquity of the fathers on the children to the third and fourth generations of those who hate Me, but showing mercy to thousands, to those who love Me and keep My commandments. (Exodus 20: 2-7)

The Bible has many terms for idolatry, and constantly reaffirms the contempt the biblical writers held for idolatrous practices. Pagan idols were described as being made of gold, silver, wood, and stone; they are only the work of men's hands, unable to speak, see, hear, smell, eat, grasp, or feel, and powerless either to injure or to benefit (Ps. 135:15-18).

In stark contrast to paganism, the early Christian church, like Judaism, was exceedingly careful not to trespass against this one central commandment: many were persecuted or martyred on exactly this point. In addition, the Christian God had no need of sacrificial offerings. Many Christians, such as the apologist

Marcianus Aristides, distinguished their beliefs as rational and wise, in contrast with the foolishness of Greek idolatry, based on the Christian refusal to practice idolatry. In a letter to the emperor from the early-mid second century, Marcianus makes this case pointedly:

> But it is a marvel, O King, with regard to the Greeks, who surpass all other peoples in their manner of life and reasoning, how they have gone astray after dead idols and lifeless images. And yet they see their gods in the hands of their artificers being sawn out, and planed and docked, and hacked short, and charred, and ornamented, and being altered by them in every kind of way. And when they grow old, and are worn away through lapse of time, and when they are molten and crushed to powder, how, I wonder, did they not perceive concerning them, that they are not gods? And as for those who did not find deliverance for themselves, how can they serve the distress of men? But even the writers and philosophers among them have wrongly alleged that the gods are such as are made in honour of God Almighty. And they err in seeking to liken (them) to God whom man has not at any time seen nor can see unto what He is like. Herein, too (they err) in asserting of deity that any such thing as deficiency can be present to it; as when they say that He receives sacrifice and requires burnt-offering and libation and immolations of men, and temples. But God is not in need, and none of these things is necessary to Him; and it is clear that men err in these things they imagine. (Apology of Aristides, 13)[74]

Around 170 AD, Melito, bishop of Sardis (considered a saint by both Roman Catholics and the Eastern Orthodox), also spoke against worshipping the invisible and omnipresent God in the form of an idol:

> There are, however, persons who say: It is for the honour of God that we make the image: in order, that is, that we may worship the God who is concealed from our view. But they are unaware that God is in every country, and in every place, and is never absent, and that there is not anything done and He knoweth it not. Yet thou, despicable man! within whom He is, and without whom He is, and above whom He is, hast nevertheless gone and bought thee wood from the carpenter's, and it is carved and made into an image insulting to God. To this thou

offerest sacrifice, and knowest not that the all-seeing eye seeth thee, and that the word of truth reproves thee, and says to thee: How can the unseen God be sculptured? Nay, it is the likeness of thyself that thou makest and worshippest. Because the wood has been sculptured, hast thou not the insight to perceive that it is still wood, or that the stone is still stone? The gold also the workman: taketh according to its weight in the balance. And when thou hast had it made into an image, why dose thou weigh it? Therefore thou art a lover of gold, and not a lover of God.[75]

Early Christian communities stood out for having "no altars, no temples, no acknowledged images" (Minucius Felix, *Octavius*, chapter 10).[76] They "assembled in houses appointed for the purpose, and, in times of persecution, in solitary places."[77]

New converts who had previously worked as artisans servicing pagan religions were forced to quit their trade and find new means of employment. Hippolytus of Rome commands, "If someone is a sculptor or a painter, let them be taught not to make idols. Either let them cease or let them be rejected."[78]

According to Frend, the second commandment forbidding Israel to make any graven image was accepted by Christian leaders in East and West alike, including Tertullian, Clement and Eusebius. The early Church showed rare unanimity in considering this prohibition absolute and binding on Christians. "The principal crime of the human race, the highest guilt charged upon the world, the whole procuring case of judgment, was idolatry."[79]

In the early third century, Origen tried to explain the tenacity with which the Christians followed this central doctrine:

Christians and Jews have regard to this command, "You shall fear the Lord your God, and serve Him alone;" and this other, "You shall have no other gods before Me: you shall not make unto you any graven image, or any likeness of anything that is in heaven above, or that is in the earth beneath, or that is in the water under the earth: you shall not bow down yourself to them, nor serve them;" and again, "You shall worship the Lord your God, and Him only shall you serve." It is in consideration of these and many other such commands, that they not only avoid temples, altars, and images, but are ready to suffer death when it is necessary, rather than debase by any such impiety the conception which they have of the Most High God (Origen, *Contra Celsum*, VII, 64).[80]

The third century Catholic theologian Arnobius confirms that his faith had no statues or images of any god, did not offer incense or libations of wine, slew no victims in sacrifice, and built no temples for ceremonies of worship. For this Christianity was often charged with impiety (atheism). In defense of his faith, Arnobius is harshly critical of pagan idolatry:

> We worship the gods, you say, by means of images. What then? Without these, do the gods not know that they are worshipped, and will they not think that any honour is shown to them by you? ... Those images which fill you with terror, and which you adore prostrate upon the ground in all the temples, are bones, stones, brass, silver, gold, clay, wood taken from a tree, or glue mixed with gypsum... Blush, then, even though it is late, and accept true methods and views from dumb creatures, and let these teach you that there is nothing divine in images, into which they do not fear or scruple to cast unclean things in obedience to the laws of their being, and led by their unerring instincts. (Arnobious, *Against the Heathen*)[81]

However, with the growing popularity of Christianity among pagans – especially after being appropriated by Constantine and his mother Helena – keeping the pagan practice of idolatry out of the movement became impossible. When Eusebius was asked for an image of the Savior by Constance, the sister of Constantine, he told her that painting holy images was a pagan custom.[82] He also told Empress Helena directly that "such images are forbidden by the Jewish law and should not be found in churches." He continues:

> Some poor woman brought me two painted figures like philosophers, and ventured to say that they represented Paul and the Saviour – I do not know on what ground. But to save her and others from offence, I took them from her and kept them by me, not thinking it right, in any case, that she should exhibit them further, that we may not seem idolaters to carry our God about with us.[83]

Constantine appointed his mother Helen as Augusta (Empress of the World), and gave her unlimited access to the imperial treasury in order to locate the relics of Judeo-Christian tradition.[84] She set out in the year 324AD with great zeal and fervor to build churches, to restore and adorn older ones and to find precious relics.[85] Around 405, images of saints and martyrs began to appear in the churches, which were to be worshiped. The adoration of the Virgin Mary was substituted for the worship of Venus and Diana.[86]

But the debate was not yet settled. In 599, Bishop Serenus of Marseille, shocked by the cult of images in his diocese, ordered their destruction. Pope Gregory (reigned 590-604) wrote him that he was correct to prevent their adoration, but should preserve them as "books for the illiterate."[87] For the general public, he reasoned, the stories of the gospels would be unapproachable without visuals.

The controversy reached its peak in 726 when Leo the Isaurian, Patriarch of Constantinople, issued his first edict against the veneration of images.[88] On one side of the debate were the Iconoclasts, also called "icon-smashers." They were suspicious of any art depicting God or humans and demanded the destruction of icons because they were forms of idolatry. On the other side were the Iconodules, or "venerators of icons." They defended the place of icons in the Church. It is worth pointing out that just prior to the iconoclast outbreak Muslim Caliph Yezid ordered the removal of all icons within his territory: the decisions regarding idolatry made by the Catholic Church may have been driven by the desire for Christianity to differentiate itself from Islam.

The controversy was more than just a struggle over different views of Christian art; in fact, it concerned the primary distinction between flesh and spirit that had always troubled Christian doctrine. Was matter, including the flesh, inherently evil (or at least distracting), compared to the glory of God? Could material components be used to reflect or reveal divine presence? What was the true meaning of Christian redemption and the salvation of the entire material universe? The answers to these questions were tied to the character of Christ's human nature.

Crucial to the discussion was the work of St. John of Damascus (759-826AD). Housed in Muslim-controlled lands and therefore outside the reach of the empire, he addressed the charges of the iconoclasts concerning the charges of idolatry:

Icons are not idols but symbols, therefore when an Orthodox venerates an icon, he is not guilty of idolatry. He is not worshipping the symbol, but merely venerating it. Such veneration is not directed toward wood, or paint or stone, but towards the person depicted. Therefore relative honor is shown to material objects, but worship is due to God alone.

We do not make obeisance to the nature of wood, but we revere and do obeisance to Him who was crucified on the Cross... When the two beams of the Cross are joined together I adore the figure because of Christ who was crucified on the Cross, but if the beams are separated, I throw them away and burn them. (St. John of Damascus)[89]

Icons were "open books to remind us of God." Those who lacked the time or learning to study theology needed only to enter a church to see the mysteries of the Christian religion unfold before them. Further, icons were necessary and essential because they protected the full and proper doctrine of the Incarnation. While God could not be represented in his eternal self, he could be depicted simply because he became human and took flesh; in so taking a material body, God proved that matter can be redeemed. He *deified* matter, making it spirit-bearing; and if flesh can be a medium for the Spirit, so can wood or paint, although in a different fashion:

I do not worship matter, but the Creator of matter, who for my sake became material and deigned to dwell in matter, who through matter effected my salvation.[90]

The seventh and last Ecumenical Council (which, like the first, was convened at Nicea) upheld the Iconodules' postion in 787AD. Icons, it was proclaimed, are to be kept in churches and honored with the same relative veneration as is shown to other material symbols, such as the "precious and life-giving Cross" and the Book of the Gospels. From 815 through 843AD Empress Theodora stamped out the attacks against icons permanently.

## Conclusions and Summary

This final chapter revealed that the history of the Church is a *human* history – as was demonstrated time and time-again by lack of consensus, political power struggles, and the elaborate definitions that were constructed and enforced (and sometimes later revoked) concerning divine matters; not to mention the many evils (persecutions, wars, genocide) done in the name of God under the protection of the Church. During nearly seven hundred years of disagreement, mostly concerning the divine and physical nature of Jesus Christ, a church doctrine was established for the Catholic Church – one which did not include the sects who refused the mantle of Rome.

Can the history and existence of the church prove that Jesus was historical? No – in fact it reveals that the theology regarding Jesus did not come from a historical founder but was the result of centuries of theological development, based on reaction to popular "heresies." The final result, rather than a clear and understandable vision of Jesus, is a walking impossibility and eternal mystery: a divine-but-human godman with two natures that are distinct but totally unified, two wills that are separate but always in agreement, two bodies that are flesh and not flesh, who has existed eternally but was begotten of God and born in the flesh.

There is a great deal more to the history of Christianity than I've briefly sketched; many revolutions, controversies, movements and beliefs. And there are excellent books that explore those movements in much more detail than this one. What I've attempted to show in this final chapter is a rough outline of the history of the literary Jesus; how the literature was developed, how the theology and doctrine was expanded, and why those beliefs in a historical founder actually survived. In short, the presence of the church, along with its 2,000 year phenomenon and continued existence today, although aided by its insistence on a historical Jesus, can be explained without one. This revelation allows us to confidently resolve the underpinning question of this book: Is Jesus Christ different from Harry Potter because he was historical? It can now be maintained that Jesus is only unique in that he is *claimed to be* historical. This is a crucial and fundamental distinction.

On the other hand, despite Christianity's early conflicts with paganism, heresies and schisms, from early times it began incorporating features of classical worship: celebration of the solstices, sacrifice, religious iconography, incense, candles, temples, and kneeling for prayer. By the Seventh Ecumenical Council, Christianity had become an different movement altogether from the faith for which the martyrs had been killed.

In this sense, we could argue that Christianity is the world's *greatest religion*: born in a period of unparalleled religious synthesis, fusing together the best of many centuries of spiritual wisdom, Christianity finally became everything to everybody. Like Hercules or Apollo, Jesus is the "light" of God, symbolized by a lion, who destroys "darkness" in the form of a serpent. Like the mysticism of the early mystery traditions, Jesus is the divine Logos, the Son of God living in us; who is also the tail of the serpent or the fallen women. Like Dionysus, Attis or Prometheus, Jesus is the suffering god who pays the sacrifice for our sins and releases us from death. Jesus can be portrayed, like Horus, as an infant God who rules "with his thumb in his mouth." Like the rituals of Osiris we search for the lost body parts of Jesus in the spring (in the form of eggs, representing new life), just before he is found and resurrected. Like Tammuz, we bring a pine tree into our homes each year, representing our savior's life cut short, but seeding the birth of a new savior born on Christmas day. Like Serapis, Jesus is both the infant and the father (hence he has no father and is considered to be "virgin-born"), whose mother and consort is a powerful goddess who is full of love and compassion. The success and popularity of the Christian movement cannot be traced to the "personality" of a historical founder, but rather in its completion and inclusion of already popular forms of spiritual worship.

# Final Conclusion

*"If the Jesus of faith is not also the Jesus of history, he's powerless and he's meaningess. Unless he's rooted in reality, unless he established his divinity by rising from the dead, he's just a feel-good symbol who's as irrelevant as Santa Claus" –Lee Strobel, The Case for Christ[1]*

Many people assume that by making the claim that Jesus was mythical it means I think he was worthless. That's not true at all; in the same sense, nobody would argue that Harry Potter is worthless just because he's a fictional character. People love Harry Potter – he's had a profound, meaningful and inspiring affect on the lives of countless children. Literature can be very edifying and should be praised as such. The story of Jesus Christ is robust, full of powerful spiritual and astrological symbolism, which can be appreciated on many levels. The same, however, cannot be said of the "history" of Jesus Christ, which is an outdated concept that may need to be relinquished.

Strobel's reaction to the claim that Jesus was not historical is the same (failed) attempt of the early church to justify the historical Jesus: if he was not historical, he would have been no different from other myths and fables. Ergo, he was a historical. Rather than evidence, it is based on the passionate belief and the experiential consequences of that belief. The true heart of the Christianity's attachment to a historical Jesus is this: If Jesus was not historical, he would be meaningless, and it is impossible for him to be meaningless, *because he is meaningful to me.* Therefore he is historical.

However, this way of thinking centers on the opinion that without a historical body, Jesus would be without meaning. Why does this have to be the case? Gnostics and many heretics refused to believe Jesus had a physical body, but still found him profoundly meaningful. Truthfully, to accept and appreciate Jesus Christ's literary legacy, very little about Christianity has to change. Christ's spiritual significance, importance, and active role as an ever-present moral guide could be maintained with much less conflict with reason or science. One could still believe in a Divine Being that, at the beginning of time, emptied itself in its creation, and that we are somehow mystically tied to this being. Most of the rituals could remain the same.

Jesus Christ could still serve as our higher self, our voice of reason and guidance, our intuition and goodness. This concept of Jesus would truly be eternal and universal: it has many names, and the expressions of its faith are as diverse as the world's many distinct cultures.

Moreover, just because something is a myth does not make it meaningless – in fact myths can be much more powerful than historical reality. Joseph Campbell claimed that the tendency to interpret mythology as history is one of the greatest failings of Christianity:

> Wherever the poetry of myth is interpreted as biography, history, or science, it is killed. The living images become only remote facts of a distant time or sky. Furthermore, it is never difficult to demonstrate that as science and history mythology is absurd. When a civilization begins to interpret its mythology in this way, the life goes out of it, temples become museums, and the link between the two perspectives is dissolved. Such a blight has certainly descended on the Bible and on a great part of the Christian cult.[2]

Rather than attempting to distinguish Jesus Christ from Harry Potter by referring to the non-proof that Jesus was *real,* a more profitable enterprise might be to analyze the two characters as literary influences and ask, which is *better*. In other words, in light of the discovery that claims of historicity cannot separate the literature of Jesus from Harry, the important thing to analyze is how the stories make people feel and act.

As a living spirit that is believed to be real and omnipresent, Jesus provides comfort and inspiration. He can also motivate his followers to great acts of charity and self-sacrifice. But as a "historical" savior, he creates dissension and conflict between various cultures and ideologies. Christ teaches suffering, meekness and humility; renounce this life and look forward to the next. Harry reminds us to embrace each small moment of happiness. Jesus says anything that happens is God's will: God is in control. Harry takes full responsibility for this world – God (Dumbledore) is dead, and there is no one else to stop the evil in the world except us. Also, while Jesus knew he would come back, and then live forever, Harry had no such hope; hence his sacrifice was much more courageous.

Religion provides comfort to get us through suffering, and endure pain and misfortune in hopes of a better afterlife. Literature like Harry Potter inspires us to stand up and fight against injustice. Jesus, as son of God and divine being, represents a level we can never reach. He is perfect, but we are sinners. He is not an example that we can model; he is the sun that makes us feel ashamed of our shadows.

Harry, in contrast, is fully human; he doubts, sins, expresses emotions, makes poor decisions, and he eventually makes the ultimate sacrifice – which importantly he had no desire to make. By his example we can compare ourselves, and through his mistakes we can recognize our own. His determination is an inspiration to us, through which we can learn that justice means taking action without guarantee, without a promise of salvation, without the support of a supernatural being that promises redemption. True ethics are not found in following law, but in making difficult decisions and being willing to act regardless of the consequences.

Most importantly, Harry Potter is popular in a way that Jesus is not. Harry Potter's movies have made billions, while Mel Gibson's *The Passion of the Christ* (2004) was disturbing, bloody and ultimately unsatisfying, riddled with the unresolved complexities in a system where the all powerful and all knowing God has to trick or deceive his creation, Satan. Harry's popularity is crucial – he is the gospel of our time; the best selling story. Yes, he is a repacking of the Jesus Christ story, but one that eclipses that story completely. While we can sift through Harry and trace back to Jesus, why would we? Harry is a much more humane, in depth, vibrant character than the Jesus of the gospels, infinitely easier to identify with, champion, and even love.

After 2,000 years, in a time of unparalleled technological and scientific advancement, when researchers have challenged the notion of an historical Jesus and logic conflicts with central tenets of Christian belief, the passion of Christ is still considered a historical fact by Christians and non-believers alike. Those who keep the faith continue to cling desperately to the historicity of Jesus rather than explore and appreciate his spiritual message.

In Mel Gibson's version, the story of Christ's Passion is repeated, full of human emotion, gore, grief, and touching kindnesses between strangers. Subtly reasserting the message of Christ's historicity are objects which will later become prize relics in Cathedrals throughout Europe; the cloth that caught an imprint of his face, the crown of thorns and the nails used on the cross, laid out and ready to be enshrined. This really happened, the story cries, and there is a surplus of evidence to prove it. The bloody figure of Jesus is triumphantly raised to life in the body, still bearing his wounds from the crucifixion, continually ignoring the obvious disadvantages of spending eternity in our physical bodies.

Like the early communities who strayed from Paul's teachings, Christians today maintain that Jesus was a historical man, who urged us to share his message and spread the good news. They are also wary of any investigation, whether rational or scientific, which may conflict with their beliefs. Finding solidarity with one another against those mysterious forces of evil that are seeking to disrupt, they inspire each other to keep believing, despite the criticism, despite the questions, despite reason.

Many Christian communities are also waiting, some a little too eagerly, for the end of the world. They are excited to receive their rewards, to be greeted by Jesus at the final judgment; excited to be proved right after all these years. Although Jesus says many times in the Bible that the kingdom of God is within them now, and not somewhere in the future, they rely on another passage, which reads, "I will be with you until the end of the age."

Usually assumed to mean that Jesus will be present until the end of time, the word "age" was an astrological concept that corresponded to one zodiac rotation caused by the precession of the equinoxes. 4,000 years ago Mithras conquered the age of Taurus by slaying a bull, initiating the age of Aries. 2,000 years ago Jesus slaughtered a lamb, and began the age of Pisces. The sun continues to burn, and the earth continues its annual orbit. For 2,000 years, the myth of Jesus Christ, the lamb of God, crucified for the sins of the world, has been mistakenly viewed as a historical figure.

Perhaps we are finally ready, after all this time, to remove the training wheels and appreciate the spiritual meaning of the Christian myth. Maybe we can move from milk to solid food. However, if we are going to start the story all over again, it is time to take down the lamb from the cross. The age of Pisces is ending. This time, we need to crucify a fish.

# About the Author

**Derek Murphy** is a writer and artist from Portland, Oregon, whose interest in Christian history began as a theology student on the Mediterranean island of Malta. His passion for religious history and existential realization has led him to the ancient megaliths of Europe, the pyramids of Egypt, the glaciers of the southern tip of Argentina, the catacombs of Rome, and the ruins Jordan, Cambodia and Thailand. He's now in Taiwan finishing his PhD in Comparative Literature and working on his second book.

# Spread the Word

*Who do you think Jesus was? Visit JPHC's website or Facebook page to follow the online discussion and share your opinion.*

This book is meant to generate discussion. You can affect the impact and direction of this discussion by posting your own review. If you liked this book, share your thoughts online and recommend the book to others. If you didn't like it, point out where I went wrong or what evidence I missed. Your comments will be helpful to the thousands of people who are also searching for the truth about the historical Jesus.

If you think this topic is important, please help us share it – visit the website (www.jesuspotterharrychrist.com) and Like, Digg, Tweet, or Stumble it.

**Please leave comments or feedback on Amazon.com.**

# Bibliography

Abbott, John. S. C. *Italy*. New York: P.F. Collier, 1882.

"Acts of Pilate." Translated by M.R. James *The Apocryphal New Testaments*. Reprint of the 1924 Oxford Clarendon Press edition, 1995. http://www.earlychristianwritings.com/text/gospelnicodemus.html.

Aeschylus. *Agamemnon*. Translated by E.D.A. Morshead. Reprint of 1909 Harvard Classics edition, Internet Classics Archive. http://classics.mit.edu/Aeschylus/agamemnon.html.

Allison, Dale C. *The Historical Christ and the Theological Jesus*. Grand Rapids, MI: Eerdmans, 2009.

Andréa, Hans. "Exploring the Spiritual Foundation of Harry Potter." *Harry Potter for Seekers,* http://harrypotterforseekers.com/alchemy.

Armstron, Karen. *The Bible: A Biography*. New York: Atlantic Monthly Press, 2007.

Arnold, Clinton E. *Ephesians Power and Magic*. Cambridge: Cambridge University Press, 1989.

Assmann, Jan. *Moses the Egyptian: The Memory of Egypt in Western Monotheism*. Cambridge: Harvard University Press, 1997.

Badiou, Alain. *Being and Event*. Translated by Oliver Feltham. New York: Continuum, 2005.

———. *St. Paul: The Foundation of Universalism*. Translated by Ray Brassier. Stanford, CA: Stanford University Press, 2003.

Billings, Bradly S. *Do This in Remembrance of Me: The Disputed Works in the Lukan Institution Narrative*. London: T&T Clark, 2006.

Bonnefoy, Yves. *Mythologies*. Translated under the direction of Wendy Doniger. Chicago: University of Chicago Press, 1992.

Bowie, A. M. *Aristophanes: Myth, Ritual and Comedy*. Cambridge: Cambridge University, 1993.

Bremmer, Jan N. *The Rise and Fall of the Afterlife*: The 1995 Read-Tuckwell Lectures at the University of Bristol. London: Routledge, 2002.

Brown, H.O.J. *Heresies: Heresy and Orthodoxy in the History of the Church*. Peabody, MA: Hendrickson, 1988.

Bulfinch, Thomas. *The Age of Fable*. New York: Airmont, 1965.

Bultmann, Rudolf. *History of the Synoptic Tradition*. San Francisco: Harper, 1976.

Burkert, Walter. *Ancient Mystery Cults*. Cambridge, MA: Harvard University Press, 1987.

———. *Greek Religion*. Translated by John Raffan. Cambridge, MA: Harvard University Press, 1985.

Campbell, Joseph. *The Hero With a Thousand Faces*. 3rd ed. Novato, CA: New World Library, 2008.

Carmichael, Joel. *The Birth of Christianity*. New York: Hippocrene Books, 1989.

Carpenter, Edward. *Pagan & Christian Creeds: Their Origin and Meaning*. New York: Harcourt, Brace and Howe, 1920. Digital reprint by NuVision Publications, 2007.

Case, Shirley Jackson. *The Mythical Christ of Radical Criticism*. Chicago: University of Chicago Press, 1912. http://www.christianorigins.com/case/ch2.html.

Celsus. *On the True Doctrine: A Discourse Against Christians*. Oxford: Oxford University, 1987.

Cooper, William Ricketts. *The Horus Myth in Its Relation to Christianity*. London: Hardwicke & Bogue, 1877.
http://books.google.com/books?id=EA4GAAAAQAAJ&pg=PA3&lpg=PA3&dq=horus+myth+in+its+relation+to+chri#v.

"Cúchulainn." *Wikipedia*. http://en.wikipedia.org/wiki/C%C3%BAchulainn.

Cumont, Franz. *The Mysteries of Mithra*. Chicago: Open Court, 1903.

Dawkins, Richard. *The God Delusion*. New York: Houghton Mifflin, 2006.

Deley, David W. "Solar Mythology and the Jesus Story." http://members.cox.net/deleyd/religion/solarmyth/christ2002.htm.

Detering, Hermann. *Der gefälschte Paulus: das Urchristentum im Zweilicht*. Düsseldorf: Patmos Press, 1995. Translated by Darrell J. Doughty and reprinted as "The Falsified Paul: Early Christianity in the Twilight." *The Journal of Higher Criticism*, 10 no. 2 (Fall 2003): 2–199. http://www.radikalkritik.de/FabricatedJHC.pdf.Page numbers refer to the English edition.

*Didache*. Translated by Alexander Roberts and James Donaldson. *Early*

*Christian Writings.* http://www.earlychristianwritings.com/text/didache-roberts.html.

Doane, T.W. *Bible Myths And Their Parallels In Other Religions: Being A Comparison Of The Old And New Testament Myths And Miracles With Those Of Heathen Nations Of Antiquity, Considering Also Their Origin And Meaning.* New York: Commonwealth, 1882. http://www.archive.org/details/biblemythsandthe00doanuoft.

Doherty, Earl. *The Jesus Puzzle.* Ottawa: Age of Reason, 2005.

Douglas, Tracy. "Harry Potter and the Goblet of Colonialism." In Goetz, *Phoenix Rising,* 280-292.

Dowden, Ken. *Religion and the Romans.* Classical World Series. London: Bristol Classical Press, 1992.

Dupuis, Charles Francois. *The Origin of All Religious Worship... Containing Also a Description of the Zodiac of Denderah.* New Orleans, 1872; Ann Arbor: University of Michigan Library, 2005. *MOA Digital Library.* http://name.umdl.umich.edu/ajf3298.0001.001.

Edelstein, Emma J. and Ludwig. *Asclepius.* Baltimore: John Hopkins University Press, 1945.

Eliade, Mircea. *The Sacred and the Profane: The Nature of Religion.* San Diego, CA: Harcourt, 1987.

Ellerbe, Hellen. *The Dark Side of Christian History.* San Raphael, CA: Morningstar Books, 1995.

Fear, A.T. "Cybele and Christ." In *Cybele, Attis & Related Cults: Studies in Memory of M.J. Vermaseren,* ed. Eugene N. Lane, 37–50. Leiden: Brill, 1996.

Frazer, James George. *The Golden Bough.* New York: Macmillan, 1956.

Freke, Timothy and Peter Gandy. *The Jesus Mysteries: Was the 'Original Jesus' a Pagan God.* New York: Three Rivers Press, 1999.

Frend, W.H.C. *The Rise of Christianity.* Philadelphia: Fortress Press, 1984.

Freud, Sigmund. *The Interpretation of Dreams.* New York: Avon Books, 1980.

Funk, Robert, et al. *The Five Gospels: What Did Jesus Really Say? The Search for the Authentic Words of Jesus.* New York: Macmillan, 1993.

Garrett, Greg. "Magic, Faith, and Belief In Harry Potter." *The Other Jesus: A Blog for the Other Christians,* http://theotherjesus.com/?p=233.

———. *One Fine Potion: The Literary Magic of Harry Potter.* Waco, TX:

Baylor University, 2010.

George, Andrew, trans. *The Epic of Gilgamesh: The Babylonian Epic Poem and Other Texts in Akkadian and Sumerian*. London: Penguin, 1999.

Gerberding, Richard and Jo Ann H. Moran Cruz. *Medieval Worlds: An Introduction to European History, 300–1494*. New York: Houghton Mifflin Company, 2004.

Gieseler, Johann C.L. [Karl Ludwig]. *A Text-book of Church History*. Vol. 1, *A.D. 1–726*. New York: Harper & Brothers, 1857.http://books.google.com/books?id=G7hAAAAAYAAJ&printsec.

Glover, T.R. *Conflict of Religions in the Early Roman Empire*. London: Methuen, 1909. Reprinted by Boston: Beacon, 1960.

Godwin, Joscelyn. *Mystery Religions in the Ancient World*. London: Thames and Hudson, 1981.

Goetz, Sharon K. *Phoenix Rising: Collected Papers on Harry Potter*. Sedalia, CO: Narrate Conferences, 2007.

Goguel, Maurice. *Jesus the Nazarene: Myth or History*. Translated by Frederick Stephens. London: T. Fisher Unwin, 1926. http://www.christianorigins.com/goguel/ch1.html.

Gordon, Cyrus H. and Gary A. Rendsburg. *The Bible and the Ancient Near East*. 4th ed. New York: W.W. Norton and Company, 1997.

Grant, Robert M. *Greek Apologists of the Second Century*. Philadelphia: Westminster, 1988.

Graves, Kersey. "All History Ignores Him." In *The World's Sixteen Crucified Saviours*. Reprint of the 1875 edition, Forgotten Books, 2007. http://books.google.com/books?id=9ysYffLU-mcC&pg=PA260&lpg=PA260&dq=Kersey+graves+all+history+ignores+him. Also: http://members.cox.net/solarmyth/appendixd3.htm.

———. "Preface." In *The World's Sixteen Crucified Saviour*s. http://www.infidels.org/library/historical.

Guthrie, W.K.C. *Orpheus and Greek Religion*. London: Methuen, 1952. Reprinted with a new preface by Larry J. Alderink. Princeton, NJ: Princeton, 1993.

Hamilton, Edith. *Mythology*. New York: Warner Books, 1999.

Hermann, Arnold. *To Think Like God: Pythagoras and Parmenides*. Las Vegas: Parmenides, 2004.

Hoehne, Marcia. "Letters the the Editor." *Christianity Today*. March 27,

2000.http:/www.christianitytoday.com.

Hotema, Hilton. *The Secret of Regeneration*. Life Science Institute, 1963.

Hurlbut, J.L. *The Story of the Christian Church*. Grand Rapids, MI: Zondervan, 1967.

Ignatius. "Epistle to the Philadelphians." *Early Christian Writings*. http://www.earlychristianwritings.com/text/ignatius-philadelphians-longer.html.

———. "Epistle to the Smyrnaeans." *Early Christian Writings*.

http://www.earlychristianwritings.com/text/ignatius-smyrnaeans-lightfoot.html.

———. "Epistle to the Tarsians." *New Advent*. http://newadvent.org/fathers/0114.htm.

"Infancy Gospel of Thomas." Translated by Alexander Roberts and James Donaldson. *Early Christian Writings*. http://www.earlychristianwritings.com/text/infancythomas-b-roberts.html.

Jabbar, Malik H. *The Astrological Foundation of the Christ Myth*. Dayton, OH: Rare Books Distributor, 1995.

Jacobsen, Thorkild. *The Treasures of Darkness: A History of Mesopotamian Religion*. New Haven, CT: Yale University Press, 1978.

Johari, Harish. *Chakras: Energy Centers of Transformation*. Rochester, VT: Desiny Books, 1987. http://www.sanatansociety.org/yoga_and_meditation/seven_chakras.htm.

Johnston, Sarah Iles. "Magic." Chapter in *Ancient Religions*, ed. Sarah Iles Johnston, 139–153. Cambridge, MA: Belknap Press of Harvard University Press, 2007.

Josephus. *Antiquities of the Jews*. Translated by William Whiston. *Project Gutenberg*. http://www.gutenberg.org/files/2848/2848-h/2848-h.htm.

———. *Wars of the Jews*. Translated by William Whiston. *Project Gutenberg*. http://www.gutenberg.org/files/2850/2850-h/2850-h.htm.

Jung, Carl Gustav. *The Archetypes and the Collective Unconscious*. Translated by R.F.C. Hull. Princeton, NJ: Princeton University Press, 1959.

———. *Civilization and Transition*. Translated by R.F.C. Hull. New York: Routledge, 1964.

Justin Martyr. *First Apology*. Translated byAlexander Roberts and James Donaldson. http://www.earlychristianwritings.com/text/justinmartyr-discourse.html.

Käsemann, Ernst. "The Problem with the Historical Jesus *Essays on New Testament Themes*. Translated by W.J. Montague. Philadelphia: Fortress Press, 1982.

Kerényi, Carl. [Karoly / Karl]. *Eleusis: Archetypal Image of Mother and Daughter*. Translated by Ralph Manheim. Bollingen Series 65, vol. 4. Reprinted, Mythos Series. New York: Bollingen Foundation, 1967. Reprinted by Princeton, NJ: Princeton University Press, 1991.

Killinger, John. *God, The Devil, and Harry Potter: A Christian Minister's Defense of the Beloved Novels*. New York: Thomas Dunne Books, 2002.

King, Stephen. "J.K. Rowling Ministry of Magic." *Entertainment Weekly*. August 10, 2007. http://www.ew.com/ew/article/0,,20050689,00.html.

Knight, Kevin. "Mithraism." *New Advent Catholic Encyclopedia*. http://www.newadvent.org/cathen/10402a.htm.

Kuhn, Alvin Boyd. *Who is This King of Glory? A Critical Study of the Christos-Messiah Tradition*. Elizabeth, NJ: Academy, 1944.

Laertius, Diogenes. "Pythagoras: The Lives and Opinions of Eminent Philosophers." Translated by C.D. Yonge. *Classic Persuasion*.

http://classicpersuasion.org/pw/diogenes/dlpythagoras.htm.

Larson, Jennifer. *Ancient Greek Cults: A Guide*. New York: Routledge, 2007.

Lee-Allen, Nancee. "Understanding Prejudice Utilizing the Harry Potter Series." In Goetz, *Phoenix Rising*, 350-353.

Leet, Leonora. *The Universal Kabalah: Deciphering the Cosmic Code in the Sacred Geometry of the Sabbath Star Diagram*. Rochester, VT: Inner Traditions, 2004.

Lewis, C.S. *God in the Dock: Essays on Theology and Ethics*. Grand Rapids, MI: Eerdmans, 1970.

———. *Mere Christianity*. O.C.R. December 12, 2003; revised July 1, 2005. http://www.lib.ru/LEWISCL/mere_engl.txt.

Littleton, C. Scott, ed. *Gods, Goddesses, and Mythology*. Tarrytown, NY: Marshall Cavendish: 2005.

http://books.google.com.tw/books?id=HC93q4gsOAwC&pg=PA1057&lpg #v=onepage&q&f=false

Logan, Mitchell. *The Christian Mythology Unveiled*. Whitefish, MT: Kessinger Publishing, 2004.

MacMullen, Ramsay. *Christianizing the Roman Empire: A.D. 100–400.* New Haven, CT: Yale University Press, 1984.

Massey, Gerald. "The Historical Jesus and the Mythical Christ." Gerald Massey's Lectures. http://www.hermetics.org/pdf/Gerald_Masseys_Lectures. pdf.

Mead, G.R.S. *Did Jesus Live 100BC? An Enquiry into the Talmud Jesus Stories, the Toldoth Jeschu, and Some Curious Statements of Epiphanius— Being a Contribution to the Study of Christian Origins.* London: Theosophical Publishing Society, 1903. http://www.christianorigins.com/mead/.

Medwin, Thomas. "Argument." In Aeschylus, *Prometheus Bound.* Translated by T. Medwin. London: William Pickering, 1832.http://books. google.com/books?id=6DoBAAAAMAAJ&pg.

Meyer, Marvin W. and Richard Smith. *Ancient Christian Magic: Coptic Texts of Ritual Power.* San Francisco: Harper San Francisco, 1994.

Minzesheimer, Bob. "10 Years of Best-Sellers." *USA Today.* March 10, 2004. Revised March 31, 2004. http://www.usatoday.com/lifedecade-main_x.htm.

Morford, Mark P.O. and Robert J. Lenardon. *Classical Mythology.* 8th ed. New York: Oxford University Press, 2007.

Mugglenet.com. "Biblical Symbolismin the World of Harry Potter." *Mugglenet.com.* November 28, 2004. http://www.mugglenet.comah01.shtml.

Mynott, Debbie. *Scholarly Studies in Harry Potter: Applying Academic Methods to a Popular Text.* http://www.amazon.co.uk/ Scholarly-Studies-Harry-Potter-Literature/dp/0773460101.

Neal, Connie. *What's a Christian to Do with Harry Potter?* Colorado Springs, CO: Waterbrook Press, 2001.

Neilson, Janet. "World Influences on Harry Potter from Asiatic Anti-Venoms to Zombies." Paper presented at Phoenix Rising, New Orleans, LA, May 17–21, 2007.

*New Jerusalem Bible.* London: Doubleday, 1989.

Newman, John Henry [Cardinal Newman]. *An Essay on the Development of Christian Doctrine.* London: James Toovey, 1945. http://books.google.com/ books?id=yE47AAAAYAAJ&printsec.

Nigg, Walter. *The Heretics: Heresy Through the Ages.* New York: Dorset Press, 1962.

Noel-Smith, Kelly. "Harry Potter's Oedipal Issues." *Psychoanalytic Studies 3* (2001): 199-207.

O'Rahilly, Cecile, trans. and ed. *Táin Bó Cúalnge from the Book of Leinster*. Dublin: Institute for Advanced Studies, 1970.

Origen. "Contra Celsum." Translated by Frederick Crombie. *The Ante-Nicene Fathers*. Vol. 4, *Tertullian (IV), Minucius Felix, Commodian, Origen*. Buffalo, NY: Christian Literature, 1885. Revised and edited for New Advent by Kevin Knight. http://www.newadvent.org/fathers/04166.htm.

Ovid. *The Metamorphoses*. Translated by Horace Gregory. New York: Viking Press, 1958.

Pagels, Elaine. *The Gnostic Gospels*. New York: Random House, 1979.

Pearse, Roger. "Mithras: All The Passages in Ancient Texts That Refer to the Cult." 'Nonnus', Comm. in Greg. Nazian. http://www.tertullian.org/rpearse/Mithras/index.htm.

Perkins, Pheme. *Gnosticism and the New Testament*. Minneapolis, MN: Augsburg Fortress, 1993.

Perrin, Norman. *Rediscovering the Teaching of Jesus*. New York: Harper & Row, 1967.

Placher, William C. *Readings in the History of Christian Theology. Vol. 1, From Its Beginnings to the Eve of the Reformation*. Philadelphia: Westminster, 1988.

Plato. *Phaedo*. Translated by Benjamin Jowett. *Project Gutenberg*. http://www.gutenberg.org/files/1658/1658-h/1658-h.htm.

"Polycarp: A Relevant Testimony for our Lives." *All About Religion*. http://www.allaboutreligion.org/polycarp.htm.

"Pseudo-ClementineLiterature." *Ante-Nicene Fathers, Vol VIII*. http://www.sacred-texts.com/chr/ecf/008/index.htm.

Roberts, MarkD. "How Can We Know Anything About the Real Jesus?" http://www.markdroberts.com/htmfiles/resources/knowaboutjesus.htm.

Robertson, Noel. "Orphic Mysteries and Dionysiac Ritual." In *Greek Mysteries: The Archaeology and Ritual of Ancient Greek Secret Cults*, ed. by Michael B. Cosmopoulos, 218–240. London: Routledge, 2003.

Robinson, James M. *The Nag Hammadi Library*. New York: Harper & Row, 1977.

Roob, Alexander. *Alchemy and Mysticism*. Italy: Taschen, 1996.

Rothfuss, Patrick. "Let's Not Play Find-the-Jesus." *Belief Net*. July 27, 2007. http://blog.beliefnet.com/blogalogue/2007/07/harry-potter-fans

Rothschild, Clare K. *Luke-Acts and the Rhetoric of History*. Tubingen, Germany: Mohr Siebeck, 2004.

Rowling, J.K. *Harry Potter and the Sorcerer's Stone*. New York: Scholastic, 1998.

———. *Harry Potter and the Chamber of Secrets*. New York: Scholastic, 1999.

———. *Harry Potter and the Prisoner of Azkaban*. New York: Scholastic, 1999.

———. *Harry Potter and the Goblet of Fire*. New York: Scholastic, 2000.

———. *Harry Potter and the Order of Phoenix*. New York: Scholastic, 2004.

———. *Harry Potter and the Half Blood Prince*. New York: Scholastic, 2005.

———. *Harry Potter and the Deathly Hallows*. New York: Scholastic, 2007.

Russell, Bertrand. *Why I Am Not a Christian*. 1927. Reprinted in *Why I Am Not a Christian and Other Essays* by Paul Edwards. New York, 1957. http://users.drew.edu/~jlenz/whynot.html.

S., Acharya [D.M. Murdock]. *Suns of God: Krishna, Buddha and Christ Unveiled*. Kempton, IL: Adventures Unlimited, 2004.

———. "The Origins of Christianity and The Quest for the Historical Jesus Christ." http://www.truthbeknown.com/origins2.htm.

———. "The Jesus Forgery: Josephus Untangled." http://www.truthbeknown.com/josephus.htm.

"Sappho, Poems of." Translated by Julia Dubnoff. http://www.uh.edu/~cldue/texts/sappho.html.

Scholasticus, Socrates. *The Ecclesiastical History*. Edited by A. C. Zenos. http://www.sacred-texts.com/chr/ecf/202/2020100.htm.

Seaford, Richard. *Dionysus*. New York: Routledge, 2006.

Segal, Robert A. *Jung on Mythology*. London: Routledge, 1998.

Shu-P'Ing Teng. "The Original Significance Of *Bi* Disks: Insights Based On Liangzhu Jade *Bi* With Incised Symbolic Motifs." *Journal of East Asian Archaeology* 2, no. 1-2 (2000): 165-94.

Sindel-Arrington, Tricia. "Gothic Harry: Connecting to Teens' Self-Discovery Journeys." Paper presented at Phoenix Rising, New Orleans, LA, May 17–21, 2007.

Stopple, Jeffrey. *A Primer of Analytic Number Theory: From Pythagoras to*

*Riemann*. Cambridge: Cambridge University Press, 2003.

Strobel, Lee. *The Case for Christ*. Grand Rapids, Michigan: Zondervan, 1998.

Stucky, Mark D. *Middle Earth's Messianic Mythology Remixed*. http://www.usask.ca/relst/jrpc/art13-middleearthmyth.html.

Tacitus. "Annals." *Perseus*. http://www.perseus.tufts.edu/cgi-bin/ptext?doc =Perseus:text:1999.02.0078&loc=15.44.

*Táin Bó Cúalnge from the Book of Leinster*. Translated and edited by Cecile O'Rahilly. Dublin: Institute for Advanced Studies, 1970.

Tarbox, Gwen A. "J. K. Rowling's Narrative Turn: *Harry Potter* and 'The War on Terror.'" Paper presented at Phoenix Rising, New Orleans, LA, May 17–21, 2007.

Taylor, Robert. *The Diegesis*. Boston: Abner Kneeland, 1834. Kessinger, 1992.

Tertullian. *Prescription Against Heretics*. Translated by PeterHolmes. *Ante-Nicene Fathers*. Vol. 3, *Tertullian*. Buffalo, NY: Christian Literature Publishing Co., 1885. Revised and edited for New Advent by Kevin Knight. http://www.newadvent.org/fathers/0311.htm.

Theissen, Gerd and Dagmar Winter. *The Search for the Plausible Jesus*. Translated by M. Eugene Boring. Louisville, KY: Westminster John Knox, 2002.

*Time Magazine*. "The New Search for The Historical Jesus." June 21, 1963. http://www.time.com/time/magazine/article/0,9171,874918,00.html.

Trigilio, John, and Kenneth Brighenti. *The Catholicism Answer Book: The 300 Most Frequently Asked Questions*. Naperville, IL: Sourcebooks, 2007.

Turcan, Robert. *The Gods of Ancient Rome*. Translated by Antonia Nevill. Edinburgh: Edinburgh University Press, 2000.

Vermaseren, M. J. *Mithras, The Secret God*. Translated by Therese and Vincent Magaw. London: Chatto and Windus, 1963.

Wallace, Daniel. "The Synoptic Problem." http://bible.org/article/ synoptic-problem.

Wasson, R. Gordon, Albert Hofmann, and Carl A. P. Ruck. *Road to Eleusis: Unveiling the Secret of the Mysteries*. New York: Harcourt Brace Jovanovich, 1978. http://www.telesterion.com/roadto.htm.

Watkins, Jon. "Harry Potter, a New Twist to Witchcraft." *Exposing Satanism* http://www.exposingsatanism.org/harrypotter.htm.

White, L. Michael. *From Jesus to Christianity: How Four Generations of Visionaries & Storytellers Created the New Testament and Christian Faith.* San Francisco: HarperCollins, 2004.

Williams, Rita. *Satanism in Harry Potter Books.* http://www.cephasministry.com/save_our_children_harry_potter_booklet.html.

Witt, R.E. *Isis in the Ancient World.* Baltimore: John Hopkins University Press, 1971.

Wright, Wilmer Cave. "Introduction to *Against the Galileans.*" In *The Works of the Emperor Julian* with an English translation by Wilmer Cave Wright, 313–317. London: Heinemann, 1923. http://www.archive.org/stream/workswithenglish03juliuoft.

"Why We Like Harry Potter." *Christianity Today.* 10 Jan. 2000. http://www.ctlibrary.com/ct/2000/january10/29.37.html.

# Index

<br>

# Notes

## Chapter One

1. "J.K. Rowling Biography." J.K. Rowling Official Site - Harry Potter and more. http://www.jkrowling.com/textonly/en/biography.cfm (accessed February 5, 2011).
2. Stephen King, "J.K. RowlingMinistry of Magic," *Entertainment Weekly*, August 10, 2007, http://www.ew.com/ew/article/0,,20050689,00.html, emphasis in the original.
3. Tracy Douglas, "Harry Potter and the Goblet of Colonialism," in *Phoenix Rising: Collected Papers on "Harry Potter," 17–21 May 2007*, ed. Sharon K. Goetz (Sedalia, Colorado: Narrate Conferences, 2008), 280–92.
4. Gwen A. Tarbox, "J. K. Rowling's Narrative Turn: *Harry Potter* and 'The War on Terror'" (paper, Phoenix Rising, New Orleans, LA, May 17–21, 2007).
5. Nancee Lee-Allan, "Understanding Prejudice Utilizing the Harry Potter Series," in Goetz, *Phoenix Rising*, 350–54.
6. Tricia Sindel-Arrington, "Gothic Harry: Connecting to Teens' Self-Discovery Journeys" (paper, Phoenix Rising, New Orleans, LA, May 17–21, 2007).
7. Janet Neilson, "World Influences on Harry Potter from Asiatic Anti-Venoms to Zombies" (paper, Phoenix Rising, New Orleans, LA, May 17–21, 2007).
8. Quoted in Jaime Bates, "'Hogwarts Professor' to Lecture on Harry Potter and the Christian Faith," Baylor University, news release, September 18, 2008, accessed January 9, 2011, http://www.baylor.edu/pr/news.php?action=story&story=52844.
9. Cynthia Whitney Hallett, *Scholarly Studies in Harry Potter: Applying Academic Methods to a Popular Text* (Lewiston, New York: Edwin Mellen, 2005).
10. Cited by M. O. Grenby, review of *Scholarly Studies in Harry Potter*, by C.H. Hallett, Amazon web page, accessed January 9, 2011, http://www.amazon.com/Scholarly-Studies-Harry-Potter-Literature/dp/0773460101.
11. Guy Dammann, "Harry Potter Breaks 400m in Sales," *The Guardian*, June 18, 2008, http://www.guardian.co.uk/books/2008/jun/18/harrypotter.news.
12. Jonathan Zimmerman, "Harry Potter and His Censors," *Education Week*, August 2, 2000, http://www.edweek.org/ew/articles/2000/08/02/43zimmer.h19.html?qs=august+2+2000+harry+potter (accessed February 5, 2011).
13. "Harry Potter Books Spark Rise in Satanism Among Children," *The Onion*, July 26, 2000, http://www.theonion.com/articles/harry-potter-books-spark-rise-in-satanism-among-ch,2413/ (accessed February 5, 2011).
14. As seen on CNN.com and BBC.com news.
15. Domenic Marando, "*Harry Potter*: The Warnings," *Everyday For Life Canada: A Blog on Canadian Life, Family and Cultural Issues*, October 28, 2010, http://everydayforlifecanada.blogspot.com/2010/10/harry-potter-warnings.html.
16. Robert S. McGee and Caryl Matrisciana, *Harry Potter: Witchcraft Repackaged; Making Evil Look Innocent* (Menifee, CA: Jeremiah Films and Caryl Productions,

2001).

17. "Emergency JESUS YOUTH Memo Regarding Release of Half-Blood Prince—July 2009," *The Landrover Baptist Church*, accessed January 9, 2011, http://www.landoverbaptist.org/news1199/potter.html.

18. Domenic Marando, "Harry Potter, the Occult Controversy," *Everyday For Life Canada*, October 24, 2010, http://everydayforlifecanada.blogspot.com/2010/10/harry-potter-occult-controversy.html.

19. Judy Blume, "Is Harry Potter Evil?" Op-Ed, *New York Times*, Oct 22, 1999, http://www.judyblume.com/censorship/potter.php (accessed February 5, 2011).

20. Connie Neal, *What's a Christian to Do with Harry Potter?* (Colorado Springs, CO: Waterbrook Press, 2001), 88. The emphasis is original.

21. Michael D. O'Brien, preface to *Harry Potter and the Paganization of Culture* (Rzeszow, Poland: Fides et Traditio, 2010); February 10, 2010, http://www.studiobrien.com/writings_on_fantasy/preface-to-harry-potter.html.

22. Alison Lentini, "Harry Potter: Occult Cosmology and the Corrupted Imagination," quoted in Connie Neal, *What's a Christian to Do*, 24.

23. Alan Jacobs, "Harry Potter's Magic," quoted in Connie Neal, *What's a Christian to Do*, 22.

24. Jon Watkins, "Harry Potter, a New Twist to Witchcraft," *Exposing Satanism*, accessed January 11, 2011, http://www.exposingsatanism.org/harrypotter.htm.

25. Richard Abanes, quoted in John Killinger, *God, The Devil, and Harry Potter: A Christian Minister's Defense of the Beloved Novels* (New York: Thomas Dunne Books, 2002), 3.

26. Linda Beam, quoted in Connie Neal, *What's a Christian to Do*, 165.

27. Connie Neal, *What's a Christian to Do*, 172-173.

28. "Editorial: Why We Like Harry Potter," *Christianity Today*, January 10, 2000, http://www.christianitytoday.com/ct/2000/january10/29.37.html.

29. John Killinger, *God The Devil, and Harry Potter*, 11.

30. Connie Neal, *What's a Christian to Do*, 119.

31. Quoted in Connie Neal, *What's a Christian to Do*, 121.

32. Chuck Colson, "Witches and Wizards: The Harry Potter Phenomenon," quoted in Connie Neal, *What's a Christian to Do*, 16.

33. Connie Neal, *What's a Christian to Do*, 176.

34. John Killinger, *God, The Devil, and Harry Potter*, 50.

35. John Killinger, *God, The Devil, and Harry Potter*, 11.

36. John Killinger, *God, The Devil, and Harry Potter*, 35.

37. Trudy Ardizzone, "Wizards and Wonders: Introduction and Sample Session," accessed December 28, 2010, http://leaderresources.org/downloads/A-All_Samples/Wizards_and_Wonders.pdf.

38. Quoted in Michael Paulson, "Harry Potter and the Admiring Faithful," Opinion, Sunday Commentary, *Dallas Morning News*, August 28, 2009, http://www.dallasnews.com/sharedcontent/dws/dn/opinion/points/stories/DN-paulson_30edi.State.Edition1.2385323.html.

39. The article by Michael Paulson is available for purchase at http://www.boston.com/bostonglobe/ideas/articles/2009/08/16/how_the_boy_wizard_won_over_

religious_critics/?page=full. A version of the article can be viewed at the *Dallas News* website in the preceding note.

40. Mary E. Hess, "Resisting the Human Need for Enemies, or What Would Harry Potter Do?" *Word and World: Theology for Christian Ministry* 28/1 (2008) 47-56; quoted by Michael Paulson in the *Dallas Morning News* article noted above.

41. Greg Garrett, *One Fine Potion: The Literary Magic of Harry Potter* (Waco, TX: Baylor University, 2010).

42. Jana Riess, "Harry Potter, Christian Hallows, and C.S. Lewis: A Q&A with Greg Garrett," Flunking Sainthood, October 6, 2010, http://blog.beliefnet.com/flunkingsainthood/2010/10/harry-potter-christian-hallows-and-cs-lewis-a-qa-with-greg-garrett.html.

43. Ernest Tucker, "No End in Sight for Pottermania," *Chicago Sun-Times*, October 22, 1999, http://www.accio-quote.org/articles/1999/1099-chictimes-tucker.html.

44. Max Wyman, "'You Can Lead a Fool to a Book But You Can't Make Them Think': Author Has Frank Words for the Religious Right," *Vancouver Sun* (British Columbia), October 26, 2000, http://www.accio-quote.org/articles/2000/1000-vancouversun-wyman.htm (accessed February 5, 2011).

45. Abigail BeauSeigneur, "Is Harry Potter the Son of God?" July 13, 2007, http://www.mugglenet.com/editorials/editorials/edit-beauseigneura01.shtml.

46. J.K. Rowling, interview, *TodayShow/Dateline NBC*,NBC, July 29, 2007, http://www.the-leaky-cauldron.org/books/postdh.

47. Auslan Cramb, "Harry Potter is 'Christ-like' Claims Theologian," *Telegraph,* October 24, 2010, http://www.telegraph.co.uk/culture/harry-potter/8083870/Harry-Potter-is-Christ-like-claims-theologian.html.

48. Celsus, *On the True Doctrine: A Discourse Against Christians* (Oxford: Oxford University Press, 1987), http://www.earlychristianwritings.com/text/origen161.html.

49. The Ante-Nicene Fathers, Volume VIII, Pseudo-Clementine Literature, The Clementine Homilies, Homily II, Ch. XXXII, http://en.wikisource.org/wiki/Ante-Nicene_Fathers/Volume_VIII/Pseudo-Clementine_Literature/The_Clementine_Homilies/Homily_II/Chapter_32.

50. Homily II, Ch. XXV, http://en.wikisource.org/wiki/Ante-Nicene_Fathers/Volume_VIII/Pseudo-Clementine_Literature/The_Clementine_Homilies/Homily_II/Chapter_25.

51. Amanda, "Biblical Symbolismin the World of Harry Potter," November 24, 2004, http://www.mugglenet.com/editorials/editorials/edit-amandah01.shtml.

52. Jeff Diamant, "The Gospel According to Rowling," *Star,* July 14 2007, http://www.thestar.com/Religion/article/235813 (accessed February 5, 2011).

53. Quoted in Hans Andréa, "Exploring the Spiritual Foundation of Harry Potter," *Harry Potter for Seekers,* accessed November 4, 2009, http://harrypotterforseekers.com/alchemy

54. Hans Andréa, http://harrypotterforseekers.com/index.php.

55. Hans Andréa, "Alchemy," accessed January 11, 2011, http://www.harrypotterforseekers.com/alchemy/alchemy.php.

56. John Killinger in "Harry Potter, Christ Figure?" a discussion, accessed January 11, 2011, http://www.beliefnet.com/Entertainment/Books/2002/11/Harry-Potter-Christ-Figure.aspx.
57. John Killinger, *God, The Devil, and Harry Potter,* 14.
58. Thomas L. Martin in "Harry Potter, Christ Figure?" a discussion, accessed January 11, 2011, http://www.beliefnet.com/Entertainment/Books/2002/11/Harry-Potter-Christ-Figure.aspx.
59. Andrew Blake in "Harry Potter, Christ Figure?"
60. Richard Abanes in "Harry Potter, Christ Figure?"
61. Patrick Rothfuss in "Harry Potter, Christ Figure?"

## Chapter Two

1. Robert Taylor, *The Diegesis,* facs. ed. (Boston: Abner Kneeland, 1834; Kessinger,1992), 254.
2. T.R. Glover, *Conflict of Religions in the Early Roman Empire* (London: Methuen, 1909; rpt. Boston: Beacon, 1960), 146
3. Quoted in Timothy Freke and Peter Gandy, *The Jesus Mysteries: Was the 'Original Jesus' a Pagan God* (New York: Three Rivers Press, 1999), 27.
4. Justin Martyr, *First Apology,* trans. Alexander Roberts and James Donaldson, http://www.earlychristianwritings.com/text/justinmartyr-discourse.html.
5. R.E. Witt, *Isis in the Ancient World* (Baltimore: John Hopkins University Press, 1971), 267.
6. Maurice Goguel, *Jesus the Nazarene: Myth or History,* trans. Frederick Stephens (London: T. Fisher Unwin, 1926), 14, http://www.christianorigins.com/goguel/ch1.html.
7. Charles François Dupuis, *The Origin of All Religious Worship* (New Orleans, 1872; Ann Arbor: University of Michigan Library, 2005), 251, *MOA Digital Library,* http://name.umdl.umich.edu/ajf3298.0001.001.
8. Maurice Goguel, *Jesus the Nazarene,* 15.
9. Shirley Jackson Case, *The Mythical Christ of Radical Criticism* (Chicago: University of Chicago Press, 1912), 33, http://www.christianorigins.com/case/ch2.html.
10. L. Michael White, *From Jesus to Christianity* (San Francisco: HarperCollins, 2004), 101.
11. Maurice Goguel, *Jesus the Nazarene,* 16.
12. Bruno Bauer, *Christ and the Caesars: The Origin of Christianity from Romanized Greek Culture* (Christus und die Caesaren, 1877), trans. Frank E. Schacht (Charleston, SC: A. Davidonis, 1998).
13. Hermann Detering, "The Falsified Paul: Early Christianity in the Twilight," in *The Journal of Higher Criticism,* 10 no. 2 (Fall 2003):47, http://www.radikalkritik.de/FabricatedJHC.pdf.
14. Kersey Graves, *The World's Sixteen Crucified Saviors: Christianity Before Christ,* 9, http://www.infidels.org/library/historical/kersey_graves/16/.
15. William Ricketts Cooper, *The Horus Myth in its Relation to Christianity* (London:

Hardwicke & Bogue, 1877), 49, http://books.google.com/books?id=EA4GAAAAQ
AAJ&pg=PA3&lpg=PA3&dq=horus+myth+in+its+relation+to+chri#v.

16. Gerald Massey, "The Historical Jesus and the Mythical Christ," Gerald Massey's Lectures, accessed January 11, 2011, http://www.hermetics.org/pdf/Gerald_Masseys_Lectures.pdf.

17. Shirley Jackson Case, *The Mythical Christ of Radical Criticism*, 43.

18. Shirley Jackson Case, *The Mythical Christ of Radical Criticism*, 41.

19. Goguel, *Jesus the Nazarene*, 28.

20. R. Bultmann, *Jesus and the World*, (1926; ET New York: Scribners, 1935) 8.

21. Bertrand Russell, *Why I Am Not a Christian* (1927; rpt. in *Why I Am Not a Christian and Other Essays*, ed. Paul Edwards [New York, 1957]), http://users.drew.edu/~jlenz/whynot.html.<http://users.drew.edu/~jlenz/whynot.html.

22. Robert A. Segal, *Jung on Mythology* (London: Routledge, 1998), 4.

23. Sigmund Freud, *The Interpretation of Dreams* (New York: Avon Books, 1980), 296.

24. Kelly Noel-Smith, "Harry Potter's Oedipal Issues," *Psychoanalytic Studies* (2001)3: 199-207.

25. Jan Assmann, *Moses the Egyptian: The Memory of Egypt in Western Monotheism* (Cambridge: Harvard, 1997), 167.

26. Carl Gustav Jung, *The Archetypes and the Collective Unconscious*, trans. R.F.C. Hull (Princeton, NJ: Princeton University Press, 1959), 154.

27. Robert A. Segal, *Jung on Mythology*, 14.

28. Carl Gustav Jung, *Civilization and Transition*, trans. R.F.C. Hull (New York: Routledge, 1964), 265.

29. Quoted in Robert A. Segal, *Jung on Mythology*, 38.

30. Joseph Campbell, *The Hero With a Thousand Faces* ed. (Novato, CA: New World Library, 2008), 197–98.

31. C.S. Lewis, *God in the Dock: Essays on Theology and Ethics* (Grand Rapids, MI: Eerdmans, 1970), 66-67.

32. Rudolph Bultmann, *The History of the Synoptic Tradition* (1921; trans. and rpt. San Francisco: Harper, 1976), 71.

33. Ernst Käsemann, "The Problem with the Historical Jesus *Essays on New Testament Themes*, trans. W.J. Montague (Philadelphia: Fortress Press, 1982), 36-37.

34. Norman Perrin, *Rediscovering the Teaching of Jesus* (New York: Harper & Row, 1967), 43.

35. Gerd Theissen and Dagmar Winter, *The Search for the Plausible Jesus*, trans. M. Eugene Boring (Louisville, KY: Westminster John Knox, 2002).

36. "The New Search for The Historical Jesus," *Time Magazine*, June 21, 1963, http://www.time.com/time/magazine/article/0,9171,874918-1,00.html.

37. Dale C. Allison, *The Historical Christ and the Theological Jesus* (Grand Rapids, MI: Eerdmans, 2009).

38. McKnight, Scot. "The Jesus We'll Never Know." *Christianity Today*, 9 Apr. 2010. http://www.christianitytoday.com/ct/2010/april/15.22.html.

39. McKnight, Scot. "The Jesus We'll Never Know." *Christianity Today*, 9 Apr. 2010. http://www.christianitytoday.com/ct/2010/april/15.22.html.

40. Acharya S [D.M. Murdock], "The Origins of Christianity and the Quest for the Historical Jesus Christ," http://www.truthbeknown.com/origins.htm.

**Chapter Three**

1. Lee Strobel, *The Case for Christ* (Grand Rapids, Michigan: Zondervan, 1998), 99.
2. Richard Dawkins, *The God Delusion* (New York: Houghton Mifflin, 2006), 94.
3. *Drive Thru History with Dave Stotts*, (Palmer Lake, CO: Coldwater Media, 2005), http://www.allaboutreligion.org/polycarp-video.htm.
4. W.H.C. Frend, *The Rise of Christianity* (Philadelphia: Fortress Press, 1984), 138.
5. W.K.C. Guthrie, *Orpheus and Greek Religion* (London: Methuen, 1952; rpt. Princeton, NJ: Princeton, 1993), 3.
6. Walter Burkert, *Ancient Mystery Cults* (Cambridge, MA: Harvard University Press, 1987), 53.
7. Bertrand Russell, *Why I Am Not a Christian*, http://users.drew.edu/~jlenz /whynot.html.
8. Alvin Boyd Kuhn, *Who is This King of Glory? A Critical Study of the Christos-Mesiah Tradition* (Elizabeth, NJ: Academy, 1944), 258–59.
9. Acharya S. [D.M. Murdock], "The Jesus Forgery: Josephus Untangled," http://www.truthbeknown.com/josephus.htm.
10. Mitchell Logan, *Christian Mythology Unveiled* (1842; rpt. Whitefish, MT: Kessinger Publishing, 2004), 79.
11. T.W. Doane, "Appendix D," in *Bible Myths And Their Parallels In Other Religions* (New York: Commonwealth,1882), 564-568, http://www.archive.org/details/biblemythsandthe00doanuoft.
12. (*Jesus of Nazareth, King of the Jews*, page 249)
13. Quoted in Acharya S. [D.M. Murdock], "The Jesus Forgery: Josephus Untangled," http://www.truthbeknown.com/josephus.htm.
14. Jan Assmann, *Moses the Egyptian*, 43.
15. T.W. Doane, "Appendix D," in *Bible Myths And Their Parallels*, 566 n. 1.
16. Kersey Graves, "All History Ignores Him," in *The World's Sixteen Crucified Saviours* (Reprint of the 1875 edition, Forgotten Books, 2007) 260, http://books.google.com/books?id=9ysYffLU-mcC&pg=PA260&lpg=PA260&dq=Kersey+graves+all+history+ignores+him
17. G.R.S. Mead, *Did Jesus Live 100BC?* (London: Theosophical Publishing Society, 1903), 48, http://www.christianorigins.com/mead/ch3.html.
18. Mark D. Roberts, "How Can We Know Anything About the Real Jesus?" http://www.markdroberts.com/htmfiles/resources/knowaboutjesus.htm.
19. Gordon and Rendsburg, *The Bible and the Ancient Near East*, 4th ed. (New York: W.W. Norton, 1997), 48.
20. Cyrus H. Gordon and Gary A. Rendsburg, *The Bible and the Ancient Near East*, 50.
21. Gordon and Rendsburg, *The Bible and the Ancient Near East*, 78.
22. Karen Armstrong, *The Bible: A Biography* (New York: Atlantic Monthly Press, 2007), 5.
23. Robert Funk, et al. *The Five Gospels: What Did Jesus Really Say? The Search for the*

*Authentic Words of Jesus* (New York: Macmillan, 1993).

24. Daniel Wallace, "The Synoptic Problem," http://bible.org/article/synoptic-problem.
25. W.H.C. Frend, *The Rise of Christianity*, 243.
26. *Didache*, 44, http://www.earlychristianwritings.com/text/didache-roberts.html.
27. W.H.C. Frend, *The Rise of Christianity*, 137.
28. Hermann Detering, "The Falsified Paul," 43.
29. W.H.C. Frend, *The Rise of Christianity*, 136.
30. Karen Armstrong, *The Bible*, 68.
31. Karen Armstrong, *The Bible*, 68.
32. *Didache*, 45.
33. *Didache*, 46–47.
34. Karen Armstrong, *The Bible*, 66.
35. *Didache*, 48.
36. W.H.C. Frend, *The Rise of Christianity*, 135.
37. Quoted in Lee Strobel, *The Case for Christ*, 40.
38. C.H. Dodd (b.1884; d.1993); quoted in W.H.C. Frend, *The Rise of Christianity*, 55.
39. Richard Dawkins, *The God Delusion* (New York: Houghton Mifflin, 2006), 253.
40. W.H.C. Frend, *The Rise of Christianity*, 25.
41. W.H.C. Frend, *The Rise of Christianity*, 28.
42. Quoted in T.R. Glover, *Conflict of Religions in the Early Roman Empire* (London: Methuen, 1909; rpt. Boston: Beacon, 1960), 50.
43. W.H.C. Frend, *The Rise of Christianity*, 29.
44. Quoted in T.R. Glover, *Conflict of Religions*, 61-63.
45. W.H.C. Frend, *The Rise of Christianity*, 55.
46. Elaine Pagels, *The Gnostic Gospels* (New York: Random House, 1979), xxii – xxiii.
47. W.H.C. Frend, *The Rise of Christianity*, 282.
48. W.H.C. Frend, *The Rise of Christianity*, 160.
49. Cited in T.R. Glover, *Conflict of Religions*, 299.
50. W.H.C. Frend, *The Rise of Christianity*, 210.
51. W.H.C. Frend, *The Rise of Christianity*, 216.
52. W.H.C. Frend, *The Rise of Christianity*, 217.
53. W.H.C. Frend, *The Rise of Christianity*, 230.
54. W.H.C. Frend, *The Rise of Christianity*, 202.
55. W.H.C. Frend, *The Rise of Christianity*, 203.
56. W.H.C. Frend, *The Rise of Christianity*, 160.
57. Detering, "The Falsified Paul," 159.
58. Greg Garrett, "Magic, Faith, and Belief In Harry Potter," *The Other Jesus: A Blog for the Other Christians*, http://theotherjesus.com/?p=233.

**Chapter Four**

1. Cecile O'Rahilly, trans. and ed., *Táin Bó Cúalnge from the Book of Leinster* (Dublin: Institute for Advanced Studies, 1970), 82-84.
2. Sir James George Frazer, *The Golden Bough* (New York: Macmillan, 1956), 419.

3.   Andrew George, trans., *The Epic of Gilgramesh*, Great Britain: Penguin, 1999), xxvii.
4.   Andrew George, trans., *The Epic of Gilgramesh*, xl.
5.   Andrew George, trans., *The Epic of Gilgramesh*, xxxi.
6.   Gordon and Rendsburg, *The Bible and the Ancient Near East*, 45.
7.   Andrew George, trans., *The Epic of Gilgramesh*, li.
8.   Richard Seaford, *Dionysus* York: Routledge, 2006), 126.
9.   Mark P.O. Morford, and Robert J. Lenardon, *Classical Mythology*, 8th ed. (New York: Oxford University Press, 2007), 385.
10.  W.K.C. Guthrie, *Orpheus and Greek Religion*, 83.
11.  Morford and Lenardon, *Classical Mythology*, 313.
12.  W.K.C. Guthrie, *Orpheus and Greek Religion*, 83.
13.  Joscelyn Godwin, *Mystery Religions in the Ancient World* (London: Thames and Hudson, 1981), 133.
14.  Morford and Lenardon, *Classical Mythology*, 384.
15.  Morford and Lenardon, *Classical Mythology*, 294.
16.  Richard Seaford, *Dionysus*, 44.
17.  Richard Seaford, *Dionysus*, 124-25.
18.  Richard Seaford, *Dionysus*, 24.
19.  James George Frazer, *The Golden Bough*, 567.
20.  James George Frazer, *The Golden Bough*, 470.
21.  Richard Seaford, *Dionysus*, 23.
22.  Morford and Lenardon, *Classical Mythology*, 313.
23.  Richard Seaford, *Dionysus*, 29.
24.  Richard Seaford, *Dionysus*, 27.
25.  Richard Seaford, *Dionysus*, 55.
26.  Richard Seaford, *Dionysus*, 115.
27.  Richard Seaford, *Dionysus*, 3.
28.  Richard Seaford, *Dionysus*, 21.
29.  Richard Seaford, *Dionysus*, 4.
30.  Richard Seaford, *Dionysus*, 122.
31.  Arnold Hermann, *To Think Like God: Pythagoras and Parmenides* (Las Vegas: Parmenides, 2004), 17.
32.  Arnold Hermann, *To Think Like God*, 43.
33.  Laertius, Diogenes. "Pythagoras: The lives and Opinions of Eminent Philosophers." Translated by C.D. Yonge. Classic Persuasion. http://classicpersuasion.org/pw/diogenes/dlpythagoras.htm
34.  Arnold Hermann, *To Think Like God*, 25.
35.  Jan N. Bremmer, *The Rise and Fall of the Afterlife: The 1995 Read-Tuckwell Lectures at the University of Bristol* (London: Routledge, 2002), 12.
36.  Alexander Roob, *Alchemy and Mysticism* (Italy: Taschen, 1996), 92.
37.  Arnold Hermann, *To Think Like God*, 49.
38.  Arnold Hermann, *To Think Like God*, 19.
39.  Jan N. Bremmer, *The Rise and Fall of the Afterlife*, 13.
40.  As quoted in Arnold Hermann, *To Think Like God*, 50.

41. Arnold Hermann, *To Think Like God*, 51.
42. Arnold Hermann, *To Think Like God*, 53.
43. Arnold Hermann, *To Think Like God*, 53–54.
44. Arnold Hermann, *To Think Like God*, 55.
45. Arnold Hermann, *To Think Like God*, 59.
46. Jan N. Bremmer, *The Rise and Fall of the Afterlife*, 24.
47. Yves Bonnefoy, *Mythologies*, trans. Wendy Doniger (Chicago: University of Chicago Press, 1992), 161.
48. Joscelyn Godwin, *Mystery Religions*, 146.
49. W.K.C. Guthrie, *Orpheus and Greek Religion*, 28.
50. Noel Robertson, "Orphic Mysteries and Dionysiac Ritual," in *Greek Mysteries: The Archaeology and Ritual of Ancient Greek Secret Cults*, ed. by Michael B. Cosmopoulos (London: Routledge, 2003), 218.
51. W.K.C. Guthrie, *Orpheus and Greek Religion*, 29.
52. C. Scott Littleton, *Gods, Goddesses, and Mythology* (Tarrytown, NY: Marshall Cavendish, 2005), 1062, http://books.google.com.tw/books?id=HC93q4gsOAwC&pg=PA1057&lpg#v=onepage&q&f=false.
53. Jan N. Bremmer, *The Rise and Fall of the Afterlife*, 5.
54. Jan N. Bremmer, *The Rise and Fall of the Afterlife,* 22.
55. W.K.C. Guthrie, *Orpheus and Greek Religion*, 183.
56. W.K.C. Guthrie, *Orpheus and Greek Religion*, 40.
57. W.K.C. Guthrie, *Orpheus and Greek Religion*, 23.
58. C. Scott Littleton, *Gods, Goddesses, and Mythology*, 1058.
59. W.K.C. Guthrie, *Orpheus and Greek Religion*, 264.
60. W.K.C. Guthrie, *Orpheus and Greek Religion*, 50.
61. Morford and Lenardon, *Classical Mythology*, 385.
62. Emma J. and Ludwig Edelstein, *Asclepius* (Baltimore: John Hopkins University Press,    1945), 9.
63. Emma J. and Ludwig Edelstein, *Asclepius*, 75.
64. Emma J. and Ludwig Edelstein, *Asclepius*, 1617.
65. Emma J. and Ludwig Edelstein, *Asclepius*, 16.
66. Robert Turcan, *The Gods of Ancient Rome*, trans. Antonia Nevill (Edinburgh: Edinburgh University Press, 2000), 108.
67. Emma J. and Ludwig Edelstein, *Asclepius*, 74.
68. Emma J. and Ludwig Edelstein, *Asclepius*, 113.
69. Emma J. and Ludwig Edelstein, *Asclepius*, 224.
70. Quoted in Emma J. and Ludwig Edelstein, *Asclepius*, 176.
71. Quoted in Emma J. and Ludwig Edelstein, *Asclepius*, 162.
72. Quoted in Emma J. and Ludwig Edelstein, *Asclepius*, 338.
73. Quoted in Emma J. and Ludwig Edelstein, *Asclepius*, 150.
74. Quoted in Emma J. and Ludwig Edelstein, *Asclepius*, 150.
75. Emma J. and Ludwig Edelstein, *Asclepius*, 136.
76. Emma J. and Ludwig Edelstein, *Asclepius*, 136.
77. Thomas Bulfinch,*The Age of Fable* (New York: Airmont, 1965), 238.

78. R.E. Witt, *Isis in the Ancient World*, 27.
79. Jan Assmann, *Moses the Egyptian*, 145.
80. R.E. Witt, *Isis in the Ancient World*, 38.
81. Quoted in R.E. Witt, *Isis in the Ancient World*, 44.
82. R.E. Witt, *Isis in the Ancient World*, 38.
83. Jan Assmann, *Moses the Egyptian*,129.
84. James George Frazer, *The Golden Bough*, 443.
85. Yves Bonnefoy, *Mythologies*, 246.
86. R.E. Witt, *Isis in the Ancient World*, 213.
87. Ken Dowden, *Religion and the Romans*, 72.
88. Gordon and Rendsburg, *The Bible and the Ancient Near East*, 60.
89. Jan Assmann, *Moses the Egyptian*, 68; de dea Syria, 1058.
90. R.E. Witt, *Isis in the Ancient World*, 210.
91. R.E. Witt, *Isis in the Ancient World*, 210.
92. R.E. Witt, *Isis in the Ancient World*, 211.
93. R.E. Witt, *Isis in the Ancient World*, 214.
94. R.E. Witt, *Isis in the Ancient World*, 215.
95. R.E. Witt, *Isis in the Ancient World*, 16.
96. R.E. Witt, *Isis in the Ancient World*, 92.
97. R.E. Witt, *Isis in the Ancient World*, 22.
98. R.E. Witt, *Isis in the Ancient World*, 135.
99. R.E. Witt, *Isis in the Ancient World*, 134.
100. R.E. Witt, *Isis in the Ancient World*, 134.
101. R.E. Witt, *Isis in the Ancient World*, 85.
102. R.E. Witt, *Isis in the Ancient World*, 67.
103. R.E. Witt, *Isis in the Ancient World*, 129.
104. Jan Assman, *Moses the Egyptian*, 145.
105. Andrew George, trans., *The Epic of Gilgramesh*, 137.
106. Andrew George, trans., *The Epic of Gilgramesh*, 68.
107. Thorkild Jacobsen, *The Treasures of Darkness: A History of Mesopotamian Religion* (New Haven, CT: Yale University Press, 1978), 26.
108. Thorkild Jacobsen, *The Treasures of Darkness*, 26.
109. Thorkild Jacobsen, *The Treasures of Darkness*, 72.
110. Jennifer Larson, *Ancient Greek Cults: A Guide* (New York: Routledge, 2007), 124.
111. Edith Hamilton, *Mythology* (New York: Warner Books, 1999), 94.
112. Jennifer Larson, *Ancient Greek Cults*, 124.
113. Walter Burkert, *Greek Religion*, trans. John Raffan (Cambridge, MA: Harvard University Press, 1985), 177.
114. Julia Dubnoff, trans. "Poems of Sappho," http://www.uh.edu/~cldue/texts/sappho.html.
115. Quoted in Jennifer Larson, *Ancient Greek Cults*, 124.
116. James George Frazer, *The Golden Bough*, 401.
117. James George Frazer, *The Golden Bough*, 401.
118. Robert Turcan, *The Gods of Ancient Rome*, 111–112.

119. Robert Turcan, *The Gods of Ancient Rome*, 113.

120. Joscelyn Godwin, *Mystery Religions*, 112.

121. James George Frazer, *The Golden Bough*, 408.

122. Joscelyn Godwin, *Mystery Religions*, 111.

123. Cited by Walter Burkert, *Ancient Mystery Cults*, 98.

124. A. T. Fear, "Cybele and Christ," in *Cybele, Attis & Related Cults: Studies in Memory of M.J. Vermaseren*, ed. Eugene N. Lane (Leiden: Brill, 1996), 39.

125. A. T. Fear, "Cybele and Christ," 40.

126. Robert Turcan, *The Gods of Ancient Rome*, 111.

127. A. T. Fear, "Cybele and Christ," 38.

128. Joscelyn Godwin, *Mystery Religions*, 111.

129. Kevin Knight, "Mithraism *New Advent Catholic Encyclopedia*, http://www.newadvent.org/cathen/10402a.htm.

130. 'Nonnus', Comm. in Greg. Nazian; quoted in Roger Pearse, "Mithras: All the Passages in Ancient Texts That Refer to the Cult," *The Tertullian Project*, http://www.tertullian.org/rpearse/mithras/index.htm.

131. Clauss, p. 102: 'Nonnus,' Comm. in Greg. Nazian. *Oratio* 4. 70 (Migne, PG 36: 989), as cited by Roger Pearse, http://www.tertullian.org/rpearse/mithras/.

132. W.H.C. Frend, *The Rise of Christianity*, 277.

133. T.R. Glover, Conflict of Religions, 106.

134. T.R. Glover, Conflict of Religions, 99.

135. M.J. Vermaseren, *Mithras The Secret God*, trans. Therese and Vincent Magaw (London: Chatto and Windus, 1963).

136. Ken Dowden, *Religion and the Romans*, Classical World Series (London: Bristol Classical Press, 1992), 79.

137. Charles François Dupuis, *The Origin of All Religious Worship*, 248.

138. Jan N. Bremmer, *The Rise and Fall of the Afterlife*, 55.

139. Kevin Knight, "Mithraism."

## PART II

1. C.S. Lewis, *Mere Christianity*, Chapter 3, O.C.R, December 12, 2003, revised July 1, 2005, http://www.lib.ru/LEWISCL/mere_engl.txt.

2. C.S. Lewis, *God in the Dock*, 66-67.

3. Walter Burkert, *Ancient Mystery Cults*, 75.

### Chapter Five

1. Clinton E. Arnold, *Ephesians Power and Magic* (Cambridge: Cambridge University Press, 1989), 28.

2. Quoted in Jan Assmann, *Moses the Egyptian*, 84.

3. Jan Assmann, *Moses the Egyptian*, 64-65.

4. Edward Carpenter, *Pagan & Christian Creeds: Their Origin and Meaning* (New York: Harcourt, Brace and Howe, 1920; NuVision Publications, digital rpt. 2007), 20.

5. Hans Andréa, http://www.harrypotterforseekers.com/.
6. John J. Miller, "Have Yourself a Merry Little Aslanmas?",
7. http://old.nationalreview.com/miller/miller200512220847.asp
8. As cited in R.E. Witt, *Isis in the Ancient World*, 220.
9. Malik H. Jabbar, *The Astrological Foundation of the Christ Myth* (Dayton, OH: Rare Books Distributor, 1995), 37.
10. David Ulansey, "The Mithraic Mysteries", http://www.well.com/~davidu/sciam.html, (accessed February 5, 2011).
11. Ibid.
12. Walter Burkert, *Ancient Mystery Cults*, 84.
13. Ken Dowden, *Religion and the Romans*, 78.
14. Cited by Jan Assmann, *Moses the Egyptian*, 202.
15. Cited in Mircea Eliade, *The Sacred and the Profane: The Nature of Religion* (Orlando: Harcourt, 1987), 75.
16. Joscelyn Godwin, *Mystery Religions*, 99.
17. Available at http://www.newadvent.org/fathers/0103220.htm.
18. Available at http://www.compassionatespirit.com/Homilies/Book-2.htm.

## Chapter Six

1. http://www.eurekalert.org/pub_releases/2006-11/trco-wor112906.php.
2. Mircea Eliade, *The Sacred and the Profane*, 48.
3. Cited in Mircea Eliade, *The Sacred and the Profane*, 54.
4. Shu-P'Ing Teng, "The Original Significance Of *Bi* Disks: Insights Based On Liangzhu Jade *Bi* With Incised Symbolic Motifs," *Journal of East Asian Archaeology* 2, no. 1-2 (2000): 165-94.
5. "Teaching the Golden Age of Chinese Archaeology: Celebrated Discoveries from the People's Republic of China, object 3," National Gallery of Art, Washington D.C.; http://www.nga.gov/education/chinatp_sl03.shtm.
6. "Snakes and Ladders," Wikipedia. http://en.wikipedia.org/wiki/Snakes_and_ladders#cite_ref-Augustyn_2-1
7. (accessed February 5, 2011).
8. Joseph Campbell, *The Hero With a Thousand Faces*, 25.
9. Mircea Eliade, *The Sacred and the Profane*, 39.
10. Mircea Eliade, *The Sacred and the Profane*, 44.
11. Steve Conor, "Astronomer's say Draco's glow is the beginning of time," *The Independent*, October 4, 2005, http://www.independent.co.uk/news/science/astronomers-say-dracos-glow-is-the-beginning-of-time-513852.html.
12. Gordon and Rendsburg, *The Bible and the Ancient Near East*, 43.
13. Gordon and Rendsburg, *The Bible and the Ancient Near East*, 43.
14. Mircea Eliade, *The Sacred and the Profane*, 77.
15. Cited by Jan Assmann, *Moses the Egyptian*, 199.
16. Cited by Jan Assmann, *Moses the Egyptian*, 198.
17. Qtd. In Emma J. and Ludwig Edelstein, *Asclepius* (Baltimore: John Hopkins

University Press, 1945), 151.

18. Quoted in Hilton Hotema, *The Secret of Regeneration* (Life Science Institute, 1963), 130.

19. Thomas Medwin, "Argument," in Aeschylus, *Prometheus Bound*, trans. T. Medwin (London: William Pickering, 1832), 3, http://books.google.com/books?id=6DoBAAAAMAAJ&pg.

20. Joscelyn Godwin, *Mystery Religions*, 134.

21. Joscelyn Godwin, *Mystery Religions*, 167.

22. Quoted in Sextus Empiricus, http://www.wsu.edu/~dee/GREECE/HERAC.HTM.

23. Qtd. In Emma J. and Ludwig Edelstein, *Asclepius* (Baltimore: John Hopkins University Press, 1945), 153.

24. Qtd. In Emma J. and Ludwig Edelstein, *Asclepius* (Baltimore: John Hopkins University Press, 1945), 152.

25. R.E. Witt, *Isis in the Ancient World*, 206.

26. Joscelyn Godwin, *Mystery Religions*, 29.

## Chapter Seven

1. Joscelyn Godwin, *Mystery Religions*, 139.

2. Joscelyn Godwin, *Mystery Religions*, 5.

3. *Sophia of Jesus Christ*, trans. Douglas M. Parrott; available at http://www.gnosis.org/naghamm/sjc.html.

4. Joscelyn Godwin, *Mystery Religions*, 79.

5. R.E. Witt, *Isis in the Ancient World*, 194.

6. Charles F. Haanel, You, Wilder Publications, 7.

7. "Little Mermaid Symbolism." Little Mermaid. http://www.the-little-mermaid.com/symbolism.php (accessed February 5, 2011).

8. Harish Johari, *Chakras: Energy Centers of Transformation* (Rochester, VT: Destiny Books, 1987), http://www.sanatansociety.org/yoga_and_meditation/seven_chakras.htm.

9. Leonora Leet, *The Universal Kabalah: Deciphering the Cosmic Code in the Sacred Geometry of the Sabbath Star Diagram* (Rochester, VT: Inner Traditions, 2004), 315.

## PART III

1. James Patrick Holding, "Dionysus. Not an influence on Christianity." Tekton Education and Apologetics Ministries. http://www.tektonics.org/copycat/dionysus.html (accessed February 5, 2011).

## Chapter Eight

1. Walter Burkert, *Ancient Mystery Cults*, 21.

2. Available at http://www.completepythagoras.net/ofpythagoras.html.

3. Iamblichus, *On the Pythagorean Life*, as quoted in Jeffrey Stopple, *A Primer of*

*Analytic Number Theory: From Pythagorus to Riemann* (Cambridge: Cambridge University Press, 2003), 5.

4. Joscelyn Godwin, *Mystery Religions*, 9.
5. Cited in Walter Burkert, *Ancient Mystery Cults*, 79.
6. Cited in Walter Burkert, *Ancient Mystery Cults*, 79.
7. Quoted in Jan Assmann, *Moses the Egyptian*, 83.
8. As cited inWalter Burkert, *Ancient Mystery Cults*, 156 n. 44.
9. Carl [Karoly / Karl] Kerényi, *Eleusis: Archetypal Image of Mother and Daughter*, trans. Ralph Manheim, Bollingen Series 65, vol. 4; rpt. Mythos Series(New York: Bollingen Foundation 1967; rpt. Princeton, NJ: Princeton University Press, 1991), 24.
10. Walter Burkert, *Ancient Mystery Cults*, 75.
11. Joscelyn Godwin, *Mystery Religions*, 26.
12. Walter Burkert, *Ancient Mystery Cults*, 69.
13. Karoly [Karl] Kerényi, *Eleusis*, 113.
14. R.E. Witt, *Isis in the Ancient World*, 91.
15. A. M. Bowie, *Aristophanes: Myth, Ritual and Comedy* (Cambridge: Cambridge University, 1993), 234 n. 36.
16. Cited by Walter Burkert, *Ancient Mystery Cults*, 98.
17. Walter Burkert, *Ancient Mystery Cults*, 98–99.
18. Franz Cumont, *The Mysteries of Mithra* (Chicago: Open Court, 1903), 116.
19. Jan Assmann, *Moses the Egyptian*, 98.
20. R. Gordon Wasson, Albert Hofmann, and Carl A. P. Ruck, *Road to Eleusis: Unveiling the Secret of the Mysteries* (New York: Harcourt Brace Jovanovich, 1978), http://www.telesterion.com/roadto.htm.
21. Ibid.
22. Ibid.
23. Quoted in Emma J. and Ludwig Edelstein, *Asclepius*, 202-203
24. Walter Burkert, *Ancient Mystery Cults*, 45.
25. Walter Burkert, *Ancient Mystery Cults*, 99.
26. Firmicus Err. 18.1, cited in Walter Burkert, *Ancient Mystery Cults*, 166.
27. Joscelyn Godwin, *Mystery Religions*, 23.
28. Walter Burkert, *Ancient Mystery Cults*, 75.
29. Joscelyn Godwin, *Mystery Religions*, 27.
30. Quoted in Walter Burkert, *Ancient Mystery Cults*, 78.
31. Walter Burkert, *Ancient Mystery Cults*, 156.
32. Jan Assmann, *Moses the Egyptian*, 185.
33. Joscelyn Godwin, *Mystery Religions*, 28.
34. Jan Assmann, *Moses the Egyptian*, 156.
35. Quoted in Jan Assmann, *Moses the Egyptian*, 156.
36. Quoted in Jan Assman, *Moses the Egyptian*, 156.
37. Quoted in Jan Assman, *Moses the Egyptian*, 156.
38. Quoted in Jan Assmann, *Moses the Egyptian*, 78.
39. Walter Burkert, *Ancient Mystery Cults*, 87.

40. Walter Burkert, *Ancient Mystery Cults*, 87.
41. Walter Burkert, *Ancient Mystery Cults*, 87.
42. Sophocles, *Frag.* 719 (Dindorf) (translation by G. E. Mylonas, *Eleusis and the Eleusinian Mysteries* [Princeton: Princeton University Press, 1961], P. 284)
43. Joscelyn Godwin, *Mystery Religions*, 37.
44. Walter Burkert, *Ancient Mystery Cults*, 21-22.
45. Joscelyn Godwin, *Mystery Religions*, 49.
46. R.E. Witt, *Isis in the Ancient World*, 152.
47. R.E. Witt, *Isis in the Ancient World*, 152.
48. W.H.C. Frend, *The Rise of Christianity*, 2.
49. W.H.C. Frend, *The Rise of Christianity*, 200.
50. "The Secret Gospel of Mark." The Gnosis Archive. http://www.gnosis.org/library/secm.htm (accessed February 5, 2011).
51. Rick Renner, "Who Was the Naked Boy in the Garden of Gethsemene?" at http://www.cfaith.com/index.php?option=com_content&view=article&id=1070.
52. http://www.gnosis.org/library/secm.htm.
53. http://www.metalog.org/files/philip.html.
54. http://www.gnosis.org/library/marygosp.htm.
55. Cited in Mircea Eliade, *The Sacred and the Profane*, 133.
56. Cited inW.H.C. Frend, *The Rise of Christianity*, 223.
57. Joscelyn Godwin, *Mystery Religions*, 106.
58. Joscelyn Godwin, *Mystery Religions*, 106.
59. "Tertullian." History Department, Hanover College. http://history.hanover.edu/courses/excerpts/260ter.html (accessed February 5, 2011)
60. Cited in Lee Strobel, *The Case for Christ*, 121–122.
61. W.H.C. Frend, *The Rise of Christianity*, 33.
62. Joscelyn Godwin, *Mystery Religions*, 78.
63. W.H.C. Frend, *The Rise of Christianity*, 35.
64. W.H.C. Frend, *The Rise of Christianity*, 35.
65. Robert M. Price, "Review - D.M. Murdock (Acharya S.), Christ in Egypt," http://www.robertmprice.mindvendor.com/reviews/murdock_christ_egypt.htm (accessed February 5, 2011).
66. Joscelyn Godwin, *Mystery Religions*, 78.
67. Jan Assmann, *Moses the Egyptian*, 99.
68. Quoted in T.R. Glover, *Conflict of Religions*, 16.
69. Quoted in T.R. Glover, *Conflict of Religions*, 16–17.
70. Sarah Iles Johnston, "Magic," chapter in *Ancient Religions*, Sarah Iles Johnston (Cambridge, MA: Belknap Press of Harvard University Press, 2007), 144.
71. Cited in Jan Assmann, *Moses the Egyptian*, 197.
72. Ilil Arbel in *Encyclopedia Mythica*, March 3, 1997, http://www.pantheon.org/articles/y/yahweh.html.
73. R.E. Witt, *Isis in the Ancient World*, 193.
74. R.E. Witt, *Isis in the Ancient World*, 193.
75. Cited in Jan Assmann, *Moses the Egyptian*, 204.

76. Clinton E. Arnold, *Ephesians Power and Magic*, 24.
77. "Avada Kedavra Curse" Main Page - Harry Potter Wiki. http://harrypotter.wikia. com/wiki/Killing_Curse (accessed February 5, 2011).
78. Clinton E. Arnold, *Ephesians Power and Magic*, 34.
79. Clinton E. Arnold, *Ephesians Power and Magic*, 31.
80. "Chrest Magus." History Hunters International. http://historyhuntersinternational. org/2010/05/31/christ-magus/
81. Ibid.
82. W.H.C. Frend, *The Rise of Christianity*, 368.
83. W.K.C. Guthrie, *Orpheus and Greek Religion*, 25.
84. Jan N. Bremmer, *The Rise and Fall of the Afterlife*, 24.
85. R.E. Witt, *Isis in the Ancient World*, 52.
86. Quoted in R.E. Witt, *Isis in the Ancient World,* 53.
87. R.E. Witt, *Isis in the Ancient World*, 55.
88. R.E. Witt, *Isis in the Ancient World*, 190.
89. Quoted in Clinton E. Arnold, *Ephesians Power and Magic*, 66.
90. Quoted in Clinton E. Arnold, *Ephesians Power and Magic*, 66.
91. R.E. Witt, *Isis in the Ancient World*, 235.
92. Cited in R.E. Witt, *Isis in the Ancient World*, 54.
93. Monica Stecchini, Steven Stecchini and Jan Sammer, *The Gospel According to Seneca*, http://www.nazarenus.com/0-4-tragospel.htm
94. Available at http://www.newadvent.org/fathers/0103115.htm.
95. Clinton E. Arnold, *Ephesians Power and Magic,* 54.
96. "Debunking Religion: Jesus Christ is the Pythagorean Theorem," Zeitgeist Movement, http://thezeitgeistmovement.com/joomla/index.php?option=com_ku nena&Itemid=99999&func=view&catid=8&id=131336&limit=10&limitstart=30.

**Chapter Nine**

1. Ante-Nicene Fathers Vol. VIII, Pseudo-Clementine Literature, The Clementine Homilies, Homily II, Anonymous, translated by Thomas Smith,Chapter 23, http://en.wikisource.org/wiki/Ante-Nicene_Fathers/Volume_VIII/ Pseudo-Clementine_Literature/The_Clementine_Homilies/Homily_II/ Chapter_23.
2. W.H.C. Frend, *The Rise of Christianity*, 101.
3. W.H.C. Frend, *The Rise of Christianity*, 101.
4. R.E. Witt, *Isis in the Ancient World*, 188.
5. Quoted in Clinton E. Arnold, *Ephesians Power and Magic*, 98.
6. Epictetus, quoted in T.R. Glover, *Conflict of Religions*, 52.
7. Marvin W. Meyer and Richard Smith, *Ancient Christian Magic: Coptic Texts of Ritual Power* (San Francisco: HarperSanFrancisco, 1994), 64.
8. W.K.C. Guthrie, *Orpheus and Greek Religion*, 269.
9. R.E. Witt, *Isis in the Ancient World*, 42.
10. Quoted in W.K.C. Guthrie, *Orpheus and Greek Religion*, 148.

11. Available at http://www.ewtn.com/library/patristc/anf2-3.txt.
12. Ibid., Chapter 13.
13. Ibid.
14. Quoted in W.H.C. Frend, *The Rise of Christianity*, 443.
15. Quoted in W.H.C. Frend, *The Rise of Christianity*, 442.
16. New Advent, The Life of Origen. http://www.newadvent.org/cathen/11306b.htm
17. Quoted in Philip Gardiner, *Gnosis: The Secret of Solomon's Temple Revealed*, 207
18. Quoted in Blatavsky, *The Secret Doctrine Vol. 4*. Available at http://www.theosociety.org/pasadena/sd/sd2-2-01.htm
19. As described in Lee Strobel, *The Case for Christ*, 48.

## Chapter Ten

1. Justin Martyr, *Dialogue with Trypho* II. 2-7, trans. Alexander Roberts and James Donaldson, http://www.earlychristianwritings.com/text/justinmartyr-dialoguetrypho.html.
2. Cited in W.H.C. Frend, *The Rise of Christianity*, 170.
3. Cited in Timothy E. Byerley, *The great commission: models of evangelization in American Catholicism*, 108.
4. John Anthony McGuckin, *On the unity of Christ: Saint Cyril (Patriarch of Alexandria)*, 61.
5. Joel Carmichael, *The Birth of Christianity* (New York: Hippocrene Books, 1989), 170-171.
6. W.H.C. Frend, *The Rise of Christianity*, 179.
7. Lucian, quoted in W.K.C. Guthrie, *Orpheus and Greek Religion*, 270.
8. Lucian, *De Morte Peregrini* 19, 20; W.H.C. Frend, *The Rise of Christianity*, 176.
9. W.H.C. Frend, *The Rise of Christianity*, 134.
10. William C. Placher, *Readings in the History of Christian Theology, vol. 1, From Its Beginnings to the Eve of the Reformation* (Philadelphia: Westminster, 1988), 35.
11. "Exhortation to the Heathen, Chapter 2 (Clement of Alexandria)." New Advent. http://www.newadvent.org/fathers/020802.htm (accessed February 5, 2011).
12. W.H.C. Frend, *The Rise of Christianity*, 178.
13. Smith, *Death of Classical Paganism*, 5; Cited in Helen Ellerbe, *The Dark Side of Christian History* (San Raphael, CA: Morningstar Books, 1995), 15.
14. John S. C. Abbott, *Italy* (New York: P.F. Collier, 1882), 325.
15. W.H.C. Frend, *The Rise of Christianity*, 110.
16. John S. C. Abbott, *Italy*, 326.
17. W.H.C. Frend, *The Rise of Christianity*, 132.
18. For information on this source, see Robert M. Grant, *Greek Apologists of the Second Century* (Philadelphia: Westminster, 1988), 178-79.
19. Clare K. Rothschild, *Luke-Acts and the Rhetoric of History* (Tubingen, Germany: Mohr Siebeck, 2004), 94.
20. John Henry Newman [Cardinal Newman], *An Essay on the Development of Christian Doctrine* (London: James Toovey, 1945), 207, http://books.google.com/

books?id=yE47AAAAYAAJ&printsec.

21. Bradly S. Billings, *Do This in Remembrance of Me: The Disputed Works in the Lukan Institution Narrative* (London: T&T Clark, 2006),151.

22. Cited in W.H.C. Frend, *The Rise of Christianity*, 12.

23. Robert M. Grant, *Second-Century Christianity: A Collection of Fragments,* 2nd ed (Louisville, KY: Westminster John Knox, 2003), 48.

24. W.H.C. Frend, *The Rise of Christianity*, 481.

25. W.H.C. Frend, *The Rise of Christianity*, 184.

26. W.H.C. Frend, *The Rise of Christianity*, 458.

27. Clare K. Rothschild, *Luke-Acts and the Rhetoric of History*.

28. Quoted in W.H.C. Frend, *The Rise of Christianity*, 110.

29. W.H.C. Frend, *The Rise of Christianity*, 34.

30. W.H.C. Frend, *The Rise of Christianity*, 42.

31. Walter Burkert, *Ancient Mystery Cults*, 52.

32. W.H.C. Frend, *The Rise of Christianity*, 232.

33. W.H.C. Frend, *The Rise of Christianity*, 279.

34. Walter Burkert, *Ancient Mystery Cults*, 48.

35. R.E. Witt, *Isis in the Ancient World*, 140.

36. W.H.C. Frend, *The Rise of Christianity*, 556.

37. Quoted in W.H.C. Frend, *The Rise of Christianity*, 556.

38. W.H.C. Frend, *The Rise of Christianity*, 556.

39. W.H.C. Frend, *The Rise of Christianity*, 458.

40. Quoted in Helen Ellerbe, *The Dark Side of Christian History*, 6.

41. Interviewed in Lee Strobel, *The Case for Christ*, 165.

42. Helen Ellerbe, *The Dark Side of Christian History*, 3.

43. Helen Ellerbe, *The Dark Side of Christian History*, 36.

44. W.H.C. Frend, *The Rise of Christianity*, 440.

45. Jan Assmann, *Moses the Egyptian*, 88.

46. W.H.C. Frend, *The Rise of Christianity*, 477.

47. W.H.C. Frend, *The Rise of Christianity*, 484.

48. W.H.C. Frend, *The Rise of Christianity*, 488.

49. Richard Gerberding and Jo Ann H. Moran Cruz, *Medieval Worlds: An Introduction to European History, 300–1494* (New York: Houghton Mifflin Company, 2004), 55–56; and Ramsay MacMullen, *Christianizing the Roman Empire: A.D. 100–400* (New Haven, CT: Yale University Press, 1984), 49.

50. Ibid.

51. W.H.C. Frend, *The Rise of Christianity*, 477.

52. W.H.C. Frend, *The Rise of Christianity*, 479.

53. W.H.C. Frend, *The Rise of Christianity*, 420.

54. W.H.C. Frend, *The Rise of Christianity*, 492.

55. Karen Armstrong, *The Bible*, 118.

56. St. Nicholas Center, *Bishop Nicholas Loses His Cool (At The Council of Nicaea),* http://www.stnicholascenter.org/Brix?pageID=57.

57. W.H.C. Frend, *The Rise of Christianity*, 541.

58. W.H.C. Frend, *The Rise of Christianity*, 595.
59. http://www.ccel.org/ccel/pearse/morefathers/files/julian_apostate_1_sun.htm.
60. W.H.C. Frend, *The Rise of Christianity*, 597.
61. W.H.C. Frend, *The Rise of Christianity*, 601.
62. W.H.C. Frend, *The Rise of Christianity*, 597.
63. Wilmer Cave Wright, "Introduction to Against the Galileans," in *The Works of the Emperor Julian* with an English translation by Wilmer Cave Wright (London: Heinemann, 1923), 313–317, http://www.archive.org/stream/workswithenglish03juliuoft.
64. Quoted in W.H.C. Frend, *The Rise of Christianity*, 606.
65. W.H.C. Frend, *The Rise of Christianity*, 602.
66. Zonara, *Epitome Historiarum*, XIII 12 –c-d; quoted in W.H.C. Frend, *The Rise of Christianity*, 421.
67. Quoted in W.H.C. Frend, *The Rise of Christianity*, 349–50.
68. Chris Armstrong, "Controversies about Christ in the early church, part III: The werewolf Jesus and the third council," http://gratefultothedead.wordpress.com/2010/10/21/controversies-about-christ-in-the-early-church-part-iii-the-werewolf-jesus-and-the-third-council/.
69. Walter Nigg, *The Heretics: Heresy Through the Ages* (New York: Dorset Press, 1962), 138.
70. "The Great Heresies." *Catholic Answers*. http://www.catholic.com/library/Great_Heresies.asp.
71. Chris Armstrong, "Controversies about Christ in the early church, part IV: The divine swallowing the human and the fourth council's 'four fences,'"
72. http://gratefultothedead.wordpress.com/2010/10/21/controversies-about-christ-in-the-early-church-part-iv-the-divine-swallowing-the-human-and-the-fourth-councils-four-fences/.
73. Ibid.
74. "Early Church Controversies." ORB: The Online Reference Book for Medieval Studies. http://www.the-orb.net/encyclop/religion/early/orb-councils3.index.htm (accessed February 5, 2011).
75. "Apology of Aristides the Philosopher," trans. and ed. D.M. Kay, *Ante-Nicene Fathers*, Volume 9, ed. Allan Menzies (Edinburgh: T&T Clark, 1896), 274 [translated from the Syriac], http://www.sacred-texts.com/chr/ecf/009/0090187.htm.
76. Melito, *A Discourse Which Was in the Presence of Antoninus Caesar, And He Exhorted the Said Caesar to Acquaint Himself With God, And Showed to Him the Way of Truth*, trans. Alexander Roberts & James Donaldson, http://www.earlychristianwritings.com/text/melito.html.
77. "The Octavius of Minucius Felix" in *Ante-Nicene Fathers*, Volume 4, ed. and trans. Alexander Roberts & James Donaldson (Grand Rapids, MI: Eerdmans, 1885), http://www.sacred-texts.com/chr/ecf/004/0040034.htm.
78. Johann C.L. [Karl Ludwig] Gieseler, *A Text-book of Church History*, vol. 1, A.D. 1–726 (New York: Harper & Brothers, 1857), 161, http://books.google.com/books?id=G7hAAAAAYAAJ&printsec.

79. "The Apostolic Tradition of Hippolytus of Rome," trans. Kevin P. Edgecomb, based on the work of Bernard Botte and Gregory Dix, http://www.bombaxo.com/hippolytus.html.

80. W.H.C. Frend, *The Rise of Christianity*, 415.

81. "Contra Celsus, Book VII (Origen)." New Advent. http://www.newadvent.org/fathers/04167.htm (accessed February 5, 2011).

82. "The Seven Books of Arnobius Against the Heathen," (Book VI) in *Ante-Nicene Fathers*, Volume 6, ed. and trans. Alexander Roberts & James Donaldson, rev. Arthur C. Cox (Buffalo, NY: Christian Literature Co, 1886), revised and edited by Kevin Knight, http://www.newadvent.org/fathers/06316.htm.

83. (*PG* 20,1545), Bellarmino Bagatti, *The Church from the Gentiles in Palestine*, trans. Eugene Hoade (Jerusalem: Franciscan Printing Press, 1970), 120.

84. Paul Carus, *The Open Court*, Volume 22 (Chicago: Open Court Publishing Co., 1908), 663-664.

85. John Trigilio and Kenneth Brighenti, *The Catholicism Answer Book: The 300 Most Frequently Asked Questions* (Naperville, IL: Sourcebooks, 2007), 258.

86. J.C. Cruz, *Relics* (Our Sunday Visitor Publishing, 1984), 255.

87. J.L. Hurlbut, *The Story of the Christian Church* (Grand Rapids, MI: Zondervan, 1967), 62.

88. H.O.J. Brown, *Heresies: Heresy and Orthodoxy in the History of the Church* (Peabody, MA: Hendrickson, 1988), 212.

89. J.B. O'Connor. "St. John Damascene," in *The Catholic Encyclopedia*, Volume VIII (Robert Appleton Company, 1910).

90. Bishop Kallistos (Ware) of Diokleia, *The Orthodox Church*, cited http://orthodoxwiki.org/Seventh_Ecumenical_Council

91. Ibid.

**Final Conclusion**

1. Lee Strobel, *The Case for Christ*, 127.

2. Joseph Campbell, *The Hero With a Thousand Faces*, 213.

Find us online:
http://www.jesuspotterharrychrist.com
http://www.holyblasphemy.net

Made in the USA
Charleston, SC
31 March 2011